FINANZIERUNG, KAPITALMARKT UND BANKEN

Herausgegeben von Prof. Dr. Hermann Locarek-Junge, Dresden, Prof. Dr. Klaus Röder, Regensburg, und Prof. Dr. Mark Wahrenburg, Frankfurt

Band 88
Chris Hoffmann
Selbstbehalt und Beziehungsstrukturen bei Verbriefungstransaktionen – Eine empirische Analyse US-amerikanischer Hypothekenverbriefungen
Lohmar – Köln 2014 ♦ 196 S. ♦ € 49,- (D) ♦ ISBN 978-3-8441-0307-6

Band 89
Christian Langkamp
Corporate Credit Risk Management
Lohmar – Köln 2014 ♦ 324 S. ♦ € 62,- (D) ♦ ISBN 978-3-8441-0309-0

Band 90
Sven Loßagk
Die Bewertung nicht börsennotierter Unternehmen – Eine empirische Untersuchung zur Erklärung des systematischen Risikos mittels rechnungswesenbasierter Daten
Lohmar – Köln 2014 ♦ 336 S. ♦ € 63,- (D) ♦ ISBN 978-3-8441-0313-7

Band 91
Hauke Christian Öynhausen
Nutzung Kollektiver Intelligenz am Kapitalmarkt – Entwicklung eines alternativen Informations- und Entscheidungsmodells für das Asset Management
Lohmar – Köln 2015 ♦ 392 S. ♦ € 66,- (D) ♦ ISBN 978-3-8441-0433-2

Band 92
Marion Hippchen
Anleihefinanzierung im Mittelstand – Eine empirische Analyse zu Mittelstands- und Fananleihen
Lohmar – Köln 2016 ♦ 436 S. ♦ € 80,- (D) ♦ ISBN 978-3-8441-0487-5

Band 93
Eva Maria Kreibohm
The Performance of Socially Responsible Investment Funds in Europe – An Empirical Analysis
Lohmar – Köln 2016 ♦ 316 S. ♦ € 68,- (D) ♦ ISBN 978-3-8441-0482-0

JOSEF EUL VERLAG

Reihe: Finanzierung, Kapitalmarkt und Banken · Band 93

Herausgegeben von Prof. Dr. Hermann Locarek-Junge, Dresden, Prof. Dr. Klaus Röder, Regensburg, und Prof. Dr. Mark Wahrenburg, Frankfurt

Dr. Eva Maria Kreibohm

The Performance of Socially Responsible Investment Funds in Europe

An Empirical Analysis

With a Preface by Prof. Dr. Ulrich Pape, ESCP Europe Business School Berlin

Bibliografische Information der Deutschen Nationalbibliothek

Die Deutsche Nationalbibliothek verzeichnet diese Publikation in der Deutschen Nationalbibliografie; detaillierte bibliografische Daten sind im Internet über <http://dnb.d-nb.de> abrufbar.

Dissertation, ESCP Europe Business School Berlin, 2016

ISBN 978-3-8441-0482-0
1. Auflage November 2016

© JOSEF EUL VERLAG GmbH, Lohmar – Köln, 2016
Alle Rechte vorbehalten

JOSEF EUL VERLAG GmbH
Brandsberg 6
53797 Lohmar
Tel.: 0 22 05 / 90 10 6-80
Fax: 0 22 05 / 90 10 6-88
https://www.eul-verlag.de
info@eul-verlag.de

Bei der Herstellung unserer Bücher möchten wir die Umwelt schonen. Dieses Buch ist daher auf säurefreiem, 100% chlorfrei gebleichtem, alterungsbeständigem Papier nach DIN 6738 gedruckt.

Preface

In recent years Socially Responsible Investments (SRI) have gained a significant degree of popularity among international investors; at the same time, the once clear-cut distinction between financial and social investment objectives is increasingly fading. Nowadays even those investors who pursue social goals expect to receive an appropriate return on their investments while, conversely, investors whose goals are primarily financially orientated have begun to take up social objectives among their investment criteria. Having said that, the question how much return SRI can generate is acquiring new relevance.

Pursuing both conceptual and empirical aims, Eva Kreibohm here analyses the performance of SRI funds in Europe. After giving a precise delineation of the SRI concept, she provides an overview of theoretical as well as empirical SRI literature. The empirical analysis answers the question whether or not investors must sacrifice part of their financial return when investing in SRI funds. In contrast to the majority of such studies undertaken up to present, this analysis places a strong focus on Europe. Furthermore, the investigation extends the scope of previous studies to include further types of funds: besides equity funds, the study deals with fixed income funds as well as balanced funds. With regard to the methodology, the author makes use of single- and multiple-factor regression models for the period of investigation chosen (2003-2013).

The results of the investigation into the various types of funds reveal that, in general terms, SRI performs neither better nor worse than traditional investments. Thus, from the perspective of capital market theory the results, differentiated according to fund type, point to the need for further research. From a practical point of view, the study provides investors and fund managers with valuable information for their investment decisions.

Eva Kreibohm's study stands out not only due to its broad theoretical foundation but also because of a convincing empirical investigation which is highly suited to practical application in the capital market sphere. For this reason, the study is just as interesting for investors and fund managers as it is for the academic world. I wish the publication every success in gaining a wide circle of interested readers!

Berlin, September 2016   Prof. Dr. Ulrich Pape

Acknowledgements

I have written this thesis while being a doctoral student at ESCP Europe, Campus Berlin. A lot of people – professors, fellow students, colleagues, friends, and family members – have accompanied me along the way. Although I cannot thank everyone individually, there are a few persons that deserve special consideration.

First and foremost, I would like to express my gratitude towards my supervisor, Prof. Dr. Ulrich Pape, owner of the Chair of Finance at ESCP Europe, Campus Berlin. He enabled me in choosing a research topic none of us two has touched before and was always approachable for me when I needed someone to discuss the status of my research project. His guidance and the constructive dialogues we had helped me to push the thesis further and refine it from the first draft until the final version.

I also would like to thank Prof. Dr. Barbara Scheck for taking the time to be my second supervisor and connecting me to research fellows at the University of Hamburg. The meetings in Hamburg helped me to further sharpen my research focus and exchange experiences with academics whose research interest are similar to mine.

Special thanks also to Prof. Dr. Houdou Basse Mama, owner of the Chair of International Financial Markets at ESCP Europe, Campus Berlin for being the chairman of the doctoral committee as well as all the other professors and research fellows from ESCP Europe for challenging me during PhD colloquiums and with this, helping me to further refine my research project.

I would also thank Morningstar and Vigeo for providing me information on the available SRI funds in Europe. Without this information, I could not have made the empirical analysis and thus, a significant part of my thesis would be missing.

Finally, I also would like to thank all my friends and family members for their unfailing and unrestricted support and motivation. They accompanied me through the good and also through the rather challenging times of writing a thesis; without their encouragement I certainly would not have been able to finish this work.

Berlin, September 2016   Eva Maria Paula Kreibohm

Table of Contents

Preface V

Acknowledgements VII

Table of Contents IX

List of Figures XIII

List of Tables XV

List of Abbreviations XVII

List of Symbols XIX

1 Introduction 1
    1.1 Research motivation and relevance 1
    1.2 Research objectives 5
    1.3 Structure of the thesis 8

2 The market for socially responsible investing 11
    2.1 The term socially responsible investing (SRI) 11
    2.2 Historical development 15
    2.3 Current market size 17
    2.4 Regulatory background 20
        2.4.1 State regulations 20
        2.4.2 Non-state regulations 24
    2.5 Investor base 29
        2.5.1 Investor characteristics 29
        2.5.2 Investor motivation 31
            2.5.2.1 Motivation to invest in a socially responsible way 31
            2.5.2.2 Financial objectives 32
            2.5.2.3 Non-financial objectives 34
    2.6 Investment strategies 36
    2.7 Excursus: Impact investing 40
    2.8 Interim conclusion 44

3 Opportunities for investors to get exposed to SRI 47
    3.1 Direct investments 47
        3.1.1 Definition of corporate social responsibility (CSR) 47

	3.1.2	CSR activities and business operations 50

- 3.1.2 CSR activities and business operations 50
  - 3.1.2.1 Arguments against the implementation of CSR activities 50
  - 3.1.2.2 Arguments in favor of the implementation of CSR activities 54
- 3.1.3 CSR activities and company financial data 58
  - 3.1.3.1 Overall company performance 58
  - 3.1.3.2 Cost of capital 64
- 3.1.4 Interim conclusion 66

3.2 Indirect investments 69
- 3.2.1 Definition of SRI funds 69
- 3.2.2 Investment screens applied 73
- 3.2.3 SRI fund categories 77
  - 3.2.3.1 SRI equity funds 77
  - 3.2.3.2 SRI fixed income funds 80
  - 3.2.3.3 SRI balanced funds 82

3.3 Interim conclusion 84

4 Literature review 87

4.1 Investor risk aversion 87

4.2 Fund characteristics 90
- 4.2.1 Measuring return 90
  - 4.2.1.1 Security return 90
  - 4.2.1.2 Portfolio return 93
- 4.2.2 Measuring risk 94
  - 4.2.2.1 Security risk 94
  - 4.2.2.2 Benefits of diversification 96
  - 4.2.2.3 Portfolio risk 102

4.3 Fund performance measurement 105
- 4.3.1 Excess returns 105
- 4.3.2 Performance measures 106
  - 4.3.2.1 Treynor ratio 106
  - 4.3.2.2 Sharpe ratio 108
  - 4.3.2.3 Jensen's alpha 109
- 4.3.3 Single-factor models 111
- 4.3.4 Multi-factor models 115
  - 4.3.4.1 Basic model 115
  - 4.3.4.2 Equity performance models 117
  - 4.3.4.3 Fixed income performance model 118

4.4 Theoretical debate on SRI fund performance 120

4.5 Empirical results on SRI fund performance 127
- 4.5.1 Results obtained using single- and two-factor models 127

		4.5.2	Results obtained using multi-factor models 131

4.5.2 Results obtained using multi-factor models 131
    4.5.2.1 Single-country analyses 131
    4.5.2.2 Multi-country analyses 133
4.5.3 Additional studies on SRI fund performance 135
4.6 Interim conclusion 139

5 Assessing the performance of European-based SRI funds 141

5.1 Hypotheses development 141
  5.1.1 SRI-screened relative to SRI-unscreened investments 141
  5.1.2 Performance across different SRI fund categories 144
  5.1.3 SRI fund performance over time 146

5.2 Methodology 150
  5.2.1 General description of the empirical analysis 150
  5.2.2 Description of the single-factor regression models 154
  5.2.3 Description of the multi-factor regression models 155
      5.2.3.1 SRI equity funds 156
      5.2.3.2 SRI balanced funds 156
      5.2.3.3 SRI fixed income funds 157

5.3 Data set 158
  5.3.1 Sample of SRI funds 158
  5.3.2 Indices used to assess SRI fund performance 164
      5.3.2.1 Market proxies 164
      5.3.2.2 Additional proxies 166

6 Empirical Results 173

6.1 Summary statistics 173
  6.1.1 SRI funds 173
  6.1.2 Benchmark indices 179
  6.1.3 Correlation coefficients 183

6.2 SRI fund performance 186
  6.2.1 Performance measures for SRI funds 186
  6.2.2 Testing residuals 187
      6.2.2.1 Normality of residuals 187
      6.2.2.2 Homoscedasticity of residuals 190
      6.2.2.3 Autocorrelation of residuals 193
  6.2.3 Results of single-factor models 196
  6.2.4 Results of multi-factor models 199
  6.2.5 Sub-period analyses 202

		6.2.6	Interim conclusion	205
	6.3	Additional analyses		208
		6.3.1	Index regression	208
		6.3.2	Gross return analysis	210
		6.3.3	Individual SRI fund performance	212
		6.3.4	Interim conclusion	215
	6.4	Summary of results		216
	6.5	Discussion of results		220
		6.5.1	Implications	220
			6.5.1.1 Investors	220
			6.5.1.2 Fund managers	222
			6.5.1.3 Researchers	224
		6.5.2	Limitations of the empirical study	225
		6.5.3	Areas for future research	228
7	Conclusion			233
Appendices				239
References				271

List of Figures

Figure 1: Investor motivation to engage in SRI 32
Figure 2: Share of SRI investment strategies on European SRI market 40
Figure 3: Balance between financial return and impact orientation 43
Figure 4: Arguments against a company's engagement in CSR activities 52
Figure 5: Arguments in favor of a company's engagement in CSR activities 58
Figure 6: Number of SRI funds domiciled in Europe between 2003 and 2013 71
Figure 7: SRI fund assets under management by country 72
Figure 8: Number of screens applied by SRI funds 76
Figure 9: Breakdown of SRI funds by category 77
Figure 10: Indifference curves for investors with different attitudes towards risk 88
Figure 11: Indifference curves for investors with different levels of risk aversion 90
Figure 12: Risk reduction due to diversification 98
Figure 13: Relation between correlation coefficient and changes in security return 102
Figure 14: Statements on the performance difference between SRI and conventional funds 121
Figure 15: Hypotheses to be tested 150
Figure 16: SRI funds with domestic or international investment strategies 152
Figure 17: SRI funds with Europe-only and global investment strategies 152
Figure 18: Derivation of the final data set 160
Figure 19: Number of SRI funds per country 161
Figure 20: Breakdown of data set by SRI fund category 163
Figure 21: Return distributions for SRI funds 177
Figure 22: Average monthly returns for benchmark indices between 2003 and 2013 ... 181
Figure 23: Distributions of residuals for SRI funds 189
Figure 24: Scatterplots to test for heteroscedasticity of residuals 192
Figure 25: Scatterplots to test for autocorrelation of residuals 194
Figure 26: Overview of accepted and rejected hypotheses 207

List of Tables

Table 1: SRI market size per region 18
Table 2: Development of SRI market size in the US and Europe 19
Table 3: SRI regulations by national governments 22
Table 4: Global voluntary SRI guidelines and reporting standards 26
Table 5: Definitions of CSR 48
Table 6: Number of CSR reports published globally 68
Table 7: Investment screens applied by SRI fund managers 74
Table 8: Types of equity funds 79
Table 9: Types of fixed income funds 82
Table 10: Overview of the theoretical debate on SRI fund performance 124
Table 11: Overview of existing studies on SRI fund performance 137
Table 12: Number of SRI funds established per period 163
Table 13: Overview of indices used in the regression analysis 169
Table 14: Summary statistics of SRI funds 174
Table 15: Summary statistics of benchmark indices 180
Table 16: Return differences between conventional and SRI benchmark indices 183
Table 17: Correlation coefficients 184
Table 18: Variance inflation factors 185
Table 19: SRI fund performance measures 186
Table 20: Summary of quantitative residuals tests 195
Table 21: Single-factor analyses for monthly return data Jan 2003 - Dec 2013 196
Table 22: Three-factor analyses for monthly return data Jan 2003 - Dec 2013 201
Table 23: Four-factor analyses for monthly return data Jan 2003 - Dec 2013 202
Table 24: Single-factor analyses for monthly return data in sub-periods 204
Table 25: Three-factor analyses for monthly return data in sub-periods 205
Table 26: Index regression 209
Table 27: Regression analysis with excess returns net and gross of management fees ... 210
Table 28: Individual fund performance for the European fund portfolio 213
Table 29: Individual fund performance for country-specific fund portfolios 214

List of Abbreviations

APT	Arbitrage Pricing Theory
AuM	Assets under Management
ASIC	Australian Securities and Investments Commission
bp	basis point
CAGR	Compound Annual Growth Rate
CAPM	Capital Asset Pricing Model
CRSP	Chicago Center for Research in Security Prices
CSR	Corporate Social Responsibility
DE	Deutschland (Germany)
DSI	Domini Social Index
EC	Environmental Conscientiousness
EP	Equator Principles
ESG	Environmental, Social, Corporate Governance
EUR	Euro
Euribor	Euro Interbank Offered Rate
EUROSIF	European Social Investment Forum
FR	France
FSRA	Financial Services Reform Act
FTSE	Financial Times Stock Exchange
GIIN	Global Impact Investing Network
GRI	Global Reporting Initiative
HML	High-Minus-Low portfolio
ICI	Investment Company Institute
IRIS	Impact Reporting & Investment Standards
ISIN	International Securities Identification Number

NL	The Netherlands
OECD	Organization for European Economic Cooperation
PRI	Principles of Responsible Investment
PwC	PriceWaterhouseCoopers
RIA	Responsible Investment Association
RIAA	Responsible Investment Association Australasia
RQ	Research Question
SEE	Social, Environmental and Ethical
SIF	Social Investment Forum
SMB	Small-Minus-Big portfolio
SRI	Socially Responsible Investing/Investment
T-bills	US Treasury bills
TNA	Total Net Assets
UK	United Kingdom
UKSIF	UK Sustainable Investment and Finance Association
UN	United Nations
US	United States of America
USD	US-Dollar
USSIF	US Social Investment Forum
VBDO	Vereniging van Beleggers voor Duurzame Ontwikkeling (Dutch Association for Sustainable Development)
VIF	Variance Inflation Factor
WLS	Weighted Least Squares

List of Symbols

α_i	Abnormal return
β_{ij}	Factor loading for each factor included in the regression model
CF_i	Cash flow paid by security i
ε_i	Error term or idiosyncratic return
$E(\bar{r}_i)$	Expected return of security i
$E(\bar{r}_p)$	Expected return of a portfolio
K	Number of factors in the regression model
N	Total number of securities in a portfolio
$P_{i,t}$	Price of security i at time t
r_f	Return of a risk-free investment
$r_{i,t}$	Realized return of security i
r_{jt}	Return of each factor included in the regression model
$\bar{r}_{i,j}$	Average of annual returns for security i and j
r_m	Return generated by the market portfolio m
$\rho_{i,j}$	Correlation coefficient between securities i and j
$\sigma_{i,j}$	Covariance between securities i and j
σ_i	Standard deviation of security i
σ_i^2	Variance of security i
σ_m^2	Variance of the market portfolio m
σ_p^2	Variance of the portfolio's returns p
T	Number of years in the sample
w_i	Proportion of security i in the whole portfolio
$x_{i,j}$	Weights assigned to security i and j

1 Introduction

1.1 Research motivation and relevance

"You cannot both have your cake and eat it".[1] This phrase that goes back to 1546 and was first used by the dramatist John Heywood, has dominated investors' investment decisions even until the new millennium: Investors are taught to decide between either maximizing financial return of their investments or using their investment money to achieve positive impact for society. While for-profit investments traditionally focus on optimizing financial return, investors, who seek to address social and environmental problems, are recommended to donate their money to charity. Typically, such donations do not yield any financial profits. Thus, conventionally, investment decisions are made on the basis of two factors: Portfolio or investment return and investors' individual attitude towards risk. Other factors, such as personal preferences or societal impact of the investments are faded out. The same has been true for companies: Managers' main responsibility is to increase shareholder value by, e.g., optimizing business operations, maximizing profits or distributing dividends. The company and its managers, in turn, should not care too much about spending corporate resources on socially responsible considerations and activities. It is rather up to the shareholders themselves to donate parts of their dividends to charity, but not something companies or their managers should be concerned with.

However, this notion seems to change and the clear-cut separation of business and society no longer strictly holds today. An increasing number of investors are no longer willing to take the either-or decision between doing well (= focusing on financial impact) and doing good (= focusing on societal impact). In fact, the opposite seems to be true: Investors increasingly look for investments, with which they can still generate solid financial returns, but at the same time intentionally address problems the society has to cope with. Investors systematically seem to deviate from the standard risk-return optimization problem as stated by neo-classical financial theory. As socially responsible investments (SRI)[2] continually move forward in making their

---

[1] The expression is taken from Heywood's (1546) work "A dialogue Conteinyng the Nomber in Effect of All the Prouerbes in the Englishe Tongue". Originally the saying was *"Wolde you bothe eate your cake, and haue your cake?"* (see Zimmer, 2011).

[2] The terms *socially responsible investments* and *socially responsible investing* are used as synonyms in the following sections and chapters.

way into investment portfolios, investors – socially conscious or not – now face the decision if they should jump onto this bandwagon or not.

Investors can participate in the SRI movement by either directly investing into companies that implement activities classified as corporate socially responsible (CSR) or indirectly by placing their money into SRI funds. These funds incorporate financial and non-financial criteria into their security selection process and only invest in companies that meet their investment criteria.[3] The non-financial criteria can either be targeted towards the inclusion of companies that perform well on ethical, social or environmental dimensions (positive screening) or towards the exclusion of companies that underperform in these dimensions (negative screening).[4] Positive screening sometimes is also combined with a best-in-class approach: Fund managers, who apply this approach, try to ensure that the fund portfolio not only meets the SRI criteria defined, but also is balanced across industries.[5] Negative screening, in turn, can result in the exclusion of entire industries such as gambling, alcohol or tobacco from the SRI funds' portfolios.[6] Thus, security selection is a stepwise process that begins with the definition of the criteria that are in line with investors' or fund managers' ethical, social, environmental or other non-financial preferences. These criteria are then applied to all securities available in the investment universe and finally only those securities that meet the (financial and non-financial) criteria are the ones that will be included in the SRI fund portfolio.[7]

The screening applied by the funds when selecting the securities that are to be included or excluded has led to a controversial discussion among academics on potential effects of such constraints on the funds' financial performance. According to portfolio theory developed by Markowitz (1952), the imposition of additional constraints in the security selection process should lead to an inferior performance of a SRI-screened relative to a SRI-unscreened fund portfolio.[8] In SRI-unscreened fund portfolios, the securities are selected from the entire investment universe. Conversely, in SRI-screened fund portfolios, only the securities that meet the pre-defined SRI criteria are available for inclusion in the portfolio. Thus, the number of securities that can potentially be part of the SRI fund portfolio is lower compared to a SRI-unscreened portfolio.

---

[3] See Goldberg et al. (2008), p. 54.
[4] See Leite & Cortez (2014), p. 251, Renneboog et al. (2008a), p. 1728 and Schwartz (2003), p. 197.
[5] See Kempf & Osthoff (2007), p. 909 and Vandekerckhove (2007), p. 403.
[6] See Haigh & Hazelton (2004), p. 61 and Humphrey & Lee (2011), p. 519.
[7] See Benson et al. (2006), p. 337.
[8] See Bello (2005), p. 41 and Cortez et al. (2009), p. 573.

Proponents of portfolio theory argue that the limited number of securities available will lead to a sub-optimal performance of the SRI fund portfolio relative to a portfolio built solely based on economic or financial screening criteria.[9]

There are, however, also arguments in favor of a superior performance of SRI funds compared to a conventional or SRI-unconstrained fund portfolio. Advocates of the SRI movement argue that it makes sense for investors to include both, non-financial and financial criteria, in the portfolio selection process: A sound performance on both dimensions indicates high managerial quality, which not only translates into lower employee turnover rates and litigation frequency, but also superior long-term financial performance compared to the market average.[10] Thus, companies with a high rating on environmental, social and governance (ESG) themes should have a comparative advantage over less socially responsible companies. This advantage is assumed to lead to a superior performance of SRI funds that invest in companies with a high rating on ESG themes relative to conventional funds that do not explicitly apply ESG screening criteria when selecting the companies to invest in.[11]

Empirical evidence on SRI fund performance is mixed. Some studies document significant levels of underperformance of SRI funds relative to their conventional counterparts, others find evidence of outperformance.[12] Other studies find no significant difference between the performances at all.[13] Thus, neither the theoretical discussion, nor the empirical studies provide consistent evidence in favor of or against a significant difference between the performance of SRI-screened and SRI-unscreened investments.

---

[9] See Benson et al. (2006), p. 338, Derwall & Koedijk (2009), p. 211, Grossman & Sharpe (1986), p. 27 and Rudd (1981), p. 57.

[10] See Bollen (2007), p. 684, Goldreyer & Diltz (1999), p. 23, Leite & Cortez (2014), p. 249 and Renneboog et al. (2008a), p. 1724.

[11] See Cortez et al. (2009), p. 573.

[12] See Cummings et al. (2000), Derwall & Koedijk (2009) and Luther et al. (1992) for studies that find evidence of SRI fund underperformance and Bauer et al. (2007), Goldreyer & Diltz (1999), Gregory et al. (1997), Jones et al. (2008), Lean et al. (2015) and Renneboog et al. (2008b) for studies that find evidence of SRI fund outperformance.

[13] See, for example, Bauer et al. (2005), Derwall & Koedijk (2009), Goldreyer & Diltz (1999), Hamilton et al. (1993), Kreander (2005), Lee et al. (2010), Reyes & Grieb (1998) and Sauer (1997).

Most of the studies published so far, however, have focused on analyzing the performance of SRI equity funds that have been established in the US or the UK. Only few studies have extended their data set and also include SRI equity funds from other countries.[14] Moreover, there is hardly any study that analyzes the performance of SRI balanced and fixed income funds.[15] Indeed, most of the studies explicitly mention that the data set consists of SRI equity funds only.[16] Thus, while there is already some evidence on the relative performance of US- or UK-based SRI equity funds, the performance of SRI balanced and fixed income funds in other geographical region has been less explored.

The empirical analysis in this thesis is an attempt to reduce this research gap by analyzing and comparing the performance of European-based SRI funds in all three fund categories. Consequently, the data set not only includes SRI equity funds, but also SRI balanced and fixed income funds that have been established in Europe. As equity funds only account for about half of the market for SRI, a data set that only includes SRI equity funds would not be representative for the entire European SRI market. Focusing on European-based SRI funds is mainly motivated by the fact that the European market is the biggest market for SRI globally.[17] Specifically, the final data set used in the analysis consists of SRI equity, balanced and fixed income funds from four European countries: The UK, France, the Netherlands and Germany. These four countries account for about 60% of the European SRI market. Moreover, as the share of SRI equity, balanced and fixed income funds in these countries is almost equal to the share obtained for all

---

[14] Kreander et al. (2005), for example, analyze the performance of SRI funds in the UK, Sweden, Germany and the Netherlands. Bauer et al. (2006) and Jones et al. (2008) focus on SRI funds from Australia.

[15] Hutton et al. (1998), p. 297 calculate the average monthly returns of SRI bond portfolios and compare it to the return of bond indices, while D'Antonio et al. (2000), p. 68 calculate the returns of SRI portfolios with varying mixes of equity and bond securities and compare it to the average returns generated by two benchmark indices. However, both studies assess performance merely based on the average returns generated by the portfolios and indices but do not account for other factors, e.g., the portfolio's exposure to systematic risk, the book-to-market ratio or the default and risk premium, that potentially also influence the realized returns. Derwall & Koedijk (2009), p. 211 are the first to compare the performance of US-based SRI balanced and fixed income funds to that of conventional funds using multi-factor regression models as also applied in this thesis.

[16] See Bauer et al. (2005), p. 1754 and (2006), p. 36, Humphrey & Lee (2011), p. 526, Kempf & Osthoff (2008), p. 1277 and Renneboog et al. (2011), p. 566.

[17] See EUROSIF (2014), p. 21 and USSIF (2012), p. 11.

SRI funds established in Europe, the funds used in the analysis can be considered to be a representative sample for the entire SRI fund market in Europe.[18]

1.2 Research objectives

The thesis aims at providing insights on a conceptual and empirical level. Thus, the research objectives of the thesis can be structured according to the level – theoretical or empirical – they refer to.

On the conceptual level, there are two objectives the thesis focusses on. First, the thesis aims at providing a comprehensive introduction to the SRI market in general and the various definitions of SRI that can be found in reports published by practitioners and in empirical studies conducted by academic researchers. Although the roots of the SRI movement can be traced back to the early 1900's, there is still no clear definition among practitioners and researchers about what SRI is and what it is not.[19] This thesis reviews the numerous definitions available, highlights the definition used as basis for the empirical analysis and presents the historical development of the SRI investment alternative. Second, with increasing market size of the SRI industry, academic interest in this field has emerged as well. The thesis gives an in-depth overview of the scientific work on SRI that has already been conducted and published in recent years. The empirical models used in the existing empirical studies are presented and the results obtained are summarized. The literature review is used as a basis for deriving of the hypotheses that are to be tested and developing the models applied in the empirical part of this thesis.

The empirical part focusses on providing an answer to the question if investors have to sacrifice parts of their financial return when investing into SRI funds or not. Given the ongoing debate on the performance expectation of SRI-screened investment alternatives, the analysis in this thesis is set out to empirically assess how the SRI-screened investment alternatives perform relative to SRI-unscreened or conventional ones. More precisely, the analysis examines if the SRI-screened investment alternatives perform better, as good as or worse than conventional investments. Thus, the main research objective of the study is to provide empirical evidence if

---

[18] The share of SRI equity funds is 59% in the sample and 54% in Europe. For SRI balanced (fixed income) funds, the share is 17% (24%) in the sample and 13% (33%) in Europe. For details on the breakdown of the European SRI fund market see Vigeo (2013a), p. 10.

[19] See Capelle-Blancard & Monjon (2012), p. 239, Schueth (2003), p. 189, Sparkes (2001), p. 195, Taylor (2000), p. 174 and Vandekerckhove (2007), p. 403.

it is in fact possible for investors to be doing good while doing well or if investors rather have to sacrifice parts of the expected financial return when investing into SRI-screened investment alternatives.

In order to find evidence on the relative performance of SRI-screened investment alternatives, the research objective is split up into three research questions that guide the empirical study in this thesis. The first research question deals with the debate if there is a significant difference between the performance of SRI-screened and conventional (SRI-unscreened) investments. In order to provide an answer to this question, the performances of SRI funds in each category are compared to the performances of conventional and SRI market indices. Additionally, the performances of the SRI market indices are compared to the performances of conventional market indices. The indices chosen serve as a benchmark for the return investors can expect when investing into passively managed market portfolios. The comparison between the returns generated by the SRI funds and the ones generated by the market indices provides insights if SRI fund managers succeed in setting up actively managed portfolios that perform better, as good as or worse than the market. Evidence of outperformance of the funds against the market would imply that SRI funds are a possibility for investors to invest in a socially responsible way and at the same time earn higher returns. Evidence in favor of a similar performance of the SRI funds would indicate that the market does not seem to price the socially responsible feature of the SRI funds and investors can expect to earn the same levels of return when investing into SRI-screened and SRI-unscreened investment alternatives. Finally, evidence of SRI fund underperformance would infer that the conventions of the traditional investment decision process still hold today and that fund managers are not able to select securities that constantly beat the market. Consequenlty, investors would be better off – at least from a financial perspective – when investing into the market portfolio and donating parts of the money generated with unscreened investments to charity in order to achieve a positive impact for society.

The comparison between the returns generated by SRI funds and that of SRI indices as well as conventional market indices ensures any difference observed between the funds' and the indices' returns are not only attributable to the active management of the funds, but to the socially responsible feature of the SRI investment alternatives. In case the empirical evidence shows that SRI funds and SRI market indices underperform (outperform) against conventional indices, the evidence suggests that the SRI-screening process does influence the performance of funds and indices alike. However, if the analysis provides evidence that only the performance of SRI funds differs from the performance of market indices, but SRI indices perform as good as conventional indices, no inference about the relationship between the screening process and the financial performance can be made. Instead, there might also be other reasons such as the active management of the funds that influence the funds' financial performance.

The second empirical research question focusses on analyzing if the performances of SRI funds from the three categories are different from each other. The data set used in the analyses is one of the few that not only includes SRI equity funds, but also SRI balanced and fixed income funds. Consequently, the performances of the SRI funds in each category cannot only be assessed relative to the market. Instead, they can also be assessed relative to each other by, e.g., comparing the performance of SRI equity funds to that of SRI fixed income funds and the performance of SRI fixed income funds to that of SRI balanced funds. As the performances of SRI funds in each category are compared with each other, the analyses provide insights on whether or not the SRI funds' performances depend on the particular fund category investors consider investing in.

Finally, the third empirical research question is targeted towards providing empirical evidence if SRI fund performance changes over time. The analyses conducted in order to answer the first two research questions examine if there is evidence suggesting any difference in the performances between SRI-screened investments themselves (e.g., SRI funds relative to SRI indices) or between SRI-screened and SRI-unscreened investments (e.g., SRI funds or indices relative to conventional indices). The first step to answer these questions is to calculate the average monthly returns generated by the SRI funds as well as the returns generated by the SRI and conventional indices. The average monthly returns, however, are calculated as an equally weighted average of the returns generated by a fund or index over the entire observation period. This implies that performance is assessed for the entire observation period from 2003 to 2013, but no inference about the relative performance of SRI funds in sub-periods can be made. However, relative performance of a SRI fund might change over time, e.g., a fund that performs worse than the market over the entire observation period might perform just as well as or even better than the market in sub-periods. Thus, the third research question is motivated by the notion that evidence in favor of or against a change in relative SRI fund performance over time provides insights on whether or not the investment horizon has an influence on the relative performance of their SRI fund portfolios. Moreover, it also generates valuable information for investors if there are SRI funds that consistently outperform the market by generating abnormal returns not only in the short, but also in the long-run.

In sum, the empirical analyses conducted in this thesis aim to provide comprehensive answers to the following three research questions (RQ):

- RQ 1: How do SRI-screened investment alternatives (SRI funds and SRI market indices) perform relative to their benchmarks (SRI and conventional indices)?
- RQ 2: Is there a difference between the performances of SRI equity, balanced and fixed income funds?
- RQ 3: Does the relative performance of the SRI funds change over time?

In order to answer these research questions, the analyses include SRI equity as well as SRI balanced and SRI fixed income funds established in the UK, France, the Netherlands and Germany – the four biggest markets for SRI in Europe. Fund performance is examined using single-factor and multi-factor regression models also applied in previous studies on SRI fund performance.[20] In order to answer the question if there is a change in SRI fund performance over time, the observation period is split up into two sub-periods and the performance of the SRI funds within each period is analyzed separately. The first sub-period ranges from January 2003 to December 2007 (the years before the global financial crisis) and the second one from January 2008 to December 2013 (the years during and after the crisis).

The results obtained in the empirical analysis are not only of interest for investors, who consider placing parts of their money into SRI funds and want to get a better understanding of the effect on the financial performance of their portfolios in case SRI funds are added. They are also relevant for SRI fund managers, who are interested in promoting their funds and attracting (new) investors and for academics, whose research interests are, e.g., located in the fields of SRI, fund portfolio performances and market efficiencies.

1.3 Structure of the thesis

The thesis is structured as follows. While the current Chapter 1 has introduced SRI as the central theme of the thesis and the research objectives, the following chapter provides an in-depth overview of the market for SRI – globally and regionally within Europe. Thus, Chapter 2 begins

---

[20] See, for example, Bauer et al. (2005), p. 1758, Betker & Sheehan (2013), p. 351, Cortez et al. (2009), p. 576, Cumby & Glen (1990), p. 503, Curcio et al. (2003), p. 81, Cuthbertson & Nitzsche (2013), p. 89, Derwall & Koedijk (2009), p. 219, Goldreyer & Diltz (1999), p. 26, Grinblatt & Titman (1989), p. 395, Mallin et al. (1995), p. 489, McDonald (1974), p. 313, Le Sourd (2010), p. 18 and Otten & Bams (2004), p. 204.

with a review of the numerous attempts made by academics and organizations to provide a definition of the term SRI. Afterwards, the historical as well as current development of the SRI market is described and regulatory standards formulated by governments and non-state organizations are presented. The chapter ends with an introduction of the different investment strategies applied by SRI investors and a brief excursus on impact investing – an investment strategy that only accounts for a fraction of the European SRI market today, but has experienced tremendous growth rates in recent years and increasingly attracts investors' and academics' interest.

Chapter 3 introduces the two possibilities investors have in order to get exposed to SRI: They either can decide to directly invest in companies that have implemented CSR activities or indirectly by investing their money in SRI funds. These funds define SRI criteria companies have to meet in order to be part of the fund's portfolio. As the empirical analysis focusses on examining the performance of SRI funds, Chapter 4 provides a review of theoretical discussions and empirical evidences found in the existing literature on SRI fund performance.

Chapter 5 starts with the derivation of the hypotheses that are to be tested in the empirical study and a brief introduction into the methodology chosen to assess SRI fund performance. The chapter ends with the description of the data set used in the empirical study and leads over to the presentation of the empirical results in Chapter 6. The description of the results in Chapter 6 is organized according to the analyses conducted: First, the results obtained in the single- and multi-factor regression models are presented. Afterwards, the results obtained in the sub-period analyses are displayed and additional analyses that have been conducted to support previous findings are introduced. The chapter closes with a discussion of the implications the empirical results might have for various stakeholder groups, critically reviews the limitations of the study and offers ideas for future research. Finally, Chapter 7 summarizes the theoretical as well as empirical observations made throughout the thesis and provides some concluding remarks.

2 The market for socially responsible investing

2.1 The term socially responsible investing (SRI)

Until today, there is no single, globally accepted definition of socially responsible investing (SRI) available. In fact, there is not even a consensus reached on the exact term used to describe SRI issues. Socially responsible investing, social investing, ethical investing, green investing and mission-based investing are examples of the terms used when asset managers, investors or academics are talking about SRI.[21] As Schueth (2003) points out, the lack of a common language to describe the process of socially responsible investing shows that the market is still developing and far away from being settled.[22]

Although there is no globally accepted definition of SRI today, the terms employed share the common theme of integrating investors' concerns about ESG issues in the investment decision process.[23] Langbein and Posner (1980), for example, define the term social investing as an investment process in which securities of financially attractive, but presumably socially irresponsible companies in a portfolio are replaced by securities of companies that are judged to have a sound record of social responsibility but are rather unattractive from a purely financial perspective.[24] According to this definition of SRI, investors have to decide between either following the conventional objective of profit maximization and with this, focusing on the financial interests of investing, or pursuing an investment strategy that puts social interests first while sacrificing some of the originally expected financial return. Clearly, this definition is a rather traditional view on the concept of social investing as it highlights the trade-off between social and financial interests investors used to face when SRI was first introduced. In light of the

---

[21] See Capelle-Blancard & Monjon (2012), p. 239, Schueth (2003), p. 189, Sparkes (2001), p. 195, Taylor (2000), p. 174 and Vandekerckhove (2007), p. 403.

[22] See Schueth (2003), p. 189.

[23] The number of definitions for SRI mentioned in the following sections are not meant to cover all definitions available. Instead, the sections are intended to provide an indication on the multitude of definitions available, but do not claim to be exhaustive.

[24] See Langbein & Posner (1980), p. 73.

increasing demand by investors to combine both, financial and non-financial interests, this definition can be considered somewhat outdated today.

About a decade later, Lowry (1993) does not provide a definition for the term social investing, but identifies four goals SRI should accomplish within the business context:[25] First, establishing a balanced and diversified working environment by hiring, retaining and promoting women and minorities in the workforce. Second, improving work conditions by promoting clean, safe and rewarding work environments. Third, continue focussing on generating profits but at the same time rethinking the way these profits are distributed to the company's shareholders. Fourth, convincing the business environment that SRI and corporate engagement in SRI is beneficial and financially attractive for all stakeholders of the company. In sum, Lowry (1993) centers his argumentation on the corporate aspects of SRI while at the same time pointing out the necessity for the socially conscious company to also have financial interests in mind when making business decisions. Contrary to the definition made by Langbein and Posner (1980), the definition provided by Lowry (1993) does not focus on the trade-off between financial and social interests managers have to take. Instead, Lowry (1993) points out that it should be possible for a company to combine both, financial and social well-being – given that the business environment realizes and acknowledges this effort.[26] This is also in line with the definition of SRI made by Cowton (1999), who clearly emphasizes that managers and investors should consider both, financial and non-financial (e.g., social or ethical) criteria, when making decisions on whether to purchase, continue holding or sell an investment security.[27]

In fact, the idea of integrating societal aspects into the investment decision process is what separates SRI from traditional investments. Knoll (2002) underlines this argumentation and determines two criteria that describe what SRI is and what it is not:[28] First and foremost, SRI is not about charity; it is about making financial investments and generating profits. Thus, SRI-investors are not willing to give away their money for free, but expect to make profits from their investments just as traditional investors do. Second – and contrary to traditional investments – financial criteria are not the only criteria relevant in the investment decision process.

---

[25] See Lowry (1993), p. 56.
[26] See Lowry (1993), p. 56.
[27] See Cowton (1999), p. 60.
[28] See Knoll (2002), pp. 689f.

2. The market for socially responsible investing

Instead, financial criteria are combined with non-financial criteria in order to accomplish the aim of generating profits (i.e. achieving financial impact) while at the same time doing something good for the society (i.e. achieving a positive social impact). The non-financial criteria incorporated into the investment process can be classified by three categories:[29]

- Social factors such as human capital, community development and labor rights
- Environmental factors such as global warming, depletion of natural resources and environmental pollution and
- Ethical factors such as violation of human rights, child labor, slavery and concerns related to certain industries like alcohol, gambling, weapons or nuclear power

Which of these factors investor consider in their investment process depends on the individual investor's preferences.[30] The only thing that is important for an investment process to be considered as socially responsible is the fact, that at least one of these factors is incorporated in the process at all. Without these factors, SRI would actually be no different than traditional investments and no separate definition would have been needed.[31]

Knoll (2002) is not the only researcher, who emphasizes the importance of considering both, the financial and the non-financial security selection criteria when talking about SRI. Goldberg et al. (2008), for example, summarize the main idea behind the SRI movement as follows:[32] SRI is an investment strategy with which investors not only try to optimize the risk and return profile of their investment but at the same time also aim improving the wellbeing of the society they live in by incorporating non-financial objectives such as their personal values and beliefs into the investment decision process.[33] In order to accomplish this goal, investors can either directly invest in companies that have implemented corporate social responsibility (CSR) activities or place parts of their investment capital into funds that pool money from different investors and apply SRI screening criteria when selecting the companies that are to be included

---

[29] See OECD (2007), p. 4.
[30] Studies conducted by Derwall et al. (2011) and Vyvyan et al. (2007) show that the preferences among SRI investors vary greatly. See Derwall et al. (2011), p. 2138 and (2007), p. 379. For further details on the individual motivation of SRI investors to engage in SRI see section 2.5.2.
[31] See Knoll (2002), p. 689.
[32] See Goldberg et al. (2008), p. 54.
[33] See Beal & Goyen (1998), p. 129 and Renneboog et al. (2008a), p. 1723.

in the fund.[34] Those funds are commonly referred to as SRI funds and introduced in more detail in section 3.2.

Apart from academic researchers, regional organizations that engage in SRI have also published their own definition of SRI. Similar to the definition made by Knoll (2002), the US Social Investment Forum (USSIF)[35] and the Canadian Responsible Investment Association (RIA)[36], for example, define SRI as an investment strategy that incorporates ESG criteria into the security selection process in order to generate both, competitive financial returns and positive impact for society.[37] Thus, SRI is an investment alternative developed for investors, who look for an investment opportunity with which they can combine their financial objectives with their personal concerns about ESG issues.[38]

The European equivalent to the USSIF and the RIA, the European Sustainable Investment Forum (EUROSIF)[39], supports this view but additionally points out the varying preferences that drive investors' investment decisions: While some investors merely focus on controlling for ESG risks when making investment decisions, others pro-actively use ESG aspects as criteria when selecting the securities for their portfolio.[40] Thus, it is difficult to identify a typical SRI investor and individual investors usually have made up own interpretation of what constitutes a socially-responsible investment and what does not. For the purpose of this thesis, SRI is defined as an investment strategy with which investors include financial objectives (i.e. optimizing the risk and return profile of their investment) and non-financial objectives (i.e. incorporating personal values and beliefs) in their investment decision process. Moreover, following the definition made by Goldberg et al. (2008), SRI as defined for this thesis can be made directly into companies that have implemented CSR activities or indirectly via SRI funds.[41]

---

[34] See Goldberg et al. (2008), p. 54.

[35] The USSIF is a membership association founded with the aim to promote the development of SRI aspects among investment professionals and institutions in the US (for more information see http://www.ussif.org).

[36] The RIA is the Canadian equivalent to the USSIF and defines itself as a membership organization for responsible investment (for more information see https://riacanada.ca/).

[37] See RIA (2013), p. 7 and USSIF (2013).

[38] See Brooks (1989), p. 32 and Mackenzie & Lewis (1999), p. 440.

[39] The EUROSIF is a not-for profit, pan-European network, whose members include institutional investors, financial service providers, academic institutes and NGOs (see http://www.eurosif.org).

[40] See EUROSIF (2012), p. 8.

[41] See Goldberg (2008), p. 54.

The multitude of definitions and interpretations of what SRI is also makes it difficult to define the global market for SRI. Nonetheless, the increasing investment volume into SRI indicates that there is a growing and non-saturated market for SRI that is worth considering in more detail.[42] Thus, the following section provides an overview of the historical development of this market as well as its current market size and regulatory initiatives taken by national governments to encourage the growth of SRI market both, regionally and globally.

2.2 Historical development

Although the idea of investing in a socially responsible way just recently gained companies' and investors' attention, the concept of SRI is not a phenomenon of the late 20th century. In fact, the origins of the SRI movement can be traced back hundreds of years when religious and philanthropic organizations started practicing it: Jewish law, for example, early on comprised several principles on how to invest in ethically correct ways.[43] Other examples include not only early Christian investors, who refrained from investing into companies that operate in putatively sinful industries such as alcohol, tobacco, gambling or pornography, but also the members of the Quaker movement in England, who refused to invest in activities related to war or slavery[44] Already in 1758, the Quakers passed a law that prohibited slavery and excluded all members from meetings that continued to import and hold slaves.[45]

For hundreds of years, there has been the notion that government and other public entities such as religious groups have the responsibility of taking care of social well-being and protecting the environment. Companies and the private sector, in turn, primarily have been responsible for generating economic wealth. Thus, it comes at little surprise that the first SRI fund that was established in the US in 1920 was fully owned by religious or charitable organizations. Financial markets, however, have paid only little attention to this fund and the funds that have been

---

[42] See Juravle & Lewis (2008), p. 287. Moreover, compounded annual growth rates of assets under management in SRI have been as high as 40% from 2003 to 2013. See USSIF (2012), p. 11, EUROSIF (2014), p. 21 and Section 2.3.

[43] See Schueth (2003), p. 189.

[44] See Knoll (2002), p. 684 and Schueth (2003), p. 189.

[45] See Cazden (2013), p. 352.

established soon after.[46] In fact, the strict separation of responsibilities first began to blur during the mid-1960s, when the political climate changed and investors got increasingly concerned about issues regarding civil rights, the environment and militarism.[47] In order to express their resentments about the military actions taken during the war in Vietnam, advocacy groups, for example, have bought shares of companies that profited from the war and forced the executives of those companies to reconsider or even terminate their engagement in military actions.[48] Others investor groups sought to address allegedly harmful business practices and put public pressure on companies with inequalities in labor-management to pass socially responsible shareholder resolutions.[49]

Only a few years later, in the 1980s, the first private investors refused to invest in companies that had business operations in South Africa. Soon after, millions of other investors joined this movement by implementing strategies aimed at pressuring the white minority government to finally end the racist system of Apartheid.[50] The group of socially conscious investors grew even further after environmental disasters such as the exploding nuclear power plant in Chernobyl in 1986 or the crash of the supertanker Exxon Valdez that spilled more than 10 million gallons of crude oil in Alaska in 1989.[51] In addition, the increased media coverage for human rights issues such as irresponsible working conditions or child labor as well as the vast amount of information on global warming and the ozone depletion caught investors' attention and led to a steady increase in the number of investors that denote themselves as socially conscious.[52]

To conclude, Schwartz (2003) lists seven factors that, in sum, have all contributed to the tremendous growth of the SRI industry since the early years in the 1960s:[53]

- Investor' growing consciousness for SRI issues

---

[46] The Pioneer Fund has been the first fund established in the US and explicitly excluded companies with business operations in or relations to the alcohol and tobacco industry. During the same era, similar funds have been established in the UK as well, but the funds could not gain popularity among investors and thus, remained in possession of the religious organizations that established them. See de Colle & York (2009), p. 84 and Sampford & Ransome (2013), p. 15.

[47] See EUROSIF (2012), p. 8, Sampford & Ransome (2013), p. 16 and Schueth (2003), p. 190.

[48] See Sampford & Ransome (2013), p. 16.

[49] The actions taken by the activists in the 1960s initiated what is today known as shareholder activism, one of the core SRI strategies defined by the USSSIF (2006), p. 1.

[50] See Dumas & Michotte (2014), p. 122 and Schueth (2003), p. 190.

[51] See Renneboog et al. (2008a), p. 1750.

[52] See EUROSIF (2010), p. 7 and Scalet & Kelly (2010), p. 70.

[53] See Schwartz (2003), p. 196.

- An increasing number of companies and organizations that engage in the CSR movement
- The growing number of empirical evidences that documents at least competitive return performance of SRI investment alternatives
- An increasing number of marketing and advertising activities tailored towards SRI investment alternatives
- Growth of media exposure devoted to CSR activities and SRI
- An increasing number of indices that only include companies with a certain CSR score and
- The growing number of national social investment organizations and their activities targeted towards SRI

This extensive list of factors highlights that it is not only increased sensitivity of investors to human rights issues that has fostered the growth of this industry. It is also the increased supply of SRI alternatives available on the market that simplified the way how investors can get involved in SRI: In fact, with an increasing number of, e.g. SRI mutual funds offered, even small investors have the chance to participate in the SRI movement. The following section provides an overview on the current global and European market for SRI and shows that this market is expected to grow further in the close future.

2.3 Current market size

According to a study on SRI done by the USSIF, the market size for assets under management (AuM) involved in sustainable and responsible investing was USD 3.74 trillion in the United States (US) in 2012.[54] This equals a proportion of almost 11% of the total assets under professional management in the US. In Europe, the market for total SRI AuM was estimated to be at approximately EUR 9.89 trillion in 2013, representing about 10% of total AuM.[55] Within the Eurozone, the biggest market for SRI is in the United Kingdom (UK, EUR 1.97 trillion), followed by France (EUR 1.73 trillion), the Netherlands (EUR 1.24 trillion) and Germany (EUR

---

[54] See USSIF (2012), p. 11.
[55] See EUROSIF (2014), p. 21.

0.89 trillion).[56] Table 1 summarizes market size estimates for SRI in five global regions (Europe, United States, Canada, Australia and Japan) and the proportion of SRI assets among total assets under professional management in each region.

Table 1: SRI market size per region

This table represents total SRI assets under management (SRI AuM) according to the core and broad definition of SRI by EUROSIF and the proportion of SRI portfolios among total AuM (in percent of total AuM) in the US, Europe, Canada, Australia and Japan. Due to data availability, numbers for Japan are from 2011 and numbers for Europe are from 2013.

Market size in 2012		Total SRI AuM	In percent of total AuM
Europe	(EUR Bn)	9.885	10%
United States	(USD Bn)	3.744	11%
Canada	(CAD Bn)	601	20%
Australia	(AUD Bn)	152	16%
Japan	(JPY Bn)	325	1%

Sources: Europe: EUROSIF (2014), United States: USSIF (2012), Canada: RIA (2013), Australia: RIAA (2013), Japan: SIF Japan (2011)

Table 1 illustrates that Europe and the US are – in absolute terms – the biggest markets for SRI globally. However, only one out of ten euros or dollars is invested into SRI in these two regions, while in Canada the SRI market constitutes about 20% of total AuM. Thus, one out of every fifth dollar is invested in SRI in Canada already today. Contrary, SRI plays only an insignificant role in Japan as the share of the SRI market currently is below 1% of total AuM in this country.[57]

Although SRI has gained considerable market share in Europe, the US, Canada and Australia already, the global market for SRI has not evolved gradually over the past few hundred years after the religious groups have introduced the idea first. Instead, the market mostly developed in the past two or three decades when the number of professionally managed SRI has increased as well.[58] Focusing on the biggest market worldwide, the US and Europe, Table 2 shows the market development and growth rates of the SRI market in the two countries.

---

[56] See EUROSIF (2014), p. 21.
[57] See SIF Japan (2011), p. 7.
[58] See Renneboog et al. (2008a), p. 1725 and USSIF (2010), p. 8.

2. The market for socially responsible investing

Table 2: Development of SRI market size in the US and Europe

This table shows the development of the SRI market in the US (Panel A) and Europe (Panel B). Numbers are in local currency: US-Dollar for the US market and Euro for the European market. Growth rates are calculated as the average growth rate of two years; for Europe, growth rates of different years have to be interpreted with caution as the number of countries included in the study varies (see note above for list of countries included in respective years).

Panel A: United States									
USD Bn	1995	1997	1999	2001	2003	2005	2007	2010	2012
Screening	162	529	1,497	2,010	2,143	1,684	2,098	2,512	3,253
Shareholder Advocacy	473	736	922	897	448	703	739	1,497	1,536
Community Investing	4	4	5	8	14	20	25	42	61
Overlapping Strategies	0	-84	-265	-592	-441	-117	-151	-981	-1,106
Total	639	1,185	2,159	2,323	2,164	2,290	2,711	3,070	3,744
Growth rate p.a.		42.7%	41.1%	3.8%	-3.4%	2.9%	9.2%	4.4%	11.0%
CAGR (1995-2012)	11.0%								
CAGR (2001-2012)	4.4%								

Note: In order to avoid double counting effects, overlapping assets involved in some combination of ESG incorporation (screening and/or community investing) and shareholder advocacy are subtracted.

Panel B: Europe							
EUR Bn	2003	2005	2007	2009	2011	2013	2013*
Core SRI	34	105	511	1,150	2,555	3,779	2,456
Broad SRI	302	1,033	2,154	3,836	4,208	6,106	5,623
Total	336	1,138	2,665	4,986	6,763	9,885	8,079
Growth rate p.a.		119.3%	67.1%	43.5%	17.8%	23.1%	
CAGR (2003-2013)	40.2%						
CAGR (2003-2013*)	37.4%						

Notes:
Core SRI: Norms- and values/ethical-based exclusions (3+ criteria); positive screening, incl. best-in-class and SRI thematic funds
Broad SRI: Simple screening (one or two exclusion criteria; norms-based or values/ethical based); engagement; integration
2003: Incl. Austria, France, Germany, Italy, Netherlands, Spain, Switzerland, United Kingdom
2005: Incl. Austria, Belgium, France, Germany, Italy, Netherlands, Spain, Switzerland, United Kingdom
2007: Incl. Austria, Belgium, Denmark, Finland, France, Germany, Italy, Netherlands, Norway, Spain, Sweden, Switzerland, United Kingdom
2009: Incl. Austria, Baltic States, Belgium, Cyprus, Denmark, Finland, France, Germany, Greece, Italy, Netherlands, Norway, Poland, Spain, Sweden, Switzerland, United Kingdom
2011/2013: Incl. Austria, Belgium, Finland, France, Germany, Italy, Netherlands, Norway, Poland, Spain, Sweden, Switzerland, United Kingdom
2013*: see 2003

Source: Own illustration based on EUROSIF (2014) and USSIF (2012)

In the US (displayed in Panel A of Table 2), the market grew from USD 0.64 trillion in 1995 to USD 2.29 trillion a decade later (+258% within 10 years) and USD 3.74 trillion in 2012. Growth rates have been as high as 40% p.a. in the mid-1990s, slowing down to a compound annual growth rate (CAGR) of 4.4% p.a. from 2001 to 2012. The market in Europe (Panel B of Table 2) also experienced phenomenal growth rates in the past ten years: Starting from EUR 0.33 trillion in 2003, the market grew by more than 100% in the two years afterwards and reached almost 30-times the initially reported market size in 2013 (EUR 9.89 trillion). The CAGR for the period 2003 to 2013 is as high as 40%, meaning that the growth rate of the SRI market repeatedly outpaced growth rates on other European investment markets.[59]

However, the number of countries included in the EUROSIF study varies from year to year: As the number of countries included in the study increased from only eight in 2003 to 17 in 2009 and fell back to 13 in 2013, the growth of the market cannot only be attributed to investors' increased interest in SRI, but is also caused by a rather simple counting-effect. Adjusting the market size for 2013 such that only those countries are taken into account that have been part of the initial EUROSIF study in 2003, the CAGR for the period 2003 to 2013 drops to 37%.[60]

Nonetheless, the SRI markets in the US and in Europe experienced a tremendous growth in the past decades and developed from a rather marginal phenomenon mainly practiced by religious institutions or social organizations to a mainstream investment alternative relevant for private and institutional investors alike.[61] Parts of the positive development of the global SRI market can and should be attributed to the regulatory initiatives taken by national governments to encourage the growth of this market. The following section reviews the regulatory framework surrounding the SRI industry in various countries worldwide.

2.4 Regulatory background

2.4.1 State regulations

Table 3 provides an overview of the SRI regulations initiated and implemented by national governments around the globe. The table illustrates that the number and intensity of state regulations varies greatly from country to country. It might be surprising, though, that the US and Australia are the only two countries outside of Europe that are included in the overview of Table 3. The reason for this is simple: Except for the countries included in the overview, hardly any other country has yet implemented national state regulations regarding SRI.[62] Companies in

---

[59] See EUROSIF (2012), p. 26.
[60] See notes to the European market in Table 2.
[61] See Jansson & Biel (2011), p. 136.
[62] See Renneboog et al. (2008a), p. 1728 and Preu & Richardson (2011), p. 872.

these countries have the choice to implement voluntary CSR and SRI guidelines that are discussed in the next section.

Australasia: In Australia, two regulations that fostered the development of the SRI market in this region have been passed in the early 2000s.[63] The first regulation relates to ethical disclosure requirements that have been introduced under the Financial Services Reform Act (FSRA). According to this regulation, issuers of financial products are obliged to report on the extent to which labor standards as well as ESG issues are considered in the selection and realization of their investment products.

The second regulation relates to SRI disclosure guidelines that have been introduced by the Australian Securities and Investments Commission (ASIC). These guidelines require personal financial advisors to get information whether and how ESG considerations are of importance to their clients. Above this, the Responsible Investment Association Australasia (RIAA)[64] conducts annual benchmarking studies on the SRI market in Australia and New Zealand. The RIAA also has developed the Responsible Investment Certification Program and the Certification Symbol to certify responsible investment products and services.

Continental Europe: Within Continental Europe, the Netherlands has been one of the first countries to introduce tax savings for sustainable investments: Already in 1995, the Dutch Tax Office passed the Green Savings and Investment Plan introducing tax advantages for green investment categories such as wind or solar energy and organic farming.[65] In the same year, institutional and private investors formed the Dutch Association for Sustainable Development (Vereniging van Beleggers voor Duurzame Ontwikkeling, VBDO). Shortly after the foundation of the organization, representatives of the VBDO attended annual shareholder meetings and explicitly asked management to report on their SRI and CSR practices. In the years thereafter, the number and quality of corporate sustainable reports for companies in the Netherlands increased significantly.[66] However, these reports are still semi-voluntary as shareholders demand them but no legal requirements have yet been put into place by national law. In fact, apart from the tax advantage mentioned in the beginning, there are no other formal legislations in place

---

[63] See Bauer et al. (2006), p. 34.
[64] The RIAA is a member organization for professionals working in the SRI industry in Australia and New Zealand. It was established as the Ethical Investment Association (EIA) in 1999, but renamed to RIAA in 2007 (see http://www.responsibleinvestment.org).
[65] See Renneboog et al. (2008a), p. 1727.
[66] See EUROSIF (2003), p. 28.

that govern the SRI market in the Netherlands.[67] Instead, institutional investors in the Dutch market have developed their own SRI policies and codes of conducts: The Pension Federation, for example, published a handbook on responsible investments and the Association for Insurers has implemented a Sustainable Investment Code (Code Duurzaam Beleggen) that requires its members to take various efforts directed towards making their investments more responsible.[68]

Table 3: SRI regulations by national governments

This table reviews legal frameworks and regulatory initiatives regarding SRI.

Country	Legal framework and SRI related regulation(s)
Australia	In March 2003, the new ethical disclosure requirements have been introduced under the Financial Services Reform Act (FSRA) requiring issuers of financial products to report on the level how labor standards as well as ESG issues are considered in the selection and realization of an investment product. In addition, under the Australian Securities and Investments Commission (ASIC), personal financial advisors are required to get information whether and how ESG considerations are of importance to their clients.
France	Since 2001, the New Economic Regulations have been passed, requiring publicly traded companies to publish information on their ESG impact in their annual reports.
Germany	In 2000, the German parliament passed the Renewable Energies Act aimed at incentivizing investments in renewable energies. The act provides above market price guarantees for companies operating plants that generate electricity out of wind, water or biomass. Since 2001, pension funds and since 2005, direct insurance companies are required to report on the ESG criteria considered in their investment savings plans. In 2002, the German Corporate Governance Code was introduced that requires companies to at least annually confirm their compliance with the code or, in case of deviations from the code, give reasons for the deviation.
Netherlands	In 1995, the Dutch Tax Office passed the Green Savings and Investment Plan introducing tax advantages for green investment categories such as wind or solar energy and organic farming. In the same year, institutional as well as private investors formed the Dutch Association for Sustainable Development (VBDO). Until today, there are no formal SRI regulations in place in the Netherlands. Nonetheless, the Pension Federation published a handbook on responsible investment and the Association for Insurers has implemented a Responsible Investment Code that requires its members to take various efforts directed towards making their investments more responsible.
United Kingdom	In 1999 (and re-published in 2005), the UK Parliament introduced The Occupational Pension Schemes (Pensions Act) that requires occupational pension funds to extend their statement of investment principles by the information on how of ESG issues are considered in their investment strategy. Since 2000, charity trustees are obliged to make sure that their investments fit their financial as well as social aims. This also includes a report on the appropriate consideration of ESG issues in the investment approach (Trustee Act). In 2001, the Association of British Insurers introduces guidelines for (primarily listed) companies encouraging them to publish significant ESG risks that might be of relevance for their business activities.
United States	In the US, several laws to address social and environmental concerns have already been passed. Examples include legislations directed towards pollution and hazardous waste control (e.g. The Clean Air Act Amendments of 1977), workplace improvement (e.g. The Equal Employment Opportunity Act of 1972) and consumer protection (e.g. The Consumer Product Safety Act). Reporting of CSR activities, however, still is voluntary for companies in the US.

Sources: Bauer et al. (2006), EUROSIF (2003, 2006, 2012, 2014), Renneboog et al. (2008a) and Tschopp (2005)

---

[67] See EUROSIF (2012), p. 47.

[68] See Pension Federation (2007) and VBDO (2012), p. 6.

2. The market for socially responsible investing 23

In Germany, several regulations on SRI have been passed as well: In 2000, for example, the German parliament passed the Renewable Energies Act aimed at incentivizing investments in renewable energies. This legislation has provided above market prices guaranties for companies operating plants that generate electricity out of wind, water or biomass.[69] Above this, pension funds and direct insurance companies are required to report on the ESG criteria considered in their investment savings plans since 2001 and 2005, respectively. This requirement is an adoption of the 1999 Pensions Act that has first been introduced in the UK and afterwards implemented in several other countries within Continental Europe.[70] Finally, the German Corporate Governance Code was introduced in 2002, requiring companies to confirm their compliance with the code at least annually or, in case of deviations from the code, give reasons for the deviation.[71] Other than that, however, there is no obligation for insurance companies to report on ESG policies in Germany. France, the second biggest market for SRI within Europe, is the only country making ESG reporting mandatory for listed companies: Since 2001 the New Economic Regulations have been passed requiring publicly traded companies to include information on their ESG impact in their annual reports.[72]

United Kingdom: The UK is a pioneer in implementing SRI legislations. It was one of the first countries to regulate the disclosure of ESG investment policies: Already in 1999 (and re-published in 2005), the UK Parliament introduced the Occupational Pension Schemes (Pensions Act) requiring occupational pension funds to extend their statement of investment principles by the information how ESG issues are considered in their investment strategy.[73] Since 2000, charity trustees are obliged to make sure that their investments fit their financial and their social objectives. This also includes the publication of a report on the appropriate consideration of ESG issues in the investment approach (Trustee Act).[74] In 2001, the Association of British Insurers introduced voluntary guidelines for listed companies encouraging them to publish ESG risks that might be of significant relevance for their business activities.[75] A decade earlier, the

---

[69] See EUROSIF (2012), p. 39.
[70] The countries that first adopted and implemented the Pension Act outside the UK are Belgium, Germany, Italy and Sweden. See Renneboog et al. (2008a), p. 1727.
[71] See EUROSIF (2003), p. 39.
[72] See Renneboog et al. (2008a), p. 1728.
[73] See EUROSIF (2012), p. 59.
[74] See EUROSIF (2003), p. 18 and Renneboog et al. (2008a), p. 1727.
[75] See EUROSIF (2003), pp. 19f.

UK Sustainable Investment and Finance Association (UKSIF), a membership network for sustainable and responsible financial services, has been launched.[76] The explicit aim of the association is to promote SRI in the UK and provide a platform for institutional and private investors to exchange best practices on how to incorporate non-financial objectives such as personal values and beliefs in their investment strategies.

United States: In the US, several legislations to address ESG concerns have already been passed: Examples of legislations that have been implemented in early stages of the SRI movement include legislations directed towards workplace improvement (e.g. the Equal Employment Opportunity Act of 1972), consumer protection (e.g. the Consumer Product Safety Act of 1972) and pollution or hazardous waste control (e.g. the Clean Air Act Amendments of 1977). Despite the various legislations already in place, reporting of CSR activities still is voluntary for companies in the US.[77]

To conclude, the total number of regulatory initiatives related to SRI is still limited and not legally binding in most of the countries worldwide. Nonetheless, there are countries that have already implemented national state regulations regarding SRI and the market for SRI has developed tremendously within the past decades. Part of this development can certainly be attributed to the national state regulations already in place. Another major driving force behind the market growth are the voluntary reporting guidelines introduced by organizations, which are active in the SRI market. Some of the guidelines that are primarily implemented on a national basis have already been mentioned briefly. Others are more globally oriented and presented in the following section.[78]

2.4.2 Non-state regulations

The lack of a common globally implemented definition of SRI not only implies that different institutions, organizations, or investors have a different understanding of what SRI is and what it is not. It also leads to a lack of standardization on how SRI is implemented and reported by

---

[76] The UKSIF was founded in 1991 as the UK Social Investment Forum but renamed to UK Sustainable Investment and Finance Association in 2009 (see http://uksif.org/about-uksif/history/).

[77] According to the Presidential Executive Order 13514, only federal agencies are required to report on their CSR performance. See KPMG (2013), p. 26, Obama (2009), p. 52119, Tschopp (2005), p. 57 and Tschopp & Huefner (2015), p. 565.

[78] The guidelines mentioned do not represent an exhausting list of all guidelines available. It is rather an extract of the most common initiatives implemented that provides a basis for further discussion.

the different actors in the market. As a consequence, with the development of the SRI market, numerous standards have been defined.[79] These standards should provide some guidance on how SRI ought to be implemented within a company and how reports should be structured in order to comprehensively display the company's CSR activities. All those standards, however, are not legally binding for the companies and continuously developed further. This, in turn, also means that the actors themselves can decide which standard to follow. Once the decision is made, the implementation of the standards and their underlying principles still remains voluntary.

Table 4 provides an overview of the set of global SRI/CSR standards and reporting frameworks actors can choose from. Again, it is important to note that this list does not claim to be collectively exhaustive: The total number of standards available is not clearly known as each organization, country, region, or SRI actor can make up its own standard. Nonetheless, the table depicts some of the well-known initiatives that have been founded in the last two decades.

In Panel A of Table 4, three voluntary CSR and SRI guidelines are presented. The first ones are the OECD Guidelines for Multinational Enterprises defined by the Organization for European Economic Cooperation (OECD).[80] These OECD guidelines comprise a multitude of voluntary standards on how companies can integrate socially and environmentally responsible behavior in their daily business operations.[81] Areas addressed are human and labor rights issues, the environment, combating bribery, consumer interests, information disclosure, competition, taxation and intellectual property rights. The guidelines are not legally binding on multinational companies, but the OECD member states are asked to ensure the implementation of those guidelines in their respective countries.[82]

---

[79] See Richardson (2008), p. 32.
[80] See OECD Watch (2013).
[81] The OECD Guidelines have been implemented in 1976 and signed by all 30 member states of the OECD as well as nine non-member states (Argentina, Brazil, Chile, Estonia, Israel, Latvia, Lithuania, Romania and Slovenia). See OECD (1976) and OECD Watch (2013), p. 32.
[82] See OECD Watch (2013), p. 8.

Table 4: Global voluntary SRI guidelines and reporting standards

This table provides an overview of voluntary CSR and SRI guidelines (Panel A) and reporting standards implemented by global SRI initiatives (Panel B).

Panel A: Voluntary CSR/SRI guidelines and principles		
Organization	Name of guideline/principle	Description
Organization for European Economic Cooperation (OECD)	OECD Guidelines for Multinational Enterprises	* Definition of multi-national principles and standards for socially and environmentally responsible corporate behavior * Areas included: Human rights, labor rights, environment, combating bribery, consumer interests, information disclosure, competition, taxation and intellectual property rights * OECD member states are responsible to ensure the implementation of the guidelines, but they are not legally binding on (multinational) companies
Principles for Responsible Investment (PRI) Initiative	UN Principles of Responsible Investment (PRI)	* UN-backed principles that serve as a voluntary guideline for SRI and are ready-to-use for (large and institutional) investors as well as signatories who aim at incorporating ESG issues in their investment decisions * Signatories commit to follow six principles: Incorporation of ESG issues in business decisions, active ownership, disclosure on ESG issues, promotion of the PRIs, collaboration and reporting on activities taken
The Equator Principles Association	Equator Principles (EP)	* Risk management framework to determine, assess and manage environmental and social risks in project finance * Member companies of the EP Financial Institutions are committed to implement the EP internally and not to provide loans or financing for companies that do not comply with the principles

Panel B: Voluntary Reporting Standards		
Organization	Reporting standard	Description
Global Reporting Initiative (GRI)	Sustainability Reporting Framework	* Implementation of a SRI reporting framework that includes SRI reporting guidelines as well as sector guidance to standardize reporting within industry sectors * Guidelines include Reporting Principles, Standard Disclosures as well as an Implementation Manual for the preparation of sustainability reports by internationally active organizations * Organizations are asked to provide information on economic, environmental and social criteria in their SRI reports
Global Impact Investing Network (GIIN)	Impact Reporting & Investment Standards (IRIS)	* Approach to standardize the way mission-driven businesses report their social and environmental impact to company stakeholders * Framework for reporting standards includes six areas companies should address in their report: Description of the organization (incl. its mission), product description, financial performance, operational impact, product impact and a glossary of IRIS terms used in the report

Sources: Equator Principles Association (2013), GIIN (2014), GRI (2013), OECD Watch (2013) and PRI Initiative (2012)

The UN Principles of Responsible Investment (PRI) are another example of SRI guidelines that are supported by a multi-state organization. Developed by the PRI Initiative[83] and backed by

---

[83] The PRI Initiative is an investor initiative in partnership with the UNEP Finance Initiative and the UN Global Compact. By 2013, almost 1,200 institutions (e.g., pension funds, insurance companies, sovereign

2. The market for socially responsible investing

the United Nations (UN), the PRIs are a ready-to use set of principles for (institutional) investors and signatories, who aim at incorporating ESG issues in their investment decisions.[84] Again, these standards are voluntary and actors themselves can decide on whether or not they integrate them into their investment decisions. Once the actors have signed the PRIs, however, they commit to adhere to the following six principles:[85]

- Consideration of ESG issues in investment analysis and decision-making processes
- Active ownership by incorporating ESG issues into the company's ownership policies and practices
- Public disclosure of ESG issues
- Promotion of the PRIs within the investment industry
- Collaboration with other companies and organizations to enhance the implementation of the PRIs and
- Reporting on SRI activities taken and the progress towards implementing the PRIs

The third example displayed in Panel A of Table 4 are the Equator Principles (EP), a risk management framework supporting companies and investors in determining, assessing and managing environmental and social risk in project finance.[86] The framework has been developed and promoted by The Equator Principles Association and is targeted primarily at financial institutions that are members of the association and provide financing for companies in almost all regions of the world and across any industry given that the requirements of the EPs demonstrably are met.

Panel B of Table 4 presents two SRI reporting initiatives that have been established in recent years. The Global Reporting Initiative (GRI) has developed the Sustainability Reporting Framework, a framework that consists of guidelines aimed at standardizing SRI reporting globally

---

development and wealth funds as well as investment managers) from more than 50 countries have signed the principles. See PRI Initiative (2013), p. 8.

[84] See PRI Initiative (2012), p. 1.
[85] See PRI Initiative (2012), p. 24.
[86] See Equator Principles Association (2013), p. 2.

and across different industry sectors.[87] The guidelines include reporting principles and disclosure requirements multinational companies can make use of when preparing a SRI report. Companies willing to prepare such a report are asked to provide information on three dimensions:[88]

- Economic aspects (e.g. economic performance, market presence and indirect economic impacts)
- Environmental aspects (e.g. materials energy, waste, emissions, products and services) and
- Social aspects (e.g. labor practices and decent work, human rights, society and product responsibility) of their activities

While the GRI targets any company interested in preparing a SRI report, the Global Impact Investing Network (GIIN) has developed the Impact Reporting & Investment Standards (IRIS) as an approach to standardize the way mission-driven companies[89] could report their social and environmental impact to company stakeholders. The framework includes six areas these companies should address in their report: [90]

- A brief description of the company itself (including its mission)
- A description of the products manufactured and promoted
- A report on the company's financial performance
- The operational impact achieved
- The impact of its products and
- A glossary of IRIS terms used in the report

To conclude, the overview provided in Table 4 on page 26 as well as the additional explanations provided illustrate that there are initiatives in place that try to introduce global SRI standards

---

[87] See GRI (2013), p. 3.
[88] See GRI (2013), p. 7.
[89] Russo (2010), p. 5 defines a mission-driven company as "*a for-profit enterprise that seeks to simultaneously meet profit goals and social and environmental goals that reflect the values of its owners.*" Usually, these values are also included in the business goals of the company, which is not necessarily the case for rather traditional companies.
[90] See IRIS (2014).

and reporting frameworks. However, no single, globally accepted standard has yet been established.[91] Instead, with increasing market size for SRI, the number of standards available has increased as well and companies and investors alike have to individually pick the ones that best match their preferences and needs.[92] This increases the effort companies and investors have to make in order to engage in SRI activities. Some of them might even get deterred from getting actively involved in the SRI movement by those numerous standards, guidelines and frameworks available. Many investors, however, are willing to make this effort and still feel confident about the idea of integrating ESG aspects into their investment decision. The next section takes a closer look at the motivation that drives investors' engagement in SRI and the characteristics some of the SRI investors have in common.

2.5 Investor base

2.5.1 Investor characteristics

Rosen et al. (1991) are among the first researchers to study the characteristics of SRI investors. Analyzing the investment behavior of about 1,500 individual investors, their study finds that while SRI investors on average have a lower median income level, they are younger and better educated than conventional fund investors: The median income level for SRI investors is USD 39,600 p.a. and USD 46,600 p.a. for conventional mutual fund investors. The median age for SRI investors and conventional fund investors is 39 and 52 years respectively. About 60% of the SRI investors have graduate degrees, compared with 22% of the conventional fund investors with graduate degrees.[93]

Barreda-Tarrazona et al. (2011) explain this finding by arguing that younger and better educated investors care more about ESG issues, which is reflected in the investment process and the way how they select the companies to invest in.[94] With increasing concern, investors inform themselves about possible investment opportunities and differences between SRI and conventional investments. The study conducted by Barreda-Tarrazona et al. (2011) also shows that the share

---

[91] See Aguilera et al. (2007), p. 851 and Tschopp (2015), p. 565.
[92] See EUROSIF (2012), p. 22.
[93] See Rosen et al. (1991), p. 226. Some studies also show that the majority (about 60%) of SRI investors are women that place a larger share of their portfolio in SRI than men do. See, for example, Nilsson (2008), p. 320 and Schueth (2003), p. 192.
[94] See Barreda-Tarrazona (2011), p. 305.

of investors, who place their money into SRI funds increases with the level of information about those funds that is provided to the investors: The publication of information on the SRI degree of the funds leads to a remarkable shift in the way investors choose their investment set – from trying to identify the most profitable funds to primarily selecting the ones with the highest SRI score.[95] Thus, irrespective of the age and level of education of potential investors, fund managers should play close attention to the way information about the SRI level of their funds is displayed.

The finding obtained by Barreda-Tarrazona et al. (2011) is also in line with the results obtained by Glac (2009), who argues that the actual investment decision is not solely influenced by the level of information available on the SRI funds but also the way how this information is transferred to the investors. As investors apply different decision frames when processing the information obtained, fund managers need to understand the frames their investors use and adjust the information they provide accordingly: Investors that have a financial decision frame are less likely to place money into SRI than investors that have a social decision frame.[96] When trying to increase the share of investors who engage in SRI, providing information on the SRI degree of funds to investors with a financial frame would be less effective than providing the same information to investors with social frames. In other words, the better fund managers understand which decision frame their investors have and the closer they adjust their information material to the frames applied, the higher the likelihood of an engagement in SRI will be.

In fact, the decision to integrate ESG criteria into the investment processes usually is not a one-time decision but rather matches the lifestyle these SRI investors already follow: More than 80% of the SRI investors donate money or belong to a cause-related group and are active in household waste recycling; almost half of the respondents (48%) regularly spend time volunteering for cause-related groups or charities.[97] Thus, and in line with the findings described above, SRI investors in general seem to act according to their personal conviction and are not primarily driven by financial considerations when placing (parts of) their money into SRI funds.

This notion, however, might not hold for all investors active in the (SRI) fund market. While the studies mentioned above primarily focused on analyzing characteristics of private investors,

---

[95] See Barreda-Tarrazona (2011), pp. 312 and 317.

[96] See Glac (2009), p. 49. In cognitive literature, decision frames are used to study how individuals react in decision situations, i.e. how they process given information and make their final decision based on the information provided. See Glac (2009), p. 42 and Tversky & Kahneman (1981), p. 453.

[97] See Rosen et al. (1991), p. 228.

Jansson and Biel (2011) also include institutional investors such as fund managers employed at investment institutions in their study. The results obtained indicate that, while investment decisions made by private and institutional investors are in fact influenced by their personal ideologies and societal values, decisions made by institutional fund managers are driven by rather strict financial information and objectives.[98]

This finding can be explained by the fact that private and – at least to some extend – institutional investors manage and invest their own money and are more liberate in defining their investment goals than fund managers are. While the latter are primarily accountable for their beneficiaries and thus, mainly deal with the concern of maximizing profits, the former can define their individual investment goals. These goals can be somewhere on the continuum that ranges from a strictly financial orientation to a strictly ethical orientation.[99] This implies that not all investors, who engage in the SRI market, are alike and no typical SRI investor can yet be identified. Consequently, the approaches used for social investing and motives that drive the socially responsible investment decisions by the individual investors are manifold. The following section reviews the reasons mentioned by investors when asked about their motivation to engage in SRI.

2.5.2 Investor motivation

2.5.2.1 Motivation to invest in a socially responsible way

Historically, the motivation to invest socially responsible has been split up into the desire of investors not to be associated with companies operating in certain industries or countries and the desire to financially benefit from a presumably financial attractive investment alternative.[100] Especially towards the beginning of the SRI movement in the mid-1980, investors got more cautious on where to invest their money and increasingly tried to avoid investing into stocks classified as sin stocks as this just *"won't look good"*[101]. Examples include the divestment strategies of investors, who refused to invest in companies with business relations in South Africa

---

[98] See Jansson & Biel (2011), pp. 137 and 139.
[99] See Hummels & Timmer (2004), p. 74.
[100] See Rivoli (2003), p. 273.
[101] Fabozzi et al. (2008), p. 83.

or the increased consciousness of investors after environmental disasters such as the exploding nuclear power plant in Chernobyl.[102]

```
                                    ┌──────────────────┐
                                    │ Performance      │
                                    │ maximization     │
                 ┌──────────────┐───┤                  │
                 │ Financial    │   └──────────────────┘
                 │ objectives   │   ┌──────────────────┐
              ───┤              │   │ Legitimization   │
┌────────────┐   └──────────────┘───┤ of conventional  │
│ Investor   │                      │ investments      │
│ motivation │───                   └──────────────────┘
│ to engage  │                      ┌──────────────────┐
│ in SRI     │   ┌──────────────┐   │ Influencing      │
└────────────┘   │ Non-financial│───┤ social change    │
              ───┤ objectives   │   └──────────────────┘
                 │              │   ┌──────────────────┐
                 └──────────────┘───┤ Personal         │
                                    │ satisfaction     │
                                    └──────────────────┘
```

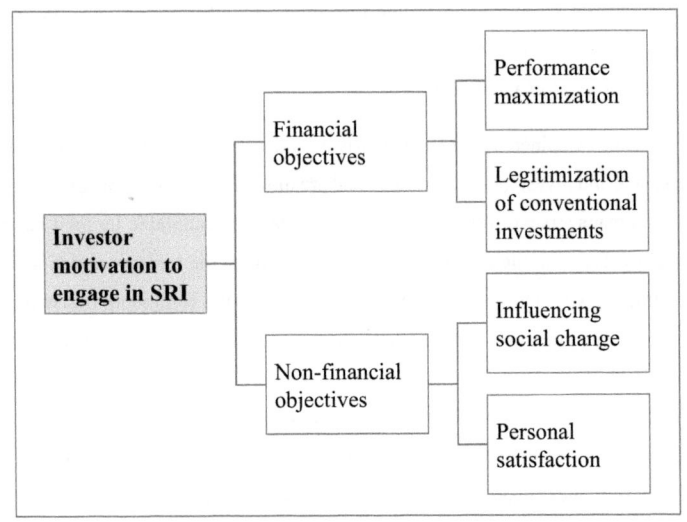

Figure 1: Investor motivation to engage in SRI
Source: Own illustration

These investors have all been driven by the idea of changing the world and making a difference through their investment – irrespective of whether financial objectives are met or not. Other investors, however, have not placed their full attention on the social or environmental consequences of their engagement in SRI. Instead, these investors mainly follow their personal conviction that SRI financially outperform other investments alternatives and thus, use the expected financial benefit as a justification why they add SRI to their portfolios.[103] In sum and even until today, investors have their own motivation to invest – at least parts of their investment capital – into the SRI alternative. Nonetheless, researchers have identified a set of financial and non-financial objectives many SRI investors mention when they are asked about their individual motivation to engage in SRI (see Figure 1).

2.5.2.2 Financial objectives

Performance maximization: While performance maximization is an objective that is definitely attributable to conventional investors, it is also of relevance for SRI investors. According

---
[102] Please refer to section 2.2 for more details on the historical development of the SRI movement.
[103] See Rivoli (2003), p. 273.

to a study done by Gevlin (2007), the majority of investors, who have placed parts of their investment capital into SRI, expects to profit from higher returns and lower levels of risk of the SRI alternative relative to conventional investments.[104] In line with this, most SRI investors – although also having ESG concerns in mind when allocating their investment capital – are not willing to sacrifice basic financial objectives just to address the ESG issues. In fact, Mackenzie and Lewis (1999) find evidence that some SRI investors are willing to trade social impact in for financial return when facing the decisions of either meeting minimum financial requirements or addressing ESG issues the society has to cope with.[105]

Moreover, the study done by Lewis and Webley (2002) shows that enthusiasm for and willingness to invest in SRI drops radically when the financial performance of SRI funds decreases relative to that of conventional investments. While about one third of the ethical investors are willing to accept lower returns (9% return p.a. generated by SRI as opposed to 10% return generated by conventional investments), only about 4% of those investors state that they would still invest in SRI when the return expectation for SRI decreases to 5% p.a., while the expectation for conventional investments remains at 10%.[106] Thus, although there seems to be a shift in the investment objectives from purely maximizing financial return to also incorporating ESG issues in the investment decision process, not all SRI investors are willing to relocate levers entirely. This finding implies that ethical investors do not classify SRI as being a primary act of charity for which they do not expect to earn significant financial returns. Instead, most SRI investors expect to achieve financial returns that are comparable to the ones generated with conventional investments.[107]

Legitimization of conventional investments: Irrespective of the financial performance of SRI investment alternatives, researchers have found evidence that investors – even if they classify themselves as being influenced by ESG concerns when making investment decisions – commonly do not place 100% of their money in SRI alternatives. Instead, SRI investors try to set up a diversified portfolio consisting of both, socially responsible as well as rather conventional

---

[104] See Gevlin (2007), pp. 56a–56b.
[105] See Mackenzie & Lewis (1999), p. 451.
[106] See Lewis & Webley (2002), p. 175.
[107] See Glac (2009), p. 42.

investment vehicles.[108] Mackenzie and Lewis (1999), for example, conduct semi-structured interviews and find that even though the investors considered themselves as being socially conscious, they place only a small part (on average about 5%) of their available capital into SRI alternatives. The other part is put into conventional investment vehicles with the explicit aim of optimizing the risk and return profiles of these investments.[109]

When they are asked about the reasons why they invest only such a small part of their money into SRI, the interviewees mention that they are uncertain about the return they can expect to generate when investing into SRI, but need to generate a certain minimum level of return with their investments in order to cover their basic financial requirements. Thus, they have split up their capital into essential capital and surplus capital. The essential capital is invested with the primary aim of generating a certain level of return – even if it means to invest in companies that are considered as being socially irresponsible. The surplus capital is then used to legitimize the conventional investment and exclusively placed into SRI that meet their personal convictions.[110] Haigh and Hazelton (2004) summarize the findings published by Mackenzie and Lewis (1999) and state that some investors (ethical or not) use SRI as a way to salve their consciences and at the same time legitimize their ongoing investment into rather conventional securities, which are primarily selected based on the perceived economic utility.[111]

2.5.2.3 Non-financial objectives

Influencing social change: The potential for influencing and achieving social change is another factor that influences investor motivation for investing in SRI. Pasewark and Riley (2010), for example, argue that some SRI investors are mainly driven by the expectation that refusing to invest in companies that have a low CSR rating might cause these companies to increase their social and environmental standards and with this, improve social and environmental conditions for society in general.[112] This rationale is based on the notion that the smaller the investor base for a company is, the more difficult it will be for the company to get access to capital.[113] Thus, managers should have a self-interest to ensure that enough investors are interested in providing

---

[108] See Michelson et al. (2004), p. 2.
[109] See Mackenzie & Lewis (1999), p. 442.
[110] See Mackenzie & Lewis (1999), pp. 449f.
[111] See Haigh & Hazelton (2004), p. 66.
[112] See Pasewark & Riley (2010), p. 239.
[113] See Heinkel et al. (2001), p. 432, Lewis & Mackenzie (2000), p. 216.

capital to their companies and align their business practices to the values and beliefs of their investors. Investors in turn can foster company's awareness for socially responsible activities by only providing capital to companies that have a minimum level of such activities.

Personal satisfaction: Wealth maximization and influencing social change are factors that drive investor motivation, but for some SRI investors they are not the primary reason to engage in SRI. In a study done by Beal et al. (2005), less than half of the investors (46.6%) indicate that wealth maximization (measured by expected corporate earnings) is the most important factor influencing their investment decision. This finding indicates that more than half of the investors focus on factors other than simply maximizing wealth when deciding how to invest their capital.[114] In line with this, Sparks (1998) documents that about one third (35%) of investors with holdings in SRI would not consider to withdraw their capital even if returns generated by SRI were lower than the returns generated by conventional investment vehicles.[115] Thus, there are SRI investors, who are driven by the exclusive desire to put their money where their mouths are and derive some non-economic utility from aligning their personal lifestyle with their investment activity – irrespective of the financial return generated with the investment.[116]

To conclude, characteristics and motives to engage in SRI differ greatly between individual SRI investors and researchers have to admit that not all SRI investors are alike.[117] In fact, profit-driven and beliefs-driven SRI investors seem to coexist in the SRI market, making it difficult to derive general conclusions on the most important and rather subordinate factors influencing the investment decision of SRI investors.[118] Even once investors have made the decision to engage in SRI, the investment strategies applied by the SRI investors vary greatly: While some investors primarily try to avoid investing in companies that operate in sin industries such as alcohol or tobacco, others define minimum criteria companies have to fulfill, e.g. equal employment opportunities for men and women or programs for environmental protection, in order

---

[114] See Beal et al. (2005), p. 68.
[115] Sparkes (1998), cited in Pasewark & Riley (2010), p. 240.
[116] See Auer & Schuhmacher (2016), p. 51 , Beal & Goyen (1998), p. 140, Bollen (2007), p. 706 and Glac (2009), p. 42.
[117] See Derwall et al. (2011), p. 2140.
[118] Nilsson (2009), p. 5 differentiates three different investor segments: (i) The primary concerned about profits investors, who assign higher weights to the financial returns than the social responsibility of the investment; (ii) the primary concerned about social responsibility investors, who over-value social responsibility relative to financial return; and (iii) the socially responsible and return driven investors, who assign equal weights to social responsibility and financial return when making their investment decision.

to be considered as part of their investment set.[119] Consequently, there is a broad variety of investment strategies applied by SRI investors and the selection of an individual's strategy is a rather subjective decision.[120] The next section introduces some commonly applied investment strategies in Europe and shows how these strategies have developed within the previous years.

2.6 Investment strategies

In its report on the SRI market in Europe, the EUROSIF (2014) differentiates seven investment strategies that SRI investors most commonly apply:[121]

- Sustainability themed investments
- Best-in-class selection
- Norms-based screening
- Exclusion of holdings from investment universe
- Integration of ESG factors in financial analysis
- Engagement and voting on sustainability matters and
- Impact investing

Sustainability themed investments are investments made with the explicit aim of supporting companies that contribute to addressing social and/or environmental issues such as food security, air pollution and climate change.[122] Thus, investors that decide to implement this strategy attach particular importance to the development of sustainability aspects while at the same time put less focus on governance issues. Today, sustainability themed investments account for about 1% of the total market for SRI in Europe, but experience above-average growth rates compared to other SRI investment strategies.[123] The positive development of this strategy is

---

[119] See Sampford & Ransome (2013), p. 16.
[120] See Michelson (2004), p. 4.
[121] See EUROSIF (2014), p. 8. The USSIF differentiates between three main investment strategies: Screening, shareholder activism and community investing. See USSIF (2006), p. 3.
[122] See EUROSIF (2014), p. 11 and VBDO (2012), p. 19.
[123] See EUROSIF (2014), pp. 11 and 21.

fostered by institutional investors in France and Sweden, who continuously increased the share of sustainability themed assets in their portfolios.[124]

Best-in-class selection is an investment strategy aimed at selecting only such companies that belong to the best-performing companies within a particular industry or asset class.[125] ESG criteria are used to generate a relative ranking of all companies within the industry or asset class. Only those companies that pass a certain threshold level are included in the investor's portfolio. The aim of investors that apply best-in-class selection is to assure that not only companies with a minimum level of ESG activities are included in the portfolio but also that the portfolio is balanced across different industries and/or asset classes.[126] Although best-in-class selection has experienced a CAGR of about 12% from 2011 to 2013, it still accounts for less than 2% of the total market for SRI in Europe, but is most commonly applied by investors in France and Sweden.[127]

Norms-based screening refers to the selection of investments based on their compliance with regional or international guidelines on SRI. Examples of such guidelines include the OECD Guidelines for Multinational Enterprises and the UN Principles of Responsible Investment that have been introduced in section 2.4.2. Investors, who apply a norms-based screening strategy, rely on such guidelines as a form of external validation of a company's adherence to commonly accepted standards of good business behavior.[128] While the origins of norms-based screening can be traced by to the Nordic countries, the strategy has a significant share of the total market

---

[124] The CAGR for sustainability themed investments in Europe was +38% from 2009 to 2011 and +11% from 2011 to 2013. The growth was mainly driven by an increase of such investments in France (CAGR 2011-2013:+166%) and Sweden (CAGR 2011-2013: +124%). See EUROSIF (2014), p. 11.

[125] An asset class is defined as a homogenous group of securities that have similar risk and return characteristics and thus, correlate highly with the other securities of this asset class, but also have other economical attributes that clearly differentiate the securities of one asset class from the securities that are part of other asset classes (see Greer (1997), p. 86, Kritzman (1999), p. 80 and Sharpe (1992), p. 8). In general, two types of asset classes can be differentiated: Super classes of assets and alternative asset classes. Super classes include capital assets such as equity, fixed income and real estate, consumable and transformable assets such as grain/wheat and metal and store of value assets such as fine art and foreign currency (see Greer (1997), pp. 87f). Alternative assets include hedge funds, private equity, credit derivatives and corporate governance (see Anson (2008), p. 3 and Lo (2010), p. 1).

[126] See Kempf & Osthoff (2007), p. 909 and Renneboog et al. (2008a), p. 1728.

[127] See EUROSIF (2014), p. 12.

[128] See EUROSIF (2014), p. 12 and Leite & Cortez (2015), p. 136.

size in almost all European countries and accounts for about 20% of the total SRI market in Europe.[129]

Exclusions of holdings from investment universe are the most commonly applied investment strategies in Europe: More than one third of the total market size for SRI is allocated to this type of investment strategy.[130] Investors, who apply this strategy, try to exclude companies with business operations in presumable undesirable industries such as pornography, tobacco, alcohol or gambling.[131] Exclusions are often also referred to as negative screening and one of the earliest strategies applied by SRI investors.[132]

While negative screening has been applied by investors for hundreds of years, the **integration of ESG factors in financial analysis** is a strategy that mainly evolved in recent years. Investors, who apply this strategy, base their investment decision not only on traditional financial performance analysis, but also consider the potential impact (positive and negative) ESG criteria might have on a company's future financials.[133] Thus, financial criteria are combined with ESG criteria and companies are not only assessed by looking at their current performance, but also by considering projections on their future performance on both dimensions. In Europe, integration strategies rank second in the total market for SRI in terms of absolute market size and account for about 27% of the total market.[134]

Engagement and voting on sustainability matters is also referred to as shareholder activism or shareholder stewardship.[135] It involves the active engagement of socially conscious investors in corporate relations issues.[136] Examples include getting in dialogue with companies about social and environmental issues in general, but also filing, co-filing and voting on shareholder resolutions.[137] These resolutions are usually aimed at improving long-term corporate policies

---

[129] Compared to the market size in 2011, norms-based screening has grown by +31% p.a. from 2011 to 2013, with significant increases in Poland (+671% p.a.), Switzerland (+638% p.a.) and Spain (+257% p.a.). See EUROSIF (2012), p. 13 for a break-down of the market sizes per country.

[130] See EUROSIF (2014), p. 14.

[131] See de Colle & York (2009), p. 85, EUROSIF (2014), p. 14, Fowler & Hope (2007), p. 244 and Humphrey & Lee (2011), p. 519.

[132] See section 2.2 for a detailed description of the historical development of SRI.

[133] See EUROSIF (2014), p. 17.

[134] The market for integration grew by +29% p.a. from 2011 to 2013. See EUROSIF (2014), p. 18.

[135] See EUROSIF (2014), p. 19.

[136] See Eisenhofer & Barry (2005), pp. 3–8, Sparkes (2001), p. 202 and Taylor (2000), p. 174.

[137] See RIA (2013), p. 8 and Schwartz (2003), p. 195.

to promote good shareholder and employee relationships. Moreover, they also serve as an ad hoc measure to address social and environmental issues investors are deeply concerned about.[138] Although shareholder activism is historically more common in the US, investors in Europe increasingly make use of their power as shareholders and owners of companies and actively engage dialogue with management of the companies, e.g. at general meetings.[139] In terms of market size, engagement and voting in Europe ranks four in the total market for SRI and experienced a growth rate of 36% p.a. from 2011 to 2013.[140]

All strategies introduced in this section offer investors the possibility to individually decide on the level of engagement in SRI activities they are willing to bear. Screening, either negative through exclusions or positive by implementing best-in-class selection, norms-based screening or sustainability themed investments, allows investors to align personal and financial goals while at the same time anonymously investing into funds or companies that implement CSR activities. Contrary, strategies such as the integration of ESG factors in financial analysis or engagement and voting are a means to directly influence a company's management and its board of directors regarding the ESG issues addressed in the corporate policies. Taken together, integration and engagement/voting account for more than half (44%) of the total market for SRI in Europe. One third (35%) is attributed to exclusions, while norms-based and positive screening make up about one fifth (19%) of the market.[141]

Impact investing does not appear in Figure 2 as it is an investment strategy that still accounts for less than 1% of the total market for SRI in Europe. Nonetheless this strategy increasingly attracts investors' interest and has grown from almost zero to a total volume of about EUR 8.75 billion in Europe by 2011 and EUR 20.269 billion by 2013.[142] The underlying principle of this investment strategy is to combine social activities with financial interests by achieving a measureable impact for society and at the same time generating a pre-defined target return.[143] The strategy has increasingly gained investors' and politicians' attention in the past few years. As the number of studies on impact investing issues is still limited, the literature review on SRI in chapter 4.4 and the empirical analysis in this thesis does not incorporate this relatively new

---

[138] See Haigh & Hazelton (2004), p. 60.
[139] See J.P. Morgan (2014), p. 2.
[140] See EUROSIF (2014), p. 20.
[141] See EUROSIF (2014), p. 21.
[142] See Bugg-Levine & Emerson (2011), p. 4 and EUROSIF (2012), p. 26 and (2014), p. 25.
[143] See EUROSIF (2014), p. 26.

aspect of the SRI movement. However, as it increasingly gains public interest, it is still worth mentioning as a brief excursus in this thesis.[144]

2013, in percent (100% = 19,408 EUR Bn)

- Best-in-class and sustainability themed: 2
- Engagement/Voting: 17
- Exclusions: 35
- Norms-based screening: 19
- Integration: 27

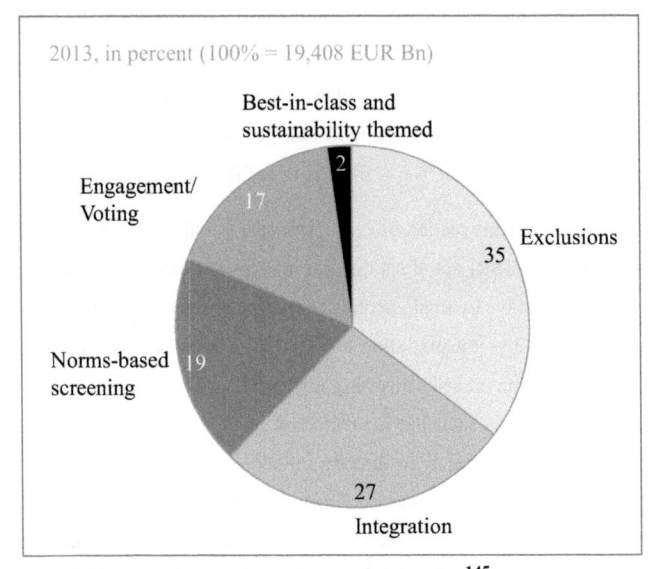

Figure 2: Share of SRI investment strategies on European SRI market[145]
Source: Own illustration based on EUROSIF (2014), p. 10

2.7 Excursus: Impact investing

The term impact investing has first been introduced in 2007 in a discussion between Antony Bugg-Levine, a pioneer in impact investing and, at that time, managing director at the Rockefeller Foundation and socially conscious investors, who have already been active in these fields for some years.[146] A few years later Bugg-Levine and Emerson (2011) define impact investing as *"investment strategies that generate financial return while intentionally improving social and environmental conditions."*[147] The authors argue that, traditionally, financial investors merely have focused on maximizing financial impact of their investments and have considered

---

[144] Although the market for impact investing is still in its infancy, it is expected to grow to about 1% of total assets under management by 2020. See Freireich & Fulton (2009), p. 9.

[145] Total market size is not adjusted for double counting as overlays between the different investment strategies have not been reported by EUROSIF (2014).

[146] See Rockefeller Foundation (2012), p. 1.

[147] See Bugg-Levine & Emerson (2011), p. 4.

2. The market for socially responsible investing

governments and charities as being responsible for achieving positive social impact. In contrast to this, philanthropists have focused on promoting equality and justice and refused the notion that they should also include financial considerations into their investment strategies. As the sharp separation of maximizing financial returns and social, ethical or environmental impact is gradually fading away today, the authors conclude that there is an ever increasing amount of investors, who use their capital not only to generate financial returns, but also to intentionally create a positive and measurable impact for society.[148]

Similar to this, the Rockefeller Foundation (2010) defines impact investments as *"investments intended to create positive impact beyond financial return."*[149] In other words, the term impact investment formalizes the concept of providing capital – mainly in the form of venture investing, private equity and direct lending – to companies, whose business strategy explicitly states the intent to make a positive social, ethical or environmental impact. Such impact cannot only be achieved through the business operations and processes employed, but also through the products manufactured and the services provided. However, it is crucial that the companies, who receive the impact investments, also have a system in place that enables them to measure the achieved impact for society as this serves as one success factor for investment.[150] Another success factor is the financial return generated as expressed by the latter part in the above definition of impact investments. With impact investments, the intent to achieve a positive impact for society co-exists with the aim to also generate expected returns that are at least comparable to the returns generated by the market. In other words, while donations are excluded as form of investments, market-rate or market-beating returns are in line with investors' ambitions.[151]

Impact investing, however, does not determine in advance if investors should focus more on the financial returns of their investments or the positive societal impact achieved. In fact, there might be some investors, who care more about the financial return their investments generate – so-called financial first investors – while there are others, who attach higher value to achieving maximum social, ethical or environmental impact – so-called impact first investors.[152] While

---

[148] See Bugg-Levine & Emerson (2011), p. 9.
[149] See Rockefeller Foundation (2010), p. 5. See EUROSIF (2014), p. 23 for an overview of alternative definitions provided by various organizations that engage in impact investing.
[150] See EUROSIF (2014), p. 24.
[151] See Rockefeller Foundation (2010), p. 7.
[152] See Freireich & Fulton (2009), p. 31.

both kinds of investors share the belief that it is possible to achieve competitive levels of financial return and at the same time face social, ethical or environmental challenges, Freireich and Fulton (2008) use the primary investment objective to differentiate the investor types:[153]

Financial first investors seek to optimize financial returns and generate a minimum level of social and/or environmental impact: These investors are typically institutional and commercial investors like pension funds, who are looking for subsectors that provide market-rate returns while at the same time achieving some social, ethical or environmental impact. Conversely, **impact first investors** seek to optimize social, ethical or environmental impact while at the same time trying to generate a minimum level of financial return: These investors primarily aim to generate social, ethical or environmental good and might also be willing to give up some financial return if needed, as long as their social, ethical or environmental objectives are met.

Irrespective of the fact on which of the two aspects – financial return or social impact – investors primarily place their attention on, the concept of impact investing tries to restore the balance between investors' financial return and social/environmental impact orientation. Traditionally, there has been an imbalance between the financial return and the impact orientation of investors: While traditional financial investors on the one hand heavily overweighed the importance of generating financial returns, philanthropists on the other hand, were rather purely impact oriented without paying close attention to generating financial returns at all. As illustrated in Figure 3, impact investors now try to find a balance between maximizing financial returns and pure impact concern. Impact investors argue that financial investments and philanthropic engagement do not exclude each other. Instead, investors can and should pursue financial objectives while also intentionally improving social, ethical or environmental conditions for society.

Recalling the definition of socially responsible investing, one might be tempted to assume that impact investing is a modern term that – at its core – represents exactly the same investment process as SRI does. Taking a closer look at the definition of SRI used in this thesis,[154] however, it becomes clear that SRI refers to almost all kinds of investments that consider ESG issues the global investment community has to deal with. This includes activities like social screening (e.g. the application of positive and negative selection criteria to either exclude or actively select specific investments for a portfolio) or engagement and voting (e.g. sustainable and responsible

---

[153] See Freireich & Fulton (2009), p. 31.
[154] See section 2.1.

investors, who actively engage in dialogues with management and are involved in filing resolutions for the companies they invested in). Thus, SRI not only includes investments that are made with the explicitly stated intend of having a positive impact. It also comprises investments that exclude investments in companies, which act in presumably harmful industries like alcohol, weapons or tobacco, and investments that are solely driven by investors' values, but are not necessarily tied to also having a social, ethical or environmental impact.[155]

	Maximize return	Traditional financial investors	Impact investors
Financial return orientation			
		Traditional philanthropists	
	No return	No impact concern	Impact orientation	Pure impact concern

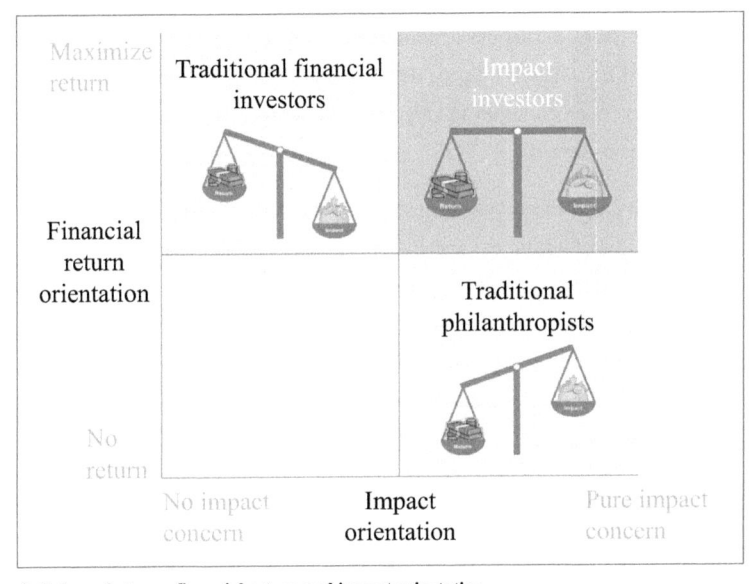

Figure 3: Balance between financial return and impact orientation
Source: Own illustration

Impact investors, however, attempt to go one step further. They strive not only to exclude investments in companies, but rather actively select individual investment opportunities that meet their perception of social responsibility. Thus, when drawing a continuum between purely profit-driven and beliefs-driven SRI investors, impact investors are located in the middle of this continuum. As there is no definition of the perfect impact investor, investors have to decide individually where on the continuum they consider themselves to be. Additionally, impact investments typically are project-specific and the investors are often publicly known, especially to the company or project receiving investors' money.[156] Thus, impact investing is a type of investment strategy within the SRI market and only refers to those investments, which are made

---

[155] See Freireich & Fulton (2009), p. 5.
[156] See EUROSIF (2012), p. 10.

with the explicit objective to generate competitive financial returns while at the same time achieving a positive and measurable social, ethical or environmental impact.

2.8 Interim conclusion

The aim of Chapter 2 was to provide an in-depth introduction to the concept of socially responsible investing. Therefore, the various definitions of SRI made by academics and organizations have been reviewed first. Afterwards, the development of the global as well as the European markets for SRI have been discussed and regulatory standards formulated by governments and public organizations presented.

Overall, the market for SRI has evolved enormously over the past two decades – from a niche market only a minority of institutions and investors used to care about into a market hardly any investor or fund manager can afford to ignore any further. In fact, the SRI market is a growth market that affects investors, companies and fund managers around the globe. The recent growth of the market has been fostered by factors such as investors' increased interest in ESG issues in general and regulatory standards in favor of SRI that have been implemented on a national, regional or global basis.

However, a global regulatory framework for SRI is not yet implemented and investors have to decide for themselves what SRI means to them and which guideline fits best to their preferences. Consequently, the investor base and the strategies applied by SRI investors are quite diverse: Some investors focus on the financial aspect of SRI and expect this investment alternative to generate competitive or even higher returns relative to conventional alternatives; others put social interest first and take financial returns as a rather positive side effect, but do not bother too much in case returns generated with SRI are lower than expected. The chapter concludes with a brief excursus on impact investing, a trend on the SRI market that is still in its infancy, but has developed considerably in recent years.

Irrespective of the investment strategy followed by an individual investor, there are two alternative ways of getting exposed to SRI: One alternative is to directly invest in public companies that have integrated CSR activities into their business operations. If SRI investors decide to follow this approach, they have to decide for themselves which companies they want to invest their money in, e.g. they first have to pick the investment strategy that matches their preferences, then select the companies that fit to the respective strategy and finally, manage the investment by themselves. An alternative way would be to invest in SRI funds that pool money from various investors and invest the collected money into companies that meet the fund manager's criteria of social responsibility. In this case, the fund managers will be responsible for identifying and selecting the companies the fund invests in. Investors, in turn, have to find a SRI fund that invests according to their individual ESG preferences and the fund managers will then take care of managing the investments. As both alternatives are of importance when trying to get an understanding on how the market for SRI works, the following chapter now introduces CSR and SRI funds in more detail.

3 Opportunities for investors to get exposed to SRI

3.1 Direct investments

3.1.1 Definition of corporate social responsibility (CSR)

Although various suggestions to define the field of corporate social responsibility have been made already, there is no formal definition of the term available until today.[157] Matten and Moon (2008) offer three possible explanations why corporations across the globe might have a different understanding of what CSR is and what it is not.[158] First, there are no formal rules how CSR should be implemented by corporations. Thus, managers have the choice to decide how CSR is applied in their corporation without having to follow any formal guidelines or normative principles. Second, CSR is used as a collective term that comprises various concepts of a corporation's social engagement. As such, the meaning of CSR is determined by the concepts researchers or practitioners define as being part of CSR rather than a term defined by governments or national institutions. Third, CSR activities implemented by corporations change over time and with this, also the meaning of CSR. Consequently, CSR is a dynamic phenomenon.[159]

Despite the difficulty to provide a general understanding for the term CSR, there are a few researchers and practitioners that have made an attempt to define the term CSR. Table 5 provides an overview of definitions that can be found in academia and practice.[160]

---

[157] See Bassen (2006), p. 5 and Matten & Moon (2008), p. 405.
[158] See Matten & Moon (2008), p. 405.
[159] See Matten & Moon (2008), p. 405.
[160] The definitions mentioned do not represent an exhausting list of all definitions available. They are rather an extract of commonly cited definitions that can be found in articles published by academics or reports issued by practitioners. For an overview of earlier definitions of CSR see Carroll (1999).

Table 5: Definitions of CSR

This table shows definitions of CSR. Panel A provides an overview how CSR is defined by academics, while Panel B depicts definitions provided by (non-profit) organizations and governmental institutions.

Panel A: CSR definition by academics		
Author(s)	Year	CSR can be defined as...
Davis	1973	"[...] the firm's considerations of, and response to, issues beyond the narrow economic, technical, and legal requirements of the firm. It is the firm's obligation to **evaluate** [...] the **effects of its decisions on external social system** in a manner that will accomplish social benefits along with the traditional economic gains which the firm seeks."
Anderson	1986	"[...] three major ares: **Complying with laws, setting** - and abiding by - moral and **ethical standards** and **philanthropic giving**."
Wood	1991	"[...] a business organization's **configuration of principles of social responsibility**, process of **social responsiveness** and policies, programs and observable outcomes as they **relate to the firm's societal relationships**."
Heal	2005	"[...] taking actions that **reduce the extent of externalized costs** or avoid distributional conflicts."
Menz	2010	"[...] a corporate policy that **includes social, ethical and ecological aspects**."

Panel B: CSR definition by organizations/institutions	
Institution	CSR can be defined as...
Vigeo	"[...] a managerial commitment according to which the **rights, interests and expectations of the stakeholders are considered** and which aims at the continuous improvement of its performance and risk control."
The European Commission	"[...] the responsibility of enterprises for their impacts on society. [...] To fully meet their corporate social responsibility, enterprises should have in place a process to **integrate social, environmental, ethical, human rights and consumer concerns** into their business operations and core strategy in **close collaboration with their stakeholders**."
United Nations	[...] a management concept whereby companies integrate social and environmental concerns in their business operations and interactions with their stakeholders. CSR is generally understood as being the way through which a company **achieves a balance of economic, environmental and social imperatives** (Triple-Bottom-Line- Approach), while **at the same time addressing the expectations of shareholders and stakeholders**.

Sources: Anderson (1986), p. 22, Davis (1973), p. 312, European Commission (2013), Heal (2005), p. 393, United Nations (2013), Vigeo (2013b), Wood (1991), p. 693

Panel A of Table 5 depicts definitions provided by academic researchers. Back in the mid-1970s, Davis describes CSR as a management's duty to look beyond the pure economic results of its decisions and also bear in mind the potential impact these decisions might have on the social environment the company operates in.[161] Anderson (1986), in turn, does not touch on the economic perspective of CSR activities in his definition. Instead, he determines the main areas a CSR program of a company should comprise of:[162]

- Obeying laws

---

[161] See Davis (1973), p. 315.
[162] See Anderson (1986), p. 22.

- Establishing and abiding ethical standards and
- Engaging in philanthropic giving

For Anderson (1986), there is no doubt that companies must – at any time – operate in compliance with the legal requirements given by international, federal, state or local law.[163] Moreover, the managers of these companies are responsible for establishing and implementing the ethical and moral standards, i.e. codes of conduct, all other members of the companies, including themselves, are obliged to abide.[164]

While the first and second aspects of CSR (obeying laws and establishing/abiding ethical standards) are set for all companies, the third aspect (engaging in philantrophic giving) is not that predefined yet. Instead, management has some degrees of freedom to make decision on the if, when, where and how to engage in philanthropic activities. However, once the decision to engage in philanthropic activity is made, the extent as well as the intent of these activities should be stated explicitly. This ensures avoiding any discrepancies – internally within the company and externally with other stakeholders – on that matter that otherwise might occur at some point in time.[165]

The relationship to external stakeholders is also an aspect other researchers focus on in their definition of CSR: Wood (1991), for example, defines the company's relationship to society as a frame that is spanned around its CSR activities.[166] This is also in line with Heal (2005), who recognizes CSR as a means to increase social value by reducing the extent to which businesses externalize (indirect) costs to the society and the environment in which they operate.[167] Finally, Menz (2010) provides a more contemporary definition of CSR by highlighting the necessity to include ESG aspects in the definition of corporate policies.[168]

More practice-oriented definitions of CSR also account for the necessity of stakeholder relationships management and the consideration of ESG aspects in a company's CSR activities. The three definitions provided in Panel B of Table 5 on page 48 all refer to the establishment

---

[163] See Anderson (1986), p. 27.
[164] See Anderson (1986), p. 27.
[165] See Anderson (1986), p. 22.
[166] See Wood (1991), p. 693.
[167] See Heal (2005), p. 393.
[168] See Menz (2010), p. 118.

of a collaborative relationship to the external social system of the companies and a balanced relation between economic and ESG aspects in a company's CSR activities. Vigeo, a corporation specialized in the assessment of a company's CSR engagement, for example, defines CSR as the management's commitment to not only focus on the interest of the shareholders of a company, but also considering the interests of all stakeholders when making business decisions.[169] In line with this, the European Commission emphasizes the necessity of integrating ESG aspects into the core business strategy in order to ensure that companies meet their responsibility towards society.[170] Finally, the UN sees CSR as a way for companies to find the right balance between meeting shareholders' expectations and at the same time addressing societal and environmental concerns of other stakeholders of the company.[171]

Thus, although a sound and broadly accepted definition of CSR is still missing, two aspects are essential parts of CSR each company should bear in mind when thinking about implementing CSR activities: The explicit incorporation of ESG aspects into business operations and the focus on maintaining sound relationships to the various stakeholders of the company.

3.1.2 CSR activities and business operations

3.1.2.1 Arguments against the implementation of CSR activities

The question whether or not companies should engage in CSR activities often goes in line with the question about the company's primary strategic goal: Is it either maximizing shareholder value (that is, total market value for the owners of the company) or stakeholder value (that is, the sum of the values generated for all groups and individuals related to the company such as employees, customers, communities and the environment)? In 1970, the American economist and Nobel Prize laureate Milton Friedman fueled this debate by publishing an article titled *"The Social Responsibility of Business is to Increase Its Profit."* As the title suspects, Friedman (1970) supports the argumentation that companies should only care about maximizing profits and not about social or environmental concerns.[172] According to Friedman (1970), managers

---

[169] See Vigeo (2013a).

[170] See European Commission (2013).

[171] See United Nations (2013).

[172] See Friedman (1970). In a recently published paper Orlitzky (2015) reviews Friedman's work and supports Friedman's claim that the concept of CSR might be advantageous for individual companies, but in sum undermines the foundations of free (capital) markets and with this, the core values of the current economic system. See Orlitzky (2015), p. 21.

of a company have sole and direct responsibility towards their employers, that is, the shareholders and owners of the company. Thus, – at least from a business perspective – managers should only be concerned with activities targeted towards maximizing shareholder return. Other activities such as social and environmental initiatives are personal interests and should be dealt with by governments, charitable organizations or the individuals themselves in their private lifes. There is no room or necessity to address these issues in the business context as *"the business of business is business."*[173]

There are other academics, who support this idea as supposed by Friedman (1970) and also take a rather skeptical view on companies' engagement in social activities. Jensen (2002), for example, argues that about 200 years of extensive research in economics and finance show that social welfare in total is maximized when companies within an economy separately aim at maximizing their firm value, or in other words, when managers take decisions entirely directed to the individual company's goal of market value maximization.[174] This argumentation is in line with Adam Smith's theorem of the invisible hand, which is based on the assumption that generating wealth can most efficiently be achieved by companies:[175] Society as a whole benefits the most in competitive and complete markets in which all companies separately aim at maximizing their own profits. Thus, companies should merely focus on making decisions in the best interest of their shareholders and not be burdened to also deal with the potential negative impact their decisions might have on society or the environment. The latter is something that is best left over to the responsibility of governments and the public sector.[176]

Despite the fact that these value-maximization theories have dominated economic and financial research for many years, there are other researchers, who take a more general perspective on CSR and support the implementation of such activities early on. Already back in the 1970s, Davis (1973), for example, came up with a discussion on what could keep companies away from engaging in CSR activities and what could encourage them to increase their engagement by going beyond the basic requirements of general law. Figure 4 provides an overview of the arguments brought forward against a company's engagement in CSR activities.

---

[173] See den Hond et al. (2007), p. 25.
[174] See Jensen (1968), p. 236.
[175] See Renneboog et al. (2008a), p. 1730.
[176] See Richardson & Cragg (2010), p. 24.

Arguments against CSR activities

• Profit maximization
   — Dilution of business' primary purpose
   — Cost of social involvement
• Competitive disadvantage and weakened international balance of payments
• Lack of social skills
• Lack of accountability

Figure 4: Arguments against a company's engagement in CSR activities
Source: Own illustration based on Davis (1973), pp. 317-321

Profit maximization: Arguments that might keep companies away from implementing CSR strategies basically are in line with the above mentioned discussion. A company's sole responsibility is profit maximization and engaging in CSR issues would dilute business' primary focus on economic productivity.[177] Proponents of this view argue that CSR puts companies into a competitive disadvantage as it incurs upfront costs that otherwise might not occur or at least be borne by other parties such as the government or the society.[178] As long as the future recovery of those costs cannot be guaranteed, transferring them from society to companies means reallocating wealth from shareholders of the company to other stakeholders, who – strictly speaking – do not even have a legal claim on the company's profits.[179] Thus, CSR is a private benefit that managers would excerpt at the costs of shareholders and that, in the end, implies lower overall financial performance of the company.

Competitive disadvantage and weakened international balance of payment: The costs associated with the implantation of CSR activities not only affects the company's financial performance. They also negatively affect the company's competitiveness on international markets. As Davis (1973) argues, the costs for CSR activities must be recovered and typically are charged-backed to the customers. As a consequence, the prices customers have to pay in order to buy the products of CSR companies are higher compared to the price they have to pay for products of companies that do not have CSR activities in place.[180] The higher prices will lead

---

[177] See Davis (1973), p. 317.
[178] See Waddock & Graves (1997), p. 305.
[179] See Humphrey et al. (2012), p. 629.
[180] See Davis (1973), p. 319.

to less sales and thus, put companies with CSR activities into a competitive disadvantage relative to companies without such activities.[181] The ultimate result will be a weakened international balance of payments for the entire economy the CSR company operates in.[182]

Lack of social skills: If management nonetheless decides to engage in CSR activities, it often lacks the necessary perceptions and skills for doing so. Usually, managers have a rather economic background and might find it difficult to set up the right programs directed to purposes other than profit.[183] Thus, it is questionable if someone, who is used to making decisions based on economic values, should be responsible to dealing with social issues as social issues require the incorporation of other perspectives than purely economic ones in the process when looking for a solution to these issues.[184]

Lack of accountability: The fact that managers do not have the qualification for dealing with social issues is also in line with the argument that managers have no direct line of accountability towards society or the public.[185] Providing managers with the task of dealing with societal issues would mean giving them responsibility for something they are not really accountable for. In fact, forcing managers to also include social objectives in their business decisions might detract them from the real fundamental objective, i.e. focus on economic priorities and maximize profits, they are obliged to achieve when acting in the best interest of the corporation and its shareholders.[186] Thus, implementing CSR on a broad basis would only make sense after society has successfully developed effective mechanisms to hold managers accountable for their economic and social actions.[187] Otherwise, CSR should rather be a niche topic, but not an integral part of each company's core strategy.

---

[181] See Gonzalez-Perez (2013), p. 8.
[182] See Davis (1973), p. 319.
[183] See Carroll & Shabana (2010), p. 88 and Davis (1973), p. 318.
[184] See Davis (1973), p. 318.
[185] See Davis (1973), p. 320.
[186] See Orlitzky (2015), p. 11.
[187] See Davis (1973), p. 320 and Orlitzky (2015), p. 11.

3.1.2.2 Arguments in favor of the implementation of CSR activities

The arguments in favor of a company's engagement in CSR activities can be sorted around four major stakeholder groups of the company: The public, customers, employees and the company's owners or shareholders.

The public: One of the main reasons often mentioned in favor of a company's engagement in CSR is the rather simple fact that this topic has become increasingly popular among policy makers and the public.[188] Representatives of both groups demand a higher level of responsibility and accountability of companies towards society and get support from (inter)national media, political debate and special interest groups such as ethical investors. In fact, the group of ethical investors has grown immensely in the past decade.[189] By now, it has reached such a critical mass that it succeeds in increasingly directing capital market's attention towards ESG performance issues.[190] Companies, in turn, can profit from this development by actively engaging in CSR issues and directing the public's attention towards the efforts made. As Fombrun and Shanley (1990) show, the public's assessment of a company increases with the level of CSR engagement of the company: The correlation coefficient between a company's reputation and the amount the company donates to charity is significantly positive at the 5%-level.[191] Thus, companies that give proportionally more to charity than others or might even have established their own foundation tend to have a higher reputation in the public.

The relationship between a company's level of engagement in CSR and its reputation also has positive effects on the company's performance data. Orlitzky & Benjamin (2001), for example, conduct a meta-analysis and find evidence that the more a company engages in CSR, the higher its reputation and the lower its financial risk.[192] Moreover, Antunovich and Laster (1998) provide evidence that the company's reputation positively influences its return characteristics: The authors find that the portfolio consisting of the most admired companies produces an abnormal return of 3.2% in the first year after portfolio formation date and 8.3% in the three following

---

[188] See Carroll and Shabana (2010), p. 85, Davis (1973), p. 313, Gonzalez-Perez (2013), p. 9 and Smith (2003), p. 53.

[189] See Cortez et al. (2012), p. 254, Gevlin (2007), p. 56a and Scalet & Kelly (2010), p. 82.

[190] See Brooks (1989), p. 31 and Vogel (2006), pp. 9 and 16.

[191] See Fombrun & Shanley (1990), pp. 248 and 251.

[192] See Orlitzky & Benjamin (2001), p. 369.

years.[193] Contrary, the portfolio consisting of the least admired companies generates a negative return of -8.6% in the first year after portfolio formation date. As the return differences between the two portfolios cannot be attributed to a higher systematic risk inherent in the portfolio of the most admired companies, the authors conclude that capital markets fail to immediately incorporate the positive reputational effect of CSR activities in the stock prices – although the public might be aware of the company's engagement and appreciate this by attributing a higher reputation to the respective company.[194] Thus, by implementing trading strategies that involve selling the losers (the portfolio with the least admired companies) and buying the winners (the portfolio with the most admired companies) investors could benefit from generating positive abnormal returns.[195]

Customers: Some of the companies use their CSR engagement not only for reputational but also trust building purposes.[196] Society expects the companies to be responsible and companies react accordingly. Thus, the engagement can be used as positive signal for current as well as prospective customers of the company that the products and services offered are reliable and of high quality. Research supports this notion. In 2011, the market research company Datamonitor published a report on best practices in CSR activities and highlights that CSR is one of the most effective tools for companies to build trust with consumers: 55% of the respondents state that they would assign a higher quality to fairly traded products or products with socially responsible attributes than other products offered in the same goods market.[197] This seems to be especially relevant for companies that are either active in industries in which a company's image is an important factor in the buying decision of a customer (e.g. industries with high levels of advertising spending or products for which consumers cannot conduct any quality checks before actually buying the product) or companies that operate in uniform markets in which it is difficult for them to differentiate their products from the offerings made by other companies in the same market.[198]

---

[193] See Antunovich & Laster (1998), p. 1.
[194] See Antunovich & Laster (1998), p. 2.
[195] This finding contradicts the findings published by DeBondt and Thaler (1985), who suggest that investors can generate positive abnormal returns by buying past losers and selling past winners.
[196] See Carroll & Shabana (2010), p. 94, Pivato (2008), p. 3 and The Corporate Register (2008), p. 46.
[197] See Datamonitor (2011), p. n/a.
[198] See Fisman et al. (2008), p. 4.

The report published by Datamonitor (2011), however, also shows that CSR is not an end in itself and companies should carefully choose their level of engagement. Again, more than half of the interviewed consumers (54%) have the perception that companies primarily introduce CSR strategies to improve their corporate image and not because they or their managers are intrinsically-motivated in doing so.[199] Thus, in order to be really authentic in their CSR engagement, companies should pay close attention to aligning all activities with their core image and business strategies. Otherwise they run the risk of a reversed effect and customers might lose trust in the company and its products. Once all strategies are aligned, CSR can be an effective means for companies to achieve consistent positive results on the perceived image among their consumers.

Employees: CSR also can be an effective tool for companies to attract highly-qualified and motivated employees and create a favorable work environment. Brekke and Nyborg (2004), for example, study the effects CSR activities have when morally motivated employees are either employed in a green or a brown company and document three main findings:[200] First, morally motivated employees demand lower wages from a green employer than from a brown employer. Second, the employees put more effort into their work if they are employed by a green company. Finally, green companies can use high levels of CSR engagement as screening device to attract more productive workers.[201] Thus, in addition to the positive effects on reputation among the public and increasing quality perception among its customers, companies also can use their CSR profile to successfully differentiate themselves in the labor market and decrease hiring costs or turnover rates.[202] This should be of special interest for companies that are active in competitive and labor-intense industries such as agriculture, hospitality or food services: These companies usually have a high demand for well-qualified and motivated employees and could use CSR to differentiate themselves from other employers in the same industry.[203]

---

[199] See Datamonitor (2011), p. n/a.

[200] Green companies are defined as companies that voluntarily undertake measures to address social and environmental concern (e.g., pollution prevention) and thus, pay a fixed amount of costs for social responsibility. In contrast to this, brown companies avoid integrating ESG issues in their business operations and consequently do not pay the costs of socially responsible. See Brekke & Nyborg (2004), p. 4.

[201] See Brekke & Nyborg (2004), p. 17.

[202] See Barnett & Salomon (2006), p. 1105.

[203] See Barnett & Salomon (2006), p. 1102.

Shareholders: The management of a company is not only responsible to the company's key stakeholders such as its employees, customers, suppliers, or the public, but also to its shareholders. In order to balance the claims of shareholders and the various other stakeholders of the company, ongoing good management practices are needed.[204] CSR can be used as a management tool to cope with this challenge supporting the argument that the implementation of CSR activities also is in the long-run self-interest of the company's shareholders.[205]

First, CSR enhances the company's reputation among their stakeholders and makes is easier for companies to attract high-quality workers or reduce turnover and absenteeism rates of their employees. Thus, CSR resembles an investment into the intangible assets of a company (e.g. human capital) that increases its competitive advantage. The competitive advantage is expected to result in higher profitability of the company and therefore, should lead to increased (financial) benefits for the shareholders.[206] Second, shareholders of companies that have voluntary CSR activities in place profit from a better reputation among their stakeholders. The reasoning behind this idea is the fact that managers of such companies are assumed to focus on managing the long-term needs of the entire company (including its stakeholders) and are less likely to get involved in short-term, value-destroying business practices.[207] Finally, company's voluntary engagement in social issues might keep government from implementing strict regulations directed towards increasing company's accountability for society and gives management the freedom to individually decide on the kind and level of engagement in CSR.[208] Figure 5 summarizes the arguments discussed in favor of a company's engagement in CSR activities.

To conclunde, the discussion in the preceding sections shows that there are argument against a company's engagement in CSR activities and arguments in favor of such engagement. However, it is important to note that the arguments presented are based on a rather theoretical debate on the effect of a company's CSR activities on its reputation. A quantitative assessment of CSR activities on the company's performance has not been discussed so far. Nonetheless, there have

---

[204] See Bassen et al. (2006), p. 9.
[205] See Davis (1973), p. 315 and Leite (2014), p. 249.
[206] See El Ghoul et al. (2011), p. 2389 and Derwall et al. (2005), p. 51.
[207] See Humphrey et al. (2012), p. 628.
[208] See den Hond & Bakker (2007), p. 908.

been attempts by academic researchers to calculate the effect of CSR activities on company performance. The following section presents an overview of some of these attempts.[209]

Arguments in favor of CSR activities
• Public: Higher reputation and positive public image • Customers: Perception of reliability and good quality products and services • Employees: Lower wages and turnover rate, higher motivation and productivity • Shareholders: Increased competitive advantage, higher profitability, increased financial benefits for shareholders

Figure 5: Arguments in favor of a company's engagement in CSR activities
Source: Own illustration

3.1.3 CSR activities and company financial data

3.1.3.1 Overall company performance

Existing studies that examine the relationship between a company's CSR activities and its financial performance can be divided into two groups: The first group consists of studies examining the overall effect of a company's CSR rating on its performance data; the second group comprises studies that try to isolate the impact of particular social factors (e.g. employee satisfaction, corporate governance mechanisms or environmental concern) on the financial performance of the company.[210]

CSR rating and company performance: Kempf and Osthoff (2007) show that stocks of companies with a high CSR rating[211] provide higher abnormal returns than those companies that have a low CSR rating. More precisely, the authors show that by implementing a long-short

---

[209] For a comprehensive literature review on the theoretical and empirical debate about the relationship between CSR and financial performance, please refer to Margolis & Walsh (2003), Margolis et al. (2009) and Orlitzky et al. (2003).

[210] This section focusses on individual (stock) returns and reviews studies that have examined the performance data of companies with a good CSR rating relative to companies with a low CSR rating. For an overview of studies examining the performance differences between portfolios of funds consisting of multiple companies with high vs. low CSR ratings, please refer to section 4.5.

[211] Rating criteria include: Community, diversity, employee relations, environment, human rights and product. See Kempf & Osthoff (2007), p. 910.

strategy, i.e. taking a long position in (buying) high-rated stocks and a short position in (selling) low-rated stocks, investors can earn abnormal returns of up to 8.7% p.a.[212] These abnormal returns also remain significant after transaction costs are taken into account.

The outperformance hypothesis is later confirmed by the study published by Statman and Glushkov (2009) and Jiao (2010). Examining stock returns in the period between 1992 and 2007, Statman and Glushkov (2009) find that stocks of companies with a high CSR score outperform stocks of companies with a rather low CSR score that operate in questionable industries such as tobacco, alcohol, gambling, firearms and nuclear operations.[213] Jiao (2010) confirms this finding and shows that stakeholder welfare is positively related to shareholder benefit and thus, company value. More precisely, the author determines Tobin's Q for each company in order to assess the effect of changes in stakeholder welfare on a company's value.[214] Tobin's Q is a ratio that measures the market value of a company relative to the book value of the same company.[215] The higher Tobin's Q, the higher is the market value of the assets and thus, the value of the entire firm. For a sample of 822 companies in the period 1992-2003, Jiao (2010) shows that an increase of one in a company's stakeholder welfare score – measured by the company's score on community and employee relations, environmental concern and diversity – is associated with a positive increase of 0.587 in Tobin's Q.[216]

However, not all studies conducted so far support the outperformance hypothesis: Guerard (1997) and Galema et al. (2008), for example, show that there is no significant difference between the returns of a SRI-screened and a SRI-unscreened portfolio in the period between 1987-1994 and 1992-2006, respectively.[217] Brammer et al. (2006) also cannot find any evidence of a significant relationship between a company's engagement in CSR activities and its financial performance. In fact, the results suggest the opposite: Stocks of companies with high CSR ratings tend to underperform the market while stocks of companies with low ratings outperform market return: While the stocks of companies with a high CSR rating underperform the equally

---

[212] See Kempf & Osthoff (2007), p. 909.
[213] See Statman & Glushkov (2009), pp. 40f.
[214] See Jiao (2010), p. 2551.
[215] Tobin's Q was first introduced by Tobin & Brainard (1977). It is calculated as the ratio between an asset's market value and its replacement costs (book value). The ratio represents the market price paid for an existing asset in the numerator relative to the market price paid for a newly produced asset of same size or physical consistency in the denominator. See Tobin & Brainard (1977), p. 235.
[216] See Jiao (2010), p. 2560.
[217] See Galema et al. (2008), p. 2647 and Guerard (1997), p. 11.

weighted benchmark by 0.01% per month, the stocks of companies with a low CSR rating outperform the respective benchmark by 0.19%.[218]

Derwall et al. (2011) extend this analysis to different periods and document that both, portfolios consisting of stocks with a low CSR rating (sin stocks) and portfolios comprised of stocks with a high CSR rating (social stocks), generate abnormal returns in the short-run. However, in the long run, the effect remains for sin stocks, but diminishes for social stocks.[219] More precisely, the authors have divided the entire sample period of 1992-2008 into four sub-periods (1992-2002, 1992-2004, 1992-2006 and 1992-2008) and document annual abnormal returns for the sin stock portfolio as well as the portfolio with social stocks that score high on employee relations. While the abnormal returns for the former portfolio are in a range between 0.215% and 0.24% per month and remain statistically significant at the 5% or 10% level for all sub-periods, the abnormal returns for the latter portfolio decrease with increasing length of the sub-period: For the period 1992-2002, the average abnormal return for the social stock portfolio is 0.46% per month (statistically significant at the 10% level), but decreases to statistically insignificant 0.23% for the period 1992-2008.[220]

Fabozzi et al. (2008) obtain similar results and find that for the period 1970-2007 sin stock portfolios consisting of companies with relations to the alcohol, gambling, tobacco, weapons or adult services industry generate abnormal annual returns of up to 19% p.a. and consistently outperform benchmark returns.[221] This finding also holds for individual years within this period and is true for all of the 21 different countries included in the study. In line with this, Hong and Kacperczyk (2007) show that a sin stock portfolio significantly outperforms a comparable portfolio of SRI-unscreened stocks by 29 basis points (bp) per month – even after adjusting for factors like market size and book-to-market ratios.[222] The authors also provide a possible explanation for the occurrence of the so-called shunned-stock hypothesis: Many investors underestimate the value of sin stocks and instead try to improve portfolio performance by focusing on socially responsible stocks. With increasing number of investors that neglect to invest in sin

---

[218] See Brammer et al. (2006), pp. 107f.
[219] See Derwall et al. (2011), p. 2137.
[220] See Derwall et al. (2011), p. 2145.
[221] See Fabozzi et al. (2008), p. 92.
[222] See Hong & Kacperczyk (2009), p. 17.

stocks, risk-sharing opportunities for the companies that issue those stocks decrease. Consequently, the price for the sin stocks decreases relative to their fundamental values and in order to remain an attractive investment alternative, companies that issue sin stocks have to pay a higher return to the investors than companies that rather are considered as being socially responsible.[223]

Employee satisfaction and company performance: The positive relationship between company performance and employee satisfaction as theoretically derived in the last section is only partially confirmed in empirical research. Edmans (2011) finds evidence that supports the notion that a portfolio consisting of stocks of the *"Best Companies to Work for in America"*[224] not only outperforms industry benchmarks but also the market.[225] However, other studies document the opposite. Scholtens and Zhou (2008), for example, find evidence in favor of a negative relationship between employee relations and company performance. The authors conclude that the costs that are associated with the investment into employee education and training outweigh the value created by loyal and committed employees.[226] This finding is also in line with the statement made by McWilliams and Siegel (2001): They argue that companies with good employee relations face higher labor costs as these companies either have to dedicate parts of the existing resources (employees) to CSR activities and fill up the gaps by other employees or hire new employees in order to effectively implement the CSR programs.[227] Although the authors did not test this statement empirically, the discussion shows that the effect of good employee relations on company performance is not as clear-cut as expected from theory.

Corporate governance and company performance: According to the agency theory, the separation of ownership within companies can lead to potential conflicts of interest between the company's management (agent) and the owners of the company (principal).[228] Corporate governance mechanisms are a means to overcome these potential conflicts by explicitly defining

---

[223] See Hong & Kacperczyk (2009), p. 17.
[224] Edmans (2011), p. 6.
[225] See Edmans (2011), pp. 9–10.
[226] See Scholten & Zhou (2008), p. 223.
[227] See McWilliams & Siegel (2001), p. 123.
[228] See Eisenhardt (1989), p. 58, Fama & Jensen (1983), p. 304, Jensen & Meckling (1976), p. 308 and Ross (1973), p. 134.

and thus, regulating shareholder rights.[229] Implementing the mechanisms, however, is voluntary for the companies and each company can define its own set of regulations. Consequently, the shareholder rights defined vary greatly across companies.

Gompers et al. (2003) have compiled a list of 24 commonly used corporate governance rules and study the effect of those rules on the firm value of 1,500 large US companies in the 1990s. Their study shows that companies benefit from strong corporate governance and shareholder rights along several performance measurements: Companies with strong shareholder rights not only exhibit higher firm values, they also have higher profits, higher sales growth, lower capital expenditures and finally, make fewer acquisitions than companies with weaker shareholder rights.[230] More precisely, implementing an investment strategy that involves buying shares of companies with the strongest shareholder rights (i.e. democracy companies) and selling shares of companies with the lowest shareholder rights (i.e. dictatorship companies) results in an abnormal return of 8.5% per annum within the sample period.[231] The authors also provide two hypotheses that explain this phenomenon and are confirmed in the course of their study: First, weak shareholder rights induce additional agency costs that negatively affect company performance measures. Second, corporate governance mechanisms are highly correlated with other characteristics such as institutional ownership, trading volume or past sales growth that have driven abnormal returns in the 1990s.[232]

Bauer et al. (2004) transfer the approach of Gompers et al. (2003) to the European market and confirm the finding that corporate governance is positively related to company performance and thus, company value. The effect weakens after accounting for country differences, but remains positive.[233] Thus, existing research supposes a positive relationship between corporate governance mechanisms and company value – although the effect does not seem to be as definite as it is with employee satisfaction.

Environmental conscientiousness (EC) and company performance: Studies that examine the relationship between a company's EC and its performance typically either analyze this re-

---

[229] See Renneboog et al. (2008a), p. 1732 and Shleifer & Vishny (1997), p. 737.
[230] See Gompers et al. (2003), p. 107.
[231] See Gompers et al. (2003), p. 109.
[232] See Gompers et al. (2003), pp. 110 and 139.
[233] See Bauer et al. (2004), p. 110.

lationship based on the company's EC (i.e. the fact that the company takes actions that go beyond the legal environmental obligations) or its environmental risk management practices. Cohen et al. (1997) focus on the effect of EC on company stock prices: The authors construct two industry-balanced portfolios, one portfolio that consist of the low pollution companies (companies with a high level of EC within their respective industry) and one portfolio that consists of the high pollution companies (companies with a low level of EC).[234] For both portfolios, the authors calculate and compare accounting and market returns.[235] The results obtained indicate that there is neither a financial penalty for investing in low pollution companies nor can investors expect to earn positive returns by investing into those companies: The portfolios that consist of low pollution companies perform better than the portfolios that consist of high pollution companies in 80% of the comparisons done in the study. The difference between the returns, however, has only been significant for about 20% of the comparison cases.[236]

In contrast to this, Diltz (1995) finds evidence that good environmental performance has a significantly positive impact on company returns: The portfolio consisting of companies with a high level of EC generated a significantly higher alpha than the portfolio of companies with a low EC rating.[237] Derwall et al. (2005) confirm the finding that environmentally responsible investing can in fact be beneficial for investors: The portfolio of stocks with a high EC score significantly outperforms the portfolio with a low EC score by 0.42% per month for the full observation period between 1995 and 2003.[238] The effect remains significant even after adjusting returns for factors such as market risk, investment style and industry effects. Similar to this, Yamashita et al. (1999) show that – at least in the short-run – the publication of information about the improvement of a company's EC score has a strong positive effect on stock prices.[239]

---

[234] See Cohen et al. (1997), p. 14.
[235] Accounting returns are measured using return on assets and return on equity for each company; market returns are measured using the total return to shareholders both, before and after risk-adjustments (see Cohen et al., 1997, p. 11).
[236] See Cohen et al. (1997), p. 14.
[237] The results are significant at the 5% level (see Diltz (1995b), p. 72). Overall, Diltz (1995b) studies return differences for good and poor rated companies on 14 different dimensions of SRI. While the returns generated by portfolios that apply environmental and military screens are significantly positive, the returns generated by portfolios that apply other screens such as charitable giving, women and minorities in management or family benefits are not significantly different from zero. See Diltz (1995b), p. 69.
[238] See Derwall et al. (2005), p. 57f.
[239] See Yamashita et al. (1999), p. 79.

This trend is even continued in the long-run, although the relation is not strong anymore. Moreover, there seems to be a strong negative effect on the stock prices of companies with a poor EC score.

The finding that a poor EC score constitutes poor financial performance – even in the long run – is also consistent with the results obtained by Scholtens and Zhou (2008). They find that poor environmental performance has a negative, although not statistically significant effect on the financial performance of a company.[240] Thus, although a high EC score is not unambiguously related to a positive price reaction by financial markets, a low EC score seems to have a severe negative effect on a company's value.

3.1.3.2 Cost of capital

Studies that examine the effect of CSR activities on a company's cost of capital can be divided into studies that either analyze the effect a company's overall CSR rating has on the components of the company's cost of capital (e.g. the cost of equity and the cost of debt) or studies that try to find an effect of individual CSR activities initiated by a company (e.g. environmental concern) on its overall cost of capital.

El Ghoul et al. (2011) examine the effect of CSR activities on the company's cost of equity. Using a sample of almost 13,000 observations for US-based companies in the period between 1992 and 2004 and controlling for company-specific or industry-related factors, the authors find that ex-ante cost of equity are lower for companies with a high CSR rating than for companies with a low CSR rating.[241] Factors contributing to the decrease in the cost of equity are: Investments in improving employee relations, environmental policies and products strategies. The study also shows that relations to the tobacco and nuclear power industry, in turn, increase equity financing cost for companies.[242]

Menz (2010) studies the relationship between a company's CSR rating and its cost of debt. Based on the assumption that CSR companies usually are less risky and more profitable than

---

[240] See Scholtens & Zhou (2008), p. 222.
[241] See El Ghoul et al. (2011), p. 2389.
[242] See El Ghoul et al. (2011), pp. 2400f.

conventional companies, the author hypothesizes that – all else being equal – socially responsible companies should also exhibit lower risk premiums.[243] The hypothesis is tested using monthly bond data for a sample of 498 bonds that have been included in the Merrill Lynch Non-Financial Corporate Bond Index at the end of May 2006.[244] The results obtained do not confirm the author's hypothesis. No difference in the risk premiums paid for bonds of CSR companies and non-CSR companies can be observed.[245] The author provides three possible explanations for this finding:[246] First, bond investors rely more on credit ratings than on CSR ratings when deciding on their investments. Second, credit ratings already include some non-financial information such as corporate governance mechanisms or environmental policies. Thus, CSR ratings do not provide additional information that is of value for the bond investors. Third, bond investors ignore CSR as valuation factor and do not recognize a good CSR score when determining the bond rating. Although Menz (2010) theoretically discusses the three explanations, he does not examine empirically which of them is weighted higher in the investment decision process of bond investors.

Sharfman and Fernando (2008) published a study on the relationship between a company's environmental risk management and its cost of capital. Their findings suggest that companies can benefit from improvements in the environmental risk management through an overall reduction of their cost of capital. The effect is related to both, a reduction in the cost of equity, which is due to a decrease of the company's volatility (measured by beta), and a shift from equity to debt financing, which is associated with additional tax benefits for the company.[247]

However, not all companies benefit from improving EC scores or environmental risk management to the same extent. In fact, the equilibrium model developed by Heinkel et al. (2001) demonstrates that companies are facing a trade-off between the higher cost of capital, if they do not exhibit EC, and the cost of reforming if transforming from a polluting to a green company.[248] While the cost of reforming can be calculated on the basis of the costs associated with

---

[243] The risk premium is defined as the excess return above the risk-free rate of return investors expect to generate by investing into a risky security. See Berk & DeMarzo (2014), p. 327, Jones (2009), p. 226 and section 4.3.2.

[244] See Menz (2010), p. 124.

[245] See Menz (2010), p. 117.

[246] See Menz (2010), p. 128.

[247] See Sharfman & Fernando (2008), p. 569.

[248] See Heinkel et al. (2001), p. 431.

the transformation, the company's cost of capital are determined by financial markets and thus, investors' willingness to place money into the company's stocks.[249] As social investors avoid investing in polluting companies, the investor base shrinks, which leads to lower stock prices and higher cost of capital for those companies. With increasing number of investors that refuse to invest in an environmentally irresponsible company, the cost of capital of this company increase and at some point exceed the costs for turning the company into a green company.[250] Only after this threshold level is achieved and the costs of capital are higher than the transformation cost, is it worthwhile for a company to invest in the transformation.

In addition to developing the model, Heinkel et al. (2001) also empirically test their statements and show that a share of about 25% social investors is necessary to overcome a company's cost of reforming.[251] This threshold has not yet been reached as only about 10-20% of AuM are dedicated to ESG issues today.[252] Thus, the majority of companies seems to have a social investor base that is below 25%, making it less attractive for those companies to turn into a green company rather than living with higher cost of capital due to the classification of being a polluting company.

3.1.4 Interim conclusion

Overall, the theoretical discussions and empirical evidences published on the relationship between a company's CSR activities and its financial performance have provided mixed results. Some researchers provide arguments in favor of a positive relationship; some find evidence for a negative relationship.[253] Some even argue that the relationship in fact should be neutral.[254] Those researchers base their argumentation on the fact that the evidences found so far are biased as they do not account for intervening variables such as expenditures for research and development that might also influence corporate performance. McWilliams and Siegel (2000), for ex-

---

[249] See Heinkel et al. (2001), pp. 431 and 438.
[250] See Heinkel et al. (2001), pp. 431 and 444f.
[251] See Heinkel et al. (2001), p. 439.
[252] See section 2.3.
[253] See, for example, Derwall et al. (2005), Jiao (2010), Kempf & Osthoff (2007), Statman & Glushkov (2009) for studies that document a positive relationship and Edmans (2011), McWilliams & Siegel (2001), Scholtens & Zhou (2008) for studies that find evidence in favor of a negative relationship.
[254] See, for example, Brammer et al. (2006), Galema et al. (2008) and Guerard (1997).

ample, argue that a relationship between a company's CSR activities and its financial performance merely exists by chance as there are too many other factors (e.g. the capital invested into research and development activities) that also influence this relationship.[255] This argumentation is also in line with the statement made by Ullmann (1985), who proposes that different CSR variables offset each other and that it therefore should not possible to determine whether a relation between CSR and financial performance exists or not.[256]

Thus, although the effect of CSR activities on a company's performance is neither clearly positive nor negative and legally-binding regulations that govern the implementation of CSR activities are still missing, the concept of CSR has become increasingly important to businesses and their managers. In line with this development, the number of companies implementing strategies targeted towards addressing ESG issues and publishing CSR reports to illustrate the social impact they have already achieved has grown tremendously. The Corporate Register[257], for example, reports that in the period between September 2006 and December 2007, about two thirds of the Financial Times Global 500 companies have published CSR reports.[258] Looking at the number of reports issued in each region as displayed in Table 6, however, there are still differences to note: While only about half of the companies in North America (56%) have issued CSR reports, the vast majority of companies in Europe and Japan did so (88% and 78%, respectively).

To conclude, for CSR to work on a long-term perspective, there are few additional requirements that have to be fulfilled: First, CSR must be clearly defined and its effect on corporate performance be measurable. Above this, a consistent documentation is needed to ensure a reliable tracking of the process made and the impact achieved.[259] Second, management must

---

[255] See McWilliams & Siegel (2000), p. 603.

[256] See Ullmann (1985), pp. 540 and 543.

[257] The Corporate Register is an online-directory of CSR reports. Companies from both, the private and the public sector, can upload their CSR reports and make it available for download to registered users (see http://www.corporateregister.com/about.html).

[258] See Lydenberg & Graham (2009), p. 49 and The Corporate Register (2008), p. 12. In 2010, the accountancy company PriceWaterhouseCoopers (PwC) published a report on CSR reporting trends displaying similar information: By the end of July 2010, about 81% of the companies in Europe produced a CSR report, while in the US and Canada this was only true for about 40% of the companies included in the report (see PwC (2010), p. 4).

[259] See Renneboog et al. (2008a), p. 1731.

acknowledge the fact that maximizing the long term value for their shareholders is not contradictory to also considering the welfare of all other stakeholders.[260] In fact, using parts of its financial resources to improve a company's social and environmental performance can result in a competitive advantage due to the more cost-efficient use of the available resources.[261] Finally, investors themselves must change their investment strategies from being purely financially oriented to also including non-financial objectives in their investment decision process or at least recognizing the positive effect CSR has on a company's reputation. Once these prerequisites are given, research shows that CSR is an effective element of corporate strategy, not only for attracting a solid customer base and highly motivated employees, but also for setting up the basis for long-term performance and profitability of the company.[262]

Table 6: Number of CSR reports published globally

This table shows the number of companies listed in the Financial Times Global 500 that have issued a CSR report in the period between September 2006 and December 2007.

Region	Number of companies	Number of CSR reporters	In percent of total companies
North America	210	118	56%
Europe	172	152	88%
Japan	49	38	78%
Asia (excl. Japan)	40	9	23%
Africa & Middle East	12	5	42%
Australasia	10	6	60%
South America	7	7	100%
Total	500	335	67%

Source: Own illustration based on The Corporate Register (2008), p. 12

---

[260] See Derwall et al. (2005), p. 51.
[261] See Porter & van der Linde (1995), p. 120.
[262] See Heal (2005), p. 408.

3.2 Indirect investments

3.2.1 Definition of SRI funds

While CSR refers to the social responsibility activities of one single company, SRI funds combine investments into multiple, as socially responsible classified companies in one portfolio.[263] The companies to include are selected based on socially responsible criteria that are individually defined by the fund managers.[264] Apart from defining the selection criteria, the main task for the fund managers is to optimize the fund's financial performance, i.e. maximizing portfolio return while maintaining a certain level of risk or minimizing the portfolio risk while achieving a certain level of return. Usually, fund managers try to meet these requirements by continually re-balancing the weights of the securities invested in.[265] This implies that, except for the fact that SRI funds incorporate socially responsible criteria when selecting the securities to be included in the fund, SRI funds are no different than conventional (mutual) funds. Mutual funds, in turn, are defined as investment vehicles that pool money from different investors and use the collected money to invest in securities such as equity, fixed income or money market instruments.[266] The funds are managed by fund managers, who have to decide which securities meet the investment policy initially defined and marketed to the investors and thus, are to be included in the fund's portfolio. Moreover, fund managers also are responsible for generating capital gains for the investors by re-balancing the fund's portfolio and buying or selling securities. The securities selected can either be of one asset category (e.g. equity securities only) or from different categories (e.g. a mixture between equity and fixed income securities).[267] Capital gains generated by the fund are split among the investors proportional to the money each investor has placed into the fund.[268]

---

[263] See Barnett & Salomon (2006), p. 1102, Haigh & Hazelton (2004), p. 68, Renneboog (2011), p. 564.

[264] See Lee et al. (2010), p. 352. Please refer to section 3.2.2 for a detailed description of commonly used screens applied as selection criteria by SRI fund managers.

[265] Due to the continuous re-balancing of the portfolio, mutual funds are also said to be actively managed. Indices, in turn, are said to be passively managed. See Ippolito (1989), p. 2.

[266] See Mobius (2007), p. 1.

[267] See section 3.2.3 for an overview of the different categories of SRI funds available for investors.

[268] See Mobius (2007), p. 1.

Investors benefit from placing money into funds in several ways:[269] First, even small (private) investors get access to securities in business sectors or industries they otherwise might not be able to invest in. Second, as funds invest in a broad variety of securities, investors can benefit from diversification effects.[270] Third, mutual funds are liquid investments and investors have the possibility to sell their share in the fund at any time and at the actual market value of the fund's securities. Finally, transaction costs per investor are lower compared to individual investments. For each transaction, commission and trading fees have to be paid. If investors trade individually, they have to bear all cost, whereas in funds, the costs are split among all investors of the funds.

There are, however, also some disadvantages associated with investments into mutual funds investors should carefully think about before placing their money into one of the funds:[271] First and foremost, investors have no direct influence on the individual securities that are included in the fund as the fund managers are responsible for managing the fund's portfolio. In order to accomplish this task, fund managers are only obliged to stick to the investment policies published in the fund's prospectus when the fund has been established. Within these policies, the fund managers are free to decide on whether or not to re-balance the portfolio and which securities to drop or add. Second, mutual funds are not riskless investments, as their value depends on the value of the securities included in the funds. As the value of these securities fluctuates, the value of the fund changes as well, making it impossible for funds to guarantee a certain level of return or risk exposure.

The characteristics of (conventional) mutual funds mentioned before also apply for SRI mutual funds. In fact, the only differentiating factor between conventional and SRI mutual funds is the integration of investors' concerns about ESG issues in the security selection process: SRI mutual funds select the securities to include in the fund's portfolio not only based on the past and prospective future financial performance of the securities, but also based on the securities' performances on diverse ESG criteria.[272] Each fund can define its own security selection criteria and SRI investors can choose to put their money solely into those funds that meet their personal

---

[269] See Mobius (2007), p. 4 and Hall (2010), p. 15.
[270] See section 4.2.2.2 for more details on the benefits of diversification.
[271] See Mobius (2007), p. 4.
[272] See Derwall & Koedijk (2009), p. 212 and Sparkes (2001), p. 196.

values and beliefs.[273] Once such a fund is identified, it offers the possibility for the investors to make a potential capital gain from a portfolio that at the same time corresponds to their social conscience.[274] Thus, in order for a fund to be attractive to a broad variety of investors, SRI fund managers have to carefully define the ESG criteria how securities are selected.

As preferences as well as values and beliefs of investors vary greatly, each fund has its own criteria how securities are selected.[275] Consequently, a heterogeneous set of SRI funds has evolved in the past few years: While there have been 313 SRI mutual funds established in Europe by 2003, the number has more than tripled to 992 funds by 2013.[276] This equals an increase of about 12% p.a. from 2003 to 2013. Figure 6 shows the development of the absolute number of SRI funds domiciled in Europe between 2003 and 2013. Although SRI funds still only represent about 3% of the total number mutual funds in Europe, the growth trend is expected to also continue in the upcoming years.[277]

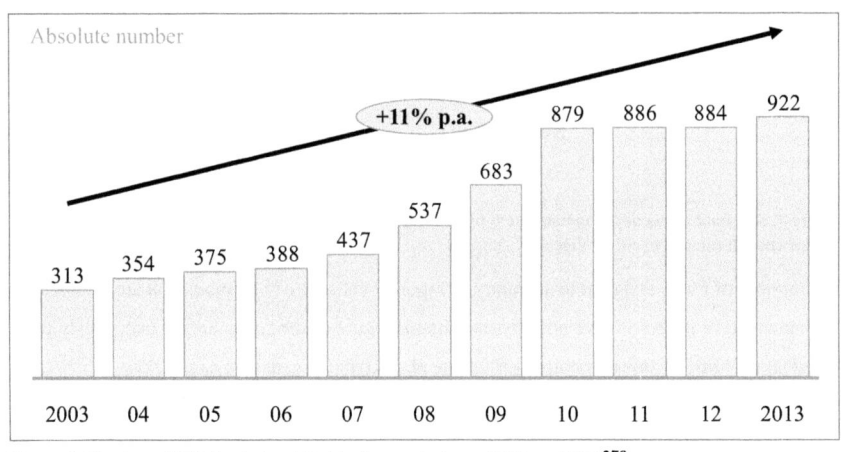

Figure 6: Number of SRI funds domiciled in Europe between 2003 and 2013[278]
Source: Own illustration based on Vigeo (2013a), p. 7

---

[273] See Humphrey & Lee (2011), p. 522 and Jones et al. (2008), p. 182.
[274] See Lee et al. (2010), p. 351.
[275] See Sandberg et al. (2008), pp. 520f.
[276] See Vigeo (2013a), p. 7.
[277] See Thomson Reuters (2013), p. 3 and Vigeo (2013a), p. 9.
[278] Figures reported as of June 30 in each year. The number of AuM grew by 24% p.a., reaching a level of EUR 107.9 billion by June 30, 2013. See Appendix I and Vigeo (2013a), p. 8.

As illustrated in Figure 7, France has the highest share (35%) of SRI fund AuM within Europe, followed by the UK (17%), Switzerland (10%), the Netherlands (10%) and Germany (8%). France, the UK, the Netherlands and Germany are also one of the biggest markets for SRI in Europe, accounting for about 60% of the total market for SRI in this region.[279] The data set used in the empirical study only includes funds from these countries.[280]

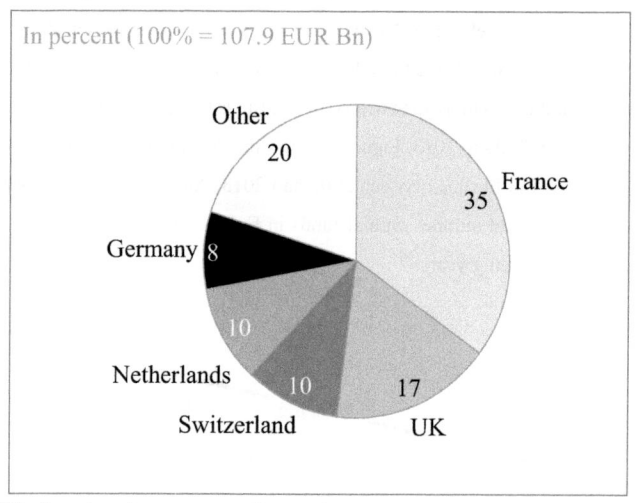

Figure 7: SRI fund assets under management by country
Source: Own illustration based on Vigeo (2013a), p. 8

The number of funds assigned to a country in Figure 7 consists of SRI funds that are established and managed in the respective country, but the managers of the funds do not necessarily only invest in securities from this country.[281] Instead, SRI fund managers can choose to not only include local securities in the fund's portfolio, but also add securities from other European countries or even from overseas – given that the securities match the selection criteria published in the fund's prospectus.[282] As screens are the most commonly applied selection criteria,[283] the

---

[279] See EUROSIF (2014), p. 21 and section 2.3 for an overview of the SRI market in Europe.

[280] Please refer to section 5.3.1 for a detailed description of the funds included in the empirical analysis.

[281] The same applies to the total number of funds displayed in Figure 6. While all funds are domiciled in Europe, the funds themselves can be sold in other countries and the securities that are included in the funds can also be issued by companies that are located overseas. See EUROSIF (2010), p. 9, Renneboog et al. (2008b), p. 306 and Vigeo (2013a), p. 6.

[282] See EUROSIF (2012), p. 12.

[283] See Statman & Glushkov (2009), p. 33 and USSIF (2006), p. 1.

following section provides an overview of the screening techniques typically applied by SRI fund managers.

3.2.2 Investment screens applied

Similar to the investment strategies used by SRI investors to select the companies or SRI funds to invest in, SRI funds themselves apply screening techniques to identify the securities that match their investment principles. Table 7 provides an overview of the most commonly applied screening techniques by SRI fund managers.

The screens can be classified as screens that are targeted at both, the inclusion or exclusion of companies or industries (listed as positive and negative screens in Panel A of Table 7)[284] or screens that only are targeted at the exclusion of certain companies or industries (listed as negative screens in Panel B of Table 7). In general, the screens included in Panel A of Table 7 not only aim at addressing investors' consciousness for ESG issues, but also dealing with ethical aspects today's societies are confronted with. Funds that apply environmental screens, for example, try to identify securities that are issued by companies, which operate environmentally friendly and, e.g. are active in the renewable energy sector or are not engaged in nuclear power activities.[285] Social and corporate governance screens are screening techniques aimed at identifying securities of companies with superior performance on equal employment opportunities, human rights issues and labor relations.[286] These screens also include faith-based or religious screening as initiated by the Quaker movement already back in the 18th-century and still practiced by Islamic funds that aim at excluding securities of companies involved in the manufacturing or marketing of pork products.[287] Finally, SRI funds that apply ethical screens try to identify and exclude securities of companies that develop and market pharmaceuticals for birth control or sell products that are tested on animals.[288]

---

[284] Fund managers can decide if they only apply positive or negative screens or a combination of both. Examples of combined screens are (i) screens that include securities of companies that demonstrate good corporate governance practices and at the same time exclude companies with documented antitrust violations or (ii) screens that try to only include securities of companies that are active in the recycling industry and also exclude those of companies that intentionally contribute to the ozone depletion. See Derwall & Koedijk (2009), p. 212 and Renneboog et al. (2008a), p. 1728.

[285] See Renneboog et al. (2008b), p. 311.

[286] See Berry & Junkus (2012), pp. 710–713 and Capelle-Blancard & Monjon (2011), p. 11.

[287] See USSIF (2006), p. 53.

[288] See Renneboog et al. (2011), p. 567.

Table 7: Investment screens applied by SRI fund managers

This table shows common investment screens applied by SRI fund managers when selecting the securities for the fund's portfolio. The minus sign (-) in the column Type relates to negative screens (i.e. the exclusion of certain companies), whereas the plus sign (+) refers to positive screens (i.e. the inclusion of certain companies). While the screens listed in Panel A can either be positive or negative; the screens listed in Panel B are all negative screens.

Panel A: Positive and negative screens			
Category	Screen	Definition	Type
Environmental	Environment	Inclusion of companies involved in activities targeted towards pollution prevention, recycling and environmental cleanup. Exclusion of companies significantly contributing to the ozone depletion or the production of hazardous waste	+/-
	Nuclear power	Exclusion of companies involved in the manufacturing of nuclear reactors or companies that operate nuclear power plants	-
	Renewable energy/ biotechnology	Inclusion of companies active in the production of power derived from renewable energy sources or promoting sustainable agriculture, biodiversity and the application of biotechnology	+
Social and corporate governance	Community impact	Inclusion of companies involved in charitable or innovative giving, affordable housing and educational as well as volunteering programs that support the local community	+
	Corporate governance	Inclusion of companies demonstrating good corporate governance practices, e.g. independence of the board and auditors as well as transparency regarding executive compensation. Exclusion of companies with antitrust violations or customer fraud	+/-
	Equal employment opportunity	Inclusion of companies demonstrating good practices related to equality and diversity issues such as work-life benefits for employees, gay and lesbian policies as well as women and minority employment	+
	Faith-based/religious screening	Inclusion or exclusion of companies based on religious reasons, e.g. the exclusion of interest-based financial institutions and companies involved in the manufacturing or marketing of pork products in accordance with Islamic principles	+/-
	Human rights	Inclusion of companies promoting human rights issues. Exclusion of companies involved in operations in countries with oppressive regimes or violation of human rights issues	+/-
	Labor relations	Inclusion of companies with strong labor or employee relation programs, high level of employee involvement, a focus on safe and healthy work environments as well as strong union relations and employee retirement benefits	+
Ethical	Abortion/birth control	Exclusion of companies involved in the production, development or manufacturing of contraceptives or companies and hospitals that execute abortion	-
	Animal testing	Inclusion of firms promoting the respectful treatment of animals. Exclusion of companies involved in animal testing activities in the research and development phase or companies that use animal ingredients in their end products	+/-
	Non-married lifestyle	Exclusion of insurance companies that cover non-married couples	-
	Pharmaceuticals	Exclusion of companies in the healthcare industry that e.g. are involved in the development and manufacturing of contraceptives	-

Panel B: Negative screens			
Category	Screen	Definition	Type
Sin	Alcohol	Exclusion of companies involved in the production, licensing, and/or retailing of alcohol products	-
	Defense/ weapons	Exclusion of companies involved in the manufacturing and retailing of firearms for personal or weapons for military use	-
	Gambling	Exclusion of casinos and companies involved in the development, production, licensing and retailing of gambling equipment	-
	Pornography/ adult entertainment	Exclusion of companies involved in the production and distribution of adult entertainment products (e.g. pornographic magazines), companies operating adult entertainment establishments and companies providing adult entertainment programming on television	-
	Tobacco	Exclusion of companies involved in the production, licensing, and/or retailing of tobacco products or products necessary for the production of tobacco products	-

Sources: Renneboog et al. (2008b), p. 311 and USSIF (2006), pp. 53f.

The screens displayed in panel B of Table 7 are used by SRI funds that aim at excluding securities of companies operating in sin industries. Similar to the exclusion strategy applied by investors, fund managers of such SRI funds try to avoid securities of companies active in the alcohol, weapons, gambling and pornography or tobacco industry.[289] Some funds also apply a best-in-class screening technique, that is, they try to invest only into securities of companies that are rated as most socially responsible compared to their peers in the same industry.[290] It is also important to note that SRI fund managers do not have to select only one of the screens displayed in Table 7, when identifying the securities that are to be included in the fund's portfolio. Instead, fund managers can – and usually do – apply a combination of screens from within one category or across different categories.[291] Figure 8 shows that about one quarter of US-based SRI fund managers apply only one screen when selecting the securities for the fund's portfolio. About 11% of the fund managers apply between two and four screens and almost two thirds (64%) of them incorporate five or more screens into the security selection process.

---

[289] See Derwall & Koedijk (2009), p. 212, EUROSIF (2014), p. 14, Statman & Glushkov (2009), p. 33.

[290] See Preu & Richardson (2011), p. 869 and section 2.6 for a detailed description of the best-in-class approach that is also implemented as investment strategy by some SRI investors.

[291] See Renneboog et al. (2011), p. 567.

Percent of total number of SRI funds

- Two to four screens: 11
- One screen: 25
- Five and more screens: 64

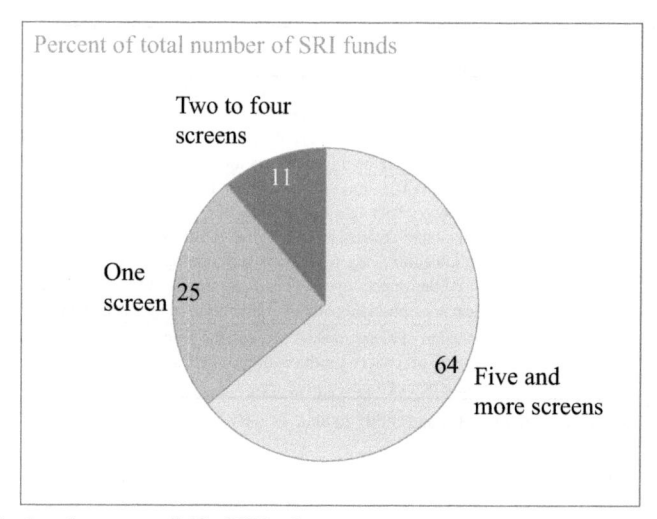

Figure 8: Number of screens applied by SRI funds
Source: Own illustration based on USSIF (2006), p. 9

Irrespective of the number of screens applied, fund managers can choose to invest in different categories of assets classes once they have identified a company that matches the fund's screening criteria: Typically, SRI funds consist of either equity or fixed income securities of a company or a combination of both categories.[292] Depending on the category of securities included in the portfolio, the funds are classified as either SRI equity, fixed income or balanced funds.[293] Figure 9 illustrates that the majority (54%) of the funds on the European SRI market are SRI equity funds. SRI fixed income funds account for about 33% and SRI balanced funds for about 13% of the total market for SRI in Europe. Thus, as all three fund categories have a significant share in the European SRI market and moreover, are part of the empirical analysis in this thesis, the next section introduces each SRI fund category in more detail.

---

[292] See Goldberg et al. (2008), p. 55.
[293] This classification is used in the course of this thesis and derived from Vigeo (2013a), p. 10 that uses a similar classification by separating the European market for SRI funds according to the asset class the securities in the fund belong to (equity, balanced and fixed income funds).

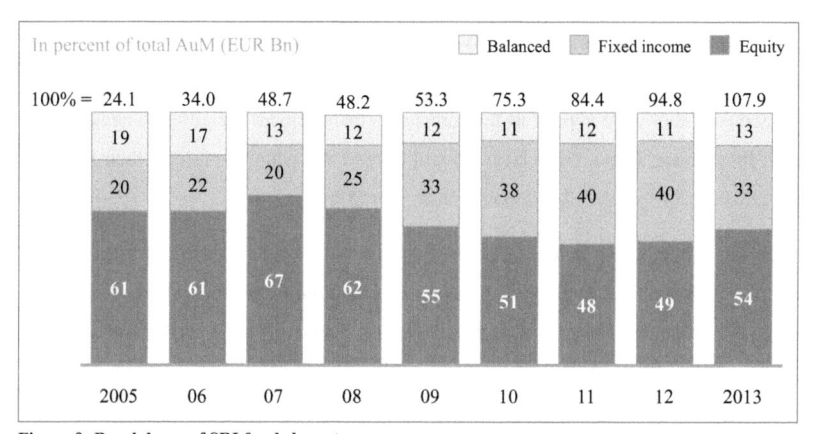

Figure 9: Breakdown of SRI funds by category
Source: Own illustration based on Vigeo (2013a), p. 10

3.2.3 SRI fund categories

3.2.3.1 SRI equity funds

Similar to conventional equity funds, SRI funds in this category invest money into equity securities issued by a public company.[294] As partial owners of the issuing company, the SRI funds – and indirectly also the funds' investors – participate in the company's profits and losses.[295] Most of the equity securities are issued as common stock, but companies can also issue preferred stock.[296] Both types of equity securities offer the investor the right to participate in the earnings and dividends distributed by the company. However, holders of preferred stock have seniority over holders of common stock when earnings and dividends are distributed and also in case of bankruptcy when assets are liquidated.[297] In contrast to common stockholders, holders of preferred stock have no or only limited voting rights. Holders of common stock have

---

[294] Equity funds can also invest smaller parts into fixed income securities and cash holdings. However, for a fund to be classified as equity fund, the share of fixed income securities or cash holdings should not exceed 30%. See Statman (2000), p. 33.

[295] See Mobius (2007), p. 19, Pozen (2002), p. 193 and Rowland (1996), p. 178.

[296] See Brealey et al. (2014), pp. 351 and 356. Convertible securities are another type of securities that have the potential of being an equity security. Strictly speaking, convertible securities are fixed income securities, but holders of these securities have – under pre-specified conditions – the right to convert the securities into common stock of the issuing company. See Dialynas & Ritchie (2005), p. 1371 and Francis (1993), p. 66.

[297] See Brealey et al. (2014), p. 356, Francis (1993), pp. 57 and 64 as well as Ross et al. (2010), p. 470.

these voting rights and thus, have the ability to directly influence decisions taken by the company's management.[298] Typically, however, common stockholders do not vote on issues related to the daily business of the company as the company's management is entitled to handle these aspects.[299] Instead, the stockholders elect a board of directors which represents their interests and only vote on major issues related to corporate governance.

Participation in earnings and dividends, however, are only two factors that determine the performance of a fund and thus, the income generated for the fund's investors. Share price appreciations (and depreciations) are a third factor that also influence a fund's performance.[300] Although there is no maturity for stock holdings and fund managers are not obliged to drop the stocks of a certain company from the fund's portfolio after a certain time, fund managers might still decide to do so at some point in time. Once the fund manager decides to liquidate the stock holding, the right to participate in earnings and dividends ceases to exist and investors of the fund either benefit from an increase in the company's stock price since the stock has been added to the portfolio (share price appreciation, i.e. the fund generates a positive return as the holding is sold for a higher price than initially paid by the fund) or suffer from a stock price decrease (share price depreciation, i.e. the return is negative as the holding is sold for less than what was initially paid).[301]

Although all equity funds invest in equity securities, there are different types of equity funds available. The funds can be differentiated according to the investment objective that they pursue. These objectives can be further divided into the regional focus of the funds' equity investment, the size of the companies that are included in the fund or the sector the companies operate in.[302] The Investment Company Institute (ICI), for example, differentiates nine different types of equity funds (see Table 8): Funds with a regional focus can be global, international, regional and emerging market equity funds; funds with a focus on company size can be aggressive growth, growth, income as well as growth and income equity funds; finally, sector funds are

---

[298] See Francis (1993), p. 58 and Pozen (2002), p. 193.
[299] See Brealey et al. (2014), p. 353, Francis (1993), p. 58 and Pozen (2002), p. 193.
[300] See Mobius (2007), p. 19 and Pozen (2002), p. 55.
[301] See Madura (2014), p. 611, Mobius (2007), p. 19 and Pozen (2002), p. 55.
[302] See Mobius (2007), p. 20 and Pozen (2002), p. 55.

funds that focus on companies active in specific industries such as financial services, health care or technology.[303]

Table 8: Types of equity funds

This table shows different types of equity funds. The funds are differentiated according to the primary investment objective of the fund (regional focus, company size or sector focus).

Investment objective	Fund type	Securities invested in by the fund
Regional focus	Global equity funds	Funds that invest primarily in worldwide equity securities
	International equity funds	At least 80 percent of the funds' portfolios are invested in equity securities of companies located outside the country in which the funds are established
	Regional equity funds	Funds that invest in equity securities of companies based in specific world regions, such as Europe, the US, Latin America, the Pacific Region, or individual countries
	Emerging market equity funds	Funds that invest primarily in equity securities of companies based in less-developed regions of the world
Company size	Aggressive growth funds	Funds that invest primarily in common stock of small, growth companies with potential for capital appreciation
	Growth and income funds	Funds that attempt to combine long-term capital growth with steady income dividends. These funds pursue this goal by investing primarily in common stocks of established companies with the potential for both growth and good dividends
	Growth funds	Funds that invest primarily in common stocks of well-established companies with the potential for capital appreciation. These funds' primary aim is to increase the value of their investments (capital gain) rather than generate a flow of dividends
	Income equity funds	Funds that seek income by investing primarily in equity securities of companies with good dividends. Capital appreciation is not an objective
Sector focus	Sector equity funds	Funds that seek capital appreciation by investing in companies in related fields or specific industries, such as financial services, health care, natural resources, technology or utilities

Sources: ICI (2007a), p. 12 and Pozen (2002), p. 55

---

[303] See ICI (2007a), p. 12. Another approach would be to group the funds according to their actual holdings instead of using the investment objective as primary criteria to differentiate between the different types of equity funds. Morningstar and Lipper, for example, use two factors to classify funds and group them according to the size of the companies included in the funds (large, mid or small market capitalization) and the investment style of the funds (value, blend/core or growth). See Thomson Reuters Lipper (2012), p. 8, Morningstar (2004), p. 1 and Pozen (2002), p. 57.

3.2.3.2 SRI fixed income funds

SRI fixed income or bond funds account for about one third of the funds available on the European SRI market (see Figure 9). These funds invest in fixed income securities that can either be issued by companies or governmental institutions.[304]

While companies that issue stocks are not obliged to pay dividends or let investors participate in their earnings and the stock holding is not limited to a certain time, fixed income securities have a predefined payment schedule and also a clearly determined maturity date: The amount and date for the periodic interest (coupon) payments the issuing company has to make to the investors and the date for the repayment of the initially borrowed capital (principal) are already determined when the security is first issued.[305] Moreover, the issuers of fixed income securities are obliged to make the interest payments and repay the principal at maturity before any payment to holders of equity securities are made.[306] As the payments to holders of fixed income securities are senior to any claims holders of equity securities have, fixed income securities are considered less risky than equity securities.[307] At the same time, however, holders of fixed income securities are only entitled to receive the predefined periodic interest payments and the principal at maturity, but they cannot benefit from higher dividends or earnings the issuing company distributes to its holders of (common or preferred) stock.[308]

The amount of the coupon payments and thus, the return investors can expect from holding fixed income securities varies with the time to maturity of the investment and the creditworthiness of the issuing company or government: The longer the time to maturity or the lower the creditworthiness of the issuing company/government, the higher are the coupon payments investors can expect.[309] Although the maturity date for the fixed income securities is pre-defined and the issuing company has to repay the face value at this date, investors in fixed income funds can sell their share in the funds at any time irrespective of the time left until maturity. As with equity securities, the price of the fixed income security can change during the period between

---

[304] See Mobius (2007), p. 29 and Pozen (2002), p. 146.

[305] See ICI (2007b), p. 7, Pozen (2002), p. 146 and Rowland (1996), p. 177. Investors in fixed income securities can be individual or institutional investors as well as funds. See Elton et al. (2009), p. 14.

[306] See Mobius (2007), p. 29.

[307] See Francis (1993), p. 19 and Pozen (2002), p. 147.

[308] See Pozen (2002), p. 147.

[309] See Elton et al. (2009), p. 14.

its purchase and sale.[310] The price for which the security can be sold varies with the interest rates: If interest rates increase, the price for the security decreases and vice versa.[311]

To sum it up, companies and governmental institutions can issue fixed income securities. The coupon payment and price of the security depends on the time to maturity of the security as well as the creditworthiness of the issuer. The ICI (2007a) uses these three criteria (issuer, time to maturity and credit quality) to classify funds that invest into fixed income securities (see Table 9).

While general funds (corporate or governmental) have no specific requirement regarding the maturity of the fixed income securities they invest in, intermediate-term funds invest in securities with a maturity of five to ten years and short-term funds invest in securities with a maturity of one to five years.[312] High-yield funds invest primarily into fixed income securities issued by companies with a low credit-rating and thus, companies that are considered to be at a high credit risk.[313] Mortgage-backed funds seek to invest in a pool of home mortgages and have been especially popular in the US in the early 2000s.[314] World bond funds aim at allocating parts of their investment capital to securities issued by foreign companies and governments. Some of these funds even restrict their investment to fixed income securities from emerging markets.[315] Contrary to world bond funds, strategic income funds invest into securities issued by domestic companies with a focus of providing high periodic income.[316]

---

[310] See Pozen (2002), p. 147.

[311] See ICI (2007b), p. 7, Lavine (1994), p. 40 and Pozen (2002), p. 147. The sensitivity of the fixed income security to changes in interest rates is measured by the securities' duration. The duration measures how much the price will change, if interest rates change by 1%. The longer the duration, the more it is affected by changes in interest rates. See Mobius (2007), p. 29.

[312] See ICI (2007a), p. 13. Funds that invest into securities with a maturity of less than one year are defined as money market funds. As the average maturity of these fund is 90 days or less, money market funds are considered to be a relatively safe investment. See Lavine (1994), p. 120.

[313] The securities issued by companies with low creditworthiness are also called junk bonds. See Lavine (1994), p. 125 and Pozen (2002), p. 151.

[314] See Mobius (2007), p. 30 and Pozen (2002), p. 149.

[315] See ICI (2007a), p. 13.

[316] See ICI (2007a), p. 13.

Table 9: Types of fixed income funds

This table shows different types of fixed income funds, differentiated according to the issuer of the underlying fixed income security, the maturity and the credit risk of the issuer.

Issuer	Fund type	Securities invested in by the fund
Corporation	Corporate bond - general funds	Funds that seek a high level of income by investing 80 percent or more of their portfolios in corporate bonds and have no explicit restrictions on average maturity
	Corporate bond - intermediate-term funds	Fund that seek a high level of income with 80 percent or more of their portfolios invested at all times in corporate bonds. Their average maturity is five to ten years
	Corporate bond - short-term funds	Funds that seek a high level of current income with 80 percent or more of their portfolios invested at all times in corporate bonds. Their average maturity is one to five years
	Global fund - general funds	Funds that invest in worldwide fixed income securities and have no stated average maturity or an average maturity of more than five years. Up to 25 percent of their portfolios' securities (not including cash) may be invested in companies located in the country in which the fund is established
	Global funds - short-term funds	Funds that invest in worldwide fixed income securities and have an average maturity of one to five years. Up to 25 percent of their portfolios' securities (not including cash) may be invested in companies located in the country in which the fund is established
	High-yield funds	Funds that seek a high level of current income by investing at least 80 percent of their portfolios in lower-rated corporate bonds
Governmental institutions	Government bond - general funds	Funds that invest at least 80 percent of their portfolios in government securities and have no stated average maturity
	Government bond - intermediate-term funds	Funds that invest at least 80 percent of their portfolios in government securities and have an average maturity of five to ten years
	Government bond - short-term funds	Funds that invest at least 80 percent of their portfolios in government securities and have an average maturity of one to five years
Other	Mortgage-backed funds	Funds that invest at least 80 percent of their portfolios in pooled mortgage-backed securities
	Other world bond funds	Funds that invest at least 80 percent of their portfolios in a combination of foreign government and corporate debt. Some funds in this category invest primarily in debt securities of emerging markets
	Strategic income funds	Funds that invest in a combination of domestic fixed-income securities to provide high current income

Source: ICI (2007a), p. 13

3.2.3.3 SRI balanced funds

SRI balanced funds are funds that simultaneously invest in equity and fixed income securities.[317] The share assigned to each of the security varies greatly between the funds. Bogle (2015) differentiates three types of balanced funds, depending on the funds' investment in equity and

---
[317] See Blake et al. (1993), p. 371, Comer et al. (2009), p. 484 and Smith & Smith (2005), p. 148.

fixed income securities as well as the underlying objectives of generating ongoing income, preserving capital and participating in potential capital growth:[318]

- **Equity-oriented balanced funds** that invest about 55-65% in equity securities and 35-45% in fixed income securities. These funds try to achieve a sound balance between the three investment objectives and generate reliable periodic income for their investors while at the same time preserving the capital invested in the securities and in best cases also benefit from capital growth.

- **Income-oriented funds** that assign a higher proportion of their investment money to fixed income securities and only invest about 20-35% in equity securities. The primary investment objective of these funds is to generate an ongoing stream of income to the investors; capital conservation and capital growth are subordinated goals.

- **Asset allocation funds** that consistently change the proportion of capital invested into equity and fixed income funds. The allocation is adjusted based on the fund manager's expectations regarding the future development of the equity and fixed income market.

Most of the balanced funds invest about 60% of the fund's portfolio into equity securities, and thus, according to the definition made by Bogle (2015), ought to be classified as equity-oriented funds.[319] The overweighting of equity securities can be attributed to the fact that – on a long-term perspective – equity securities generate higher returns for the investors than fixed income securities.[320] Historically, fixed income securities provide investors with a lower, but constant stream of cash inflows. Thus, while equity securities are used to increase a fund's long-term return, fixed income securities are included in the portfolio to provide ongoing income for the fund's investors. Although balanced funds are considered to provide stable returns and be less risky than equity funds[321], Figure 9 on page 77 shows that the market share for SRI balanced funds decreased from 19% in 2005 to 11-13% in the years between 2007 and 2013.

---

[318] See Bogle (2015), p. 136.
[319] See Gitman et al. (2010), p. 446, Lavine (1994), p. 15 and Pozen (2002), p. 54.
[320] See Berk & DeMarzo (2014), pp. 322–324, Fama & French (1989), p. 28 and (1993), p. 14, Francis (1993), p. 19 and Jones (2009), p. 148.
[321] See Bogle (2015), p. 137 and Lavine (1994), p. 15.

3.3   Interim conclusion

This chapter has introduced CSR and SRI funds as two alternative ways on how investors can get exposed to SRI. CSR relates to activities taken by companies to integrate ESG concerns into their daily business operations and get into dialogue with the companies' stakeholders. Although the effect of such activities on a company's performance is still unclear, there is strong evidence that CSR activities increase a company's reputation among its key stakeholders, including its employees, customers, shareholders and the public. Shareholders of companies with CSR activities in place not only benefit from a better reputation these companies have, they also have the chance to shape the companies' CSR profile by actively engaging in corporate relations issues.

Active engagement, however, requires the individual investor's attention and implies that each investor is responsible for selecting the companies to invest in and managing the investment. As this can be a time-consuming task, the number of companies that can potentially be part of the investor's portfolio, is limited. Investors, who try to diversify their portfolios across a larger number of companies that address their concerns of ESG issues, can decide to invest in SRI funds. In this case, the fund's managers are responsible for actively managing the investment, e.g. defining the SRI screening criteria, identifying the companies that meet the screening criteria and deciding when to add or drop companies from the investment portfolio.

Which alternative way SRI investors decide to follow, depends on the investor's individual preferences: Investing into only few companies that have (voluntarily) implemented CSR activities offers SRI investors the chance to directly have an impact on the actions taken by the companies to address ESG issues; investing into SRI funds, in turn, offers them the possibility to spread their engagement across many different companies and indirectly influence a company's engagement in CSR. In fact, the most important factor to increase the number of companies that integrate CSR activities in their business operations is that investors integrate ESG issues in their investment selection process at all: The more investors emphasize the importance of a company's CSR activities in the selection process, the more a company's management might get motivated to care about more than just the economic performance of the company.

The remaining part of this thesis now focuses on the indirect investment alternative via SRI funds. Specifically, the objective is to empirically analyze the performance of these funds relative to the performance of conventional and SRI benchmark indices. As the empirical study in this thesis is not the first to study the performance of SRI funds, the following chapter begins with an in-depth review of the financial background used when assessing the performance of SR funds as well as the theoretical discussion and the empirical evidence on SRI fund performance that has been documented so far. This review provides the basis for the empirical study that is introduced and discussed in the chapters thereafter.

4 Literature review

4.1 Investor risk aversion

Section 2.5 has shown that the investor base for SRI is highly diverse and no typical SRI investor has yet been identified: Some investors are motivated to engage in SRI because of the positive impact SRI are expected to generate for society as a whole. Others welcome the positive social impact of SRI, but primarily expect SRI alternatives to produce higher returns than conventional ones. Irrespective of the motivation why investors are interested in SRI, studies that examine the characteristics of SRI investors or the performance of the SRI alternative are all based on the assumption that investors are risk-averse. Thus, irrespective of their age (young/old) or status (individual/institutional), investors – socially conscious or not – are assumed to require a compensation for investing into risky securities.[322]

The assumption of risk aversion does not imply that all investors are risk-averse or that risk-averse investors are not willing to take on any risk when placing money into financial securities.[323] Instead, risk aversion means that investors want to be compensated for the risk associated with the investment. The higher the risk, the higher the return the investors expect to generate with the investment.[324] Theoretically, investors can also be risk-neutral or risk-seeking.[325] Risk-seeking investors have a positive attitude towards risk and are willing to bear the additional level of uncertainty and volatility associated with a more risky investment – even at the cost of generating lower returns. Confronted with a fair game, risk-seeking investors are assumed to accept the game as they derive some extra utility from the chance of winning that is higher than the disutility of losing in the game.[326] Risk-neutral investors, in turn, are indifferent whether or not a fair game is undertaken. These investors are more concerned about achieving a particular level of return when investing into a security rather than the risk they are taking on

---

[322] See Hearth & Zaima (1998), p. 355 and Jones (2009), p. 10.
[323] See Reilly & Brown (2011), p. 182.
[324] See Hearth & Zaima (1998), p. 355 and Jones (2009), p. 10.
[325] See Francis & Kim (2013), p. 70, Graham et al. (2009), p. 163 and Hearth & Zaima (1998), p. 355.
[326] A fair game is defined as a game for which the expected value of the game is equal to the costs associated with it. Thus, in a fair game, the chances of winning or losing are equal and the expected return is zero. See Elton et al. (2009), pp. 246f. for a detailed description of a fair game and the influence the investors' attitudes towards risk have on their behavior in such a game.

with this investment. Finally, risk-averse investors try to avoid risk or – in case risk is inevitable – need to be compensated for taking on the risk. Thus, risk-averse investors in general would reject a fair game as the disutility derived from losing in the game is higher than the utility derived from winning in the game.[327]

The trade-off between risk and utility (or expected return) any investor faces is illustrated in Figure 10: The curve for risk-averse investors is upward sloping indicating a positive relationship between risk and return. Thus, the higher the risk associated with an investment, the higher the return investors expect to generate with this investments.

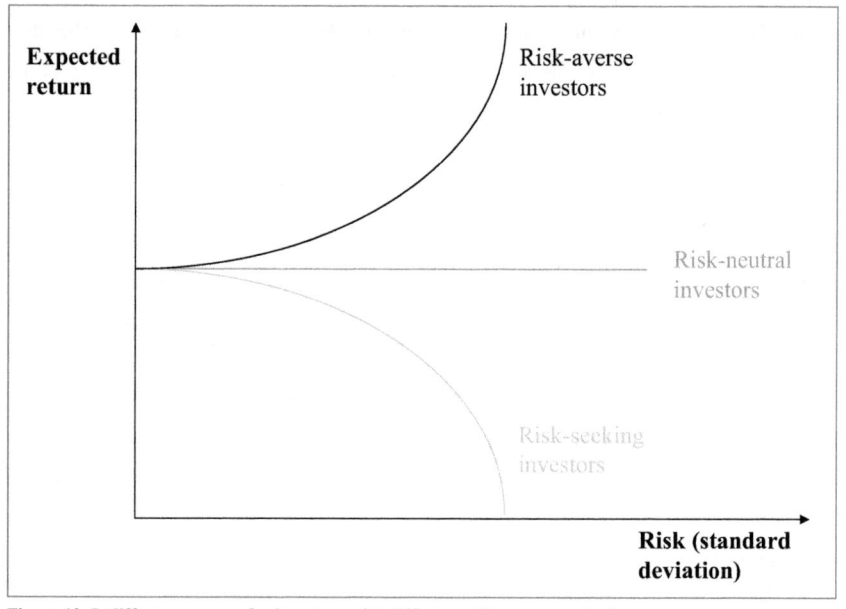

Figure 10: Indifference curves for investors with different attitudes towards risk
Source: Own illustration based on Francis & Kim (2013), p. 70

Figure 10 on page 88 also shows that risk-neutral investors would expect the same rate of return irrespective of the risk associated with an investment. The risk-neutral relationship between risk and return is indicated by the straight or horizontal line in Figure 10. Risk-seeking investors accept a negative relationship between risk and return and would expect lower returns for higher levels of risk. The negative relationship between risk and return for risk-seeking investors is indicated by the downward sloping curve in Figure 10.

---

[327] See Elton et al. (2009), p. 246 and Sharpe et al. (1995), p. 173.

Even if the basic assumption of financial theory is that investors are risk-averse rather than risk-neutral or even risk-seeking, this does not imply that all investors have the same level of risk aversion.[328] Instead, some investors might be more risk-averse than others and demand even higher expected returns for the same level of risk than less risk-averse investors do.[329] Thus, the level of compensation required by each investor depends on the individual investor's appetite for risk and is quite subjective. This implies that investors face their own trade-off between risk and the return they expect to generate with a risky investment. Figure 11 shows examples of two investors with different levels of risk-aversion. Investor A is more risk-averse and demands a higher level of return for the same level of risk than investor B (as indicated by points A and B in Figure 11). As the level of risk increases, investor A demands an even higher compensation for the same level of increase in risk than investor B does (as indicated by points C and D in Figure 11).[330] Consequently, the risk-and-return curve is steeper (flatter), the more (less) risk-averse an individual investor is.[331]

To conclude, section 2.6 has shown that SRI investors apply different criteria to select the securities for their portfolios according to the securities' compliance with their individual investment strategy. Personal values and beliefs or concerns about ESG issues, however, are not the only factors investors usually base their investment decisions on. Instead, the final selection of securities or funds to invest in also depends on financial factors such as the risk associated with an investment and the return the investors expect to generate with the respective investment.[332] The following section introduces risk and return as financial factors that influence investors' investment decision in more detail. The section also shows how both factors can be measured and how investors can reduce some level of financial risk when investing into more than just one risky security.

---

[328] See Francis & Kim (2013), p. 62.
[329] See Francis & Kim (2013), p. 32 and Reilly & Brown (2011), p. 182.
[330] See Francis & Kim (2013), p. 72 and Hearth & Zaima (1998), pp. 356f.
[331] See Francis & Kim (2013), p. 35 and Mayo (2013), p. 155.
[332] See Levy & Sarnat (1995), p. 291.

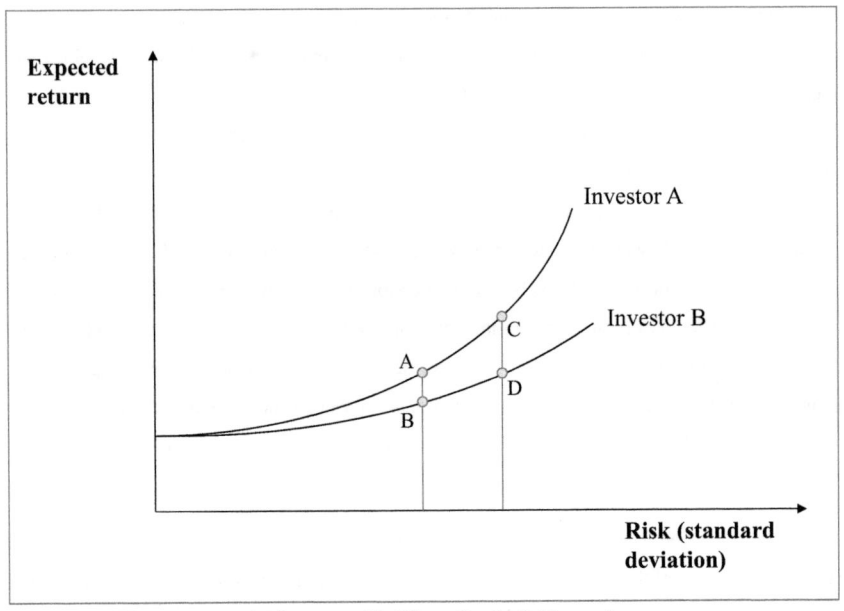

Figure 11: Indifference curves for investors with different levels of risk aversion
Source: Own illustration based on Francis & Kim (2013), p. 72 and Hearth & Zaima (1998), p. 356f.

4.2 Fund characteristics

4.2.1 Measuring return

4.2.1.1 Security return

Investments typically are made with the intent to generate some kind of (financial) return.[333] As the return investors can expect to earn with their investment cannot be predicted with certainty, the investment decisions typically are based on the investor's personal preferences as well as the likely return the investment will generate and the risk associated with the investment.[334]

---

[333] See Mayo (2013), p. 129 and Ruppert (2010), p. 5.
[334] See Berk & DeMarzo (2014), p. 316 and Francis & Kim (2013), p. 7.

4. Literature review

Generally speaking, a risky investment can generate different levels of return for the investor and each possible return can occur with a certain probability.[335] Given the probabilities with which each return can occur, the likely or expected return of that investment can be calculated as the weighted average of its possible or future returns.[336] However, as the probabilities of future returns usually cannot be determined with certainty, historical or realized returns of the security can be used to approximate its expected return.[337]

Historical or realized returns of an investment are a measure to assess how well an investment (e.g. a security, a portfolio or a fund) has performed in the past. The historical performance of portfolios or funds that consist of different investments is determined by the performance of each individual security included in the portfolio or fund.[338] For individual securities, historical returns are equal to the relative increase in the value of the respective security, including all cash flows paid by the security over some period of time.[339]

Formally, historical returns of a security can be split up into two components: The price change component (capital gain or loss) and the income component (yield) of the security.[340] The price change component equals the change in the price of the security over a period. If the price for a security has increased (decreased) over a specific period, e.g. one year, the price change component is positive (negative) and the investment is said to have generated a capital gain (loss). While the price change component can be measured for all financial securities available for investing, the income component only occurs for securities that involve periodic cash flows such as dividends from stocks or interest payments from bonds.[341] The income component can be measured by the relative value of the respective cash flow payments to the price initially paid for the security or the price of the security at the beginning of the period analyzed.

Thus, the historically return for a security can be calculated as follows:[342]

---

[335] See Berk & DeMarzo (2014), p. 316.
[336] See Berk & DeMarzo (2014), p. 316 and Mayo (2013), p. 131.
[337] See Francis & Kim (2013), p. 20 and Jones (2009), p. 129.
[338] See section 4.2.1 for details how to calculate the return of a portfolio or fund.
[339] See Berk & DeMarzo (2014), p. 316.
[340] See Berk & DeMarzo (2014), p. 319, Jones (2009), p. 129 and Ross et al. (2010), p. 301.
[341] See Jones (2009), p. 129.
[342] See Hearth & Zaima (1998), p. 357 and Jones (2009), p. 129.

$$r_{i,t+1} = capital\ gain\ or\ loss + yield$$
$$= \frac{P_{i,t+1} - P_{i,t}}{P_{i,t}} + \frac{CF_{i,t+1}}{P_{i,t}}$$
$$= \frac{P_{i,t+1} - P_{i,t} + CF_{i,t+1}}{P_{i,t}} \text{ or } \frac{P_{i,t+1} + CF_{i,t+1}}{P_{i,t}} - 1 \qquad (1)$$

where

$r_{i,t+1}$	=	the historical or realized return of security i
$P_{i,t+1}$	=	the price of security i at time $t+1$
$P_{i,t}$	=	the price of security i at time t and
$CF_{i,t+1}$	=	the cash flow paid by security i at time $t+1$.

In order to ensure comparability of the returns for different securities, the historical return of the security is calculated as a relative number and expressed in percentage terms. The expression in percentage terms is essential as each security requires a different initial investment, pays different cash flows and sells for a different price at the end of the holding period. This implies that the returns for different securities vary and it is important to ensure comparability of returns when analyzing performance of various securities.[343]

Historical returns, however, differ not only between the individual securities. Instead, returns are also different when assessing the performance of a single security over a time period of, e.g. a few years: Returns are higher in some years and lower or even negative in other years. In order to get an estimate on a security's performance, investors typically calculate an expected return for the security that is based on the historical returns generated by this security over multiple years.

Assuming that each historical return is equally likely with probability $1/T$, the expected rate of return of security i can be calculated as follows:

$$E(\bar{r}_i) = \frac{1}{T}(r_{i,1} + r_{i,2} + \cdots + r_{i,T}) = \frac{1}{T}\sum_{t=1}^{T} r_{i,t} \qquad (2)$$

where

$E(\bar{r}_i)$	=	the expected rate of return for security i in years 1 to T
T =		the number of years in the sample and
$r_{i,t}$	=	the historical return of the security i in year t.

---

[343] See Ross et al. (2010), p. 302.

In this case, the expected rate of return for a security is equal to the average of the historical returns generated by the security over T years.[344] The information on the expected return of the security can be used by investors and fund managers to assess whether the security fits into a portfolio and how the portfolio's expected return is affected when this particular security is added.

4.2.1.2 Portfolio return

The expected return of a portfolio – either set up by the investor himself or through a SRI fund that bundles different securities – is equal to the weighted average of the expected returns of the individual securities included in the portfolio.[345] The weight assigned to each security's expected return is equal to the percentage of the portfolio's total value that is invested into the security.[346] The sum of the total weights assigned to the securities' returns in a portfolio has to add up to 100%.[347] Thus,

$$w_1 + w_2 + \cdots + w_i = \sum_{i=1}^{N} w_i = 1 \qquad (3)$$

where w_i = the proportion of security i in the whole portfolio.

The expected return of the portfolio can then be calculated as follows:[348]

$$E(\tilde{r}_p) = \sum_{i=1}^{N} w_i E(\tilde{r}_i) \qquad (4)$$

where

$E(\tilde{r}_p)$ = the expected return of the portfolio
N = the total number of securities in the portfolio
w_i = the proportion of security i in the whole portfolio and

---

[344] The average historical return is calculated as arithmetic return. This approach, however, does not consider compounding effects when interest rates or cash flows are re-invested by the investor. An alternative way to calculate average historical return would be to calculate the geometric average return. The geometric average return is defined as the T-th root of the product of the historical returns over T years minus one:

$$E(\tilde{r}_i) = \sqrt[T]{(r_{i,1} \times r_{i,2} \ldots r_{i,T})} - 1.$$

See Feibel (2003), p. 59, Francis & Kim (2013), p. 20 and Reilly & Brown (2011, p. 7). For a detailed discussion on the advantages and disadvantages of the arithmetic and geometric mean see Cooper (1996) and Jacquier et al. (2003).

[345] See Elton et al. (2009), p. 51, Lo (2010), p. 173 and Reilly & Brown (2011), p. 183.

[346] See Jones (2009), p. 169 and Reilly & Brown (2011), p. 183.

[347] See Francis & Kim (2013), p. 22 and Markowitz (1952), p. 78.

[348] See Jones (2009), p. 169, Markowitz (1952), p. 81 and Reilly & Brown (2011), p. 184.

$E(\tilde{r}_i)$ = the expected return of security i.

Thus, Equation (4) shows that the impact a security's expected return has on the portfolios expected return depends on two factors that are associated with the security. First, the weight assigned to the security: The higher (lower) the weight, the greater (smaller) the impact of the security's return on the portfolio's return. Second, the expected return for the security: The higher (lower) the expected return of the security, the higher (lower) is the expected return for the entire portfolio. In general, the portfolio's return lies in between the security with the lowest expected return and the security with the highest expected return.[349] For equally weighted portfolios, the proportion assigned to each security is constant and calculated by simply dividing the sum of the weights in the portfolio (100%) by the total number of securities included in the portfolio. Consequently, for equally weighted portfolios, it follows that: $w_i = \frac{1}{N}$.[350]

4.2.2 Measuring risk

4.2.2.1 Security risk

The expected return is one component that influences an investor's perception about the possible future return development of a security. However, as the previous section has shown, this figure is an estimate that is calculated using the average of historical returns generated by the security; it is not an exact prediction how high or low any future return of that security will be. In fact, most of the historical returns generated by a security differ from the calculated average, and future returns can differ from the average as well.[351] The difference can either be positive (i.e. historical/future returns are higher than the expected return) or negative (i.e. historical/future returns are lower than the expected return).

The greater the average difference between the historical returns and the expected return, the more risky the security is expected to be. If the difference is zero, the security is assumed to have no risk and returns do not differ from the calculated average at all.[352] Thus, the expected

---

[349] See Jones (2009), p. 170.

[350] The calculations made in the empirical part of this thesis are based on equally weighted portfolios of SRI funds (see section 6.1.1).

[351] See Berk & DeMarzo (2014), p. 324.

[352] See Jones (2009), p. 216.

return that is calculated as an average of the historical returns would be an almost exact prediction of the future return of that security. However, as most of the securities available for investors bear some level of risk, future returns are expected returns that cannot be predicted with certainty. Instead, investors face the risk that the actual return generated will (positively or negatively) deviate from the expected return.

In order to calculate the risk that is associated with a security, statistical measures such as standard deviation and variance are most commonly used.[353] Both measure the deviation of historical returns around the average expected return value and are closely related: While the variance is the mean squared deviation from the expected return value, the standard deviation is the square root of the variance. Using historical returns, the variance of a security can be calculated as follows:[354]

$$Var(r_i) = \sigma_i^2 = \frac{1}{T-1}\Sigma_{t=1}^T \left(r_{i,t} - E(\bar{r}_i)\right)^2 \qquad (5)$$

where

σ_i^2 = the variance of security i
T = the number of years in the sample
$r_{i,t}$ = the historical return of the security i in year t
$E(\bar{r}_i)$ = the expected return for security i in years 1 to T.

As the variance relates to the squared difference between the historical and expected return, it has a different unit of measure than the expected return. Consequently, variance and expected return cannot be directly compared or used when analyzing a security's risk and return profile. Instead, standard deviation is used, which is the square root of the variance and thus, has the same unit of measure as the expected return.[355] Formally, the standard deviation of a security and can be calculated as follows:

$$SD(R_i) = \sigma_i = \sqrt{Var(r_i)} \qquad (6)$$

where σ_i is the standard deviation of security i's historical return.

---

[353] See Hearth & Zaima (1998), p. 361 and Reilly & Brown (2011), p. 183.

[354] The squared deviation is divided by $T-1$ instead of T as one degree of freedom is lost by estimating the expected return for the security. See Berk & DeMarzo (2014), p. 323, Francis & Kim (2013), p. 20 and Hearth & Zaima (1998), p. 362.

[355] See Berk & DeMarzo (2014), p. 317, Heath & Zaima (1998), p. 361 and Markowitz (1959), p. 71.

The standard deviation as described above measures the risk that is associated with the respective security. It is also referred to as the volatility of a security's return as it quantifies the uncertainty investors are facing when investing into a specific security.[356] Moreover, standard deviation indicates the most likely deviation of future returns from the average expected return of the security.[357] The higher the standard deviation, the more volatile the historical returns are and thus, the higher the risk associated with that security.[358] Moreover, most financial models and performance measures such as the ones applied in the empirical study of this thesis are based on the assumption that returns of a security are normally distributed, i.e., they show a symmetric pattern around the mean.[359] Given this assumption, the standard deviation not only provides useful information on the risk associated with a security, but also the range of the likely returns investors can expect to generate with that security: Assuming normal distribution of returns, there is a probability of 68 percent that the actual return of the security will be within $\pm$ 1.00 standard deviation from the historical return and a probability of 90, 95 and 99 percent that the actual return will be within $\pm$ 1.65, 1.96 or 2.58 standard deviations, respectively.[360]

4.2.2.2 Benefits of diversification

The risk of a security as calculated in the previous section is composed of two factors: The unique risk of a security and the market risk.[361] Unique risk is risk that is directly associated with the security. For equity investments like stocks, for example, unique risk refers to changes in a stock's return due to news directly associated with the company issuing the stock (e.g. increase in the stock price due to the announcement of a significant gain in market share).[362] This type of risk is also referred to as company-specific, idiosyncratic or diversifiable risk.[363] Contrarily, market risk relates to macro-economic factors that affect all securities within an

---

[356] See Brooks (2008), p. 383.
[357] See Mayo (2013), p. 141 and Ross et al. (2010), p. 314.
[358] See Jones (2009), p. 167 and Reilly & Brown (2011), p. 12.
[359] See Drobetz (2001), p. 63, Fama (1970), p. 399, Fletcher (1995), p. 128, Francis & Kim (2013), p. 201, Jensen (1972), p. 374, Lintner (1965a), p. 591, Sharpe (1987), p. 32 and Tobin (1958), p. 74.
[360] See Berk & DeMarzo (2014), p. 325, Hearth & Zaima (1998), p. 361, Jones (2009), p. 167, Markowitz (1976), p. 49, Sharpe et al. (2015), p. 311 and Stock & Watson (2007), p. 82.
[361] See Bodie et al. (2011), p. 197.
[362] See Berk & DeMarzo (2014), p. 332.
[363] See Berk & DeMarzo (2014), p. 332, Bodie et al. (2011), p. 197 and Bradfield (2007), p. 115.

economy (e.g. the announcement of a change in interest rates by the Central Bank or the inflation rate). This risk is also called systematic or non-diversifiable risk.[364]

According to portfolio theory developed by Markowitz (1952), investors should only be concerned about market risk when selecting the securities for their portfolio, but not about unique risk associated with any of the individual securities. The reasoning behind this is the fact that the unique risk is diversified away if the number of securities in the portfolio is large enough: While some news (e.g. the loss of a lawsuit) negatively affect the return development of securities issued by a specific company, the same news might positively affect the return of the securities issued by another company (e.g. a positive judgment in the same lawsuit).[365] In sum, for portfolios that consist of a large number of securities, company-specific news that positively or negatively influence the price of a particular security average out such that the overall risk and return profile of the portfolios remains constant. As the market risk, however, affects all securities in the portfolio, price changes that are caused by market-specific news do not cancel each other out. Instead, changes in prices or returns of all securities within a market also affect the risk and return profile of the portfolios. Thus, market risk is a risk that cannot be diversified away by the investors – no matter how large the number of securities in a portfolio might be.[366]

Figure 12 illustrates the relationship between the number of securities included in a portfolio and the total risk of the portfolio: With increasing number of securities included in a portfolio, the contribution of unique risk to the total risk of the portfolio decreases. In fact, with a sufficiently large number of securities in the portfolio investors can reduce or – in best cases – entirely eliminate unique risks associated with the individual securities. This is also called the diversification effect.[367] The exposure to market risk, however, remains and cannot be diversified away.[368] Figure 12 also shows that diversification effect is higher the fewer securities are included in a portfolio. Thus, with increasing number of securities in a portfolio the benefits of diversification for investors diminish and are limited to the point at which unique risk is equal to zero and total risk of the portfolio is equal to the market risk.[369]

---

[364] See Berk & DeMarzo (2014), p. 332.
[365] See Berk & DeMarzo (2014), p. 332 and Bradfield (2007), p. 115.
[366] See Bodie et al. (2011), p. 197 and Brealey et al. (2014), p. 174.
[367] See Bodie et al. (2007), p. 189 and Elton et al. (2009), p. 139.
[368] See Bodie et al. (2011), p. 197 and Statman (1987), p. 353.
[369] Statman (1987) provides empirical evidence of a decreasing diversification effect for large portfolios: Studying a portfolio that consists of 500 stocks within the US, he shows that while portfolio risk decreases from

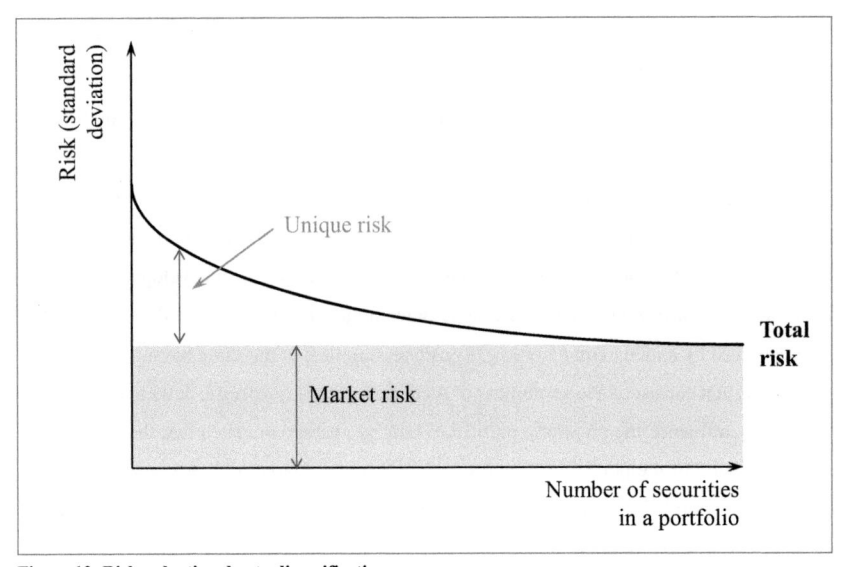

Figure 12: Risk reduction due to diversification
Source: Own illustration based on Bodie et al. (2011), p. 197 and Brealey et al. (2014), p. 174

A presumably straightforward approach to quantify the risk investors are exposed to when holding a specific portfolio would be to simply calculate the weighted average of the risks associated with the individual securities in the portfolio. Although this approach can be applied when calculating the return of the portfolio[370], it would not provide the correct result for the portfolio's risk exposure. Instead, due to the diversification effect, the risk of the portfolio is lower than the weighted average risks of the securities included in the portfolio. In most cases, the risk of the portfolio is even lower than the risk of the securities themselves.[371] The reasoning behind this notion is the fact that the unique risk of a security is (partially) diversified away when the security is combined with other securities. In a completely diversified portfolio only market risk remains. Such a portfolio is also called market portfolio.[372] In general, the market portfolio is defined as a portfolio that consists of all risky securities in a market.[373] The weight assigned to each security in the market portfolio is equal to the total market value of that security relative

---

almost 50% to 37% when the number of securities in the portfolio increases from one to two, the effect is less than 0.2% and thus, almost negligible, when the number increases from 75 to 100 securities. See Statman (1987), pp. 355 and 362.

[370] See section 4.2.1.2.
[371] See Berk & DeMarzo (2014), p. 354 and Bodie et al. (2007), p. 166.
[372] See Reilly & Brown (2011), p. 214.
[373] See Elton et al. (2009), p. 285 and Francis & Kim (2013), p. 293.

to the total market value of all securities in the market.[374] As such a portfolio that contains all securities (i.e. stocks, bonds, real estate, commodities, arts, and so forth) does not exist in reality, the performance of the market portfolio is often approximated by using substitutes such as benchmark indices in financial studies.[375]

For partially diversified portfolios, the risk is composed of market risk and some proportion of unique risk that is not diversified away. The amount of unique risk that remains depends on the amount of such risk that the securities in the portfolio have in common.[376] Securities of companies that operate in the same industry, for example, have a higher share of common risk than securities of companies that operate in different industries.[377] Thus, the diversification effect for the investors is higher, the lower the amount of risk that the securities or companies issuing the securities in the portfolio have in common. In fact, the diversification effect is maximized and with this, the portfolio risk minimized, if securities, whose returns move in the opposite direction, are combined. In this case, the risks offset each other and unique risk is canceled out in the portfolio.[378]

Two statistical measures can be used in order to quantify the amount of risk that the securities in a portfolio have in common: Covariance and correlation.[379] Covariance is a measure that shows the extent to which the returns of two securities change or move together.[380] Changes in the return of a security, in turn, determine the risk that is associated with that security.[381] The following formula can be used to calculate the covariance between securities i and j based on historical return data:[382]

---

[374] See Francis & Kim (2013), p. 292 and Reilly & Brown (2011), p. 232.
[375] See Francis & Kim (2013), p. 293.
[376] See Berk & DeMarzo (2014), p. 354.
[377] E.g. securities issued by companies in the airline industry have a high share of common risk. Thus, when securities of these companies are combined into a portfolio, the diversification effect is limited as the returns of these securities tend to move in the same directions. Conversely, the effect is higher when securities of companies that operate in the airline and apparel industry are combined into a portfolio as these two industries are not closely related to each other and returns of these securities are assumed to move in opposite directions. See Berk & DeMarzo (2014), p. 354.
[378] See Berk & DeMarzo (2014), p. 355, Bodie et al. (2007), p. 166 and Jones (2009), p. 176.
[379] See Berk & DeMarzo (2014), p. 354 and DeFusco et al. (2011), p. 152.
[380] See Berk & DeMarzo (2014), p. 354 and Jones (2009), p. 176.
[381] See section 4.2.2.1.
[382] Again, the divisor is $T-1$ instead of T as one degree of freedom is lost by estimating the expected returns for the securities. See section 4.2.2.1 as well as Berk & DeMarzo (2014), p. 354, Hearth & Zaima (1998), p. 368 and Reilly & Brown (2011), p. 93.

$$Cov(r_i, r_j) = \sigma_{i,j} = \frac{1}{T-1}\sum_{t=1}^{T}(r_{i,t} - \bar{r}_i)(r_{j,t} - \bar{r}_j) \qquad (7)$$

where

$\sigma_{i,j}$	=	the covariance between securities i and j
T	=	the number of years in the sample
$\bar{r}_{i,j}$	=	the average of annual returns for security i and j in years 1 to T and
r_t	=	the realized return of the securities in year t.

The covariance can either be positive, negative or zero and ranges from $-\infty$ to $+\infty$.[383] If the covariance is positive, the two securities exhibit a similar behavior, i.e. their returns tend to move in the same direction at the same time: When the return for one security increases, the return for the other security tends to increase as well.[384] If the covariance is negative, the securities show opposite behaviors, i.e. if the return for one security increases (decreases), the return for the other security tends to decrease (increase). Finally, if the covariance is zero, the securities are independent and do not exhibit any behavior of co-movement.[385]

However, the covariance only indicates if the securities tend to show the same behavior or not: Its value is more positive (negative), the more closely the returns of the securities move together (in opposite directions). Thus, it only provides an indication on the direction of the relationship[386], but cannot be used to quantify the strength of the relationship.[387] In order to also quantify the strength of the relationship, the covariance measure needs to be standardized and the correlation coefficient between the two securities calculated. Formally, standardization is achieved by dividing the covariance of the two securities by the product of their individual standard deviations:[388]

$$Corr(R_i, R_j) = \rho_{i,j} = \frac{\sigma_{i,j}}{\sigma_i \sigma_j} \qquad (8)$$

where

---

[383] See Jones (2009), p. 176, Markowitz (1976), p. 49 and Reilly & Brown (2011), p. 93.

[384] See Berk & DeMarzo (2014), p. 354 and Jones (2009), p. 176.

[385] See Berk & DeMarzo (2014), p. 354 and Jones (2009), p. 176.

[386] A covariance of, e.g., -5 indicates a negative relationship between the returns of two securities; but the relationship can be weak (in case the returns are highly volatile and the risk of the securities high) or strong (in case the returns are less volatile and thus, the securities less risky). See Reilly & Brown (2011), p. 188.

[387] See Berk & DeMarzo (2014), p. 355 and Reilly & Brown (2011), p. 93.

[388] See Graham et al. (2009), p. 174, Jones (2009), p. 177, Markowitz (1959), p. 85 and Reilly & Brown (2011), p. 188.

$\rho_{i,j}$ = the correlation coefficient between securities i and j
$\sigma_{i,j}$ = the covariance between securities i and j
σ_i = the standard deviation of security i and
σ_j = the standard deviation of security j.

The correlation coefficient has the same algebraic sign as the covariance. However, the unit of measure for covariance is percent squared while the correlation coefficient has no unit of measure.[389] Another difference between covariance and the correlation coefficient is the fact that the covariance can have any value between $-\infty$ and $+\infty$. Due to the standardization, the correlation coefficient always is between -1 and +1.[390] Similar to covariance, the correlation coefficient between securities of companies, which operate within the same or similar industries, typically is higher than that of companies, which operate in different business environments.[391]

Figure 13 graphically illustrates the relationship between the correlation coefficient and the co-movement of the returns of two securities. The interpretation of the correlation coefficient is similar to the one for the covariance between two securities: If the correlation coefficient between two securities is -1, the securities are perfectly negatively correlated and their returns always move in opposite directions, e.g. if the price for one security increases (decreases), the price and thus, the return for the other security is expected to decrease (increase). Contrarily, if the correlation coefficient is +1, the securities are perfectly positively correlated and thus, their returns always move together, e.g. if the price for one security increases (decreases), the price for the other security is expected to increase (decrease) as well.[392] Finally, if the correlation is 0, the securities are uncorrelated and no tendency of return or price movements can be observed.

Although negative and zero correlation coefficients between securities are possible, most of the securities within one industry have a positive correlation coefficient, as they are all affected by common factors such as changes in interest rates or inflation.[393]

---

[389] The correlation coefficient is calculated by dividing the covariance – which is measured in percent squared – by the product of the standard deviations for the two securities – which also is in percent squared. For a more detailed discussion on this, please refer to Graham et al. (2009), p. 174.

[390] See Berk & DeMarzo (2014), p. 355, Markowitz (1959), p. 85 and Reilly & Brown (2011), p. 68.

[391] See Berk & DeMarzo (2014), p. 357 and Markowitz (1952), p. 89.

[392] The covariance of a security's return with itself equals the variance of the security. The correlation of a security with itself equals +1 as the security's return is perfectly positively correlated with itself. See Berk & DeMarzo (2014), p. 355.

[393] See Graham et al. (2009), p. 174.

	Perfectly Negatively Correlated	Uncorrelated		Perfectly Positively Correlated
Correlation coefficient	-1	0		+1
Level of co-movement	Always Move Opposite	Tend to Move Opposite	No Tendency	Tend to Move Together	Always Move Together

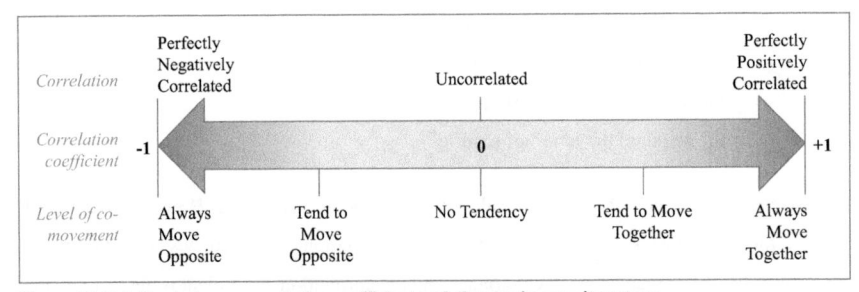

Figure 13: Relation between correlation coefficient and changes in security return
Source: Own illustration based on Berk & DeMarzo (2014), p. 355

4.2.2.3 Portfolio risk

While the return for a portfolio consisting of multiple assets equals the weighted average of the (expected or historical) returns of each security in the portfolio, the calculation of the portfolio's risk or variance is not that straightforward. Instead, due to the benefits of diversification, the overall portfolio's risk is lower than the weighted average of the individual security's risks.[394] Thus, not only the risk and weight of each security in a portfolio needs to be considered when calculating portfolio variance and risk, but also the level of co-movement or covariance between the individual securities. Taking these factors into account, the portfolio variance can be calculated as follows:[395]

$$\sigma_P^2 = \sum_{i=1}^{N} x_i^2 \sigma_i^2 + \sum_{i=1}^{N} \sum_{j=1}^{N} x_i x_j \sigma_{i,j} \qquad (9)$$

where

σ_P^2 = the variance of the portfolio's returns
N = the number of securities included in the portfolio
σ_i^2 = the variance of the return for security i
$\sigma_{i,j}$ = the covariance between security i and j
$x_{i,j}$ = the weights assigned to security i and j.

Again, the sum of the total weights assigned to the securities in the portfolio has to add up to 100%.[396] According to Equation (9) above, the variance of a portfolio with multiple assets is

---

[394] See section 4.2.2.2 for a detailed description of the benefits of diversification.
[395] See Berk & DeMarzo (2014), p. 359, Hearth & Zaima (1998), p. 377, Jones (2009), p. 181, Markowitz (1952), p. 81 and (1959), p. 94 as well as Reilly & Brown (2011), p. 190.
[396] See Equation (3).

composed of two factors: The first factor is the weighted average of the individual variances ($\sum_{i=1}^{N} x_i^2 \sigma_i^2$) and the second factor is the weighted covariance between the returns of all possible pairs of securities that are included in the portfolio ($\sum_{i=1}^{N} \sum_{j=1}^{N} x_i x_j \sigma_{i,j}$, for $i \neq j$).[397] Finally, using Equation (8), the covariance factor in Equation (9) can be replaced by the product between the correlation coefficient of the two securities i and j as well as standard deviations of both securities.

Thus, the portfolio's variance can be determined as follows:[398]

$$\sigma_P^2 = \sum_{i=1}^{N} x_i^2 \sigma_i^2 + \sum_{i=1}^{N} \sum_{j=1}^{N} x_i x_j \rho_{i,j} \sigma_i \sigma_j \qquad (10)$$

where

σ_P^2 = variance of the portfolio's returns
$\rho_{i,j}$ = the correlation between securities i and j
σ_i = the standard deviation of security i
σ_j = the standard deviation of security j
$x_{i,j}$ = the weights assigned to security i and j.

As the risk of the portfolio is measured by the portfolio's standard deviation and the standard deviation is the square root of the variance, the risk finally can be calculated as follows:

$$\sigma_P = \sqrt{\sigma_P^2} = \sqrt{\sum_{i=1}^{N} x_i^2 \sigma_i^2 + \sum_{i=1}^{N} \sum_{j=1}^{N} x_i x_j \rho_{i,j} \sigma_i \sigma_j} \qquad (11)$$

Equation (11) implies that the risk of a portfolio depends on three factors:[399]

- The weight assigned to each security ($x_{i,j}$),
- the standard deviation ($\sigma_{i,i}$) of each security and
- the correlation coefficient ($\rho_{i,j}$) between the individual securities

Equation (11) also shows that, when a security is added to the portfolio, there are two effects that cause a change in the portfolio's risk: First, the new security's own variance and second,

---

[397] The double summation sign ($\sum\sum$) in the covariance term indicates that each covariance term is included twice and all possible combinations of covariance between i and j are to be added together. See also Hearth & Zaima (1998), p. 377 and Jones (2009), p. 181.

[398] See Hearth & Zaima (1998), p. 380.

[399] See Francis & Kim (2013), p. 26.

the correlation of the new security with all other securities that are already included in the portfolio.[400] With increasing number of securities in the portfolio, the importance of the second effect increases as the relative weight of the correlations between all securities gets larger compared to the weights of the individual variances. Thus, when a security is added to a portfolio, the most important factor that drives the risk of the overall portfolio is the security's correlation with all other securities in the portfolio. The individual security's risk is less important to the overall portfolio risk.[401] Moreover, the lower the average correlation of the new security with the other securities in the portfolio is, the lower is the contribution of the new security's variance to the overall portfolio's risk – irrespective of the own variance of the new security.

Consequently, unless the correlation coefficient between the securities is +1 for all pairs of securities, the risk of the overall portfolio always is lower than the weighted average of the standard deviations of the individual securities:[402]

$$\sigma_P = \sqrt{\sum_{i=1}^{N} x_i^2 \sigma_i^2 + \sum_{i=1}^{N} \sum_{j=1}^{N} x_i x_j \rho_{i,j} \sigma_i \sigma_j} < \sum_i x_i \sigma_i \qquad (12)$$

where all notations are the same as before.

To conclude, portfolio theory suggests that investors can benefit from diversification by spreading the investment across many different securities that have a less than perfect positive correlation with each other.[403] The expected return of the portfolio is equal to the weighted average of the expected returns of the securities included in the portfolio, but the expected variability of the portfolio's return is lower than the average variability of the individual returns.[404] However, it is not possible for investors to eliminate all risk that is associated with the risky securities in the portfolio.[405] Instead, the degree to which the investors can benefit from diversification and with this, the overall risk they are exposed to when holding the portfolio, depends on the amount of common risk that the individual securities within the portfolio share. The lower the amount of common risk, measured by the correlation coefficient or covariance between the securities,

---

[400] See Reilly & Brown (2011), p. 191.
[401] See Reilly & Brown (2011), p. 191 and Rubinstein (2002), p. 1042.
[402] See Berk & DeMarzo (2014), p. 363 and Brealey et al. (2014), p. 175.
[403] See Francis & Kim (2013), p. 19, Markowitz (1952), p. 89 and Reilly & Brown (2011), p. 68.
[404] This is true under the assumption that the securities have a correlation lower than +1. See Reilly & Brown (2011), p. 69.
[405] See Bodie et al. (2011), p. 197 and Brealey et al. (2014), p. 174.

the higher the effect of diversification and thus, the more investors benefit from combining multiple securities into one portfolio.[406]

Investors and fund managers can use the information on portfolio expected return and risk when building their (fund) portfolios.[407] During the process they then have to decide how to best allocate the investment capital between the different securities available.[408] This decision is based on their views on the likely return they can earn when investing into a particular security as well as the risk involved with this securities. Using historical return data, investors and fund managers can make up their own estimate on expected returns of the portfolio and the variability that is associated with those returns.[409] Once the security is added to a portfolio or once the fund is set up, investors and fund managers are interested in tracking the financial performance of the portfolio or fund. The following section introduces commonly applied models how this performance can be assessed.

4.3 Fund performance measurement

4.3.1 Excess returns

The preceding sections have shown that risk and return are important characteristics of a financial security and risk-averse investors want to be compensated for bearing risk when investing into a risky security. Consequently, investors expect to generate higher returns for risky investments such as equity or fixed income securities issued by companies than for almost risk-free investments such as securities issued by governments. The difference between the return on a risk-free investment and a risky investment is called excess return.[410] It measures the average risk premium investors expect to generate with the risky investment.[411]

Formally, excess return for a security can be calculated as follows:[412]

---

[406] See Francis & Kim (2013), p. 38, Markowitz (1952), p. 89 and Reilly & Brown (2011), p. 196.
[407] See Mayo (2013), p. 142.
[408] See Reilly & Brown (2011), p. 39.
[409] See Francis & Kim (2013), p. 22.
[410] See Jones (2009), p. 230.
[411] See Berk & DeMarzo (2014), p. 327 and Jones (2009), p. 147.
[412] See Berk & DeMarzo (2014), p. 327 and Francis & Kim (2013), p. 171.

$$Excess\ return\ =\ E(\tilde{r}_i) - r_f \qquad (13)$$

where

$E(\tilde{r}_i)$ = the expected return of security i and

r_f = the return of a risk-free investment.

Excess return is an absolute measure of return generated by a security above the risk-free rate of return. Comparing excess returns for different securities on an absolute level, however, is difficult. For example, security A with an expected excess return of 5% p.a. might seem more attractive to investors than security B with an expected excess return of 3%. However, given the additional information that security A has an average standard deviation of 10% while security B has an average standard deviation of only 2%, for instance, the investors might change their perception on how attractive both securities are. Thus, and as already indicated in section 4.2, return and risk of a security should always be considered together when assessing the attractiveness or financial performance of an investment security. The following section introduces some of the most commonly applied performance measures that assess excess return in relation to the security's risk. While all three measures combine risk and return aspects into a single performance figure, the way with which this figure is calculated is different for each of the measures.

4.3.2 Performance measures

4.3.2.1 Treynor ratio

The Treynor ratio measures the expected excess return of a security per unit of market or systematic risk associated with this security.[413] Systematic risk is the amount of risk inherent in a security that remains even if the security is part of a fully diversified portfolio.[414] In order to quantify the systematic risk of a security, the beta-factor β_i of that security is calculated.[415] This factor measures the security's risk relative to the market portfolio and indicates the security's sensitivity to changes in the return of the market portfolio.[416] More precisely, the beta of a security indicates the expected change in the security's return after a 1% change in the return

---

[413] See Goldreyer & Diltz (1999), p. 26, Mallin et al. (1995), p. 487 and Treynor (1964), p. 74.
[414] See section 4.2.2.2.
[415] See Francis & Kim (2013), p. 168, Lhabitant (2006), p. 251, Mayo (2013), p. 159.
[416] See Elton et al. (2009), p. 137, Lhabitant (2006), p. 448, Reilly & Brown (2011), p. 216.

of the market portfolio.[417] The return of a security with a beta of 0.4, for example, is expected to change by 0.4% when the market return changes by 1%. In general, the beta of the market portfolio is 1 and securities with a beta higher than 1 are expected to be riskier than the market portfolio while securities with a beta of less than 1 are expected to be less risky than the market.[418]

Formally, systematic risk or beta of a security can be calculated as follows:[419]

$$\beta_i = \frac{\sigma_{i,m}}{\sigma_m^2} \qquad (14)$$

where

β_i = the unit of systematic risk associated with security i

$\sigma_{i,m}$ = the covariance between security i and the market portfolio and

σ_m^2 = the variance of the market portfolio.

Using beta as a measure of systematic risk, the Treynor ratio TR_i for a security can be calculated follows[420]:

$$TR_i = \frac{E(\tilde{r}_i) - r_f}{\beta_i} \qquad (15)$$

where

$E(\tilde{r}_i)$ = the expected return of security i

r_f = the return of a risk-free investment and

β_i = the unit of systematic risk associated with security i.

The Treynor ratio can be interpreted as a figure that measures the excess return (displayed in the nominator) per unit of systematic risk (displayed in the denominator) of a security.[421] Risk-averse investors aim at maximizing this ratio, e.g. they try to identify securities with which they

---

[417] See Berk & DeMarzo (2014), p. 376.

[418] See Elton et al. (2009), p. 137 and Lhabitant (2006), p. 449.

[419] See Graham et al. (2009), p. 180 and Jensen (1969), p. 177. An alternative way to calculate β_i is to use regression analysis between the realized return of the security i ($r_i - r_f$) and the return of the market portfolio ($r_m - r_f$) and estimate the slope coefficient in the following formula:
$r_i - r_f = \alpha_i + \beta_i(r_m - r_f) + \varepsilon_i$. See section 4.3.3 and Reilly & Brown (2011), p. 221.

[420] See Treynor (1964), p. 69.

[421] See Francis (1993), p. 685 and Reilly & Brown (2011), p. 963.

can generate as much excess return as possible for the same amount of systematic risk.[422] However, as a security's risk consists of systematic and unsystematic risk, the Treynor ratio only includes parts of the total risk of the security. In contrast to this, the Sharpe ratio – as introduced in the following section – includes both risk factors when assessing security return.

4.3.2.2 Sharpe ratio

The main difference between the Sharpe ratio and the Treynor ratio is the fact that the Sharpe ratio is calculated using the security's standard deviation instead of the beta-factor in the denominator. Thus, keeping the nominator constant, the Sharpe ratio can be calculated as follows:[423]

$$SR_i = \frac{E(\tilde{r}_i) - r_f}{\sigma_i} \qquad (16)$$

where

$E(\tilde{r}_i)$ = the expected return of security i
r_f = the return of a risk-free investment and
σ_i = the standard deviation of security i.

Due to the changes in the denominator, the Sharpe ratio is a measure of the expected excess return per unit of total risk (systematic and unsystematic) of a security.[424] As total risk is a measure of the variability of the security's returns around the average historical return, the Sharpe ratio is also called the reward to variability ratio.[425] Similar to the Treynor ratio, the Sharpe ratio is a relative measure that assesses portfolio performance in one single number: The higher the Sharpe ratio of a security, the more attractive the risk and return profile of the security is for the investors.[426]

---

[422] See Reilly & Brown (2011), p. 963.
[423] See Sharpe (1966), p. 130.
[424] See Jones (2009), p. 571 and Reilly & Brown (2011), p. 965.
[425] See Horowitz (1966), p. 485, Jones (2009), p. 571 and Ruppert (2010), p. 424.
[426] See Francis (1993), p. 681 and Jones (2009), p. 571.

4.3.2.3 Jensen's alpha

Jensen's alpha is another measure often used by academics and practitioners when assessing the financial performance of a security.[427] Jensen (1969) has developed a figure that measures the difference between the actually realized return of the security and the return the security was expected to generate. This difference is also called the abnormal return generated by the security and can be calculated as follows:[428]

$$\alpha_i = r_i - E(\tilde{r}_i) \qquad (17)$$

where

α_i = the abnormal return generated by security i

r_i = the realized return of security i and

$E(\tilde{r}_i)$ = the expected return of security i.

Rearranging Equation (13) implies that the expected return of a security equals the return generated by a risk-free investment plus the excess return:

$$E(\tilde{r}_i) = r_f + excess\ return \qquad (18)$$

where

$E(\tilde{r}_i)$ = the expected return of security i and

r_f = the return of a risk-free investment.

The excess return, however, is a measure for the risk premium demanded by investors when investing into the risky security.[429] The risk premium of the security is quantified by multiplying the unit of systematic risk of the security – which is a measure of the market risk the security is exposed to – with the expected risk premium paid by the market portfolio.[430]

Using the beta-factor as a measure of the systematic risk, the difference between the expected return on the market portfolio and the risk-free rate of return as a measure of the market risk premium, the formula used to derive Jensen's alpha is as follows:[431]

---

[427] See Amenc et al. (2011), p. 47, Cortez et al. (2009), p. 576, Goldreyer & Diltz (1999), p. 26, Mallin et al. (1995), p. 489, McDonalds (1974), p. 313 and Murthi et al. (1997), p. 409.

[428] See Jones (2009), p. 308.

[429] See Jones (2009), p. 226 and section 4.3.1.

[430] The calculation for the risk premium is derived from the capital asset pricing model (CAPM), which has been developed by Sharpe (1964) and is introduced in the following section 4.3.3.

[431] See Jensen (1968), p. 390.

$$\alpha_i = r_i - [r_f + \beta_i(r_m - r_f)] \qquad (19)$$

where

$\alpha_i =$ the abnormal return generated by security i
$r_i =$ the realized return of security i
$\beta_i =$ the unit of systematic risk associated with security i
$r_m =$ the return generated by the market portfolio and
$r_f =$ the return of a risk-free investment.

As alpha measures the difference between the actual and the expected performance of the security, the values obtained for alpha can be zero (actual performance equals expected performance), positive (actual performance is greater than expected performance) or negative (actual performance is lower than expected performance). A positive (negative) alpha indicates a superior (inferior) performance of the security relative to the market portfolio.[432]

When assessing portfolios that are administered by professional fund managers, alpha is also used to assess the performance of the manager.[433] In this case, a positive alpha would indicate that the fund manager successfully identifies securities that are underpriced by the market and that the fund manager is able to generate above-market returns by investing into these securities. A negative alpha would indicate that the securities selected by the fund manager are, on average, overpriced.[434] According to capital market theory, however, all alphas should be equal to zero. Thus, it should not be possible for investors or fund managers to generate abnormal returns as the notion of market efficiency suggests that securities are fairly priced and that their prices fully reflect all publicly available information.[435] This implies that it should not even be possible for investors or fund managers to identify securities that are temporarily over- or undervalued as all securities should be priced correctly at any time.[436]

As a concluding remark on this section, it is important to note that for all three measures (Treynor ratio, Sharpe ratio and Jensen's alpha) the expected return and the risk of the security can

---

[432] See Francs & Kim (2013), p. 444, Jensen (1968), p. 394 and Mayo (2013), p. 222.

[433] See Jensen (1968), p. 394 and Jones (2009), p. 582. For the purpose of this study, alpha is defined as fund manager's ability to generate abnormal return by identifying securities that are (temporarily) mispriced. Other sources of alpha generation, i.e. dividend payments, are not considered.

[434] See Francis & Kim (2013), p. 446 and Reilly & Brown (2011), p. 219.

[435] See Diderich (2009), p. 37, Fama (1970), p. 383 and (1991), p. 1575 as well as section 5.1.3.

[436] See Francis & Kim (2013), p. 446 and Jones (2009), p. 582.

be replaced by the expected return or risk of a fund or portfolio in case financial performance is assessed for aggregated measures such as funds or portfolios. Which of the three measures investors should or do apply when analyzing the performance of a security, depends on the cause of the analysis: While the Treynor and Sharpe ratios are relative measures that can be used to rank securities, Jensen's alpha is an absolute measure used to assess the individual performance of a security or fund manager.[437] Moreover, the calculation of the Treynor and Sharpe ratio has not changed over the years; the way how alpha is determined, however, has been refined since its first introduction in the 1960s. The next section introduces the different models that have been developed and thus, alternatively can be used to calculate the alpha.

4.3.3 Single-factor models

Even before the introduction of Jensen's alpha, Treynor (1961)[438], Sharpe (1964), Lintner (1965a, 1965b) and Mossin (1966) have developed what is known today as the capital asset pricing model (CAPM). The CAPM is a single-factor regression model that can be used to quantitatively assess how the risk of a security affects its expected return.[439] It builds on the notion of portfolio theory as developed by Markowitz (1952) and is based on the following assumptions:[440]

- Investors are risk-averse, i.e. they need to be compensated for bearing risk.

- Capital market are perfect, i.e. there are no transaction costs, taxes or short-selling restrictions and all investors can lend and borrow money at the risk-free rate of return.

---

[437] See Jones (2009), pp. 571 and 582 as well as Reilly & Brown (2011), p. 971 for a detailed overview of the advantages and disadvantages of each of the three performance measures.

[438] The paper written by Treynor (1961) is an unpublished manuscript that has been published as a working paper by French (2002) about 40 years after it has initially been written.

[439] See Perold (2004), p. 3. The CAPM can also be used to determine the equity cost of capital of a security and with this, the price or value of that security in an efficient market (see Berk & DeMarzo (2014), p. 401 and Francis & Kim (2013), p. 296). An alternative way to calculate the expected return of a security would be to use the arbitrage pricing theory (APT), developed by Ross (1976). Similar to the CAPM, the APT is also based on the assumption that there is a positive relationship between the systematic risk of a security and its expected return. However, contrary to the CAPM, the APT is a more general model that is based on fewer assumptions than the CAPM and that uses more than one risk factor in order to calculate the expected return of a security. See Fabozzi et al. (2002), p. 18, Francis (1993), p. 635, Mayo (2013), p. 166, Reilly & Brown (2011), p. 261, Ross (1976), pp. 347–351 and Ross et al. (2010), p. 381.

[440] See Berk & DeMarzo (2014), p. 379, Hearth & Zaima (1998), p. 400, Hirt & Block (2012), p. 453, French (2002), p. 2, Perold (2004), p. 16, Reilly & Brown (2011), p. 183, Sharpe (1964), pp. 433f.

- All investors have access to the same investment alternatives and investments are made for one period only.
- There is a positive relationship between risk and return, i.e. the higher the risk associated with a security, the higher the risk premium investors demand when investing into the security and thus, the higher the (expected) return generated by the security.
- All investors have homogenous expectations about the expected return, the standard deviation of a security and the correlation coefficients between the securities in a portfolio.

Combining the assumptions of the CAPM with the additional assumption that the expected return of a security is driven by systematic risk only, the expected return of a security according to the CAPM can be calculated as follows:[441]

$$E(\tilde{r}_i) = r_f + \beta_i(r_m - r_f) \qquad (20)$$

where

$E(\tilde{r}_i)$ = the expected return of security i
r_f = the return of a risk-free investment
β_i = the unit of systematic risk associated with security i
r_m = the return generated by the market portfolio.

Equation (20) implies that the CAPM – in its basic form – is a measure of the expected return of a security. In order to assess the performance of a security, the expected return has to be compared to the actual return the security has generated over a specific period. Thus, using Equation (20) as well as Equation (19) and rearranging terms, the excess return or performance of a security can be assessed as follows:[442]

$$r_i - r_f = \alpha_i + \beta_i(r_m - r_f) + \varepsilon_i \qquad (21)$$

where

r_i = the realized return of security i
r_f = the return of a risk-free investment
α_i = the abnormal return generated by security i
β_i = the unit of systematic risk associated with security i

---

[441] See Sharpe (1964), p. 432.
[442] Combining equation (18) and (19) it follows that $\alpha_i = r_i - E(\tilde{r}_i)$. Substituting the expected return by the CAPM-formula displayed in Equation (19) it follows that $r_i - \alpha_i = r_f - \beta_i(r_m - r_f)$. See also Francis & Kim (2013), p. 171 and Jensen (1968), p. 395.

4. Literature review

$r_m =$ the return generated by the market portfolio and

$\varepsilon_i =$ the error term that accounts for the security's unsystematic risk.

Equation (21) shows that, in order to calculate the alpha generated by a security, investors or fund managers first need to determine three main parameters:

- The actual return generated by the security over a specific period
- The return on the risk-free investment and
- The return on a market portfolio during the same period

The return on the market portfolio is the benchmark return against which the financial performance of the security is assessed. Theoretically, the market portfolio that is used as a benchmark should be the return on a value-weighted portfolio that contains all securities within an economy.[443] For equity markets, the market portfolio theoretically should consist of all stocks available in this market. However, as no such portfolio truly exists, the portfolio's return typically is approximated using the return generated by an index. For equity markets in Europe or the US, for example, the returns generated by the Dow Jones Euro Stoxx 50 or the S&P 500 are used as proxy for the market portfolio, respectively.[444]

With the information for all three parameters given, the alpha and beta of the security can then be calculated using linear regression analysis.[445] Assuming a linear relationship between the market risk premium and the risk premium paid by the security, the estimate for alpha is the intercept of the regression equation, which equals the constant return generated by the security irrespective of the market return.[446] Thus, alpha represents the average incremental return generated by the security above the return that is attributed to the level of systematic (market) risk inherent in the security. In efficient markets, alpha is assumed to be zero, but empirical research

---

[443] See Graham et al. (2009), p. 181.
[444] See Climent & Soriano (2011), p. 277, Diderich (2009), p. 16, Elton et al. (2009), p. 22, Francis & Kim (2013), p. 415, Malkiel (2003), p. 65, Reilly & Brown (2011), p. 221, Sharpe (1992), p. 17. For details on the Euro Stoxx 50 index see https://www.stoxx.com/index-details?symbol=SX5E and http://us.spindices.com/indices/equity/sp-500 for details on the S&P 500 index.
[445] See Berk & DeMarzo (2014), p. 410.
[446] See Elton et al. (2009), p. 140.

shows that it can have values that are significantly different from zero – either positive or negative.[447]

The estimate for beta, in turn, equals the slope coefficient of the regression equation and measures the expected increase in return of the security for a 1% change in the return of the market portfolio.[448] As both measures, alpha and beta, are estimates of the true parameter values, they cannot be predicted with certainty and are always subject to estimation error.[449] Thus, confidence intervals are often reported in order to determine a most-likely range for the values of alpha and beta.[450]

The CAPM has often been used to describe risk and return characteristics of *equity* securities. However, the model also can be applied to any financial security, e.g., equity, balanced or fixed income securities. The only prerequisite is that the expected return, as well as the risk and correlation coefficient between the securities can be adequately estimated.[451] As the financial performance of the securities should always be measured against an appropriate benchmark, the proxies used to measure the market return should be adjusted accordingly.[452] While the return on equity indices such as the Euro Stoxx 50 or the S&P 500 are appropriate benchmarks to measure the market return of equity securities, the return on an index from the Markit iBoxx index family such as the iBoxx EUR Corporates can be used to assess the performance of fixed income securities.[453]

Although the CAPM can be used to assess the performance for various financial securities, it also has a major drawback: It is based on the assumption that one variable – in this case, the security's exposure to systematic risk – is the main driver for security return and sufficient to

---

[447] An alpha of zero indicated that the security is fairly priced and that the return generated by the security is attributable to the security's level of systematic risk. A positive (negative) alpha indicates superior (inferior) performance of the security. See also Jones (2009), p. 575 and section 4.3.2.3.

[448] See Jones (2009), p. 229, Mayo (2013), p. 189 and Reilly & Brown (2011), p. 221.

[449] See Jones (2009), p. 230.

[450] A confidence interval provides a range of likely values for the estimated parameters of alpha and beta and specifies the probability that the true parameter will fall into this range of values. A confidence interval of 95%, for example, states that there is a 95% probability that the stated range contains the true value of the estimated parameter. The choice of the confidence interval is arbitrary, but the most commonly used confidence intervals are 95% and 99%. See Berk & DeMarzo (2014), p. 325, Francis & Kim (2013), p. 261, Ruppert (2004), p. 60 and Wooldridge (2013), p. 130.

[451] See Konno & Kobayashi (1997), p. 1427 and Reilly & Brown (2011), p. 993.

[452] See Hirt & Block (2012), p. 99.

[453] See Dietze (2009), p. 196. For an overview of the available bond indices see Markit (2014), p. 7.

explain the differences in the returns across securities.[454] However, researchers have shown that systematic risk is one but not the only driver of a security's return. Instead, factors such as the size or book-to-market ratio of the company issuing the security also influence the return generated by the security. Fama and French (1992), for example, show that securities issued by small companies or companies with a high book-to-market ratio consistently generate higher returns than securities issued by large companies or companies with a low book-to-market ratio.[455]

In order to capture these so-called anomalies that cannot be explained by the CAPM, researchers have developed multi-factor regression models that use a number of independent variables to assess the return of a security. Thus, while the CAPM is a model that only incorporates a single independent variable, multi-factor models incorporate two or more variables to assess the performance of a security. The following sections describe the general models as well the models most commonly used to assess the performance of SRI funds.

4.3.4 Multi-factor models

4.3.4.1 Basic model

The basic model that uses multiple factors in order to assess the performance of a security can be estimated as follows:[456]

$$r_i - r_f = \alpha_i + \beta_m(r_m - r_f) + \sum_{j=1}^{K} \beta_j r_j + \varepsilon_i \qquad (22)$$

where

r_i = the realized return of security i
r_f = the return of a risk-free investment
α_i = the abnormal return generated by security i
β_m = the unit of systematic risk associated with security i[457]
r_m = the return generated by the market portfolio

---

[454] See Graham et al. (2009), p. 280 and Reilly & Brown (2011), p. 993.
[455] See Bodie et al. (2007), p. 223, Fama & French (1992), p. 428, Graham et al. (2009), p. 215 and Reilly & Brown (2011), p. 231.
[456] See Elton et al. (1995), p. 1237.
[457] Due to the additional number of betas in Equation (22), the notation of β_i from Equation (20) and (21) has been adjusted. Thus, $\beta_m = \beta_i$ and measures the security's exposure to market risk.

$K =$ the number of factors in the model
$\beta_j =$ the factor loading for each factor included in the model
$r_j =$ the return on each factor and
$\varepsilon_i =$ the error term or idiosyncratic return.

In contrast to the CAPM – as shown in Equation (21) – multi-factor models include more than just one source of systematic risk when assessing the performance of a security.[458] As market risk is part of multi-factor models, these models as introduced in Equation (22) are said to be a generalization of the CAPM.[459] The number of factors that is included in multi-factor models in addition to market risk depends on the quantity of risk factors considered.[460] In general, the number of betas to be estimated in the models increases with the number of independent variables or risk factors included in the model.[461] The interpretation of the beta-factor, however, remains the same for all risk factors: Beta determines the securities sensitivity to changes in the risk factor, i.e. it specifies the expected percentage change in the excess return of the security analyzed for a 1% change in the return of the risk component.[462] The factors that commonly are used to as independent variables are, e.g., the market return, the size of the company issuing a security or the book-to-market value of the company.[463] Which of the variables are included varies between the models applied and the security analyzed – as the following sections will show.

---

[458] It is important to note that while the number of risk factors included in multi-factor models can vary between the models, all risk factors that are to be considered have to be sources of systematic and thus, undiversifiable risk that affect all securities in a market. Sources of unsystematic risk should not be included as single factors in the models, but are captured by the error term. See Berk & DeMarzo (2014), p. 461, Erhardt & Brigham (2008), p. 223 and Fama & French (1993), p. 4.

[459] See Erhardt & Brigham (2008), p. 223.

[460] See Bradfield (2007), p. 237.

[461] In a three- factor model, there are three independent variables and thus, three betas to be estimated. In a four-factor model, the number of variables and thus, betas to be estimated increases by one.

[462] See Berk & DeMarzo (2014), p. 461 and section 4.3.2 for details on the interpretation of the market beta-factor.

[463] See Fama & French (1993), p. 3.

4.3.4.2 Equity performance models

Fama and French three-factor model

Fama and French (1992, 1993) criticize that the standard CAPM fails to explain patterns in equity security market returns, such as the relationship between the average return of a company's equity and its size or book-to-market value.[464] In order to address this shortcoming, Fama and French (1993, 1996) have developed a three-factor model that captures some of the observed return anomalies when assessing security returns. The authors show that a security's expected excess return over the risk-free rate $(r_i - r_f)$ depends on three (risk) factors:[465]

- The security's exposure to systematic risk and its excess return on the market portfolio, i.e. the equity market portfolio

- The difference between the return of a portfolio consisting of securities issued by companies with a small market capitalization and the return of a portfolio consisting of securities issued by companies with a large market capitalization, i.e. the small-minus-big (SMB) portfolio

- The difference between the returns of a portfolio that includes securities with a high book-to-market ratio and the return of a portfolio that includes securities with a low book-to-market ratio, i.e. the high-minus-low (HML) portfolio

Following this description, the expected excess return of an equity portfolio over the risk-free rate $(r_e - r_f)$ can be estimated as follows:[466]

$$r_e - r_f = \alpha_e + \beta_{EQU}(r_{EQU} - r_f) + \beta_{SMB}r_{SMB} + \beta_{HML}r_{HML} + \varepsilon_e \quad (23)$$

where

β_{EQU}, β_{SMB} and β_{HML} = the factor loadings for each of the independent variables

r_{EQU} = the return on the equity market portfolio

r_{SMB} = the return on the small-minus-big portfolio and

r_{HML} = the return on the high-minus-low portfolio.

---

[464] See Fama & French (1992), p. 446 and (1993), p. 3.
[465] See Fama & French (1996), pp. 55f. and Jones et al. (2008), p. 186.
[466] See Fama & French (1993), p. 24 and (1996), p. 55.

Equation (23) shows that, in addition to systematic risk, the excess return of a security is also influenced by the risk associated with the size of the company issuing the security, and the differences in the risk associated with value companies that have a high book-to-market ratio or growth companies with a low book-to-market ratio.[467]

Carhart four-factor model

Carhart (1997) extends the Fama-French model by including one additional risk factor that accounts for the fact that equity securities with higher (lower) returns in a one-year observation period also tend to have higher (lower) returns in the following years.[468] This effect is called momentum anomaly and has first been documented by Jegadeesh and Titman in 1993.[469] Similar to the SMB and HML factors introduced in the Fama-French three-factor model, Carhart (1997) estimates the price momentum factor as the difference in the return of two portfolios: The return on the portfolio consisting of securities with the highest 30 percent one-year return (winner portfolio) minus the return on the portfolio consisting of securities with the lowest 30 percent one-year return (loser portfolio). Formally, the Carhart four-factor model can be estimated as follows:[470]

$$r_e - r_f = \alpha_e + \beta_{EQU}(r_{EQU} - r_f) + \beta_{SMB}r_{SMB} + \beta_{HML}r_{HML} + \beta_{MOM}r_{MOM} + \varepsilon_e \qquad (24)$$

where all factors and variables used in the three-factor model are also included in the four-factor model. r_{MOM} is the additional momentum factor and β_{MOM} is the factor loading on the price momentum factor.

4.3.4.3 Fixed income performance model

While the Fama-French three-factor and the Carhart four-factor model have mainly been developed and used to study the performance of equity securities, the approach to measure the (Jensen's) alpha generated by a security can also be applied to other financial securities such as fixed income securities.[471]

---

[467] See Fama & French (1993), p. 41 and (1995), p. 132 as well as Reilly & Brown (2011), p. 253.
[468] See Carhart (1997), p. 61 and Reilly & Brown (2011), p. 254.
[469] Jegadeesh and Titman (1993) show that investors can earn abnormal returns by implementing an investment strategy that sells recent loser portfolios and buys recent winner portfolios.
[470] See Carhart (1997), p. 61 and Reilly & Brown (2011), p. 254.
[471] See Reilly & Brown (2011), p. 993 and section 4.3.3.

4. Literature review

Fama and French (1993) themselves have developed a modified version of the three-factor model and expanded their model by two additional factors that relate to risk commonly associated with fixed income securities: The first factor is a default premium that equals the credit spread on a corporate bond. The credit spread is calculated as the return difference between a long-term corporate bond and a long-term government bond. The second factor is a term premium that captures unexpected changes in interest rates. The term premium is calculated as the difference between the return of a long-term and a short-term government bond.[472] Formally, the five-factor model can be estimated as follows:[473]

$$r_i - r_f = \alpha_i + \beta_{EQU}(r_{EQU} - r_f) + \beta_{SMB}r_{SMB}$$
$$+\beta_{HML}r_{HML} + \beta_{DEF}r_{DEF} + \beta_{TERM}r_{TERM} + \varepsilon_i \qquad (25)$$

where all factors and variables used in the three-factor model are the same as before and

β_{TERM} and β_{DEF} = the factor loadings on the two additional risk factors
r_{DEF} = the return on the default premium
r_{TERM} = the return on the term premium.

Although the five-factor model contains both, equity and fixed income risk factors, the findings obtained in the empirical study conducted by Fama and French (1993) show that – at least for fixed income securities – only the two additional factors (the term premium and default premium) have significant factor loadings and thus, are the dominant factors to explain variations in returns of fixed income securities.[474] Consequently, in order to assess the performance of fixed income securities, the model used for the empirical analysis can be simplified from a five to a three-factor model that contains the market risk premium as well as the term and default premium as return explaining factors.[475]

To conclude, the single- and multi-factor models described in sections 4.3.3 and 4.3.4 are models that have been used in studies that assess SRI fund performance. Not all studies, however, apply all three models in their empirical analyses. Instead, earlier studies have used the CAPM to explain SRI equity fund performance and compare the returns generated by the SRI funds to

---

[472] See Fama & French (1993), p. 71.
[473] See Fama & French (1993), p. 71 and Reilly & Brown (2011), p. 993.
[474] In the same paper, Fama & French show that for equity securities, factor loadings are only significant for the market risk premium as well as the SMB and HML factor. The factor loadings for the term and default premium are insignificant. See Fama & French (1993), pp. 26, 40 and 52.
[475] See Fama & French (1993), pp. 16f., 31, 40, 52.

those of conventional funds or benchmark indices.[476] Later studies have applied the multi-factor models also described previously.[477] Prior to presenting the results obtained in the studies, the following section reviews the theoretical debate on SRI fund performance that is used as a basis for the empirical analyses in these studies.

4.4 Theoretical debate on SRI fund performance

Researchers commonly discuss three statements on the expected performance of SRI fund portfolios compared to conventional fund portfolios:[478] Some argue that risk-adjusted expected returns of SRI fund portfolios should be lower than the ones of conventional portfolios mainly due to the additional constraints imposed when selecting the securities to be included in the portfolio. Others state that return estimates for SRI fund portfolios should be equal to the estimates made for conventional portfolios. This statement is based on the assumption that the market does not price CSR activities of companies and thus, there should not be any difference between the performance of SRI and conventional fund portfolios. Finally, some take the position that SRI fund portfolios should outperform conventional portfolios and that the expected returns for SRI fund portfolios should in fact be higher than the expected returns for conventional portfolios. Figure 14 summarizes the three statements discussed in theoretical debates on the performance of SRI fund portfolios.

Statement 1 – Doing good but not well: Risk-adjusted (expected) returns for SRI fund portfolios are *lower than* the risk-adjusted expected returns of conventional portfolios. Proponents of this view argue that the SRI fund portfolio might suffer from poorer performance due to a number of factors that negatively influence the risk and return relationship of the SRI-screened portfolio: First, there is the concern of a potential increase in volatility and lower returns of SRI funds compared to conventional funds.[479] Research indicates that, by applying SRI screens in the portfolio construction process, investors tend to exclude larger companies from the investment universe. The remaining companies, in turn, tend to be smaller and have more volatile

---

[476] See, for example, Luther et al. (1992), Hamilton et al. (1993), Sauer (1997) and Statman (2000).
[477] See, for example, Bauer et al. (2005), Jones et al. (2008), Lee et al. (2010) and Blanchett (2010).
[478] See Climent & Soriano (2011), p. 276, Hamilton et al. (1993), p. 63, Revelli & Viviani (2015), p. 3.
[479] See Fabozzi et al. (2008), p. 85 and Rudd (1981), p. 60.

returns than the companies included in conventional portfolios. The higher volatility negatively influences the risk and return characteristics of the fund portfolio.[480]

Statement 1 – Doing good but not well

Risk-adjusted (expected) returns for SRI portfolios are *lower than* the risk-adjusted (expected) returns conventional portfolios

Statement 2 – Socially responsible feature is not priced

Risk-adjusted (expected) returns for SRI portfolios are *equal to* the risk-adjusted (expected) returns conventional portfolios

Statement 3 – Doing well while doing good

Risk-adjusted (expected) returns for SRI portfolios are *higher than* the risk-adjusted (expected) returns conventional portfolios

---

Figure 14: Statements on the performance difference between SRI and conventional funds
Source: Own illustration

Second, holding a fully diversified portfolio, or at least having access to unconstrained investment opportunities, is not feasible in the SRI context. Thus, proponents of Statement 1 argue that the level of diversification of SRI-screened fund portfolios should be lower than that of SRI-unscreened fund portfolios. Financial models like portfolio theory developed by Markowitz (1952) assume that investors' primary investment objective is to optimize the relationship between risk and return in their portfolio and with this, achieve a mean-variance efficient portfolio.[481] Conventionally, this objective is met by holding a fully diversified portfolio that consists of a number of securities that are selected from the universe of all investment securities available. SRI investors, however, deliberately decide to build their portfolios by selecting securities from a subset of the universe: Securities are added and removed from the portfolio on the basis of pre-defined SRI screens. The objective of realizing diversification benefits is subordinated – if considered at all when making investment decisions.[482] Depending on the screens defined, the selection process may result in entire industries being excluded from the investment opportunity set. Thus, proponents of portfolio theory argue that the limited number of assets available for selection leads to a lower level of diversification of SRI portfolios, which is not

---

[480] See Cortez et al. (2009), p. 586, Gregory et al. (1997), p. 723 and Mallin et al. (1995), p. 485.

[481] According to Markowitz (1952), p. 87, a portfolio is efficient if it generates the highest expected return for a given level of risk or is exposed to the lowest level of risk for a given level of return. See also Benson et al. (2006), p. 338 and Humphrey & Lee (2011), p. 520 as well as sections 4.2.1.2 and 4.2.2.3 for a detailed description of the calculation of portfolio return and risk.

[482] See Langbein & Posner (1980), p. 85.

likely to be offset by an increase in returns.[483] Consequently, the performance of SRI-screened portfolios is expected to be inferior to the performance of SRI-unscreened portfolios, which are built based on economic screening criteria only.[484]

Third, the screening process applied by the SRI funds implies additional administrative and monitoring cost, which potentially also have a negative effect on the performance of the fund portfolios.[485] Langbein and Posner (1980), for example, argue that even if return expectations for SRI fund portfolios are equal to those of conventional portfolios, net returns would still be lower for SRI portfolios due to the higher administrative costs associated with SRI screening.[486]

Finally, transaction costs and management fees for SRI fund portfolios are expected to be higher than for conventional fund portfolios. This is due to the fact that SRI funds tend to be smaller than conventional funds and the funds' managers need to collect more specialized information concerning the ethical practices of companies. This information, however, is not easily available – especially for companies that are not publicly traded.[487]

To conclude, proponents of Statement 1 (i.e. the underperformance hypotheses) argue that – at least from a theoretical perspective – the performance of SR fund portfolios is negatively affected by the constraints imposed in the screening process. Goldreyer and Diltz (1999) summarize the arguments in favor of Statement 1 with the claim: *"Do not mix money and morality"*[488]. Thus, according to Statement 1, investors should be better off separating financial and non-financial objectives in their investment decision.

Statement 2 – No effect: Risk-adjusted expected returns of SRI fund portfolios are *equal to* the risk-adjusted expected returns of conventional portfolios. This statement is consistent with the argumentation that CSR activities of companies are not priced or cancel each other out when securities of such companies are combined into one portfolio.[489] In addition, the notion of market efficiency suggests that security prices in the market fully reflect all publicly available information.[490] Thus, prices of a security should be equal to the fundamental value of the security

---

[483] See Cortez et al. (2009), p. 573, Grossman & Sharpe (1986), p. 27 and Rudd (1981), p. 57.
[484] See Bello (2005), p. 42.
[485] See Cortez et al. (2009), p. 573.
[486] See Langbein & Posner (1980), p. 93.
[487] See Juravle & Lewis (2008), p. 294 and Michelson (2004), p. 5.
[488] Goldreyer & Diltz (1999), p. 23.
[489] See Derwall et al. (2011), p. 2144 and Statman (2000), p. 36.
[490] See section 5.1.3 as well as Diltz (1995b), p. 69 and Fama (1970), p. 383, (1991), p. 1575.

4. Literature review

at any time. This notion implies that investors should not be able to implement trading strategies, which are based on the idea of making profits with mispriced securities and thus, should not be able to generate abnormal returns – positive or negative – by investing into companies that have implemented CSR activities or funds that use SRI screens to select the companies to invest in.

Consequently, proponents of Statement 2 argue that SRI investors should not be able to either outperform the market by consistently picking securities of winner companies that yield higher expected returns.[491] Moreover, they also do not have to be afraid of suffering from underperformance as average returns are the same for SRI and conventional fund portfolios.[492] Yet, others argue that even if the application of SRI investments strategies in the security selection process might generate value-relevant information for SRI fund managers, conventional investment managers could simply duplicate the investment strategy of the SRI fund managers.[493] As a consequence differences in the performance of both portfolios should immediately diminish and returns generated by SRI fund portfolio would be no different than the returns generated by conventional fund portfolios.[494]

Statement 3 – Doing well while doing good: Risk adjusted (expected) returns for SRI fund portfolios are *higher than* the risk-adjusted expected returns of conventional portfolios. Advocates of the SRI movement argue that it is in fact possible to be doing well while doing good and it makes good sense for investors as well as fund managers to include both, financial and non-financial criteria in the portfolio selection process for various reasons: First, a sound performance on both criteria indicates high managerial quality, which not only translates into lower worker turnover rates and litigation frequency, but also into favorable long-term financial performance of companies with a high rating on ESG themes.[495] Consequently, these companies are expected to have a comparative advantage over less responsible companies. This advantage leads to a superior performance of SRI funds that invest in the companies with a high rating on ESG themes.[496]

---

[491] See Goldreyer & Diltz (1999), p. 23, Haigh & Hazelton (2004), p. 66, Hamilton et al. (1993), p. 62, Langbein & Posner (1980), p. 92 and Sauer (1997), p. 140.
[492] See Langbein & Posner (1980), p. 92.
[493] See Diltz (1995a), p. 64, Haigh & Hazelton (2004), p. 67 and Renneboog et al. (2008a), p. 1735.
[494] See Renneboog et al. (2008a), p. 1735.
[495] See Cullis (1992), p. 14, Cummings (2000), p. 80, Goldreyer & Diltz (1999), p. 23, Leite & Cortez (2014), p. 249 and Renneboog et al. (2008a), p. 1724.
[496] See Cortez et al. (2009), p. 573 and Kurtz (1997), p. 39.

Second, even if SRI fund portfolios underperform according to financial or economic performance criteria such as risk, return, diversification and management fees, they are expected to outperform conventional fund portfolios on non-financial criteria such as ethical, social or environmental considerations. These criteria, in turn, are assumed to entail some kind of compensating utility for SRI investors: By investing into companies with a high ESG rating or into SRI funds, socially-conscious investors might derive a consumption value that equals or even outweighs the presumably lower investment value of the SRI alternative relative to conventional securities.[497] Thus proponents of Statement 3 argue that SRI-screened investments should outperform conventional ones.

Finally, as information on companies' ESG rating becomes more easily accessible, more investors will incorporate SRI screens in their investment decision process. By screening out investment alternatives that are not consistent with their personal values and beliefs, investors can raise companies' awareness to ESG issues and might even be able to put pressure on managers of socially irresponsible companies to change their behavior and turn the company into a more socially responsible one.[498]

To conclude, there are arguments in favor of all three statements and no consensus has yet been reached whether – at least from a theoretical perspective – SRI fund portfolios tend to outperform, underperform or perform as well as conventional fund portfolios. Table 10 summarizes the arguments made in support of each of the three statements.

Table 10: Overview of the theoretical debate on SRI fund performance

This table summarizes the researchers' views on SRI fund performance relative to the performance of conventional investment alternatives. Panel A summarizes the arguments made by proponents for Statement 1 - Doing well while doing good; Panel B summarizes arguments in favor of Statements 2 - No effect; Panel C summarizes the arguments in favor or Statement 3 - Doing well while doing good.

---

[497] See Auer & Schuhmacher (2016), p. 51, Bollen (2007), p. 706, Langbein & Posner (1980), p. 94 and Renneboog et al. (2008a), p. 1723.

[498] See Sauer (1997), p. 138.

4. Literature review

Panel A: Proponents of Statement 1 - Doing good but not well		
Author(s)	Year, page	Position towards SRI fund performance
Rudd	1981, p. 60	"The imposition of social responsibility criteria may bias the portfolio and cause, except in rare circumstances, an **increase in the investment risk**. [...] Each time that a manager is constrained, the **portfolio performance suffers**. Social responsibility criteria are, merely, incremental to the traditional investment approach."
Gregory et al.	1997, p. 705f.	"[...] Studies showed [...] that ethical fund investments were skewed towards smaller market capitalization companies. [...] There may be some *a priori* reasons why **larger funds may be expected to exhibit superior performance to smaller funds**, based mainly around arguments invoking economies of scale."
Goldreyer & Diltz	1999, p. 23	"[...] Imposing **additional constraints** on the investor's portfolio selection problem **will likely lead to lower returns** than would be the case if sociopolitical information were not factored into the decision."
Bello	2005, p. 52	"[...] the **effect of socially responsible investing is to decrease diversification**, and because the decrease in diversification **is not likely to be offset by an increase in returns**, portfolio performance is impaired."
Benson et al.	2006, p. 338	"Investors may be attracted to SRI funds because they possess personal values that are consistent with the underlying philosophy of the SRI fund. In such cases, the investors are making a **deliberate choice to concentrate on a sub-set of investment assets**. In a mean-variance theoretical framework, such a strategy can result in a **sub-optimal portfolio**."
Cortez et al.	2008, p. 573	"Theoretically, portfolio theory arguments suggest that **the imposition of additional constraints will inhibit the construction of the optimal portfolio**. As the universe of investments is reduced, investors will benefit less from the potential for diversification than in an unconstrained portfolio which will result in **lower risk-adjusted returns**."
Fabozzi et al.	2008, p. 85	"Economic intuition suggests that if **an optimal portfolio is obtained** under the mean-variance framework **from a subuniverse** that has been screened by any constraints, **it will underperform**, on a risk-adjusted basis, a portfolio without constraints."
Humphrey & Lee	2011, p. 520	"The **argument against SRI funds** [...] is that these funds **will have a limited investment opportunity set**, and may even result in entire industries being excluded from funds' portfolios. [...] The result for the fund is **reduced returns and increased idiosyncratic risk** [...]. "

Panel B: Proponents of Statement 2 - Socially responsible feature is not priced		
Author(s)	Year, page	Position towards SRI fund performance
Langbein & Posner	1980, p. 92	"[...] **we are not concerned that adherence to social principles will result in portfolios that yield lower average returns** than portfolios designed to maximize the financial well-being of the investment beneficiaries. The average return will be the same [...]. **We reject the argument that the social investor can consistently pick winners** by being more sensitive to political and social factors that can impinge on corporate profitability."
Hamilton et al.	1993, p. 63	"[...[The **social responsibility feature of stocks is not priced**. [...] Socially responsible investors who sell stocks find enough conventional investors ready to buy that the prices of the stocks do not drop. [...] Factors that are not proxies for risk **do not affect expected returns**."

Author	Year, page	Position
Diltz	1995a, p. 64	"Equity markets are so large, so liquid and so efficient that **it really does not matter whether social screening is performed** when selecting firms for investment portfolios."
Diltz	1995b, p. 69	"The notion of **market efficiency would suggest that securities are priced to reflect all publicly available information**. The implication [...] is that **investors should not be able to earn abnormal returns** by screening firms for ethical behaviour in either the positive or the negative sense."
Statman	2000, p. 36	"Socially responsible investors can raise the cost of capital of [...] companies only in the absence of numerous conventional investors who stand ready to provide substitute capital at the same cost. There is **evidence** that [...] the **boycott of stocks of companies** [...] had **no detectable effect on their returns**."
Haigh & Hazelton	2004, p. 67	"**SRI funds cannot guarantee that they can alter the cost of capital for their investments**. First, SRI funds [...] command negligible market share, which discounts the argument for a direct effect on companies. Second, even if SRI funds commanded greater market share, any effects [...] would be short-lived, given liquid capital markets. Third, there are no guarantees that financial markets will look to SRI funds to signal undisclosed future revenue growth or costs and accordingly follow the investment actions of SRI funds."
Derwall et al.	2011, p. 2139	"There are some reasons to expect that the market fails to value some CSR practices [...]. First, CSR is a multidimensional [...] concept, and **investors lack the tools** [...] **to adequately measure CSR practices and their effects on the fundamental value of the firm**. Second, **accounting standards that have not adapted to a CSR-minded business environment cloud** sound judgment on the added value of CSR. [...]"

Panel C: Proponents of Statement 3 - Doing well while doing good

Author(s)	Year, page	Position towards SRI fund performance
Cullis et al.	1992, p. 14	"[...] The **acceptance of social responsibility may be indicative of more skilful management** and the ability to substitute less costly implicit claims, such as the maintenance of consumer and worker satisfaction, for more costly explicit claims, such as formal safety and regulatory constraints."
Sauer	1997, p. 138	"Good corporate citizenship is likely to create solid firm loyalty, and as a result, **responsible firms may experience increased product sales**. [...] Employee loyalty benefits a firm by improving productivity, innovation, lowering production costs, and thereby enhancing profitability."
Kurtz	1997, p. 39	"[...] **Socially responsible companies can outperform** their less responsible counterparts. [...] social responsibility can be a way for companies to improve relations with various constituencies important to their future success. [...] Socially responsible behavior is a sign of skillful management or a by-product of financial success. Some also view socially responsible behavior as a signal from management."
Cummings	2000, p. 80	"[...] There is **unlikely to be an identifiable cost to ethical investment** as it is a form of behaviour that does not restrict itself to any particular grouping. In fact, **ethical investment may involve lower long run costs** through a reduction in the risk of the investment being to externalities action exposed such as regulatory and litigation."
Michelson et al.	2004, p. 52	"There are a number of reasons why ethical investments might do better than more standard or conventional investment. [...] **Higher financial returns occur because of the adoption of social screening practices**. [...] Ethical investment operates with **longer time horizons** than more conventional investment."
Renneboog et al.	2008a, p. 1735	"[...] **Firms investing in CSR create shareholder value** [...]. Firms ignoring socially responsibility may destroy long-run shareholder value due to reputation losses and/or potential litigation costs."

Source: Own illustration

Given the theoretical discussion presented in this section, the following section now reviews existing empirical evidence on SRI fund performance and shows a similar result: Although there are numerous studies documenting a significant performance gap (positive and negative) between SRI and conventional fund portfolios, there is also a considerable number of studies showing that there is no (significant) performance difference between the two portfolios.[499]

4.5 Empirical results on SRI fund performance

4.5.1 Results obtained using single- and two-factor models

Luther et al. (1992) are among the first researchers to examine the performance of ethical equity funds in the UK. The authors apply the CAPM and use Jensen's alpha to analyze whether ethical equity funds perform differently than conventional funds. Studying risk and return characteristics for 15 funds in the UK in the period 1984-1990, the researchers find weak evidence that – on a risk-adjusted basis – ethical equity funds perform better than their conventional counterparts: The average Jensen's alpha for the ethical equity funds is 0.03% per month, but not statistically different from zero.[500] Thus, the authors conclude that there is no evidence for differences in the risk-adjusted returns of ethical and non-ethical funds. However, although the return difference is not statistically significant, Luther et al. (1992) also find evidence for a size effect as the ethical funds in the sample tended to invest in smaller companies than the conventional funds.[501]

In order to control for the size effect, Mallin et al. (1995) conduct a matched pair analysis and calculate Jensen's alphas for 29 ethical and 29 conventional equity funds that are matched based on asset size and age. The results obtained indicate that, while both funds underperform the market, ethical funds slightly outperform conventional funds in the period 1986-1993. Monthly alphas for ethical funds are in the range between -0.28% and 1.21%, whereas for non-ethical funds the range is slightly broader from -0.41% to 1.56% per month.[502] On an individual fund

---

[499] Please refer to Capelle-Blancard & Monjon (2012), Revelli & Viviani (2015) or Renneboog et al. (2008a) for a comprehensive literature review of the empirical studies that have been published on the performance of SRI funds.

[500] See Luther et al. (1992), pp. 63f.

[501] See Luther et al. (1992), pp. 65f.

[502] See Mallin et al. (1995), pp. 490f.

level, the vast majority of the alphas generated by each fund are positive, which again indicates outperformance of the ethical funds compared to the benchmark portfolio: 22 ethical funds and 23 non-ethical funds show positive alphas, although only 8 alphas (four ethical and four non-ethical ones) are statistically different from zero.[503]

Hamilton et al. (1993) compare the performance of 32 ethical funds to that of 320 randomly selected conventional funds in the US for the period 1981-1990. Dividing the observation period into two sub-periods, the authors find that the average Jensen's alpha is 0.06% per month for the 17 ethical funds and -0.14% for the 170 conventional funds that have been established prior to 1985. On the contrary, the average Jensen's alpha for the 15 ethical funds established after 1985 is -0.28% per month, which is considerably lower than the average monthly alpha of -0.04% of the corresponding conventional funds.[504] However, the differences between the average alphas are not statistically significant, meaning that there is no indication of systematic under- or outperformance for ethical funds compared to their conventional counterparts. Yet, Hamilton et al. (1993) interpret this finding as a rather positive signal for investors: The market does not seem to price the socially responsible characteristics of funds. This implies that, although investors cannot expect to earn excess returns by investing ethically, they also do not have to suffer from inferior financial performance when investing parts of their money into this investment alternative.[505]

Similar results have been obtained by Reyes and Grieb (1998) as well as Goldreyer and Diltz (1999) for the US and Cummings (2000) for the Australian SRI market. Reyes and Grieb (1998) analyze the performance of 15 SRI funds in the US and document that the Sharpe ratios for SRI funds are not significantly different than the ones for conventional funds. In fact, only four funds are found to have Sharpe ratios higher than their respective peer group, while the remaining Sharpe ratios for SRI funds are all lower than that for conventional funds.[506] Goldreyer and Diltz (1999) calculate Jensen's alphas, Sharpe ratios and Treynor ratios for 49 SRI mutual funds and 60 conventional funds and obtain mixed results regarding the performance difference be-

---

[503] See Mallin et al. (1995), p. 489.
[504] See Hamilton et al. (1993), p. 65.
[505] See Hamilton et al. (1993), p. 66.
[506] See Reyes & Grieb (1998), pp. 2–3.

tween the two fund groups: While average Jensen's alpha and Sharpe ratios are higher for conventional funds, SRI funds on average have higher Treynor ratios.[507] Cummings (2000) examines the return performance of seven ethical trusts in relation to three benchmark indices in Australia (small company index, industry index and market index). The results indicate that, on average, the ethical trusts tend to outperform their industry averages, but at the same time underperform the market average.[508] The authors all conclude that the application of social screening neither has an adverse impact on the investment performance of the funds, nor does it influence the fund's performance in any systematic manner.

Instead of analyzing only individual fund performance, Sauer (1997) examines index returns in the US for the period 1986-1994. Specifically, he compares the investment performance of the Domini Social Index (DSI)[509] – an index consisting of 400 stocks of socially responsible companies in the US – with the performance of two benchmark indices, the S&P 500 and the Chicago Center for Research in Security Prices (CRSP) Value Weighted Market Indexes.[510] The results indicate that – on average – there is neither a significant difference between the average monthly raw returns of the DSI and the benchmark indices' returns, nor the risk-adjusted returns as measured by Jensen's alpha and Sharpe ratios: The average monthly return of the DSI is 1.2%, compared to 1.1% and 1.0% for the S&P 500 and the CRSP, respectively[511]. Jensen's alpha for the DSI using the S&P 500 and the CRSP as a proxy for market returns is 0.04% and 0.1%, respectively and thus, insignificantly different from zero.[512] Finally, Sharpe ratios between the DSI and the S&P 500 or CRSP also are not statistically different.[513]

Statman (2000) confirms the finding that the performance of SRI indices does not significantly differ from the performance of conventional indices: While the average monthly raw return of the DSI (1.44%) is slightly higher than that of the S&P 500 (1.41%) and the CRSP (1.37%), the

---

[507] See Goldreyer and Diltz (1999), pp. 25 and 29.
[508] See Cummings (2000), pp. 83 and 85–86.
[509] The index has been launched in 1990 as the Domini 400 Social Index, but is now called the MSCI KLD 400 Social Index. For more details see https://www.msci.com/resources/factsheets/index_fact_sheet/msci-kld-400-social-index.pdf.
[510] See http://www.crsp.com/products/documentation/stock-file-indexes for more details on the available CRSP Value Weighted Market Indexes.
[511] See Sauer (1997), p. 142.
[512] See Sauer (1997), p. 144.
[513] See Sauer (1997), p. 146.

risk-adjusted returns are slightly lower, although not statistically significant.[514] In addition to measuring the performance of the DSI index relative to the performance of the S&P 500 and the CRSP indices, Statman (2000) also compares the performance of 31 SRI equity funds to that of 62 conventional funds with similar asset size. In line with the results obtained for the indices, the author finds no significant differences in the return performance of the individual funds. The average monthly Jensen's alpha of -0.42% for SRI equity funds is slightly higher (or less negative) than the average alpha calculated for conventional funds (-0.62%). But again, the difference is not statistically significant.[515]

In sum, early studies that use single-factor models to examine the performance of SRI investment alternatives have not found any significant difference in the returns of SRI funds compared to conventional funds or benchmark indices. However, the documented differences in fund performance have been analyzed on a raw and risk-adjusted basis, using the excess market return as the only independent variable in the regression model. Other factors that potentially influence the risk and return characteristics of the funds, such as the size effect, which is caused by differences in the market capitalization of the companies included in the funds, have not been accounted for in those studies. Gregory et al. (1997), for example, explicitly criticizes the results obtained by Mallin et al. (1995) as they have not controlled for the fact that – at least in the UK – SRI funds tend to invest in smaller companies than the ones usually included in the indices used as benchmarks.[516]

To overcome the problem of this so-called small-cap bias, Gregory et al. (1997) apply a two-factor asset pricing model that controls for the size effect in measuring excess returns of SRI funds in the UK. Specifically, the authors incorporate a size premium (the difference between the return on stocks with a low and high market capitalization) into their calculation and determine adjusted Jensen's alphas, using the Hoare Govett Small Companies Index and the Financial Times All Share Index as benchmark indices.[517] The results indicate a slightly lower performance of SRI funds compared to their benchmarks, although again, the difference is not statistically significant.[518]

---

[514] See Statman (2000), pp. 31 and 38.
[515] See Statman (2000), p. 34.
[516] See Gregory et al. (1997), p. 705.
[517] See Gregory et al. (1997), p. 707.
[518] See Gregory et al. (1997), p. 710.

Kreander et al. (2005) address the small-cap bias in a two-factor model and conduct a matched pair analysis of 60 SRI equity funds from four European countries (UK, Sweden, Germany and the Netherlands). Their findings are consistent with the results obtained by Gregory et al. (1997): Average returns are identical for SRI as well as non-SRI funds (0.13% per week) and the difference between the adjusted Jensen's alphas calculated (0.007% for SRI funds compared to -0.019% for non-SRI funds) is not statistically significant.[519] In line with this finding, the average Sharpe and Treynor ratio for the SRI funds are insignificantly higher than those for non-SRI funds: While the Sharpe ratio for SRI funds is 0.034, it is 0.024 for non-SRI funds; the Treynor ratio for SRI funds is 0.0011 and 0.0010 for non-SRI funds.[520] Thus, Kreander et al. (2005) conclude that SRI funds seem to perform just as well as non-SRI funds. There is no statistical difference in the returns of SRI and non-SRI funds, even after accounting for potential biases such as the size effect or small-cap bias.[521] This finding supports the notion that the market does not systematically price the ethical component of SRI funds, which was already expressed earlier by Hamilton et al. (1993).[522]

4.5.2 Results obtained using multi-factor models

4.5.2.1 Single-country analyses

In addition to the single- and two-factor models used in earlier studies, more recent studies applied the three- and four-factor regression models introduced in section 4.3.4. In addition to the size factor, these models also include a growth and momentum factor in the analysis of SRI fund performance. Blanchett (2010), for example, applies the four-factor regression model in order to determine the risk-adjusted returns of three social indices in the US for the period 1990-2008.[523] The regression analysis shows that only the DSI is able to generate a positive alpha (+0.14% per month), while the average monthly alpha for the Calvert Social Index and the

---

[519] See Kreander et al. (2005), pp. 1479 and 1481f.
[520] See Kreander et al. (2005), p. 1481.
[521] See Kreander et al. (2005), p. 1491.
[522] See Hamilton et al. (1993), p. 66.
[523] Indices included in the study are the Domini Social 400 Index (https://www.msci.com/resources/fact-sheets/index_fact_sheet/msci-kld-400-social-index.pdf), the Calvert Social Index (http://www.calvert.com/resources/calvert-responsible-index-series) and the FTSE4Good US Index (http://www.ftse.com/products/indices/FTSE4Good). See Blanchett (2010), p. 95.

FTSE4Good US Index are negative (-0.01% and -0.27%, respectively).[524] The author also compares the performance of SRI to non-SRI funds and finds evidence that SRI funds perform worse than their non-SRI peers on a raw-return basis[525], but perform better on a risk-adjusted basis.[526] None of the results, however, are statistically significant.

Bauer et al. (2006) and (2007) perform a similar analysis and apply the four-factor model developed by Carhart (1997) in an empirical study on the Canadian as well as Australian SRI market. For the Canadian market, Bauer al. (2007) find evidence that suggests slightly lower performance of SRI funds compared to their conventional counterparts. The average annual return generated by the SRI funds (5.12%) is lower than the average return generated by conventional funds (5.48%) in the sample period January 1994 to January 2003.[527] The authors also find evidence that the SRI funds are more risky than non-SRI funds: While SRI funds have an average standard deviation of 14.21% p.a., the standard deviation for conventional fund is 14.05% p.a.[528]

Moreover, the excess return generated by the SRI funds measured by the single-factor Jensen's alpha is lower than the alpha generated by the conventional funds. Yet, neither the individual alphas for both funds nor the difference between the two alphas are significantly different from zero.[529] In contrast to this, the alpha generated by SRI fund portfolio in the four-factor model (-3.18% p.a.) is significantly different from zero, representing strong underperformance of the SRI funds relative to the market portfolio.[530] The conventional portfolio also underperforms the market portfolio (the average monthly alpha for non-SRI funds is -2.90% p.a.). However,

---

[524] See Blanchett (2010), p. 96.

[525] The net (gross) return generated by SRI funds is -0.17% (-0.14%) per month lower than the return generated by non-SRI funds. See Blanchett (2010), p. 98.

[526] The average Jensen's alpha of the SRI funds is +0.01% and 0.10% per month when calculated using net and gross returns in the regression analysis, respectively. See Blanchett (2010), p. 100.

[527] See Bauer et al. (2007), p. 113.

[528] See Bauer et al. (2007), p. 113.

[529] The alpha generated by SRI fund is -2.93% p.a. for SRI funds and -5.59% p.a. for non-SRI funds. See Bauer et al. (2007), p. 115.

[530] See Bauer et al. (2007), p. 118.

the return difference between the SRI and the conventional fund portfolio is again not significant.[531] Thus, although both portfolios (SRI and non-SRI) underperform the market, no significant difference between the performances of the two portfolios in the Canadian market is observed.

This result is partially confirmed by the study published by Bauer et al. (2006) on SRI equity fund performance in Australia. Studying the performance of equally weighted SRI and non-SRI fund portfolios in the period between 1992 and 2003, the authors find no significant difference between the returns generated by the two portfolios.[532] However, the result is sensitive to the time period analyzed: While the SRI funds significantly underperform their conventional counterparts by -3.36% p.a. in the period from 1992 to 1996, the performance difference diminishes in the periods from 1996 to 1999 and 1999 to 2003.[533] Contrarily, Jones et al. (2008) find evidence that Australian SRI equity funds significantly underperform their conventional counterparts and that the level of underperformance gets even stronger for the most recent periods in the sample. Over the entire sample period between 1986 and 2005, SRI funds underperform their conventional peers on average by 0.07% per month. For the period from 2000 to 2005, the amount of underperformance increases to 0.12% per month.[534]

4.5.2.2 Multi-country analyses

For international markets, Bauer et al. (2005) compare the performance of SRI equity funds in the US, UK and Germany using Carhart's four factor model and find no evidence of significant under- or outperformance of SRI funds relative to their conventional counterparts in the period between 1990 and 2001.[535] The study also documents that all SRI funds included in the study are more growth-oriented and less value-oriented than conventional funds.[536] Moreover, the authors are able to document differences in the investment strategies of SRI funds in the re-

---

[531] See Bauer et al. (2007), p. 119.

[532] Relative to non-ethical funds, ethical funds generate a lower return of -1.56% p.a. during in the sample period, but the difference is not statistically significant. See Bauer et al. (2006), p. 39.

[533] See Bauer et al. (2007), p. 43.

[534] See Jones et al. (2008), p. 189.

[535] See Bauer et al. (2005), p. 1759.

[536] Growth-orientation means that the SRI funds, on average, have a low book-to-market ratio. In contrast to this, conventional funds are found to be more value-oriented, meaning that they have a high book-to-market ratio. See Bauer et al. (2005), p. 1762.

spective countries: While SRI funds in Germany and the UK tend to invest in small-capitalization companies, SRI funds domiciled in the US tend to focus their investments towards large-capitalization companies.[537]

An international study conducted by Renneboog et al. (2008b) reveals slight evidence of underperformance of SRI equity fund compared to benchmark indices and conventional funds. The authors compare the performance of SRI funds to market indices and conventional funds in 17 different countries across three regions[538] and get mixed results: While SRI equity funds in all countries perform worse than the market benchmarks, the four-factor alphas are only significantly negative for the US, the UK, France, Ireland, the Netherlands, Sweden, Canada, Japan and Malaysia.[539] Furthermore, the alphas for the SRI equity funds are lower than the alphas obtained for the conventional funds in almost all countries in the study. However, the differences in returns are not statistically significant in most of the countries. Exceptions are SRI funds in France, Ireland, Sweden and Japan where the average monthly alphas for SRI funds are 7% to 4% p.a. lower than the respective alphas for the conventional funds.[540] Overall, Renneboog et al. (2008b) cannot find evidence for significant outperformance and only slight evidence for significant underperformance of SRI funds relative to conventional funds.

The evidence of underperformance also persists when controlling for screening activities such as activism policy or community investing and other fund characteristics such as fund size, age, fee structure or reputation of the fund.[541] The authors also study the effect of screening intensity (estimated by the number of SRI screens applied by each fund) on the fund's performance. Funds that primarily invest in companies that engage in community involvement or have their own SRI research team benefit from an additional return of up to 3.6% p.a. for each additional screen applied.[542] However, fund returns decrease with increasing screening intensity on social and governance criteria: For those funds that focus on social and governance criteria, there is

---

[537] See Bauer et al. (2005), p. 1762.

[538] Countries and regions included in the study are: (i) Europe: Belgium, France, Germany, Ireland, Italy, Luxembourg, the Netherlands, Norway, Sweden, Switzerland and the UK (including Guernsey and the Isle of Man), (ii) North America: the US and Canada and (iii) Asia-Pacific: Australia, Japan, Malaysia and Singapore. See Renneboog et al. (2008b), p. 305.

[539] See Renneboog et al. (2008b), p. 308.

[540] See Renneboog et al. (2008b), pp. 312f.

[541] For details on the effect of screening activities and fund characteristics on a fund's performance, please refer to Renneboog et al. (2008b), p. 318.

[542] See Renneboog et al. (2008b), p. 320.

evidence that one additional screen is associated with a 1% lower risk-adjusted return per year.[543]

4.5.3 Additional studies on SRI fund performance

Lee et al. (2010) also find evidence that screening intensity significantly negatively influences risk-adjusted returns in the Carhart (1997) four-factor model, although it has no effect on raw returns: Their analysis shows that with each additional screen applied by a fund, the risk-adjusted return of this funds decreased by 0.7% p.a.[544] In contrast to this, Humphrey and Lee (2011) document that SRI funds that applied more screens tend to generate higher returns than funds with fewer screens.[545] This result, however, is sensitive to the type of screens applied: While positive screens improve risk-adjusted performance of SRI funds, negative screens lead to an increase in the risk associated with the SRI funds and thus, lead to a decrease in the funds' returns.[546]

Barnett et al. (2006) find evidence in favor of a curvilinear relationship between the number of screens applied by a fund and its financial performance: Analyzing the performance of 61 SRI funds in the period from 1972 to 2000, the authors show that with increasing number of social screens applied by a SRI fund, its financial return initially decreases, reaches its minimum at seven screens and recovers again until the maximum of twelve screens is reached.[547] However, the analysis also reveals that the financial return generated by funds that apply twelve screens is still lower than the return achieved by funds that apply only one screen.[548] The authors conclude that SRI funds are able to generate competitive returns only in two instances: Either by applying only one or two screens as in such cases the benefits of increased diversification can still be realized. Or by applying as many screens as possible as this helps the fund's managers to eliminate underperforming companies from the portfolio, which in turn, results in a higher

---

[543] See Renneboog et al. (2008b), p. 320.
[544] See Lee et al. (2010), p. 362.
[545] Humphrey & Lee (2011), p. 529.
[546] See Humphrey & Lee (2011), p. 529.
[547] See Barnett et al. (2006), p. 1114.
[548] The return of the fund with twelve screens is 0.2% per month lower than that for the fund with only one screen or for more-broadly diversified fund portfolios. See Barnett & Salomon (2006), p. 1114.

financial performance.[549] Only those funds that are *"stuck in the middle"*[550] generate inferior returns as their manager are not successful in setting up a sufficiently diversified portfolio or eliminating underperforming companies from the fund's portfolio.[551]

Most of the studies discussed so far examine the performance of SRI equity funds, but do not include SRI balanced or SRI fixed income funds in their analysis. However, as SRI equity funds only account for about half of the market for SRI, it is hardly possible to make inferences for the entire SRI market. Moreover, while the share of SRI equity funds decreased from about 62% in 2005 to 54% in 2013, the share of SRI fixed income funds increased from 20% to 33% within the same period.[552] Thus, SRI fixed income funds have increasingly gained market share in the recent years, but only limited research has been conducted so far that also includes other fund categories than SRI equity funds in the data samples used for the empirical analysis.

Derwall and Koedijk (2009) are one of the few researchers who address the increasing importance of SRI fixed income funds and examined the performance of socially responsible fixed income and balanced funds relative to a matched sample of conventional funds. Their findings suggest that, while there is no significant difference between the performance of SRI fixed income funds and their conventional counterparts, SRI balanced funds significantly outperform their peers by 1.3% p.a.[553] However, as the sample is restricted to SRI funds from the US, it is again difficult to draw conclusions for the European or global SRI fund market. Nonetheless, the study clearly extended previous research as it is one of the first to examine the performance of SRI fixed income and balanced funds alike.

---

[549] See Barnett et al. (2006), p. 1117.
[550] Barnett et al. (2006), p. 1118.
[551] See Barnett et al. (2006), p. 1118.
[552] See Vigeo (2013a), p. 10 and section 3.2.3.
[553] See Derwall & Koedijk (2009), p. 222.

4. Literature review

Table 11: Overview of existing studies on SRI fund performance

This table summarizes methodologies and empirical findings of studies on SRI fund performance. Panel A depicts studies that have used 1- and 2-factor models, while panel B lists studies that have used multi-factor models. The studies are sorted according to the year of publication.

Panel A: 1- and 2-factor models

Study	Regional focus	Period of analysis	Main finding of study
Luther et al. (1992)	UK	1972-1990	Weak evidence that ethical funds perform better than conventional funds: Jensen's alphas of ethical funds are positive with a mean of 0.03% per month, but the difference is **not statistically significant**.
Hamilton et al. (1993)	US	1981-1985	Excess returns of 15 out of 17 funds examined are **not statistically different from zero**. The market does not price social responsibility characteristics and investors do not have be afraid of forgoing some level of return when investing into SRI. However, they also should not expect to earn abnormal returns with this investment alternative.
Mallin et al. (1995)	UK	1986-1993	**No evidence that risk-adjusted returns of ethical and non-ethical funds are significantly different.** Conventional and ethical trusts both underperform the market. Ethical trusts seem to perform better than conventional trusts, but the difference is not statistically significant.
Gregory (1997)	UK	1986-1994	Two-factor model controls for size bias in measuring excess returns of SRI funds. The results indicate that SRI funds perform worse than conventional funds, but the **difference is not statistically significant.**
Sauer (1997)	US	1986-1994	Application of social screens does not have an adverse impact on investment performance of funds. **The costs of implementing socially responsible criteria are negligible.**
Reyes & Grieb (1998)	US	1986-1995	Risk-adjusted performance of all 15 SRI funds included in the sample is **not statistically different** from the respective conventional counterparts. SRI screens have no impact on the performance of the SRI funds.
Goldreyer and Diltz (1999)	US	1981-1997	**Social screening does not affect the investment performance of mutual SRI funds** in any systematic or predictable way.
Cummings (2000)	Australia	1986-1994	Ethical trusts perform better than their industry averages but perform worse than the market average. However, the difference is **not statistically significant.**
Statman (2000)	US	1990-1998	SRI funds perform better than conventional funds of equal asset size, but the difference is **not statistically significant.**
Kreander (2005)	Europe (UK, Sweden, Germany, Netherlands)	1995-2001	Two-factor model incorporates a small capitalization index in addition to the market index used by the previous studies. The results indicate that the risk-adjusted **performance of SRI funds is similar to that of conventional funds and the market benchmark.**

Panel B: Multi-factor models			
Study	Regional focus	Period of analysis	Main finding of study
Bauer et al. (2005)	Germany, UK and US	1990-2001	**No evidence in favor of a significant difference in risk-adjusted returns** between SRI and conventional funds after controlling for investment style.
Barnett et al. (2006)	US	1972-2000	Financial performance of SRI funds varies with the type of screens applied by the funds. There is a **curvilinear relationship between the financial performance and the number of screens applied.**
Bauer, Derwall et al. (2006)	Canada	1994-2003	Ethical mutual funds perform worse than their conventional peers over the entire observation period and are more risky. However, the **performance difference is not statistically significant,** neither for the single-factor nor the four-factor model employed in the study.
Bauer, Otten et al. (2006)	Australia	1992-2003	**No evidence of significant differences** in risk-adjusted returns between SRI and conventional funds, but the result is sensitive to the time period analyzed: While SRI funds underperform their conventional counterparts in the period 1992-1996, the performance difference diminishes in the period 1996-2003.
Jones et al. (2008)	Australia	1986-2005	**SRI funds significantly underperform the market benchmark** over the entire sample period, even after controlling for size effects, book-to-market ratio and momentum effects. The amount of underperformance is even higher for the more recent period analyzed.
Renneboog et al. (2008b)	Global	1991-2003	**SRI as well as conventional funds underperform the market benchmark.** However, risk-adjusted returns of SRI funds are not statistically different from the performance of conventional funds in most countries except for France, Ireland, Sweden and Japan.
Derwall & Koedijk (2009)	US	1987-2003	**Fixed income SRI funds perform similar than conventional funds. Balanced SRI funds outperform** their conventional peers and the difference is statistically significant.
Lee et al. (2010)	US	1989-2006	**Screening has a negative effect on financial performance of SRI funds**: Each additional screen applied by a fund is associated with an decrease in the fund's return of 0.7% p.a.
Blanchett (2010)	US	1990-2008	**SRI funds underperform** conventional funds **on a pure return basis,** but **outperform** their conventional counterparts **on a risk-adjusted basis.**
Humphrey & Lee (2011)	Australia	1990-2008	There is **a positive relationship between the number of positive screens applied by the funds and the fund's return.** But the relationship between the fund's return and the number of negative screens applied is negative.

Source: Own illustration

To summarize, the preceding discussion on existing research of SRI fund performance indicates that no consensus has yet been reached if there is a significant performance difference between SRI-screened funds and SRI-unscreened investment alternatives: While some studies document slight outperformance of SRI funds compared to conventional funds or market indices, others find evidence of slight underperformance.[554] Most of the studies, however, find no significant difference between SRI funds and conventional funds or their respective benchmarks indices.[555] Thus, and in line with Statement 2 introduced in section 4.4, the market does not seem to systematically price the social characteristics of SRI funds and investors do not have to pay a price for aligning their financial and ESG objectives. Table 11 provides a summary of the empirical findings on SRI performance presented above.

4.6 Interim conclusion

This chapter has summarized theoretical discussions and empirical evidences documented in existing literature on SRI fund performance. The theoretical discussion introduced at the beginning of this chapter has shown that there is a controversial debate among researchers on whether or not – at least from a theoretical perspective – the performance of SRI funds is expected to be similar, better or worse than the performance of conventional investment alternatives.

Some researchers argue that the market does not price the socially responsible feature of SRI-screened investment alternatives and there should be no difference in the performance between SRI-screened and SRI-unscreened investment alternatives at all. Proponents of portfolio theory, however, argue that the imposition of additional constraints in the security selection process applied by SRI funds should lead to an inferior performance of the SRI-screened relative to SRI-unscreened investments. Finally, advocates of the SRI movement argue that companies with a high rating on ESG themes have a comparative, and with this, financial advantage over less socially responsible companies. This advantage leads to a better performance of SRI funds that invest in such high ESG-rated companies relative to conventional funds that do not explicitly apply ESG screening criteria when selecting the companies to invest in. As there are reasonable arguments in favor of all statements made by the researchers, no generally accepted statement on the performance of SRI funds can yet be made – at least from a theoretical perspective.

---

[554] See Blanchett (2010), Cummings (2000), Luther et al. (1992), Mallin et al. (1995) and Statman (2000) for studies that find evidence in favor of SRI fund outperformance and Gregory (1997), Bauer et al. (2006), Jones et al. (2008) and Renneboog et al. (2008b) for studies that document evidence in favor of SRI fund underperformance.

[555] See, for example, Bauer et al. (2005), Derwall & Koedijk (2009), Goldreyer & Diltz (1999), Hamilton et al. (1993), Kreander (2005), Lee et al. (2010), Reyes & Grieb (1998) and Sauer (1997).

The empirical evidence presented in the later part of this chapter supports this finding: Some studies find no significant difference between the performances of SRI funds relative to conventional investment alternatives at all. Others document significant levels of under- or outperformance of SRI funds. Thus, neither the theoretical discussion nor the empirical studies provide consistent evidence in favor or against a significant difference between the performances of SRI-screened and SRI-unscreened investments. Although the findings are not consistent, they at least challenge the notion that SRI funds inevitably generate lower returns compared to SRI-unscreened investments. There is no doubt that the screening process applied by the SRI funds restricts the overall investment universe. However, empirical research does not support the notion that this process inevitably also leads to a superior or inferior performance of SRI-screened investments.

To conclude, the theoretical discussion on SRI fund performance presented in this chapter is relevant for the entire market – no matter if the discussion is on SRI funds that are domiciled either in the US, in Europe or globally. Most of the empirical studies published so far, however, focus on SRI funds established and promoted in the US. Moreover, the data sets used in these studies typically only include SRI equity funds. As the market for SRI includes not only SRI equity, but also SRI balanced and SRI fixed income funds, the empirical study included in this thesis is set up to analyze the performance of all three categories of SRI funds: Excess returns for European-based SRI equity, balanced and fixed income funds are determined and assessed relative to the returns generated by benchmark indices in each of the three fund categories.

Prior to presenting the results obtained in the empirical study, the following chapter first derives the hypotheses that are to be tested and introduces the methodology and the data set that are used in the analysis.

5 Assessing the performance of European-based SRI funds

5.1 Hypotheses development

5.1.1 SRI-screened relative to SRI-unscreened investments

The theoretical debate in section 4.4 has shown that no generally accepted statement on the performance of SRI funds can yet be made. The aim of the thesis is to test whether the empirical evidence supports this theoretical debate or whether there is a significant difference between the performance of SRI-screened and SRI-unscreened investment alternatives. Specifically, the empirical study aims to examine whether a difference in the performance between the two investment alternatives can be observed at all and whether this difference indicates under- or outperformance of the SRI relative to the conventional investment alternatives. While evidence that documents underperformance of SRI alternatives would support Statement 1 of section 4.4, i.e. doing good but not well, evidence in favor of outperformance of SRI against SRI-unscreened investments would support Statement 3, i.e. doing well while doing good. Finally, evidence of no significant performance differences would support Statement 2 and the notion that the market in fact does not price socially responsible features of SRI funds, i.e. no effect.[556] Thus, the first hypothesis that is to be tested in the empirical study centers on the question whether the returns generated by SRI-screened investment alternatives are significantly different from the returns generated by their SRI-unscreened counterparts.

Theoretically, portfolio theory as developed by Markowitz (1952) states that investors aim at optimizing the risk-and-return profile of a portfolio as a whole.[557] Thus, not the risk-and-return profile of an individual security is of major importance when selecting the securities that ought to be part of a portfolio. Instead, investors look at the expected return and risk of the resulting portfolio when the individual securities are combined. While the return that is (potentially) generated by the portfolio is a desirable thing for investors, risk that is associated with a certain

---

[556] See page 122.
[557] See Markowitz (1952), p. 82 and (1991), p. 470 as well as section 4.4.

level of return is an undesirable thing the risk-averse investors try to avoid.[558] Thus, when selecting the securities for a portfolio, investors try to maximize the expected mean return of their portfolio for a given level of risk or minimize the risk for a given level of return.[559]

As introduced in section 4.2, a portfolio's return equals the weighted average of the return of the securities included in the portfolio. Due to benefits of diversification, the risk of the portfolio is lower than the weighted average of the individual securities' risk. The benefits of diversification are stronger, the lower the correlation or covariance between the returns of the individual securities that are combined in the portfolio is. Thus, effective diversification means spreading the investment across a large number of securities with a low covariance and, in best cases, avoiding securities with a high covariance.[560]

Conventionally, investors select the individual securities to be included in their portfolio from the entire universe of securities available and aim at holding a fully diversified portfolio for which the benefits of diversification are maximized.[561] While the security selection process in conventional investment approaches primarily is based on financial criteria, SRI approaches also consider non-financial or ESG criteria when selecting the securities to invest in.[562] However, the screening applied by SRI alternatives in the selection process limits the number of securities that potentially can be part of the portfolio. Thus, proponents of portfolio theory argue that the imposition of additional constraints by the SRI alternatives reduces the benefits of diversification, which is not likely to be offset by an increase in returns for the investor.[563] The result is an inferior performance of the SRI-screened portfolio, relative to a SRI-unscreened portfolio.

The so-called underperformance-effect is assumed to occur for any type of SRI-screened investment alternative.[564] Examples are SRI funds and SRI market indices, whose managers apply similar screens when selecting the securities and thus, restrict the investment universe by only considering a limited set of securities that meet the fund's or manager's investment criteria.

---

[558] See Fisher (1975), p. 74 and Markowitz (1952), p. 77.
[559] See Jobson & Korkie (1980), p. 544 and Mayo (2013), p. 129.
[560] See Markowitz (1952), p. 89 and (1999), p. 8.
[561] See section 4.4.
[562] See Goldberg (2008), p. 54, Renneboog et al. (2008a), p. 1728 and Schwartz (2003), p. 197.
[563] See Bello (2005), p. 42 and Renneboog et al. (2008a), p. 1734.
[564] See Fowler & Hope (2007), p. 250 and Schroder (2003), p. 9.

Investing into SRI and optimizing one's portfolio is not necessarily a contradiction in itself. Proponents of the so-called outperformance-effect of SRI-screened alternatives compared to SRI-unscreened or conventional investments argue that the detailed screening process allows investors to get access to value-relevant information they otherwise would not be able to obtain.[565] This information helps investors to identify and select securities that generate higher expected returns or have a lower risk-profile than conventional investment alternatives.[566] Thus, advocates of the SRI movement argue that it makes good sense for investors and fund managers to include both financial and non-financial criteria in the portfolio selection process. A sound performance on both criteria indicates high managerial quality, which not only translates into lower worker turnover rates and litigation frequency, but also favorable long-term financial performance of those companies.[567] Consequently, companies with a high ESG rating should have a comparative advantage over less socially responsible companies. This advantage should lead to a superior performance of the SRI fund portfolios that consist of socially responsible companies relative to conventional fund portfolios.[568]

Considering the debate introduced in section 4.4, as well as the theoretical discussion presented in this section, the hypotheses on the performance of SRI-screened relative to SRI-unscreened investment alternatives state that there is a significant difference in the performance of SRI-screened and SRI-unscreened investments alternatives. Specifically, the following three hypotheses are tested:

- H1a: There is a significant difference in the performance of *SRI indices* compared to *conventional benchmark indices*.

- H1b: There is a significant difference in the performance of *SRI funds* compared to *conventional benchmark indices*.

- H1c: There is a significant difference in the performance of *SRI funds* compared to *SRI benchmark indices*.

The alternative hypotheses state that there is no significant effect and thus, applying SRI screens in the portfolio selection process has neither a positive nor a negative impact on the expected return of the SRI-screened investment portfolio.

---

[565] See Haigh & Hazelton (2004), p. 65, Heal (2005), p. 401 and Renneboog et al. (2008b), p. 305.
[566] See Renneboog et al. (2008a), p. 1735 and (2008b), p. 305.
[567] See Goldreyer & Diltz (1999), p. 23.
[568] See Cortez et al. (2009), p. 573.

5.1.2   Performance across different SRI fund categories

Studies on the long-term performance of financial securities show that equity securities on the one hand generate higher returns than any other asset classes, but on the other hand, are also considerably more risky than other securities such as fixed income investments.[569] Portfolio theory offers a theoretical explanation why returns and risk associated with equity securities are higher than for other securities: Investors are assumed to be risk-averse and expect to be compensated for bearing the risk that is associated with an investment security. The higher the risk associated with a security, the higher the return investors demand for bearing this risk.[570]

When investing into equity securities such as common or preferred stocks, investors become shareholders of the company they invest in. As partial owners, investors have the possibility to participate in any future earnings the company generates, but also face the risk of suffering from losses the company may face during a fiscal year.[571] In case a company generates positive earnings, these earnings may be distributed as dividends to the shareholders of the company. Although the dividends are usually paid on an ongoing basis, a company is not obliged to pay dividends to its shareholders. The management of the company can also retain some or all of the earnings in order to invest them into ongoing business operations, new projects or use the earnings to repay the company's debt obligations.[572] Thus, investors not only face the risk of losses when investing into equity securities, but also have to accept management's decision to retain earnings and to not (fully) distribute them to the company's shareholders.

Unlike equity instruments, fixed income securities such as corporate or government bonds usually have a predefined payment schedule and a clearly determined maturity date: When raising capital by using fixed income securities, the amount and date for the interest (coupon) payments

---

[569]   For example, the average annual return for small stocks in the U.S. was 18.7% and the return for the S&P 500, a measure for equity securities, was 11.7% for the period January 1926 – December 2011; the standard deviation was 39.2% and 20.3%, respectively. For fixed income securities, the average annual return on a triple-A rated corporate bond was only 6.6% with a standard deviation of 7.0%. Treasury bills had the lowest return of 3.6% and a standard deviation of 3.1% for the same period. See Berk & DeMarzo (2014), pp. 322–324.

[570]   See section 4.1 for more details on investor risk aversion.

[571]   See section 3.2.3.1 as well as Elton et al. (2009), p. 17.

[572]   The amount of money that is retained or paid-out as dividends is determined by the dividend or payout policy that is set by the board of directors of a company. See Baker (2009), p. 3 and Berk & DeMarzo (2014), p. 585.

and the date for the repayment of the initially borrowed capital (principal) are already determined when the security is first issued.[573] Debt holders, who invest in fixed income securities of a company, are preferred over equity holders in terms of payment priority. In case of positive earnings, claims of debt holders are served first and only the remaining capital can either be distributed to equity holders as dividends or retained within the company. [574] The superiority of debt holders over equity holders also holds when a company files for bankruptcy: Claims made by equity holders are residual claims and served only after all claims made by debt holders are paid.[575] Thus, the risk associated with fixed income securities is considerably lower than for equity securities. While equity holders can unlimitedly participate in the earnings paid by the company,[576] debt holders can only expect to get the interest and principal payments initially agreed upon. The lower risk level of fixed income securities also implies that the risk premium demanded by investors when investing into these securities and thus, the expected returns, are lower for fixed income securities than for equity securities.[577]

Blended capital market instruments, such as balanced funds, invest in both, equity and fixed income securities. The weight assigned to each of those securities varies from fund to fund and depends on the fund's investment objectives and style.[578] As balanced funds combine equity and fixed income securities in one portfolio, the risk and return characteristics are expected to be somewhere in between those of equity and fixed income funds.[579] Following this discussion, equity securities are assumed to be the most volatile and risky investment instruments. Moreover, the long-term return of these securities is also assumed to be higher than for other instruments such as fixed income securities, which typically have lower levels of risk. Therefore, equity funds are expected to generate the highest returns followed by balanced funds and fixed funds.[580]

---

[573] See section 3.2.3.2 as well as Elton et al. (2009), p. 14.
[574] See Elton et al. (2009), p. 17.
[575] See Jones (2009), p. 38.
[576] Dividends are distributed proportional to the number of shares an equity holder owns. The board defines the amount per share that is to be paid out. See Berk & DeMarzo (2014), p. 585.
[577] See Berk & DeMarzo (2014), pp. 322–324.
[578] See section 3.2.3.3 as well as Haslem (2009), p. 177.
[579] See Horowitz (1966), p. 487.
[580] See Brealey et al. (2014), p. 162, Fama & French (1989), p. 28 and (1993), p. 14, Francis (1993), p. 19 and Jones (2009), p. 148.

For the purpose of this thesis, the aforementioned return sequence is tested within the context of SRI. Thus, the following hypotheses address the question if there is a significant performance difference between SRI funds of different categories, i.e. SRI equity, balanced and fixed income funds:

- H2a: The *performance of SRI equity funds* is *superior* to the performance of SRI funds in other categories.

- H2b: *SRI fixed income funds underperform* other categories of SRI funds.

The alternative hypotheses states that there is no significant difference between the returns generated by the different fund categories and SRI equity funds show similar performances as SRI balanced and fixed income funds do.

5.1.3 SRI fund performance over time

The efficient market hypothesis states that the price for a security fully reflects all available information, e.g. all information that investors might need to take the decision on whether or not to invest in a security.[581] Moreover, the price also includes all future cash flows that are expected to be generated by the security.[582] Fama (1970, 1991) differentiates three forms of market efficiency:[583]

- The weak form efficiency
- The semi-strong form efficiency and
- The strong form efficiency

The weak form efficiency implies that security returns are not predictable and it should not be possible for investors generate abnormal profits by implementing trading strategies that are based on the past price performance of a security, e.g. by selling past winners and buying past losers or trading on momentum.[584] The semi-strong form efficiency states that it should not be possible to generate abnormal returns by trading on publicly available information for a security

---

[581] See Fama (1970), p. 383 and (1991), p. 1575, Jordan (1983), p. 1325 and Malkiel (2003), p. 59.
[582] See Berk & DeMarzo (2014), p. 295.
[583] See Fama (1970), p. 383 and (1991), p. 1575.
[584] See Fama (1991), p. 1576.

such as earnings announcements or analyst recommendations.[585] The underlying belief is that whenever new information on a security is available, this information is spread among investors very rapidly and immediately is reflected in the price of the security.[586] Finally, the strong form efficiency implies that it should not even be possible to generate abnormal returns by trading on private or insider information, which is not directly reflected in market prices of a security, but might still be of high relevance for investors' decision making.[587]

Irrespective which form of market efficiency truly holds, the notion of market efficiency is based on the assumptions that

- There are no transaction cost when securities are traded,
- All market participants have access to the same information at any time and
- Prices for securities only change when new information is available; the adjustment takes place immediately and the information is priced in correctly.[588]

Consequently, in efficient markets, security prices are assumed to fully reflect all available information.[589] In other words, security prices are expected to be in equilibrium at any time and it is neither possible for investors to identify securities that are constantly or temporarily mispriced and outperform the market by actively managing their investment portfolios.[590] Moreover, market efficiency also implies that even uninformed investors should be able to generate competitive returns when following passive investment strategies and investing into market portfolios such as equity or fixed income indices that are assumed to be fully diversified portfolios.[591] However, it should not be possible for investors of any kind – private, public or institutional – to identify securities such as funds that constantly perform better than the market.

---

[585] See Fama (1970), p. 383 and (1991), p. 1576.
[586] See Fama (1991), p. 1576 and Malkiel (2003), p. 59.
[587] See Fama (1991), p. 1576 and Jordan (1983), p. 1325.
[588] See Fama (1970), p. 387. Fama (1970), p. 387 also emphasizes that these assumptions are sufficient, but not necessary conditions for market efficiency. Thus, a market can still be efficient even if the given conditions are not fully met on real capital markets.
[589] See Elton et al. (2009), p. 398 and Fama (1970), p. 387.
[590] See Mayo (2013), p. 108.
[591] See section 4.2.2.2 for the definition of the market portfolio as well as Malkiel (2003), p. 59.

Jegadeesh and Titman (1993) empirically test the market efficiency hypothesis and show that it seems to be possible for investors to generate abnormal returns by implementing trading strategies that buy stocks that have performed well, i.e. winner stocks, and sell stocks that have performed poor, i.e. loser stocks, in the 6 to 12 months prior to the portfolio formation date. However, the effect only lasts for a holding period of 3 to 12 months and diminishes in the two years after the portfolio has been set up.[592] A similar result has been documented by Carhart (1997), who shows that the top-performing mutual funds in the sample generate returns that are as high as the investment expenses charged by the fund. However, most of the funds are not able to earn back their investment expenses and thus, underperform against the market.[593] Moreover, although there are funds that outperform the market in one year and the following year, the effect disappears in the years thereafter.[594] Thus, although there might be funds that temporarily outperform the market, past outperformance of a fund against the market does not provide evidence for a future (out- or under-) performance of the fund. This finding is in line with the weak form market efficiency: Any difference in security prices or returns does not persist over time and fund managers are not able to follow investment strategies with which they can consistently beat the market.[595]

Although there are a number of researchers that question the validity of the efficient market hypothesis,[596] it is still one of the fundamental principles of financial theory today and used as basic assumption in order to derive the third group of hypotheses that is to be tested in the empirical study. Specifically, using the evidence provided by Jegadeesh and Titman (1993) and Carhart (1997), the aim of the third group of hypotheses is to analyze if there is a change in SRI fund performance over time. In order to test these hypotheses, the investment period will be split up into two sub-periods. The first period comprises the years before (January 2003 to December 2007) and the second period the years during and after the global financial crisis (January 2008 to December 2013). The division into these two periods is motivated by the fact that empirical research shows that there is a difference in the relative performance of SRI funds in

---

[592] See Jegadeesh & Titman (1993), p. 89. Trading strategies that are based on the idea of buying winner stocks and selling loser stocks are called momentum strategies. See Berk & DeMarzo (2014), p. 458).

[593] See Carhart (1997), p. 80.

[594] See Carhart (1997), p. 81.

[595] See Sharpe (1966), p. 121.

[596] See Grinblatt & Titman (1992), Malkiel (2003) as well as Sharpe (1966) for an overview of the arguments against the validity of the market efficiency hypothesis.

non-crisis and crisis periods.[597] The entire observation period in this study ranges from January 2003 to December 2013. According to the information provided by the National Bureau of Economic Research, this observation period comprises one period of recession (December 2007 to June 2009) that at the same time also marks the beginning and end of the global financial crisis.[598] Thus, for the purpose of the study, the global financial crisis is used as a factor to determine the two sub-periods needed in order to assess if there are changes in relative SRI fund performance over time.

According to the efficient market hypothesis, it should not be able to document any differences in the relative performance of SRI funds over time. Instead, SRI funds that are built on active trading strategies are assumed to underperform their market benchmarks during any given period – not matter if the period under consideration is just a sub-set of the entire period or if the performance is assessed over the entire period. Moreover, even if SRI funds are able to outperform their benchmarks in sub-periods, it is assumed that the funds underperform their benchmark indices over the entire observation period. To conclude, the following hypotheses are tested:

- H3a: SRI funds that *outperform their SRI benchmarks* in the first sub-period will underperform the benchmarks in the second sub-period.

- H3b: SRI funds that *outperform their conventional benchmarks* in the first sub-period will underperform the benchmarks in the second period.

- H3c: SRI funds that *underperform their SRI benchmarks* during the entire observation period will also underperform the benchmark in sub-periods.

- H3d: SRI funds that *underperform their conventional benchmarks* during the entire observation period will also underperform in sub-periods.

The alternative hypothesis states that outperformance of SRI fund persists over time and underperformance is an effect that does not occur for SRI funds.

---

[597] See Areal et al. (2015), p. 397, Becchetti et al. (2015), p. 2543, Leite & Cortez (2015), p. 136) and Nofsinger & Varma (2014), p. 185.

[598] According to the National Bureau of Economic Research the economic activity peaked in December 2007 and declined in the months thereafter. Thus, January 2008 is marked as the end of the expansion period that began after the burst of the technology bubble in 2001 and the beginning of the recession around the global financial crisis. See National Bureau of Economic Research (2010) and Nofsinger & Varma (2014), p. 185.

Figure 15 summarizes the derived hypotheses. Prior to presenting the results obtained when testing the hypotheses, the following sections first introduce the methodology applied and the data set used in the empirical analysis.

Group of hypotheses	Description of hypotheses	
The performance of SRI screened relative to socially unscreened investments alternatives	H1a:	There is a significant difference in the performance of *SRI indices* compared to *conventional benchmark indices*.
	H1b:	There is a significant difference in the performance of *SRI funds* compared to *conventional benchmark indices*.
	H1c:	There is a significant difference in the performance of *SRI funds* compared to *SRI benchmark indices*.
The performance of SRI funds across different categories	H2a:	The *performance of SRI equity funds* is *superior* to the performance of SRI funds in other categories.
	H2b:	*SRI fixed income funds underperform* other categories of SRI funds.
The performance of SRI funds over time	H3a:	SRI funds that *outperform their SRI benchmarks* in the first sub-period will underperform the benchmarks in the second sub-period.
	H3b:	SRI funds that *outperform their conventional benchmarks* in the first sub-period will underperform the benchmarks in the second period.
	H3c:	SRI funds that *underperform their SRI benchmarks* during the entire observation period will also underperform the benchmark in sub-periods.
	H3d:	SRI funds that *underperform their conventional benchmarks* during the entire observation period will also underperform in sub-periods.

Figure 15: Hypotheses to be tested
Source: Own illustration

5.2 Methodology

5.2.1 General description of the empirical analysis

The main objective of this thesis is to provide an empirical answer to the question if it is possible for investors to be doing good while doing well or if investors have to sacrifice parts of their financial return when investing into SRI funds. In order to answer this question, a number of hypotheses have been derived in the previous section.[599] The hypotheses are tested empirically

---

[599] See section 5.1.

by running single- and multi-factor regression models on a sample of SRI funds established in Europe.[600] Specifically, the empirical study presented in this thesis investigates the performance of investment portfolios consisting of SRI equity, balanced and fixed income funds and compares the performance of these portfolios to that of benchmark indices in each category. The SRI funds included in the analysis are funds that are established in the four biggest markets within Europe: France, the UK, the Netherlands and Germany. Together, these markets account for about two thirds of the entire market for SRI in Europe as measured by total AuM.[601]

Although the funds are established locally, their performance is evaluated against European benchmark indices. SRI funds are assigned to a portfolio based on the category to which the respective fund belongs to and the country in which it has been established. Thus, SRI equity, balanced and fixed income portfolios exist for funds in all four countries (France, the UK, the Netherlands and Germany). However, the performance of each SRI fund portfolio is compared to the performance of European instead of local benchmark indices. Moreover, excess returns for both, the fund portfolios and the benchmark indices are determined using the Euro Interbank Offered Rate (Euribor) as a proxy for the interest rate.[602] Consequently, the empirical study is conducted by taking on a European rather than a local investor's perspective. The reason for this decision is twofold: First, political decisions such as the introduction of a common currency foster the integration of European financial markets. Markets no longer ought to be analyzed in isolation and merely taking local conditions into consideration. Second, and even more substantial, the funds in the sample are established in one of the four countries, but follow a European or even global investment strategy and thus, do not only invest locally. Instead, as the following analysis shows, the investment portfolio of the funds consists of companies located in different countries within Europe and sometimes even globally.

An analysis of the countries in which SRI funds that are established in France have invested in shows that 48 out of 186 SRI funds (26%) invest a higher share into companies that are based outside of France than into companies that are based within France. For Germany and the UK,

---

[600] Parts of the empirical study, especially the results obtained for SRI funds in Germany, have been summarized in an article ("*The performance of socially responsible investment funds in Germany*") that will be submitted for reviewing to the journal *Business Ethics: A European Review*.

[601] See EUROSIF (2014), p. 21 and section 3.2.1.

[602] The Euribor is an average interest rate at which European banks lend and borrow money from one another. It is one of the most important reference rates in the European markets and applied as a proxy for the risk-free interest rates in a number of previous studies on the performance of SRI alternatives in Europe, e.g. Dietze et al. (2009), van de Velde (2005) Wan-Ni (2012).

the share is even higher: 43 out of 70 SRI funds (61%) and 32 out of 67 SRI funds (48%) invest a higher proportion into companies that are based in international rather than in domestic markets. Moreover, 23 out of the 186 SRI funds in France (12%), 40 out of the 70 German SRI funds (57%) and 46 out of the 67 SRI funds in the UK (69%) follow global investment strategies, meaning that they invest heavily into companies that are located outside of Europe. Figure 16 and Figure 17 graphically illustrate investment strategies applied by the SRI funds.[603]

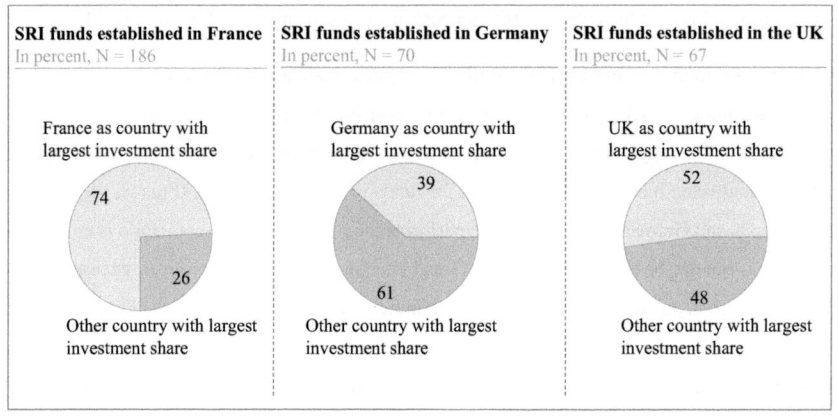

SRI funds established in France In percent, N = 186	SRI funds established in Germany In percent, N = 70	SRI funds established in the UK In percent, N = 67
France as country with largest investment share: 74 Other country with largest investment share: 26	Germany as country with largest investment share: 39 Other country with largest investment share: 61	UK as country with largest investment share: 52 Other country with largest investment share: 48

Figure 16: SRI funds with domestic or international investment strategies
Source: Own illustration

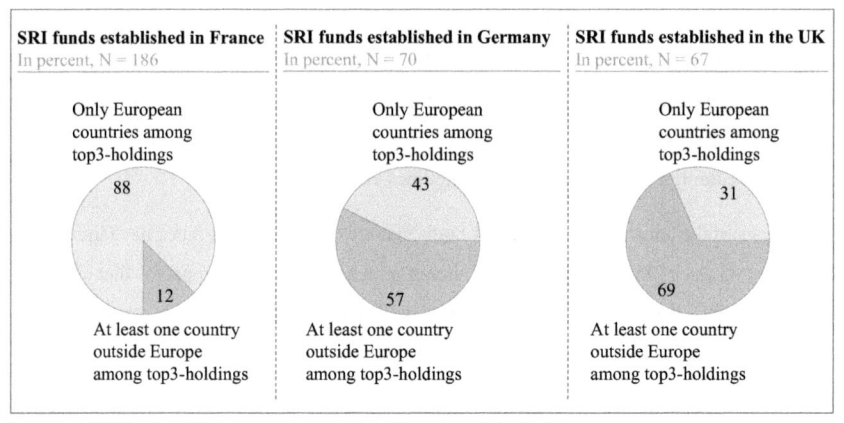

SRI funds established in France In percent, N = 186	SRI funds established in Germany In percent, N = 70	SRI funds established in the UK In percent, N = 67
Only European countries among top3-holdings: 88 At least one country outside Europe among top3-holdings: 12	Only European countries among top3-holdings: 43 At least one country outside Europe among top3-holdings: 57	Only European countries among top3-holdings: 31 At least one country outside Europe among top3-holdings: 69

Figure 17: SRI funds with Europe-only and global investment strategies
Source: Own illustration

---

[603] For SRI funds established in the Netherlands, no comprehensive investment data was available. Thus, the investment strategies of these funds cannot be displayed in Figure 16 and Figure 17.

Based on the strategies displayed in Figure 16 and Figure 17 one could argue that the performance of the SRI funds should be assessed relative to global market portfolios and consequently, the performance of global benchmark indices. However, although the majority of the SRI funds established in Germany and the UK invest into companies outside of Europe, the share of these global investments is below 50% for almost all funds. Thus, the investment is spread across companies from different countries, but most of the investments are made into domestic or European countries. Consequently, only European indices are used as benchmarks in the empirical analysis.[604]

In order to assess the relative performance of the SRI funds and test the hypotheses derived in section 5.1, four different types of analyses are conducted: First, the performance of SRI funds is evaluated relative to the performance of conventional benchmark indices of each fund category. Second, the SRI funds' performance is compared to that of SRI benchmark indices in each category. These two analyses provide an empirical answer to the question if there are differences in the performance of SRI-screened and SRI-unscreened investment alternatives (testing hypotheses H1a, H1b and H1c).[605] Third, differences between the performances of funds in the three categories – SRI equity, balanced or fixed income – are analyzed (testing hypotheses H2a and H2b).[606] Finally, the study investigates whether there are changes in relative performance of SRI funds over time. This is achieved by splitting the observation period into two sub-periods (testing hypotheses H3a, H3b, H3c and H3d).[607]

In all cases, performance is assessed using the time series of risk-adjusted monthly returns for equally weighted portfolios of SRI equity, balanced or fixed income funds as well as the returns for the respective conventional and SRI benchmark indices.[608] The risk-adjusted returns used as performance measures, in turn, are calculated by running single- and multi-factor regression models that are introduced in the following section.

---

[604] This approach is in line with other studies on fund performance that also use European benchmark indices when analyzing the performance of European funds (see, for example, Banegas et al. (2013), p. 707, Cortez et al. (2009), p. 578, Foo & Witkowska (2015), p. 4 and Leite & Cortez (2014), p. 255). For more details on the specific benchmarks used in the analyses of this thesis, please refer to section 5.3.2.

[605] See section 5.1.1.

[606] See section 5.1.2.

[607] See section 5.1.3.

[608] The performances of equally weighted fund portfolios are compared to that of value weighted indices. As the individual funds are value weighted, no additional weighting is conducted when building the portfolios. Moreover, the results for value weighted and equally weighted fund portfolios are similar. See section 4.2.1 and 6.1.1.

5.2.2 Description of the single-factor regression models

In the single-factor model, fund performance is evaluated by determining the difference between the excess return of the fund portfolio and the excess return on a single-factor benchmark, estimated by a linear regression. For equity funds, this difference is known as Jensen's alpha (1968).[609] Formally, the following regression model is estimated:[610]

$$r_{p,t} - r_{f,t} = \alpha_p + \beta_m(r_{m,t} - r_{f,t}) + \varepsilon_{p,t} \qquad (26)$$

where

$r_{p,t}$	=	the return on an equally weighted portfolio of funds in month t
$r_{f,t}$	=	the return on the European risk-free rate in month t
$r_{m,t}$	=	the return of the European market index in month t
α_p	=	the 1-factor abnormal return of the portfolio
β_m	=	a proxy for the market risk exposure of the portfolio and
$\varepsilon_{p,t}$	=	the idiosyncratic return or error term.

The monthly returns for each fund portfolio are calculated as continuously compounded net returns (free of management fees, but gross of lead fees). Excess returns $(r_{p,t} - r_{f,t})$ are calculated as the difference between a portfolio's monthly returns and the return on the 3-month Euribor, which is used as a proxy for the risk-free rate for funds in all three categories. When estimating the alpha and beta coefficient in the single factor regression analysis, a separate market proxy for each category is used: For equity and fixed income funds, the returns on the Euro Stoxx Index and FTSE Euro Corporate Index are used as proxies in the conventional index models.[611] The Euro Stoxx Sustainability Index and the FTSE4Good Index are used as proxies in the SRI index models.[612] The market proxy for balanced funds is a weighted average between

---

[609] See also section 4.3.2.

[610] A similar model has been applied by e.g., Cortez et al. (2009), p. 576, Cumby & Glen (1990), p. 503, Goldreyer & Diltz (1999), p. 26, Grinblatt & Titman (1989), p. 395, Mallin et al. (1995), p. 489, McDonald (1974), p. 313, who also analyzed the performance of (SRI) mutual funds. Although multi-factor models provide more detailed information on the factors that influence the performance of the fund portfolios, a survey conducted by Amenc et al. (2011), p. 47 shows that about 27% of the respondents use single-factor models to assess fund performance and 21% use multi-factor models.

[611] See https://www.stoxx.com/index-details?symbol=SXXE for details on the Euro Stoxx Index and http://www.ftse.com/products/indices/Global-Bonds for details on the FTSE Euro Corporate Index.

[612] See https://www.stoxx.com/index-details?symbol=SUTE sx5e for details on the Euro Stoxx Sustainability Index and http://www.ftse.com/products/indices/FTSE4Good for details on the FTSE4Good Index.

the proxy for the equity market (57.2%) and the fixed income market (42.8%).[613] Significantly positive (negative) alphas indicate superior (inferior) performance of the SRI funds relative to the respective market.[614] The beta coefficients indicate the funds' sensitivity to changes in the market proxy.

5.2.3 Description of the multi-factor regression models

In addition to the single-factor regression models, multi-factor models used in more recent empirical studies on SRI fund performance also are applied to assess SRI fund performance. The basic model is estimated as follows:[615]

$$r_{p,t} - r_{f,t} = \alpha_p + \beta_m(r_{m,t} - r_{f,t}) + \sum_{j=1}^{K} \beta_j\, r_{j,t} + \varepsilon_{p,t} \qquad (27)$$

where

$\beta_j =$ the factor loading for each factor included in the model
$r_{j,t}$ = the return on each factor in month t
$K =$ the number of factors in the model
$\varepsilon_{p,t}$ = the idiosyncratic return or error term and
$r_{p,t}, r_{f,t}, r_{m,t}, \alpha_p$ and β_m are the same as in the single-factor regression model.

While the single-factor model is based on the assumption that there is a linear relationship between the excess return of the fund portfolio and the excess return on the market index, the multi-factor model assumes that additional factors are needed to explain the variation in the excess return of the fund portfolios.[616] As the number of factors depends on the fund category the portfolio consists of, a separate regression model is estimated for each category of SRI fund portfolios.

---

[613] See section 5.3.2 for a detailed description of the benchmark indices used in the regression models and Appendix III for weights used to calculate the market proxy for balanced funds.
[614] Please refer to section 4.3.2.3 for details on the possible interpretation of positive or negative alphas.
[615] See section 4.3.4.1 as well as Elton et al. (1995), p. 1237.
[616] See Blake et al. (1993), p. 375 and Derwall & Koedijk (2009), p. 219.

5.2.3.1 SRI equity funds

For equity markets, the multi-factor model applied is similar to the Fama and French (1993, 1996) three-factor model and estimated as follows:[617]

$$r_{e,t} - r_{f,t} = \alpha_e + \beta_{EQU}(r_{EQU,t} - r_{f,t}) + \beta_{SMB}r_{SMB,t} + \beta_{HML}r_{HML,t} + \varepsilon_{e,t} \qquad (28)$$

where

$r_{e,t}$	= the realized return of the SRI equity fund portfolio in month t
$r_{f,t}$	= the return on the risk-free rate in month t
α_e	= the abnormal return generated by the SRI equity fund portfolio
$r_{EQU,t}$	= the return on the equity market index in month t
$r_{SMB,t}$	= the return on the size factor in month t
$r_{HML,t}$	= the return on the book-to-market factor in month t
β_{EQU}, β_{SMB} and β_{HML}	= the factor loadings on the three factors and
$\varepsilon_{e,t}$	= the idiosyncratic return or error term.

In addition to the excess return on the market portfolio, the three-factor regression model applied for SRI equity funds also considers the return on the small-minus-big portfolio and the return on the high-minus-low portfolio.[618] The three-factor model has already been applied in numerous studies on SRI fund performance.[619] Therefore, it is considered to be a valid model to be used in the empirical part of this thesis.

5.2.3.2 SRI balanced funds

The model used for balanced funds is based on the study published by Derwall and Koedijk (2009), who examine the performance of SRI balanced and fixed income funds:[620]

$$r_{b,t} - r_{f,t} = \alpha_b + \beta_{FIX}(r_{FIX,t} - r_{f,t}) + \beta_{DEF}r_{DEF,t} + \beta_{EQU}(r_{EQU,t} - r_{f,t}) + \varepsilon_{b,t} \qquad (29)$$

where

$r_{b,t}$	= the realized return of the SRI balanced fund portfolio in month t

---

[617] See section 4.3.4.2 as well as Fama & French (1993, p. 19) and (1996), p. 55.

[618] See section 4.3.4.2.

[619] See, for example, Bauer et al. (2005) and (2006), Betker & Sheehan (2013), p. 351, Curcio et al. (2003), p. 81, Cuthbertson & Nitzsche (2013), p. 89, Le Sourd (2010), Otten & Bams (2004), p. 204 and Renneboog et al. (2008b).

[620] See Derwall & Koedijk (2009), p. 220.

$r_{f,t}$ = the return on the risk-free rate in month t
α_b = the three-factor abnormal return of the balanced fund portfolio
$r_{FIX,t}$ = the return on the fixed income market index in month t
$r_{DEF,t}$ = the return on the default risk compensation factor in month t
$r_{EQU,t}$ = the return on the equity market index and in month t
β_{FIX}, β_{DEF} and β_{EQU} = the factor loadings on the three factors and
$\varepsilon_{b,t}$ = the idiosyncratic return or error term.

The three-factor regression model applied for balanced funds accounts for the fact that balanced funds not only invest in equity but also fixed income securities.[621] In fact, these funds, on average, invest half of their assets into equity securities and the other half into fixed income securities.[622]

Thus, the three factor model applied to assess the performance of SRI balanced fund portfolios not only considers the portfolio's sensitivity to equity market index, but also its exposure to the fixed income market.[623] In addition, the default factor captures the default risk premium investors demand as compensation for the expected loss from default that is associated with fixed income securities.[624]

5.2.3.3 SRI fixed income funds

The model used to examine the performance of SRI fixed income funds is similar to the models that have been introduced by Fama and French (1993) and Elton et al. (1995):[625]

$$r_{i,t} - r_{f,t} = \alpha_i + \beta_{FIX}(r_{FIX,t} - r_{f,t}) + \beta_{DEF}r_{DEF,t} + \beta_{TERM}r_{TERM,t} + \varepsilon_{i,t} \quad (30)$$

where

$r_{i,t}$ = the realized return of the SRI fixed income fund portfolio
$r_{f,t}$ = the return on the risk-free rate in month t

---

[621] See Geczy et al. (2005), p. 10.
[622] See Benartzi & Thaler (2001), p. 82 as well as Huberman & Jiang (2006), p. 768. Other researchers such as Haslem (2009), p. 177 argue that the standard split between equity and fixed income securities in balanced funds is 60-70% equity and 30-40% fixed income. See Gitman et al. (2010), p. 446 as well as section 3.2.3. The balanced funds included in the data set of the study in this thesis invest about 57% into equity securities and 43% into fixed income securities (see section 5.3.2).
[623] See Comer et al. (2009), p. 487.
[624] See Elton et al. (2001), p. 247.
[625] See Elton et al. (1995), p. 1237 and Fama & French (1993), p. 30.

α_i = the three-factor abnormal return of the fixed income portfolio
$r_{FIX,t}$ = the return on the fixed income market index in month t
$r_{DEF,t}$ = the return on a corporate minus a government bond index
$r_{TERM,t}$ = the return on a long-term minus a short-term government bond index
β_{FIX}, β_{DEF} and β_{TERM} = the factor loadings on the three factors and
$\varepsilon_{e,t}$ = the idiosyncratic return or error term.

While the original model developed by Fama and French (1993) contains five-factors, the empirical test shows that only the market risk factor and the term premium and the default premium are the dominant factors that explain variations in returns of fixed income securities.[626]

Similar to the regression models applied for equity and balanced funds, the market risk factor is approximated by a fixed income market index. The default factor is the additional compensation demanded by investors to cover for the default risk of (corporate) fixed income securities. The term spread accounts for changes in interest rates caused by different maturities of the fixed income securities.[627] While the default risk premium is calculated as the difference in the return of a corporate bond index and a government bond index, the term premium is calculated as the difference in the return of a long-term and a short-term government bond index.[628]

The alphas and betas are constrained to be constant in all models and during the entire sample period. This assumption is commonly made in studies on relative SRI fund performance.[629]

5.3 Data set

5.3.1 Sample of SRI funds

The data set used in the empirical analysis consists of SRI funds established in four European countries: The UK, France, the Netherlands and Germany. The UK is the biggest market for SRI in Europe. Measured by total AuM, SRI in the UK has a total market size of EUR 1,973 billion, followed by the SRI market in France with a market size of EUR 1,729 billion, the

---

[626] See Fama & French (1993), pp. 18, 40 and 52 as well as section 4.3.4.3.
[627] See Elton et al. (1995), p. 1233, Fama & French (1991), p. 1584 and Ilmanen (1995), p. 481.
[628] See Equation (30).
[629] See Cortez et al. (2009), p. 576, Fama & French (1993), p. 43, Ilmanen (1995), p. 497, Kreander et al. (2005), p. 1477 and Silva et al. (2003), p. 203.

Netherlands with a market size of EUR 1,245 billion and Germany with a market size of EUR 899 billion.[630] Together, these markets account for about two-thirds of the market for SRI within Europe. The list of SRI funds in those four countries is obtained from Morningstar and Vigeo[631] and entails a total of 477 SRI equity, balanced and fixed income funds (see Figure 18).

- Neither are listed as equity, nor fixed income or balanced funds, but labeled as "other" funds in the original sample of funds,
- Do not have an International Securities Identification Number (ISIN),[632]
- Are funds of funds, feeder funds or fed by other funds,
- Are not classified as unit trusts,
- Are established after January 01, 2011, in order to have at least two years of performance data for the respective funds,
- Funds for which Datastream does not have data prior to 2011 and
- Funds, whose ISIN appeared twice in the initial list.

Figure 18 shows the adjustments that have been made in order to derive the final sample of 361 SRI funds across all three fund categories in Europe.

The number of SRI funds in each country is displayed in Figure 19 : In total, there are 186 SRI funds established and domiciled in France, 70 SRI funds in Germany, 67 in the UK and 38 in the Netherlands.[633] Thus, France is the second biggest market according to AuM, but the number of SRI funds that have been established in France is more than twice as big as has the number of funds that have been established the UK, the leading market for SRI according to AuM. Germany only ranks number four in terms of market size, but has the second largest number of funds of all markets.

---

[630] See EUROSIF (2014), p. 21 as well as section 2.3.
[631] Vigeo is a rating company that specializes in the assessment of companies' and organizations' performance on ESG issues (http://www.vigeo.com).
[632] ISIN is a uniform identification number assigned to financial securities in order to facilitate trading procedures on capital markets (http://www.isin.org/).
[633] Please refer to Appendix II for a detailed list of all funds per country included in the analysis.

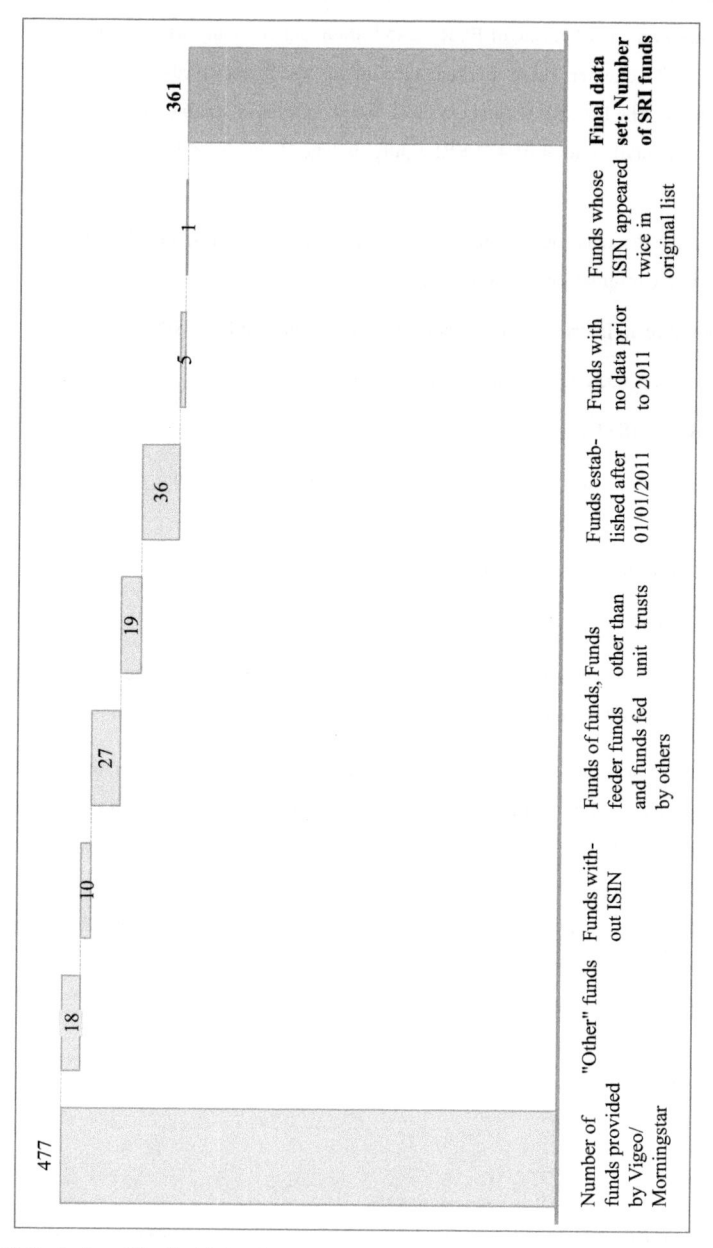

Figure 18: Derivation of the final data set
Source: Own illustration. The original list provided by Morningstar and Vigeo has been adjusted by funds that:

Differences in the ranking of the four markets relative to their market volume and number of funds can be explained by two factors: First, the share of AuM that is managed by the funds and second, the average size of the funds. In France and Germany, about 70-75% of the SRI AuM are managed by institutional investors or funds, while private investors and single mandates only account for about one quarter of the total SRI market.[634] In contrast to this, only 12% of SRI AuM in the Netherlands are invested in funds while the majority is invested via private investments or single mandated. The lower share of AuM that are invested via funds explains the fact that the total number of funds in the Netherlands is lower than it is in France and Germany.[635]

Figure 19: Number of SRI funds per country
Source: Own illustration

Another important explanation for the ranking differences is the fact the average fund size differs greatly between the four countries. Although France and Germany have the highest number of funds included in the sample (186 and 70, respectively), the average size of these funds is lower than the size of the funds in the UK and the Netherlands: While the average total net AuM for SRI funds is EUR 171 million in France and EUR 107 million in Germany, SRI funds in the Netherlands and the UK on average manage total net AuM of EUR 225 million and EUR

---

[634] See EUROSIF (2014), p. 43 for details on the French SRI market and p. 46 for details on the German SRI market.

[635] See EUROSIF (2014), p. 51. Data on the split of funds relative to single mandates is not available for the UK.

196 million, respectively.[636] Thus, although the number of SRI funds in France and Germany is relatively large, the funds manage a lower volume than the funds in the UK and the Netherlands.

To conclude, SRI funds play a dominant role on the market for SRI in France and Germany, although the average size of the funds established in these countries is smaller than the size of SRI funds in other countries such as the UK and the Netherlands. Conversely, SRI funds established in the UK and the Netherlands are bigger in size but the share of these funds relative to the total market size is lower than it is in France and Germany.

Figure 20 shows the split of the data set according to the investment category of the SRI funds (SRI equity, fixed income or balanced funds): The majority (59%) of the total funds are SRI equity funds, while SRI fixed income funds account for about one quarter (24%) and SRI balanced funds for 17% of the total funds in the sample. Thus, the share of SRI equity and balanced funds in the sample is slightly higher and the share of fixed income funds slightly lower than the shares obtained for the total number of SRI funds in Europe.[637] However, the deviations are less than 10% in each category and thus, the data set is considered to be a representative sample for the European SRI fund market.

The classification of SRI funds, according to the investment category they belong to, is also picked up in Table 12. This table shows a break-down of the SRI funds according to the year in which they have been established. Panel A of Table 12 shows that about two thirds of the funds included in the sample have been established between 2000 and 2009, while about 30% of the funds already existed before 2000. Interestingly, 142 SRI funds (about 40% of the total funds) have been established in the period between 2005 and 2009, the years before and during the global financial crisis.[638]

---

[636] See Appendix II.
[637] In 2013, the share of all SRI equity, balanced and fixed income funds established in Europe is 54%, 33% and 13%, respectively (see section 3.2.3).
[638] See section 5.1.3 and Leite & Cortez (2015), p. 134.

Composition of the SRI fund portfolio
In percent (100% = 361 funds)

- Balanced funds: 17
- Fixed income funds: 24
- Equity funds: 59

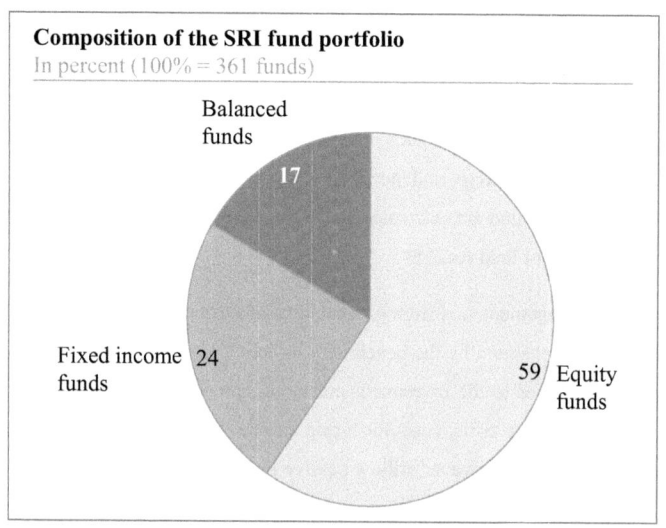

Figure 20: Breakdown of data set by SRI fund category
Source: Own illustration

Table 12: Number of SRI funds established per period

This table shows the total number of SRI funds in the sample established in France, the UK, the Netherlands and Germany. Panel A shows the total number of funds according to the five-year period in which the funds have been established. Panel B shows the number of funds established in each year for the period between 2005 and 2009, the years before and during the global financial crisis.

Panel A: Total number of SRI funds established in five different sub-periods

	prior to 1995	1995-1999	2000-2004	2005-2009	2010+	Total
Equity	31	35	58	85	5	214
Balanced	6	4	18	26	6	60
Fixed Income	21	8	20	31	7	87
Total	58	47	96	142	18	361

Panel B: Total number of SRI funds established between 2005-2009

	2005	2006	2007	2008	2009	Total
Total	14	19	46	27	36	142

Source: Own illustration

Panel B of Table 12 provides a yearly breakdown of this sub-period between 2005 and 2009. The table illustrates that the number of newly established SRI funds per year has reached its peak with 46 funds in 2007, the year in which the financial crisis started, dropped down to 27 newly established funds in 2008 and recovered to 36 funds in 2009. Thus, it seems that neither investors nor fund managers have strongly lost confidence in the investment alternative of SRI funds during the global financial crisis.

Data on the price performance of the SRI funds is obtained from Datastream, a database that provides information on the historical performance of multiple financial products. Monthly price data for each fund for the period from January 2003 to December 2013 are downloaded. To be included in the final data set, funds must have a complete time-series of monthly observations throughout the 3-year period between January 2011 and December 2013.[639] The monthly returns for each fund are calculated as continuously compounded returns net of management fees, but gross of load fees.[640]

The deduction of management fees from gross returns ensures comparability of the funds' returns and the returns generated by the benchmark indices:[641] As funds are actively managed, investors have to pay fees to the investment managing company in order to cover operating expenses such as marketing costs, costs for hiring and training fund managers or compliance cost.[642] Benchmark indices, however, follow passive investment strategies that do not involve such fees.[643] Thus, in the analysis, gross returns for the benchmark indices are compared to net returns for the SRI funds as only in this case both returns are net of management fees.[644] Excess returns are calculated for each SRI fund as the difference between the fund's return and the 3-month Euribor, the proxy for the risk-free rate.

5.3.2 Indices used to assess SRI fund performance

5.3.2.1 Market proxies

The performance of the SRI funds is assessed relative to the performance of both, conventional as well as SRI indices. The returns generated by those indices are used as a proxy for the return on the market portfolio, which – according to portfolio theory – is the portfolio that contains all

---

[639] The sample is not free of survivorship bias as no adjustment for funds that ceased to exist during the observation period has been made. For possible implications when survivorship bias is not accounted for in the analysis, please refer to the limitations of the study discussed in section 6.5.2.

[640] This is a common way of assessing fund return and applied by, e.g. Cortez et al. (2009), p. 577, Cuthbertson & Nitzsche (2013), p. 91, Dietze et al. (2009), p. 196, Henriksson (1984), p. 80, Hirt & Block (2012), p. 101, Ippolito (1989), p. 4, Jensen (1969), p. 221, Leite & Cortez (2014), p. 254, Schroder (2003), p. 10 and Silva et al. (2003), p. 213.

[641] See Ayadi & (2011), p. 384 and Fama & French (2010), p. 1915.

[642] See Gil-Bazo et al. (2010), p. 245, Malhotra & McLeod (1997), p. 182, Murthi et al. (1997), p. 411.

[643] See Pozen (2002), p. 61.

[644] See Jensen (1969), p. 225 for a detailed discussion why it is a feasible approach to compare gross benchmark returns to net fund returns when assessing fund performance.

risky securities in a market and thus, the most efficiently diversified portfolio.[645] As such a portfolio does not exist in reality, the performance of the market portfolio is approximated by using the return of substitutes such as benchmark indices.[646] However, these benchmark indices only include parts of the securities in the respective market and empirical research shows that the choice of the index has a significant effect on the correctness of the results obtained when analyzing the performance of a fund portfolio.[647]

In order to ensure that the performance of funds in different categories (equity, balanced and fixed income) is assessed relative to an appropriate benchmark, different indices for each category are used in the analysis. Moreover, the performance of the SRI funds is not only assessed relative to a conventional benchmark index, but also relative to a SRI benchmark index. As SRI funds and SRI indices restrict their investment universe by only considering a limited set of investment securities that meet their investment criteria and apply similar screening criteria when selecting their investment securities, one could expect that the application of similar investment criteria leads to a better performance of SRI indices in predicting SRI funds than of conventional indices.[648] Comparing the explanatory power of both indices (conventional as well as SRI) on the performance of SRI funds in the sample should provide insights which of the indices are a better proxy for the market portfolio and thus, more reliable when assessing the performance of the funds.

Regarding the specific indices used, the Euro Stoxx Index and Euro Stoxx Sustainability Index are used as benchmark indices for SRI equity funds. For SRI fixed income funds, the FTSE Euro Corporate Index and the FTSE4Good Europe Index are used as benchmark indices. As no market proxy for SRI balanced funds could have been identified, the market proxies used in the study are self-generated benchmark indices that consist of the index used for SRI equity funds and the index used as benchmark for the SRI fixed income funds. Thus, in order to assess the performance of SRI balanced funds relative to the SRI market index, the proxy used in the

---

[645] See section 4.2.2.2.
[646] See Francis & Kim (2013), p. 293.
[647] See Grinblatt & Titman (1994), p. 427. Roll (1980), p. 5 and (1981), p. 20 show that the application of an inappropriate benchmark negatively influences the applicability of the CAPM when assessing portfolio performance. Specifically, the author shows that an inappropriate benchmarks leads to a misleading result regarding the performance of the market portfolio and thus, an incorrect estimate of the portfolio's beta, which in turn is a measure of the portfolios risk exposure relative to the market portfolio. See also Reilly & Akthar (1995), p. 33.
[648] See Bauer et al. (2005), p. 1765 and (2007), p. 116, Cortez et al. (2009), p. 579 and Leite & Cortez (2014), p. 261.

analysis is a combination of the Euro Stoxx Sustainability Index and the FTSE4Good Europe Index. For the conventional market index, the proxy is a combination of the Euro Stoxx Index and the FTSE Euro Corporate Index. The weights assigned to each of the indices are equal to the average investment that the SRI balanced funds in the sample have in equity (57.2%) and fixed income (42.8%) securities.[649]

Similar to the SRI funds, all price information data for the indices used as market proxies are obtained from Datastream. Monthly returns for the indices are calculated as continuously compounded returns within the period January 2003 to December 2013. Excess returns for each index are determined using the 3-month Euribor. In the single-factor regression models the excess returns generated by the market proxies described in this section are used as the only independent variable when assessing SRI fund return.

5.3.2.2 Additional proxies

In addition to the market proxies, additional variables are needed to predict the SRI fund returns in the multi-factor models. The indices used as proxies to estimate the variables depend on the fund category that is analyzed: For SRI equity funds, the multi-factor regression model consists of a market factor, a size factor and a book-to-market factor.[650] While the market factor is approximated using the excess return on the Euro Stoxx Index, the size factor is calculated as the difference between the returns on a small cap index and a return on a large cap index and approximated by the return generated by the Euro Stoxx Small Index and the return generated by the Euro Stoxx 50 Index.[651] The Euro Stoxx Small Index is used as a proxy for companies with a small market capitalization as it contains stocks of the 200 companies with the lowest market capitalization among all 600 small, medium and large capitalization companies that are included in the main index, the Euro Stoxx 600 Index. Conversely, the Euro Stoxx 50 Index contains stocks of the 50 companies with the highest market capitalization in the Eurozone.[652] The book-to-market factor is calculated as the difference between the return of an index that

---

[649] See Appendix III for the average investment into equity and fixed income securities of the individual SRI balanced funds.

[650] See section 5.2.3.1.

[651] See https://www.stoxx.com/index-details?symbol=SCXE for details on the Euro Stoxx Small Index and https://www.stoxx.com/index-details?symbol=sx5e for details on the Euro Stoxx 50 Index.

[652] For further information on the Euro Stoxx equity indices, please refer to http://www.stoxx.com/indices/types/introduction.html.

represents a portfolio of high book-to-market stocks (value stocks) and the return of an index that represents a portfolio of low book-to-market stocks (growth stocks).[653] This factor is approximated by the difference between the return generated by the Euro Stoxx Large Value Index and the Euro Stoxx Large Growth Index, which – as implied by the name of the indices – are proxies for the value and growth stocks within Europe.[654]

For SRI fixed income funds, the excess market return is approximated by the return on the FTSE Euro Corporate Index and the return on the 3-month Euribor. The default factor is measured by the difference between the returns on the iBoxx Euro Corporates All Maturities Index and the iBoxx Euro Sovereign Ezone All Maturities Index.[655] Thus, the iBoxx Euro Corporates All Maturities Index is used as a proxy for the average return generated by a corporate bond index, while the iBoxx Euro Sovereign Ezone All Maturities Index is the proxy used for the average return generated by a government bond index. The term spread is calculated using the returns generated by the iBoxx Euro Sovereign 7-10 Years Index (i.e. the proxy for the average return of a long-term government bond) and the iBoxx Euro Sovereign 1-3 Years Index (i.e. the proxy for the average return of a short-term government bond). For SRI balanced funds, the proxies are derived from the ones used for the respective factor in the equity and fixed income regression models.

The aim of this chapter was to introduce the empirical analysis that has been conducted in order to assess the performance of European-based SRI funds. In the first section of this chapter, the hypotheses that are tested in the analysis have been introduced. The overarching question underlying the empirical analysis is how SRI-screened investments perform relative to SRI-unscreened investment alternatives.

In order to provide a comprehensive answer to this question, three sets of hypotheses are derived: The first set contains hypotheses that center on the question whether SRI-screened investment alternatives in fact perform different than SRI-unscreened alternatives. In order to test these hypotheses, not only the performance of SRI funds is compared to the performance of SRI-screened and SRI-unscreened benchmark indices. The performance of the SRI-screened

---

[653] See Banegas et al. (2013), p. 704, Bauer et al. (2005), p. 1758, Betker & Sheehan (2013), p. 351, Fama (1993), p. 9, Hong & Kacperczyk (2009), p. 21 and Leite & Cortez (2015), p. 136.

[654] See https://www.stoxx.com/index-details?symbol=SLVE for details on the Euro Stoxx Large Value Index and https://www.stoxx.com/index-details?symbol=SLGE for details on the Euro Stoxx Large Growth Index.

[655] See https://www.markit.com/Product/File?CMSID=915f800efc0643f3bbf8c064c9715c2e for an overview on the iBoxx Indices and details on the composition and performance of those indices.

benchmarks indices themselves are also compared to the performance of the SRI-unscreened indices. The second set includes hypotheses that aim at answering the question if SRI funds from the three categories perform differently relative to each other. As the study contains more than just one fund category, the aim is to examine if there is one SRI fund category that consistently under- or outperforms other fund categories or if there is no significant difference between the performance of the SRI funds at all. Finally, the third set of hypotheses aims to test if SRI fund performance changes over time. These analyses offer insights on whether there is a difference in the short- or long-term performance of the funds or not.

The second section of this chapter has introduced the methodology that has been chosen in order to test the hypotheses. The single- and multifactor regression models are based on the models that have already been applied by other researchers that studied SRI fund performance before. As funds of each category are exposed to different factors, the models have been adjusted to reflect market-specifics accordingly.

The data set used in the empirical analysis has been described in the third and final section of this chapter. The data set consists of SRI funds that are established in the four biggest markets for SRI in Europe (France, the UK, the Netherlands and Germany) as well as European indices that are used as proxies in the regression models of each fund category. The decision to use European instead of local indices is mainly motivated by the fact that although the funds are established in one of the countries, most of them invest in European-based companies. Moreover, using the same benchmark indices for SRI funds from different countries ensures comparability of the funds' returns.

To conclude, this chapter has set the basis for the detailed description and discussion of the empirical results in the following chapter. After providing information on the descriptive statistics of the funds and benchmark indices, the following chapter focusses on the presentation of the regression results as well as the additional analyses that have been conducted in order to answer the overarching research question and test the hypotheses.

Table 13 summarizes the proxies used for each category of SRI funds. The table also illustrates that for single-factor regression models, conventional and SRI indices are used as market proxies. For multi-factor models, however, only conventional indices are used. From theory one would expect that the SRI indices perform better in predicting SRI fund return than conventional indices would do. Both, SRI indices and SRI funds restrict their investment universe by only considering a limited set of investment securities that meet their investment screening criteria. Thus, one could expect that the application of similar investment criteria leads to a more realistic prediction of SRI fund returns when SRI rather than conventional indices are used in the regression models.[656] In fact, the empirical results show that explanatory power of the conventional index model is higher than that of the SRI index models.[657] Consequently, only conventional indices are used in the multi-factor regression analyses. Again, all price information data for the indices mentioned are obtained from Datastream and monthly returns for each index are calculated as continuously compounded returns.

The aim of this chapter was to introduce the empirical analysis that has been conducted in order to assess the performance of European-based SRI funds. In the first section of this chapter, the hypotheses that are tested in the analysis have been introduced. The overarching question underlying the empirical analysis is how SRI-screened investments perform relative to SRI-unscreened investment alternatives.

In order to provide a comprehensive answer to this question, three sets of hypotheses are derived: The first set contains hypotheses that center on the question whether SRI-screened investment alternatives in fact perform different than SRI-unscreened alternatives. In order to test these hypotheses, not only the performance of SRI funds is compared to the performance of SRI-screened and SRI-unscreened benchmark indices. The performance of the SRI-screened benchmarks indices themselves are also compared to the performance of the SRI-unscreened indices. The second set includes hypotheses that aim at answering the question if SRI funds from the three categories perform differently relative to each other. As the study contains more than just one fund category, the aim is to examine if there is one SRI fund category that consistently under- or outperforms other fund categories or if there is no significant difference between the performance of the SRI funds at all. Finally, the third set of hypotheses aims to test if SRI fund performance changes over time. These analyses offer insights on whether there is a difference in the short- or long-term performance of the funds or not.

The second section of this chapter has introduced the methodology that has been chosen in order to test the hypotheses. The single- and multifactor regression models are based on the models that have already been applied by other researchers that studied SRI fund performance

---

[656] See section 5.3.2.1 as well as Cortez et al. (2009), p. 579 and Leite & Cortez (2014), p. 261.

[657] The explanatory power is measured by the adjusted R^2, which is higher for the conventional than for the SRI regression models for all three fund categories (see section 6.2.1). This finding is in line with the findings made by Bauer et al. (2005), p. 1765 and (2007), p. 116, Cortez et al. (2009), p. 579 and Leite & Cortez (2014), p. 261.

before. As funds of each category are exposed to different factors, the models have been adjusted to reflect market-specifics accordingly.

The data set used in the empirical analysis has been described in the third and final section of this chapter. The data set consists of SRI funds that are established in the four biggest markets for SRI in Europe (France, the UK, the Netherlands and Germany) as well as European indices that are used as proxies in the regression models of each fund category. The decision to use European instead of local indices is mainly motivated by the fact that although the funds are established in one of the countries, most of them invest in European-based companies. Moreover, using the same benchmark indices for SRI funds from different countries ensures comparability of the funds' returns.

To conclude, this chapter has set the basis for the detailed description and discussion of the empirical results in the following chapter. After providing information on the descriptive statistics of the funds and benchmark indices, the following chapter focusses on the presentation of the regression results as well as the additional analyses that have been conducted in order to answer the overarching research question and test the hypotheses.

Table 13: Overview of indices used in the regression analysis

This table shows the indices that have been used in the single- (Panel A) and multi-factor regression models (Panel B) for each SRI fund category. While the risk-free rate of return is the same for all regression models, the indices used as proxies for the individual factors differ for each fund category.

Panel A: Single-factor regression

	Market factor		Risk-free rate
	Conventional	SRI	
Equity funds	Euro Stoxx Index	Euro Stoxx Sustainability Index	3-month Euribor
Balanced funds	57.2% Euro Stoxx Index, 42.8% FTSE Euro Corporate Index	57.2% Euro Stoxx Sustainability Index, 42.8% FTSE4Good EU Index	3-month Euribor
Fixed income funds	FTSE Euro Corporate Index	FTSE4Good EU Index	3-month Euribor

Panel B: Multi-factor regression

	Market factor		SMB		HML	
	Market proxy	Risk-free rate	Small Cap Index	Large Cap Index	Value Index	Growth Index
Equity funds	Euro Stoxx Index	3-month Euribor	Euro Stoxx Small Index	Euro Stoxx 50 Index	Euro Stoxx Large Value Index	Euro Stoxx Large Growth Index

	Market factor		Default		Equity market exposure	
	Market proxy	Risk-free rate	Corp. Bond Index	Gov. Bond Index	Equity Index	Risk-free rate
Balanced funds	57.2% Euro Stoxx Index, 42.8% FTSE Euro Corporate Index	3-month Euribor	iBoxx Euro Corporates All Maturities Index	iBoxx Euro Sovereign Ezone All Maturities Index	Euro Stoxx Index	3-month Euribor

	Market factor		Default		Term	
	Market proxy	Risk-free rate	Corp. Bond Index	Gov. Bond Index	Long-term Gov. Bond iBoxx Euro Sovereign 7-10 Years Index	Short-term Gov. Bond iBoxx Euro Sovereign 1-3 Years Index
Fixed income funds	FTSE Euro Corporate Index	3-month Euribor	iBoxx Euro Corporates All Maturities Index	iBoxx Euro Sovereign Ezone All Maturities Index		

Source: Own illustration

Interim conclusion

6 Empirical Results

6.1 Summary statistics

6.1.1 SRI funds

The regression models applied in the empirical analysis of this thesis are based on the assumption that returns of the SRI fund portfolios and benchmark indices included in the sample are normally distributed, i.e., the returns show a symmetric pattern around the mean.[658] This assumption is the basis on which financial models such as the CAPM or multi-factor regression models such as the ones used in this thesis are built on.[659] Prior to presenting the results obtained when running the regression models, this section will review if the assumption of normally distributed returns holds true for the data set used.

In order to test if the returns of the fund portfolios and benchmark indices are normally distributed, typically not only the basic characteristics such as the mean return generated or the standard deviation of the returns are reported. Instead, also the descriptive statistics such as the skewness and kurtosis values and the Shapiro-Wilk (1965) W-statistic for the funds and benchmarks are assessed.[660] Merely looking at average returns and standard deviations of the returns – the first and second central moment of a normal distribution – would not be sufficient to test if the returns are in fact distributed normally.[661] The reasoning behind this approach is the fact that the average return and standard deviation are static values that do not provide any indication if the return distribution is in fact symmetric around the mean or if there are outliers that cause a deviation from the normal distribution.[662] Thus, the skewness and kurtosis values – the third and fourth central moment of a normal distribution – should also to be assessed, ideally in conjunction with a more formal statistical test such as the Shapiro-Wilk (1965) test.[663]

---

[658] See section 4.2.2.1.
[659] See Francis & Kim (2013), p. 201 and Tsay (2005), p. 14.
[660] See, for example, Cortez et al. (2009), p. 577, Derwall et al. (2005), p. 54, Francs & Kim (2013), p. 202 and Wan-Ni (2012), p. 428.
[661] See Tsay (2005), p. 9.
[662] See section 4.2.2.1 and Franke et al. (2011), p. 47.
[663] See DeCarlo (1997), p. 296 and Tsay (2005), p. 10.

The skewness value measures the degree to which the return distribution deviates from symmetry.[664] The normal distribution is symmetric around the mean and thus, has a skewness of zero.[665] A negative (positive) skewness indicates that the tails on the left (right) of the distribution are longer than they are for the normal distribution.[666] The kurtosis value measures the peakedness of the return distribution.[667] The normal distribution has a kurtosis of three.[668] Values greater than three indicate that the tails of the distribution are too thin or too peaked in the middle and that the distribution of the returns tends to contain more extreme values or outliers than the normal distribution does.[669] In order to formally assess the assumption that returns are normally distributed, the Shapiro-Wilk (1965) W-statistic is also calculated.[670] Shapiro and Wilk (1965) have developed a statistical measure (W-statistic) that combines the information obtained when looking at standard deviation, skewness and kurtosis values of the return distribution. The W-statistic is calculated in order to test the null hypothesis that returns are normally distributed and provides reliable results even when the sample size is small (e.g., for $n < 20$).[671] In general, the W-statistic can take values between zero and one. For small values, the null hypothesis would be rejected; a value of one would indicate normality of the distribution.[672]

Table 14 shows the characteristics and descriptive statistics for the excess returns generated by equally weighted portfolios of SRI funds in each category included in the sample.

Table 14: Summary statistics of SRI funds

This table presents the characteristics and summary statistics for equally weighted portfolios of SRI funds in each category. Panel A illustrates the results on an aggregated level, Panel B shows the detailed results for each category and country. Management fees, mean excess return and standard deviation are given in percentage per month. All data are reported for the period from January 2003 to December 2013. ***, ** indicates significance at the 1% and 5% level, respectively.

---

[664] See Franke et al. (2011), p. 47 and Stock & Watson (2007), p. 27.
[665] See Wooldridge (2013), p. 731.
[666] See Franke et al. (2011), p. 47 and Neter et al. (1993), p. 85.
[667] See Neter et al. (1993), p. 87.
[668] See Franke et al. (2011), p. 48 and Stock & Watson (2007), p. 28.
[669] See D'Agostino et al. (1990), p. 317 and Tsay (2005), p. 9.
[670] See Shapiro & Wilk (1965), p. 592 for a detailed description how the W-statistic is calculated.
[671] See Villasenor Alva & Estrada (2009), p. 1871 and Shapiro & Wilk (1965), p. 602.
[672] See Razali & Wah (2011), p. 25 and Ruppert & Matteson (2015), p. 64.

6. Empirical Results

Panel A: Europe

		Fund characteristics			Descriptive statistics of excess returns			
Category	Number of funds	Average TNA[1] (in EUR Mn)	Mean management fee (%)	Mean excess return (%)	Standard deviation (%)	Skewness	Kurtosis	Shapiro-Wilk (W-statistic)
Equity	214	152.30	0.12	0.09	4.29	-1.04	5.12	0.937 ***
Balanced	60	137.53	0.10	-0.07	1.75	-0.97	4.93	0.945 ***
Fixed Income	87	231.62	0.05	-0.11	0.59	-0.29	2.55	0.978 **
Total	361	168.96	0.10	0.01	2.90	-1.02	5.24	0.939 ***

Panel B: Country split

		Fund characteristics			Descriptive statistics of excess returns			
Category	Number of funds	Average TNA* (in EUR Mn)	Mean management fee (%)	Mean excess return (%)	Standard deviation (%)	Skewness	Kurtosis	Shapiro-Wilk (W-statistic)
Equity								
FR	103	155.01	0.13	0.09	4.59	-0.80	4.16	0.952 ***
UK	52	183.86	0.12	0.16	4.10	-1.07	5.80	0.933 ***
NL	24	153.49	0.10	0.04	4.26	-1.28	5.70	0.914 ***
DE	35	96.60	0.11	0.02	4.35	-1.33	6.35	0.910 ***
Balanced								
FR	22	39.94	0.10	-0.02	1.81	-0.77	4.37	0.959 ***
UK	7	239.83	0.13	0.11	3.22	-0.95	4.73	0.949 ***
NL	8	373.57	0.08	-0.03	1.81	-0.63	3.46	0.971 ***
DE	23	117.64	0.09	-0.18	1.46	-1.33	6.25	0.911 ***
Fixed Income								
FR	61	244.85	0.05	-0.03	0.39	-0.19	2.69	0.986
UK	8	239.86	0.09	-0.28	2.67	-0.85	5.20	0.958 ***
NL	6	310.99	0.06	-0.21	0.01	-0.84	4.46	0.953 ***
DE	12	119.13	0.05	-0.24	0.81	-0.23	2.52	0.986

[1] Total net assets
Source: Own illustration

Panel A of Table 14 shows the summary statistics on an aggregated level for all 361 SRI funds included in the sample. The average fund size, measured by total net assets (TNA) of the funds, is EUR 168.96 million. SRI balanced funds are the smallest funds with an average size of EUR 137.53 million and SRI fixed income funds are the biggest funds with an average size of EUR 231.62 million. SRI equity funds charge the highest monthly management fees (0.12% per month), but at the same time generate the highest mean excess net return of 0.09% per month. In fact, SRI equity funds are the only funds that, on average, generate a positive mean excess return: Although fixed income funds charge the lowest management fees (0.05% per month), they generate an average negative return of -0.11% per month. Balanced funds charge 0.10% per month and generate a negative return of -0.07% per month.

The negative skewness values obtained for all three fund portfolios indicate that the excess return distribution is skewed to the left.[673] Moreover, the kurtosis values that deviate from three, the value for the normal distribution, and the highly significant W-statistic provide evidence that excess returns for the equity and balanced funds in particular are not normally distributed.[674]

Figure 21 illustrates deviations of the return distributions from the normal distribution. The black line in each graph of Figure 21 shows the estimated return distribution for the SRI funds in each category; the grey line shows the normal distribution.[675] As indicated by the skewness and kurtosis values, the return distributions deviate from the normal distribution for all three categories of funds. This finding, however, applies to most fund return data and does not imply that linear regression – which is based on the assumption that returns are normally distributed – cannot be conducted.[676] Instead, it rather implies that additional tests – especially on the residuals of the regression – have to be conducted prior to running the regression analysis. These tests and the results obtained are presented in section 6.2.

---

[673] See Acock (2008), p. 229 and Vose (2008), p. 97.

[674] See Acock (2008), p. 229, DeCarlo (1997), p. 292 and Vose (2008), p. 99.

[675] The graphs illustrated in Figure 21 as based on the output provided by the STATA, the data analysis and statistical software program that is used to run the regression analyses. For more information on the software, please refer to www.stata.com/.

[676] See Affleck-Graves (1989), p. 892, Cortez et al. (2009), p. 577 and Studenmund (2011), p. 100.

6. Empirical Results

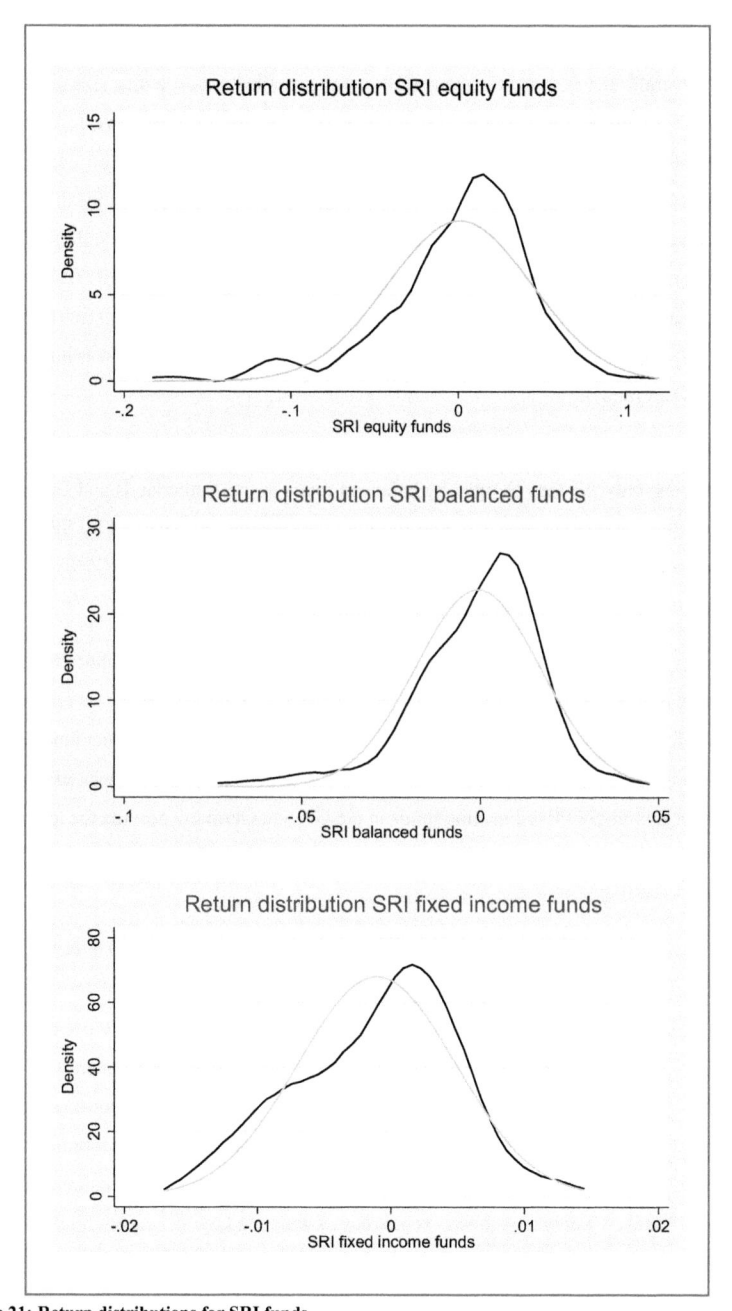

Figure 21: Return distributions for SRI funds
Source: Own illustration based on STATA output

The detailed characteristics for SRI funds per country are displayed in Panel B of Table 14 on page 174. Overall, SRI funds in Germany (DE) are the smallest funds, with a size that is below the average TNA for all funds: SRI equity funds in Germany, for example, have an average size of EUR 96.60 million, compared to a total average of EUR 152.30 million for the entire sample. The SRI funds in the UK and the Netherlands are bigger than the average European SRI funds: While the average fund size of balanced funds in the sample is EUR 137.53 million, SRI balanced funds in the UK have an average size of EUR 239.83 million and EUR 373.57 million in the Netherlands. SRI balanced funds in France on average have the smallest size (EUR 39.94 million), although the number of balanced funds in France (22 funds) is almost as high as in the Netherlands (23 funds).

Management fees for SRI equity and balanced funds are between 0.10% and 0.13% per month in all countries; only the fees charged by balanced funds in the Netherlands and Germany are slightly below 0.10% per month. Conversely, the management fees charged by SRI fixed income funds are below 0.10% per month in all countries (0.09% in the UK, 0.06% in the Netherlands and 0.05% in France and Germany).

Mean excess returns for SRI equity funds are positive in all countries. SRI equity funds in the UK generate a mean excess return of 0.16% per month, the highest mean excess return of SRI funds in all four countries. While the returns for balanced and SRI fixed income funds are negative in almost all countries, balanced funds in the UK generate a positive mean excess return of 0.11% per month. SRI fixed income funds in the UK and Germany provide the lowest average mean return during the entire observation period (-0.28% and -0.24% per month, respectively).

Standard deviations for the mean excess returns of the funds in the UK also deviate from the average for the funds in the other three countries: While the average standard deviation of the excess returns generated by SRI balanced funds in the total sample is 1.75% per month, it is 3.22% per month in the UK. For fixed income funds, the spread is even higher: The average standard deviation for SRI fixed income funds in the UK is 2.67% per month, compared to 0.59% per month for SRI fixed income funds in the total sample. Mean excess returns generated by SRI fixed income funds in the Netherlands have the lowest standard deviation (0.01% per month) of all funds. Conversely, mean excess returns generated by SRI equity funds in France have the highest standard deviation (4.59% per month). Finally, for each country and category of funds, the returns distributions are negatively skewed (as indicated by the negative skewness values) and not normally distributed (as indicated by the kurtosis values that deviate from the value of three).[677]

6.1.2 Benchmark indices

Table 15 presents the summary statistics for the benchmark indices used in the analyses. Similar to the results obtained for SRI fund returns, the skewness and kurtosis values as well as the Shapiro-Wilk (1965) test for normality indicate that excess returns are not normally distributed for the benchmark indices used. However, contrary to the mean excess returns generated by the SRI funds, all benchmarks have positive mean excess returns during the observation period. The FTSE Euro Corporate Index provides the highest monthly excess return (0.25%) and at the same time has the lowest standard deviation (0.89%) of all benchmark indices. Equity benchmarks generate the lowest returns, but at the same time also have the highest standard deviations during our observation period. As the indices used as benchmarks for balanced funds are weighted averages of the equity and fixed income indices the values obtained for the balanced indices are between those that are obtained for equity and fixed income indices.

The finding that equity indices generate the lowest mean excess returns and at the same time have the highest standard deviations of all indices in the sample is rather surprising: Studies on the long-term performance of financial securities show that equity securities are not only the riskiest investment instrument, but also have the highest risk premiums and thus, offer the higher returns than other financial securities.[678] The lower mean returns for equity benchmarks relative to fixed income benchmarks in our sample are caused by the highly negative returns generated by the equity markets during the global financial crisis in 2007/2008. Figure 22 shows that, while the average monthly returns during the entire observation period from 2003 to 2013 alternate between -2.14% and +2.08% per month for the FTSE Corporate Index (the benchmark for the fixed income market), the average monthly returns for the Euro Stoxx Index (the benchmark for the equity market) are more volatile and as low as -16.68% per month at the end of 2008.

---

[677] The normal distribution is defined to have a skewness of zero and a kurtosis of three. See Acock (2008), p. 229, Lee et al. (2000), p. 110, Ruppert (2004), p. 27, Sclove (2012), p. 24 and Vose (2008), pp. 97–99.

[678] See Berk & DeMarzo (2014), pp. 322–324, Brealey et al. (2014), p. 162, Fama & French (1989), p. 28 and (1993), p. 14, Francis (1993), p. 19 and Jones (2009), p. 148.

Table 15: Summary statistics of benchmark indices

This table shows the summary statistics for the conventional and SRI indices used as market benchmarks. The reporting period is January 2003 to December 2013.
Monthly returns are continuously compounded returns and reported in percentage terms. ***, ** indicates significance at the 1% and 5% level, respectively.

Benchmark for...		Mean excess return (%)	Standard deviation (%)	Skewness	Kurtosis	Shapiro-Wilk (W-statistic)
Euro Stoxx	Conventional equity market	0.14	5.33	-0.79	3.94	0.950 ***
57.2% EuroStoxx, 42.8% FTSE Corp	Conventional balanced market	0.19	3.06	-0.75	4.03	0.957 ***
FTSE Corp	Conventional fixed income market	0.25	0.89	-0.42	2.51	0.973 ***
Euro Stoxx Sust.	SRI equity market	0.08	5.42	-0.61	3.72	0.964 ***
57.2% EuroStoxx Sust., 42.8% FTSE4Good	SRI balanced market	0.10	5.02	-0.67	3.99	0.955 ***
FTSE4Good EU	SRI fixed income market	0.11	4.61	-0.75	4.44	0.948 **

Source: Own illustration

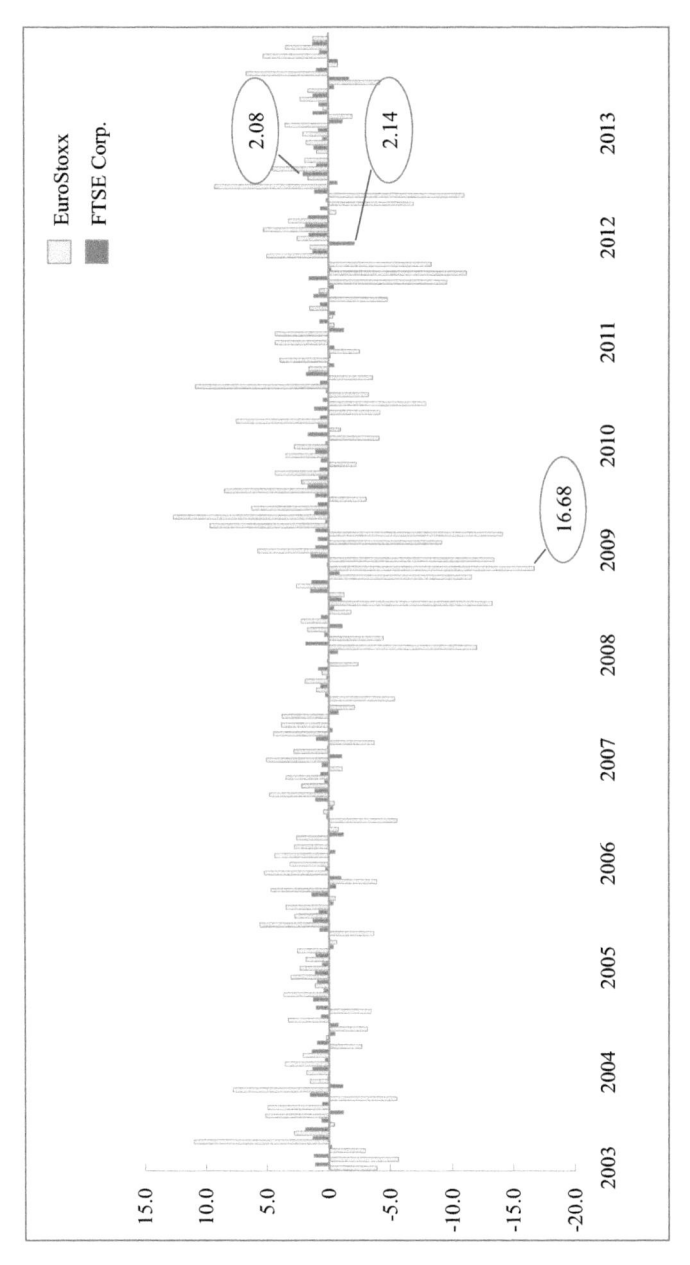

Figure 22: Average monthly returns for benchmark indices between 2003 and 2013
Source: Own illustration

The graphs displayed in Figure 22 also illustrate that the volatility of the Euro Stoxx Index has increased considerably with beginning of the financial crisis in 2008:[679] The volatility, measured by standard deviation of the monthly returns, for the Euro Stoxx Index is 3.56% per month for the period between January 2003 and December 2007, but increases to 6.32% per month for the period between January 2008 and December 2013. In order to study the potential impact the financial crisis has had on the returns generated by the indices and SRI funds, the empirical study examines the performances over two sub-periods: The first period ranges from January 2003 to December 2007 (before the crisis) and the second one from January 2008 to December 2013 (during and after the crisis). The separation into sub-periods also allows studying changes in fund performance over time and thus, testing hypotheses H3a to H3d.

Comparing excess returns and standard deviations between the conventional indices and SRI indices in Table 15 on page 180 indicates that, on a pure risk and return basis, the SRI indices underperform against the conventional indices: The returns of the conventional indices are higher and standard deviations are lower than the ones obtained for the SRI indices. The average monthly return for the Euro Stoxx Index, the index used for the conventional equity market, is 0.14% compared to 0.08% for the Euro Stoxx Sustainability Index, the index used for the SRI equity market. The difference between the fixed income indices is even more remarkable: While the average monthly return for the FTSE Corporate Index, the index used for the conventional fixed income market, is 0.25%, it is only 0.11% for the FTSE4Good Index, the index used for the SRI fixed income market.

Table 16 summarizes the differences between the excess returns for the conventional and SRI benchmarks per category: For equity benchmarks, the difference between the excess returns of the conventional index and the SRI index is 0.06% per month, for balanced funds it is 0.09% per month and for fixed income funds 0.03% per month. Thus, there are differences in the average returns between the SRI and the conventional benchmark indices and SRI benchmark indices provide lower mean excess returns than conventional indices. However, as none of the differences is significantly different from zero, hypothesis *H1a: There is a significant difference in the performance of SRI indices compared to conventional indices* has to be rejected at the 1% level.

---

[679] See section 5.1.3 for a classification of the period of the global financial crisis as well as National Bureau of Economic Research (2010) and Nofsinger & Varma (2014), p. 185.

Table 16: Return differences between conventional and SRI benchmark indices

This table shows the differences in monthly excess returns between the conventional and SRI indices for the entire observation period from Jan 2003 to Dec 2013. Monthly returns are continuously compounded returns and reported in percentage terms.

Benchmark	Difference in excess returns (%)	t-stat.
Equity fund benchmarks	0.06	0.880
Balanced fund benchmarks	0.09	0.517
Fixed income fund benchmarks	0.03	0.354

Source: Own illustration

6.1.3 Correlation coefficients

Table 17 shows the correlation coefficients between the SRI fund returns and the explanatory variables (market indices and additional factors) used in the regression analysis. The results show that for equity and balanced SRI funds, the correlation coefficient between the SRI fund portfolio return and the conventional market index is higher than the coefficient between the fund portfolio return and the SRI index: The correlation coefficient between the return generated by the equity SRI fund portfolio and the SRI equity market index is 0.930; the correlation coefficient between the return generated by the SRI equity fund portfolio and the return generated by the conventional equity index is 0.944. For balanced funds, the correlation between the fund portfolio return and the SRI market index is 0.892 and 0.915 between the fund portfolio and the conventional market index. This finding indicates that – at least for equity and balanced SRI funds – the fund returns tend to move closer together with the returns generated by the conventional market indices than they do with the returns generated by the SRI market indices.[680]

For fixed income SRI funds, the correlation coefficient between the SRI fund portfolio return and the conventional index is also higher (0.854) than the coefficient between the fund portfolio return and the SRI index (0.096). Moreover, the low correlation coefficient between the fund portfolio return and the SRI index indicate that this index only has little power to explain SRI fund return – not only relative to the conventional market index but also in absolute terms when looked at separately.

---

[680] See section 4.2.2.2 for a detailed description of the interpretation of the correlation coefficient.

Table 17: Correlation coefficients

This table shows the correlation coefficients between the returns of the SRI funds and the returns of the explanatory variables used in the regression analysis. Panel A shows the coefficient for the equity market, Panel B for the balanced market and Panel C for the fixed income market.

Panel A: Equity market					
	SRI equity funds	SRI equity index	Conv. equity index	SMB	HML
SRI equity funds	1.0000				
SRI equity index	0.9304	1.0000			
Conv. Index	0.9447	0.9907	1.0000		
SMB	0.1524	-0.0533	0.0015	1.0000	
HML	0.3479	0.4729	0.4800	-0.0554	1.0000

Panel B: Balanced market					
	SRI balanced funds	SRI balanced index	Conv. balanced index	Conv. FI index	DEF
SRI balanced funds	1.0000				
SRI balanced index	0.8919	1.0000			
Conv. balanced index	0.9152	0.9841	1.0000		
Conv. fixed income index	0.2776	-0.0027	0.1239	1.0000	
DEF	0.5828	0.4935	0.5281	0.1930	1.0000

Panel C: Fixed income market					
	SRI fixed income funds	SRI fixed income index	Conv. fixed income index	DEF	TERM
SRI fixed income funds	1.0000				
SRI fixed income index	0.0968	1.0000			
Conv. fixed income index	0.8542	0.0438	1.0000		
DEF	0.1403	0.5397	0.1930	1.0000	
TERM	0.6693	-0.1663	0.6750	-0.3657	1.0000

Source: Own illustration

The low correlations coefficients between the explanatory variables for each of the fund categories indicate that there is no evidence of multicollinearity between the variables used in the multi-factor analyses.[681] As the regression analysis is based on the assumption that neither the explanatory variables nor the residuals are correlated with each other, multicollinearity between the explanatory variables would have led to distortions in the estimates obtained for the individual variables.

In order to provide more robust evidence on the presence of multicollinearity, the variance inflation factor (VIF) for each explanatory variable is also calculated. The VIF quantifies how

---

[681] See Brooks (2008), p. 170 and El Ghoul et al. (2011), p. 2394.

much the correlation between the explanatory variables used in the regression model increases the variances of the respective variables and thus, decreased the exactness of the estimate obtained for each variable.[682] In other words, the higher the VIF for a variable, the less precise the estimate of the variable obtained in the regression.[683] It is calculated as $VIF = (1 - R_i^2)^{-1}$ where R_i^2 is the R^2 obtained when running a regression of the i-th variable (dependent variable) on all the other explanatory variables used in the regression model (independent variables).[684] A VIF of 10 would indicate that the variance for the respective variable is strongly influenced by the correlation of this variable with the other variables in the model and thus, provide an indication that multicollinearity is present.[685] The results of the VIF obtained for each explanatory variable used in the multi-factor regression models of this thesis are displayed in Table 18.

Table 18: Variance inflation factors

This table shows the variance inflation factors (VIF) calculated for the explanatory variables used in the multi-factor regression models in each market.

Equity market	VIF	Balanced market	VIF	Fixed income market	VIF
Equity index	1.30	Fixed income index	1.05	Fixed income index	3.12
SMB	1.00	DEF	1.42	DEF	1.96
HML	1.30	Equity index	1.37	TERM	3.46

Source: Own illustration

As the VIF is smaller than 10 for all variables, the results provide further evidence that there is no multicollinearity between the explanatory variables used in the regression models.[686] Even if multicollinearity were present, it could have been the case that the model fit (measured by R^2) were high. However, the intervals obtained for the estimates of explanatory variables would have been large, which potentially lead to insignificant t-statistics and thus, inappropriate conclusions on the values of the estimates. However, as multicollinearity does not occur for the variables used in this study, regression analysis can be applied without making adjustments to the models.[687]

---

[682] See Freund et al. (2006), p. 190 and Maindonald & Braun (2010), p. 201.
[683] See Bu & Lacey (2007), p. 36.
[684] See Kennedy (2003), p. 213 and Kleinbaum et al. (2013), p. 363.
[685] See Freund et al. (2006), p. 191, Kennedy (2003), p. 213 and Kleinbaum et al. (2013), p. 363.
[686] See Benson et al. (2006), p. 355, Dietze et al. (2009), p. 201, Kennedy (2003), p. 213 and Orlitzky & Benjamin (2001), p. 406.
[687] See Brooks (2008), p. 172.

6.2 SRI fund performance

6.2.1 Performance measures for SRI funds

In order to assess SRI fund performance, individual performance measures for the funds in each category are calculated. Table 19 shows the Treynor and Sharpe ratios for SRI equity, balanced and fixed income funds. The Treynor ratios are calculated as introduced in section 4.3.2 and by using the respective conventional benchmark index in each category of funds as a proxy for the market portfolio, e.g. the Euro Stoxx Index for SRI equity funds and the FTSE Corporate Index for SRI fixed income funds. The results obtained show that both measures lead to a similar conclusion: Equity funds are more attractive for the investors than balanced or fixed income funds.

Table 19: SRI fund performance measures

This table shows the Treynor and Sharpe ratios calculated as individual performance measures for each SRI fund category. The Treynor ratio has been calculated using the conventional indices as a proxy for the market portfolio.

	Mean excess return (%)	Treynor ratio	Sharpe ratio
Equity SRI funds	0.09	0.12	0.02
Balanced SRI funds	-0.07	-0.14	-0.04
Fixed income SRI funds	-0.11	-0.19	-0.18

Source: Own illustration

Although the Treynor ratios only account for the systematic risk inherent in the SRI funds and the Sharpe ratios consider both, systematic and unsystematic risk,[688] both ratios are positive for SRI equity funds and negative for SRI balanced and SRI fixed income funds. This is due to the fact that the excess returns for balanced and fixed income funds are negative. As the excess returns are in the numerator when calculating the ratios, the resulting quotient between the excess returns and the risk measures is negative as well.

Jensen's alpha, a third performance measure that has been introduced in section 4.3.2, is a constant factor that results from running single- and multi factor linear regression models. Prior to presenting the results obtained in the regression models, the following section first describes

---

[688] See section 4.3.2 for a detailed description of the Treynor and Sharpe ratios as performance measures.

the analyses that have been conducted in order to test whether the residuals used in the analyses are normally distributed and thus, meet the requirements of general linear regression models.[689]

6.2.2 Testing residuals

6.2.2.1 Normality of residuals

The summary statistics for SRI funds presented in section 6.1.1 have already indicated that the returns generated by the SRI funds are not normally distributed. Normal distribution of the return data, however, is not a necessary condition that linear regression models can be estimated in order to assess SRI fund performance. Instead, the residuals obtained in the regression analysis should be normally distributed in order to correctly estimate the (single- and multi-factor) regression models.[690] If the residuals are not normally distributed, the regression models have to be adjusted. Thus, prior to introducing the adjustments made and the results obtained thereby, this section first shows the results obtained when testing the residuals.

In order to test if the residuals are normally distributed, a graphical and a numerical test is conducted.[691] The results of the graphical test are displayed in Figure 23. Similar to the return distribution displayed in Figure 21, the black line shows the distribution of the residuals for each portfolio of funds and the grey line indicates the normal distribution. In general, the graphs for all SRI fund categories deviate from the normal distribution. Specifically, the distributions have higher peaks and fatter tails than the normal distribution for all fund categories. Thus, the distributions are said to be leptokurtic instead of normal in shape.[692]

Comparing the three graphs with each other indicates that the graphs obtained for the residuals of SRI equity and balanced funds seem to deviate more from the normal distribution than the graph for SRI fixed income funds. This finding is also supported by the W-statistic obtained when conducting the Shapiro-Wilk (1965) test: The W-statistic for the residuals of SRI equity and balanced funds are almost identical (0.969 and 0.967, respectively), but the W-statistic for the residuals of SRI fixed income funds is lower (0.907). However, as all values obtained for

---

[689] See Francis & Kim (2013), p. 201 and Lee et al. (2000), p. 560.
[690] See Affleck-Graves (1989), p. 892 and Studenmund (2011), p. 100.
[691] The residual tests are based on regression models that are estimated with conventional indices used as proxies for the market portfolio. The results obtained in the single-factor regression models indicate the conventional indices perform better in predicting SRI fund returns than SRI indices do (see section 6.2.3).
[692] See Brooks (2008), p. 162, Sheskin (2003), p. 20, Spanos (1999), p. 20 and Tsay (2005), p. 9.

the *W*-statistic are significant, the null hypothesis that the residuals are normally distributed has to be rejected at the 1%-level.

Typically, non-normality of returns and residuals is caused by outliers, e.g. a small number of return data that take on extreme negative (or positive) values. These extreme values lead to a deviation of the return and residual distribution from the normal distribution.[693] Linear regression models usually are based on the assumption that returns and residuals are normally distributed.[694] Applying such models although the assumption of normality is violated can cause misleading interpretations of the results.[695]

There are several possibilities to deal with the non-normality of the residuals, which ensure that linear regression models still can be applied. The first possibility is to simply ignore the finding of non-normality and estimate the linear regression models without making any modifications. This approach, however, would lead to wrong inferences of, e.g., the *t*-statistic used to test the significance of the coefficient or the *F*-statistic used to assess the fit of the model.[696]

The second possibility is to identify the outliers that cause deviations from normality and remove them by, e.g. including dummy variables to the regression.[697] However, as the return data used in this study are historical time-series data, the individual data points relate to each other. Extreme (positive or negative) returns are part of the historical return development of the funds and benchmark indices. Removing these extreme values would be equal to manually adjusting the return development. This would, in turn, result in a distorted image of the actual return development of the funds and indices. Therefore, manually manipulating results is considered as being no feasible option to deal with non-normality of the residuals – at least in the course of this study.[698]

---

[693] See Brooks (2008), p. 163, Montgomery et al. (2015), p. 139 and Ruppert (2004), p. 199.
[694] See Francis & Kim (2013), p. 201 and Lee et al. (2000), p. 560.
[695] See Crown (1998), p. 71 and Montgomery et al. (2015), p. 129.
[696] See Crown (1998), p. 71.
[697] See Brooks (2008), p. 165.
[698] See Brooks (2008), p. 166 and Freund et al. (2006), p. 63.

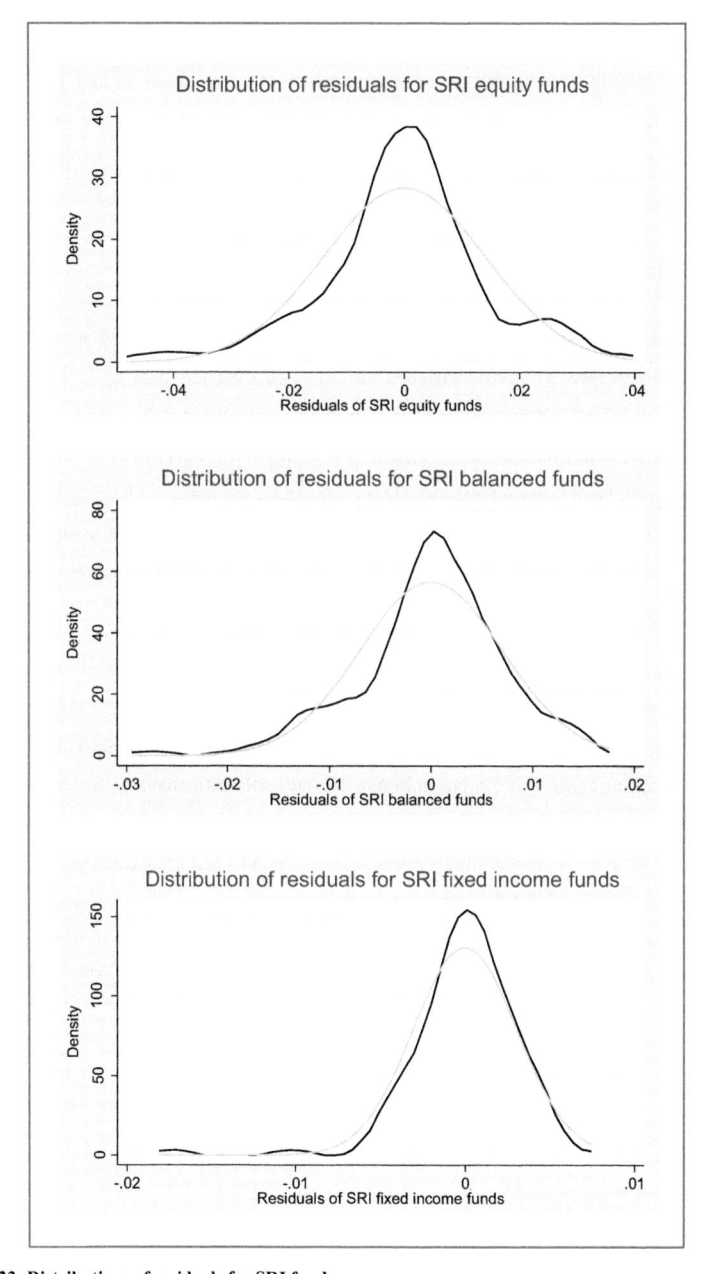

Figure 23: Distributions of residuals for SRI funds
Source: Own illustration based on STATA output

The third possibility is to test if the data set is homoscedastic or if there is any type of heteroscedasticity that influences the finding of non-normality of the residuals. In fact, if evidence of heteroscedasticity is found, non-normality is inherent in all data points and thus, the removal of the outliers would not result in normality of the residual distribution.[699] Therefore, the following section shows the results obtained when testing the data set for homoscedasticity.

6.2.2.2 Homoscedasticity of residuals

Homoscedasticity implies that the variance of the residuals is homogeneous or constant.[700] If the residuals do not have a constant variance, they are said to be heteroscedastic. Linear regression models as applied in this study are based on the assumption that the variances are homoscedastic. In case heteroscedasticity is present, the regression models need to be adjusted by, e.g. estimating the regression with standard errors that are robust against heteroscedasticity.[701] Applying the regression models despite the presence of heteroscedasticity would reduce the efficiency of these models and thus, result in incorrect estimates of the variances of the regression coefficients.[702]

A graphical test to detect heteroscedasticity is to plot the residuals against the dependent variable as displayed in Figure 24. If the assumption of homoscedasticity is not violated, the single dots in the plot should rather look like a random cloud instead of being organized in a systematic manner.[703] Looking at the three graphs in Figure 24, one could infer that the plots for SRI equity and balanced funds are indeed random clouds of data points, which would imply that the residuals for SRI equity and balanced funds are in fact assumed to be homoscedastic. The plot obtained for the residuals of SRI fixed income funds, however, implies that there could in fact be a pattern in the data points. Specifically, there seems to be an upward shift in the plot for SRI fixed income funds, which would imply that these residuals are heteroscedastic.

---

[699] See Brooks (2008), p. 167.
[700] See Brooks (2008), p. 132, Freund et al. (2006), p. 163, Ruppert (2004), p. 453 as well as Verbeek (2012), p. 95.
[701] See Brooks (2008), p. 138.
[702] The implication is that the estimated variances and thus, standard errors for the constant or alpha-coefficient in the regression, would be too large and – typically – too low for the beta-coefficients. For more details see Brooks (2008), p. 135.
[703] See Crown (1998), p. 80.

6. Empirical Results 191

In order to quantitatively test the inferences that residuals are homoscedastic for SRI equity and balanced funds and heteroscedastic for SRI fixed income funds, the White (1980) test is used. While most tests for homoscedasticity assume normality of returns, White (1980) has developed an approach that can be applied to test the hypothesis that residuals are homoscedastic even if the returns are not normally distributed.[704] As section 6.2.2.1 has shown, the residuals for the sample at hand are not normally distributed. Thus, the White (1980) test is used in this setting. A small p-value obtained for the White statistic would mean that the null hypothesis has to be rejected and the alternative hypothesis, which states that residuals are heteroscedastic, has to be accepted.[705]

The results obtained for the residuals of SRI equity, balanced and fixed income funds that are displayed in Table 20 support the findings obtained in the graphical test: The F-values for SRI equity and balanced funds are highly significant and thus, too large to reject the null hypothesis. The F-value for SRI fixed income funds, however, is not significant. Consequently, the assumption that residuals are homoscedastic only holds true for SRI equity and balanced funds, but not for fixed income funds.

In order to deal with the finding of heteroscedasticity of residuals, the linear regression model in this study uses Newey-West (1994) standards errors that are robust against heteroscedasticity and autocorrelation.[706] Prior to introducing the method applied when using Newey-West (1994) standard errors, the following section first introduces what autocorrelation of residuals means and how it is detected.

---

[704] An alternative test for detecting heteroscedasticity would be the Breusch-Pragan (1979) test. However, this test assumes that residuals are normally distributed with a mean and variance value of zero. For further details on the assumptions of the tests see also Breusch-Pragan (1979), p. 1288 and White (1980), p. 817.

[705] See Baltagi (2002), p. 110 and Brooks (2008), p. 135.

[706] See Newey & West (1994). An alternative for dealing with heteroscedasticity would be to use weighted least squares (WLS) instead of ordinary least squares. However, this approach requires knowledge of what causes the heteroscedasticity. As this knowledge is barely available, the WLS approach becomes less feasible in practice than simply using heteroscedasticity-robust standard errors as introduced by Newey & West (1994), p. 644. See Brooks (2008), p. 136.

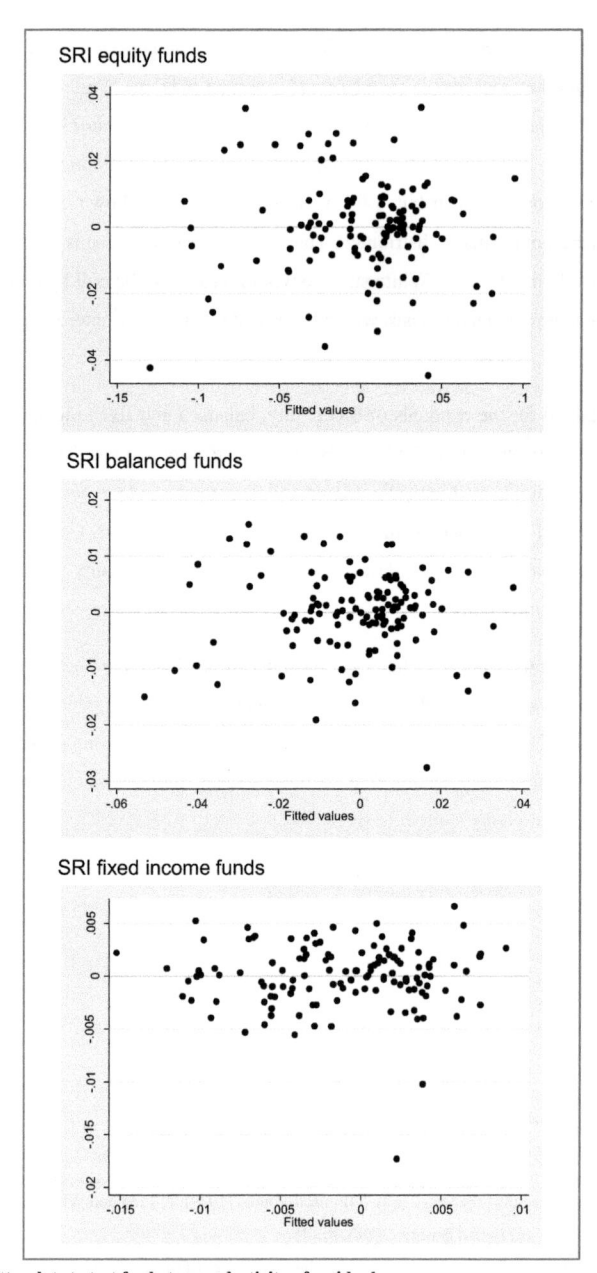

Figure 24: Scatterplots to test for heteroscedasticity of residuals
Source: Own illustration based on STATA output

6.2.2.3 Autocorrelation of residuals

Linear regression models that are based on ordinary least squares assume that the residuals are not only normally distributed or homoscedastic, but also uncorrelated with one another.[707] Uncorrelated residuals imply that the covariance between the residuals over time is assumed to be zero. If the covariance is different from zero, the residuals are said to be autocorrelated or serially correlated.[708] In general, autocorrelation is more likely to appear in studies that use time-series data than it is in cross-sectional studies.[709] The reason for this is the fact that the data points in time series data are collected during adjacent time periods, e.g. monthly fund returns that are measured over a period of two or more years. Thus, an effect such as the financial crisis that influences the return data in one month might spill over to the next months and might impact the return development of the respective fund for more than just one month.

As the empirical study in this thesis uses time-series data, a test for autocorrelation of residuals is performed. In order to detect autocorrelation, again, a graphical illustration and a quantitative test is conducted. The residuals are plotted against the time variable in Figure 25. If residuals were autocorrelated, the graphs should exhibit any type of systematic order between the data points. Examples of systematic order would be large magnitudes of the residuals relative to the uncorrelated residuals.[710] However, no plot of uncorrelated residuals is available for comparison in this case, which makes it is difficult to classify the magnitude of the residuals plots as being small or large. Thus, graphical illustrations require a lot of experience for making reliable estimations if autocorrelation in time-series data is present or not.[711] In fact, except for the upward shift that can be observed for the residuals of SRI fixed income funds, it is difficult to identify a pattern in the data points displayed in Figure 25.

---

[707] See Brooks (2008), p. 139, Lindström et al. (2015), p. 10 and Studenmund (2011), p. 97.

[708] See Freund et al. (2006), p. 160.

[709] Data that is used in cross-sectional studies are collected based on the assumption of random sampling. Random sampling, in turn, implies that the observations for the individual data points and with this, the residuals of the observations, are independent from each other. Given this assumption, autocorrelation typically is not a potential problem in cross-sectional studies. See Baltagi (2002), p. 115 and Wooldridge (2013), p. 350.

[710] See Freund et al. (2006), p. 165.

[711] See Brooks (2008), p. 143 and Chatfield (2013), p. 28.

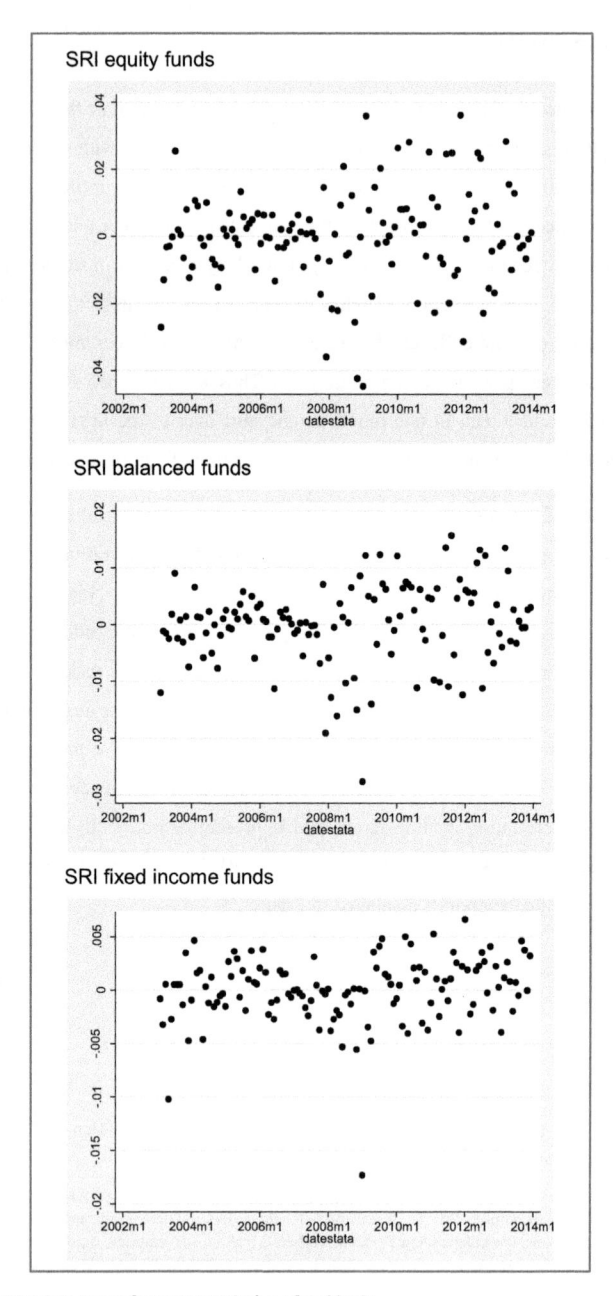

Figure 25: Scatterplots to test for autocorrelation of residuals
Source: Own illustration based on STATA output

The quantitative test that is conducted to detect autocorrelation is the Durbin-Watson (1950, 1951a, 1951b) test. Durbin and Watson have developed a test that allows assessing first order autocorrelation, which is the relationship between the residual and its immediately previous value.[712] The null hypothesis of the Durbin-Watson test states that residuals are independent and thus, not affected by autocorrelation.[713] The D-statistic obtained when conducting the test is between 0 and 4. In case of no autocorrelation, the D-statistic is equal to 2.[714] Deviations of the D-statistic for the residuals from 2 imply positive (i.e. for values between 2 and 4) or negative (i.e. for values between 0 and 2) autocorrelation of the residuals.

For values between 1.69 and 2.31 (D-statistic), the null hypothesis would have to be accepted and for values below 1.65 and above 2.35 it would have to be rejected.[715] For values between 1.65 and 1.69 as well as 2.31 and 2.35, the null hypothesis of no autocorrelation could neither be accepted nor rejected. As displayed in Table 20, the D-statistic for SRI equity and fixed income funds are 2.21 and 1.84, respectively. Thus, the null hypotheses cannot be rejected for those categories of funds and there is no evidence that the residuals are (positively or negatively) autocorrelated. For SRI balanced funds, the D-statistic is equal to 2.38, which is above 2.35 and leads to the rejection of the null hypothesis. Consequently, there is significant evidence of negative autocorrelation of SRI balanced funds in the sample.

Table 20: Summary of quantitative residuals tests

This table summarizes the residual tests that have been conducted prior to estimating the regression models. The Shapiro-Wilk statistics tests if residuals are normally distributed; the White statistics tests if returns are homoscedastic; the Durbin-Watson statistic tests for autocorrelation of the residuals.

Test for...	Shapiro-Wilk (W-statistic) Normal dist.	White statistic (F-Value) Heterosc.	Durbin-Watson (D-statistic) Autocorr.
Equity SRI funds	0.969 ***	13.72 ***	2.210
Balanced SRI funds	0.967 ***	7.830 **	2.382
Fixed income SRI funds	0.907 ***	0.500	1.836

Source: Own illustration

---

[712] See Brooks (2008), p. 144, Lee et al. (2000), p. 712 and Montgomery (2015), p. 477.
[713] See Durbin & Watson (1950), p. 417 and (1951b), p. 161.
[714] See Brooks (2008), p. 147, Freund et al. (2006), p. 166 and Studenmund (2011), p. 316.
[715] The critical values are derived for the time series data on a European level and at a significance-level of 5%. See Durbin & Watson (1951b), p. 173.

Even though heteroscedasticity and autocorrelation of residuals are present, the linear regression models as introduced in section 5.2 nevertheless are estimated when assessing SRI fund performance. However, the estimates for the residuals are reported according to the Newey-West (1994) regression analysis, which accounts for heteroscedasticity and autocorrelation.[716] This approach has already been applied in previous studies on SRI fund performance and has proven to be successful in predicting SRI fund returns.[717] The following sections will present the empirical results obtained when running the single- and multi-factor regression models.

6.2.3 Results of single-factor models

Table 21 shows the results obtained when running the single-factor regression models. The performance of equally weighted portfolios of SRI funds is compared to the performance of respective benchmark indices. All results reported in Table 21 are for the entire observation period from 2003 to 2013.

Panel A of Table 21 summarizes the results per SRI fund category on an aggregated level; Panel B shows the results per category and country. Overall, the negative alphas obtained in almost all categories indicate lower performance of the SRI funds relative to the chosen benchmark indices. Moreover, the relative performance of SRI funds is lower when conventional indices are used as benchmarks instead of SRI indices: In fact, the results displayed on the left in Panel A of Table 21 indicate that SRI balanced and fixed income funds significantly underperform their benchmark by -0.17% and -0.25% per month, respectively. The alpha obtained for SRI equity funds is also negative (-0.02% per month), but statistically not significant. Thus, when single-factor regression models are applied on an aggregated level for the entire sample of SRI funds, evidence of underperformance is only documented for SRI balanced and fixed income funds, but not for SRI equity funds.

Table 21: Single-factor analyses for monthly return data Jan 2003 - Dec 2013

This table shows the results for the single-factor regression analyses in the period from Jan 2003 to Dec 2013. Returns are calculated for equally weighted portfolios of SRI funds in each fund category. Panel A illustrates the results for Europe on an aggregated level and Panel B for each country. The estimates for alphas (α) are expressed in percentage terms per month. The t-statistics reported below the coefficients are calculated using Newey-West (1994) standard errors and lags of order 3 to account for heteroscedasticity and autocorrelation. ***, ** indicates significance at the 1% and 5% level, respectively.

---

[716] See Newey & West (1994), p. 648.
[717] See, for example, Benson et al. (2006), p. 349, Climent & Soriano (2011), p. 280, Galema et al. (2008), p. 2651, Jones et al. (2008), p. 189 and Renneboog et al. (2008b), p. 313.

6. Empirical Results

Panel A: Europe	Conventional indices			SRI indices		
Category	Alpha	Beta	Adj. R^2	Alpha	Beta	Adj. R^2
Equity	-0.017	0.759 ***	0.892	0.028	0.735 ***	0.865
	(-0.14)	(20.15)		(0.20)	(17.09)	
Balanced	-0.170 ***	0.520 ***	0.836	-0.101	0.309 ***	0.794
	(-2.72)	(16.73)		(-1.53)	(14.37)	
Fixed Income	-0.249 ***	0.564 ***	0.728	-0.107 *	0.012	0.002
	(-8.40)	(19.02)		(-1.89)	(1.06)	
Panel B: Country-split	Conventional indices			SRI indices		
Category/Country	Alpha	Beta	Adj. R^2	Alpha	Beta	Adj. R^2
Equity						
FR	-0.025	0.839 ***	0.949	0.025	0.817 ***	0.932
	(-0.32)	(36.34)		(0.26)	(27.09)	
UK	0.063	0.651 ***	0.715	0.103	0.625 ***	0.682
	(0.31)	(12.13)		(0.47)	(11.17)	
NL	-0.056	0.704 ***	0.773	-0.013	0.676 ***	0.738
	(-0.31)	(12.77)		(-0.07)	(11.61)	
DE	-0.080	0.735 ***	0.810	-0.036	0.709 ***	0.780
	(-0.48)	(12.55)		(-0.19)	(11.44)	
Balanced						
FR	-0.132 ***	0.570 ***	0.935	-0.056	0.340 ***	0.894
	(-3.87)	(34.06)		(-1.38)	(24.04)	
UK	-0.038	0.778 ***	0.548	0.064	0.477 ***	0.552
	(-0.18)	(8.84)		(0.32)	(8.58)	
NL	-0.122	0.485 ***	0.674	-0.057	0.287 ***	0.634
	(-1.47)	(13.35)		(-0.65)	(12.39)	
DE	-0.262 ***	0.408 ***	0.736	-0.207 ***	0.237 ***	0.668
	(-4.06)	(10.33)		(-2.98)	(9.11)	
Fixed Income						
FR	-0.127 ***	0.395 ***	0.809	-0.027	-0.001	-0.008
	(-8.87)	(25.12)		(-0.71)	(-0.09)	
UK	-0.654 ***	1.460 ***	0.230	-0.299	0.146 **	0.056
	(-2.81)	(6.78)		(-1.25)	(2.49)	
NL	-0.369 ***	0.644 ***	0.318	-0.202 **	-0.032	0.014
	(-5.41)	(9.24)		(-2.27)	(-1.60)	
DE	-0.414 ***	0.701 ***	0.587	-0.235 ***	-0.007	-0.006
	(-9.15)	(13.71)		(-3.13)	(-0.45)	

Source: Own illustration

Looking at the results per country as summarized in Panel B of Table 21, SRI balanced funds significantly underperform their conventional benchmark in France (-0.13% per month) and Germany (-0.26% per month). For SRI fixed income funds, the underperformance effect against the conventional benchmark is statistically significant in all four countries: Negative alphas range from -0.13% per month in France up to -0.65% per month in the UK. When SRI indices are used as benchmarks, the alphas for the SRI funds are also negative for almost all categories of funds, but statistically only significant for SRI balanced (alpha of -0.21% per month) and fixed income (alpha of -0.24% per month) funds in Germany. SRI equity funds in France and the UK as well as SRI balanced funds in the UK are able to generate positive alphas (0.03%, 0.10% and 0.06% per month, respectively), but the values are not statistically significant.

The higher beta factors for conventional indices in Table 21 indicate that the returns generated by SRI funds are not only lower compared to conventional indices; they are also more sensitive to conventional than to SRI indices. For SRI equity funds, the beta factor is 0.795 when conventional indices are used and 0.735 when SRI indices are used as benchmarks in the regression model (Panel A of Table 21). For fixed income funds, the difference is even more pronounced: While the beta factor is 0.012 in the SRI index model, it is 0.564 in the conventional index model. The observation that betas are higher when conventional indices are used as benchmarks also applies on the individual country level as displayed in Panel B of Table 21.

Comparing the results obtained for each category of funds, SRI equity funds have higher betas than SRI balanced and fixed income funds in all countries, except the UK. For conventional index models, SRI fixed income funds in UK have the highest beta-factor (1.46), followed by SRI balanced funds (0.778) and SRI equity funds (0.651). Overall, most beta factors are greater than zero, indicating a positive relationship between changes in the market return and changes in SRI fund return.[718]

Finally, the higher adjusted R^2 obtained for the conventional index models for all three categories of SRI funds indicates that the explanatory power of the conventional index models is higher than that for the SRI index models.[719] This finding is rather astonishing as SRI indices and SRI funds restrict their investment universe by only considering a limited set of investment securities that meet their investment criteria and apply similar screening criteria when selecting their investment securities. Thus, one could expect that the application of similar investment criteria leads to a better performance of SRI indices in predicting SRI funds than of conventional indices.[720]

However, the adjusted R^2 for the SRI index model is only 0.79 for SRI balanced funds in Europe whereas for the conventional index model it is 0.84. For equity funds, the difference is less pronounced (the adjusted R^2 for the SRI index model is 0.87 and 0.89 for the conventional index model), but even more extreme for fixed income funds: While the adjusted R^2 is almost zero in

---

[718] The beta-factor for SRI equity funds displayed in Panel A is 0.759. Thus, a 1%-change in market return is expected to result in a 0.759%-change in SRI fund return (see section 4.3.2.1).

[719] See Brooks (2008), p. 109 and Cortez et al. (2009), p. 579.

[720] See section 5.3.2.2 as well as Bauer et al. (2005), p. 1765 and (2007), p. 116, Cortez et al. (2009), p. 579 and Leite & Cortez (2014), p. 261.

the SRI index model, it is 0.73 in the conventional index model. Thus, the explanatory power of the conventional index models is higher than that for the SRI index models. As a consequence, only conventional indices are used as benchmarks in the multi-factor regression models. The results obtained are discussed in the following section.

To conclude this section on SRI fund performance, the results obtained when estimating the single-factor regression models indicate that SRI funds underperform their respective benchmark only in rare cases: When conventional indices are used as benchmarks, significant underperformance of SRI funds can been documented for the portfolio of SRI balanced and fixed income funds, but not for SRI equity funds in the overall European portfolio. On a country-specific level, only the SRI balanced funds in the France and Germany underperform their benchmarks. Thus, hypothesis *H1b: There is a significant difference in the performance of SRI funds compared to conventional indices* can only be accepted for SRI fixed income funds and partially also for SRI balanced funds, but has to be rejected for SRI equity funds. In line with this, hypothesis *H1c: There is a significant difference in the performance of SRI funds compared to SRI benchmark indices* also has to be rejected for all SRI funds except SRI balanced and fixed income funds in Germany. Thus, although the alphas for the SRI funds in the SRI regression models have mainly been negative, no evidence of significant underperformance of the SRI funds relative to their benchmarks can been documented.

6.2.4 Results of multi-factor models

The results summarized in Table 22 indicate that the explanatory power of the models increases when three-factor regression models are applied: The adjusted R^2 improves for all categories of SRI funds and in all countries. For SRI equity funds, for example, the adjusted R^2 increases from 0.89 in the single-factor to 0.93 in the three-factor regression model (Panel A of Table 22). Consequently, the three-factor regression models are more reliable in predicting SRI funds returns than the single-factor models applied previously.[721]

However, the results obtained by the three-factor regression model are similar to the ones obtained when applying the single-factor regression models: For the overall European portfolio, alphas are negative for all categories of SRI funds and statistically significant for SRI balanced

---

[721] Adjusted R^2 instead of R^2 is used to compare the goodness of fit between the single- and multi-factor models. The value obtained for R^2 depends on the number of regressors in the model; the more regressors are used, the higher R^2 will be. Adjusted R^2, in turn, accounts for the losses in the degrees of freedom when more regressors are added to the model and thus, is a more reliable estimate of the model fit when comparing regression models with a different number of regressors. See Brooks (2008), p. 110.

(-0.24% per month) and fixed income funds (-0.24% per month), only SRI equity funds do not exhibit significant negative alphas (-0.15% per month). On the country-specific level, SRI fixed income and balanced funds – except for the fund in the UK – significantly underperform their benchmarks. Again, SRI equity funds generate negative alphas, but no evidence of significant underperformance can be observed.

Overall, the alphas generated by the funds are lower in the three-factor than in the single-factor regression model: For the overall European fund portfolio, the alpha generated by SRI equity funds, for example, is -0.02% per month in the single-factor model and -0.15% per month in the three-factor model. For SRI balanced funds, the statistically significant alpha decreases from -0.17% per month in the single-factor model to -0.24% per month in the multi-factor model. Only the significantly negative alpha for SRI fixed income funds is almost the same in both models (-0.24% per month). On a country-specific level, the alphas obtained in the three-factor models are also lower than those obtained in the single-factor models. Interestingly, for SRI equity funds in the UK, the alpha is positive in the single-factor model (+0.06% per month), but negative in the three-factor regression model (-0.13% per month).

The results obtained for the adjusted R^2 in the three-factor regressions model show that the overall fit of the regression model increases with an increasing number of regressors or factors in the model. This finding could lead to the conclusion that a four-factor regression model would be even better in predicting SRI fund return than the single- or three factor regression models. In section 4.3.4.2 the Carhart (1997) four-factor model has been introduced. This model is an extension of the three-factor model developed by Fama and French (1993, 1996)[722] and accounts for the momentum anomaly documented by Jegadeesh and Titman (1993).[723]

---

[722] See Fama & French (1993), p. 19 and (1996), p. 55.

[723] Jegadeesh and Titman show that trading strategies that buy stocks that have performed well (winner stocks) and sell stocks that have performed poor (loser stocks) in the past 6 months prior to the portfolio formation date and hold this portfolio for a period of 6 months generate significant abnormal returns for the years 1965 to 1989. See section 5.1.3 and Jegadeesh & Titman (1993), p. 89.

6. Empirical Results

Table 22: Three-factor analyses for monthly return data Jan 2003 - Dec 2013

This table shows the results for the three-factor regression analysis for the period from Jan 2003 to Dec 2013. Returns are calculated for equally weighted portfolios of SRI funds in each fund category. Panel A illustrates the results for Europe on an aggregated level and Panel B for each country. The estimates for alphas (α) are expressed in percentage terms per month. The t-statistics reported below the coefficients are calculated using Newey-West (1994) standard errors and lags of order 3 to account for heteroscedasticity and autocorrelation. ***, **, * indicates significance at the 1%, 5%, and 10% level, respectively.

Panel A: Europe	Conventional indices				
Category	Alpha	Beta 1	Beta 2	Beta 3	Adj. R^2
Equity	-0.151	0.808 ***	0.214 ***	-0.185 ***	0.926
	(-1.39)	(28.44)	(3.91)	(-4.56)	
Balanced	-0.242 ***	0.503 ***	0.175 ***	0.272 ***	0.871
	(-4.66)	(8.80)	(3.37)	(15.22)	
Fixed Income	-0.239 ***	0.426 ***	0.062 *	0.142 ***	0.747
	(-8.81)	(8.27)	(1.90)	(3.37)	

Panel B: Country-split	Conventional indices				
Category/Country	Alpha	Beta 1	Beta 2	Beta 3	Adj. R^2
Equity					
FR	-0.099	0.874 ***	0.107 ***	-0.134 ***	0.960
	(-1.36)	(40.07)	(3.32)	(-4.21)	
UK	-0.128	0.714 ***	0.313 ***	-0.241 ***	0.788
	(-0.70)	(17.74)	(3.54)	(-3.39)	
NL	-0.250	0.769 ***	0.317 ***	-0.248 ***	0.844
	(-1.57)	(20.01)	(3.75)	(-4.57)	
DE	-0.254	0.791 ***	0.288 ***	-0.216 ***	0.864
	(-1.63)	(17.71)	(3.46)	(-3.97)	
Balanced					
FR	-0.171 ***	0.397 ***	0.041	0.319 ***	0.941
	(-4.96)	(7.03)	(0.94)	(32.51)	
UK	-0.105	0.588 ***	0.754 ***	0.357 ***	0.604
	(-0.57)	(3.10)	(3.21)	(6.02)	
NL	-0.228 ***	0.630 ***	0.128	0.255 ***	0.724
	(-3.01)	(6.69)	(1.42)	(10.72)	
DE	-0.353 ***	0.537 ***	0.142 **	0.210 ***	0.801
	(-6.81)	(9.20)	(2.17)	(10.79)	
Fixed Income					
FR	-0.117 ***	0.245 ***	0.017	0.168 ***	0.919
	(-10.18)	(11.41)	(0.99)	(9.98)	
UK	-0.635 ***	1.431 ***	0.649 **	-0.146	0.308
	(-3.27)	(4.29)	(2.47)	(-0.72)	
NL	-0.362 ***	0.457 ***	-0.213 ***	0.275 ***	0.490
	(-6.29)	(3.69)	(-3.17)	(2.98)	
DE	-0.413 ***	0.642 ***	-0.102 **	0.096 *	0.629
	(-9.93)	(8.26)	(-2.32)	(1.69)	

Source: Own illustration

Table 23: Four-factor analyses for monthly return data Jan 2003 - Dec 2013

This table shows the results for the four-factor regression analyses for the period Jan 2003 - Dec 2013 and the adjusted R^2 obtained in the three-factor regression analyses. Returns are calculated for equally weighted portfolios of SRI funds in each category of funds. The estimates for alphas (α) are expressed in percentage terms per month. The t-statistics reported in parentheses below the coefficients are calculated using Newey-West (1994) standard errors and lags of order 3 to account for heteroscedasticity and autocorrelation. ***, **, * indicates significance at the 1%, 5%, and 10% level, respectively.

Equity funds	Conventional indices					4-factor adj. R^2	3-factor adj. R^2
	Alpha	Beta 1	Beta 2	Beta 3	Beta 4		
Europe	-0.109	0.799 ***	0.222 ***	-0.193 ***	-0.160 **	0.930	0.926
	(-1.00)	(24.04)	(3.88)	(-4.68)	(-2.49)		
FR	-0.076	0.869 ***	0.111 ***	-0.138 ***	-0.088 *	0.960	0.960
	(-1.09)	(36.96)	(3.45)	(-4.25)	(-2.06)		
UK	-0.025	0.693 ***	0.333 ***	-0.262 ***	-0.388 ***	0.816	0.788
	(-0.14)	(14.02)	(3.62)	(-3.87)	(-3.36)		
NL	-0.220	0.763 ***	0.323 ***	-0.254 ***	-0.113	0.845	0.844
	(-1.32)	(17.84)	(3.72)	(-4.45)	(-0.99)		
DE	-0.239	0.788 ***	0.291 ***	-0.219 ***	-0.057	0.863	0.864
	(-1.47)	(16.10)	(3.40)	(-3.99)	(-0.56)		

Source: Own illustration

In order to test if the overall model fit increases with an additional factor, a four-factor regression analysis similar to the one developed by Carhart (1997) has been estimated for all SRI equity funds as well. This model is a representative test if the inclusion of one additional factor leads to a significant improvement of the overall fit of the regression model for SRI funds in all categories. Table 23 shows the results obtained for the factor loadings and adjusted R^2 for the four- and three-factor regression models. Again, the factor loadings for the estimated alphas are negative, but statistically not significant – neither on an aggregated European-level nor for the funds in the four countries separately. As the adjusted R^2 do also not improve significantly compared to the results obtained in the three-factor regression model, the remaining analyses for all categories of funds are based on the three-factor models introduced in section 4.3.4.

6.2.5 Sub-period analyses

Figure 22 on page 181 shows that returns for the Euro Stoxx index have been highly volatile after the start of the global financial crisis in mid-2007. In order to test hypotheses H3a to H3d and thus, to assess whether the financial crisis also had an effect on the relative performance of the SRI funds compared to their benchmarks, the funds' performances are analyzed over two sub-periods: The first period ranges from January 2003 to December 2007 (before the crisis) and the second one from January 2008 to December 2013 (during and after the crisis). For each period, single-factor and multi-factor regression analyses are estimated in the same ways as done previously when the performance has been assessed for the entire observation period. The results obtained in the sub-period analysis are displayed in Table 24 for the single-factor models and Table 25 for the three-factor models.

The sub-period analysis for the single-factor models in Table 24 shows that the underperformance effect seems to be slightly more pronounced in the years before than during or after the global financial crisis. Compared to the one-period analysis, all alphas obtained are lower in the first period from 2003 to 2007 and higher in the second period from 2008 to 2013: While SRI balanced funds underperform their conventional benchmark in the one-period analysis by -0.17% per month, the effect is -0.29% per month for the period 2003 to 2007 and only -0.11% per month for the period 2008 to 2013. SRI equity funds even generate a positive alpha in the second period (+0.06% per month), but the effect is not statistically significant. The negative alphas for SRI balanced and SRI fixed income funds are statistically significant at the 1% level.

When SRI indices are used as benchmarks, the alphas are lower in the first period as well. While the alpha generated by SRI equity funds is 0.03% per month in the whole-period, it is only 0.01% per month in the sub-period from 2003 to 2007, but 0.04% per month in the sub-period from 2008 to 2013. The negative alphas for SRI balanced (-0.17% per month) and fixed income (-0.18% per month) funds in the sub-period 2003 to 2007 are even statistically significant, which has not been the case in the one-period analysis. Thus, SRI fund underperformance occurs in the short-run, but diminishes in the long-run – at least for SRI balanced funds in the single-factor and three-factor model. This finding leads to the rejection of hypotheses H3c and H3d for SRI balanced funds, which state that SRI funds that underperform their (SRI and conventional) benchmarks in the short-run will also underperform their benchmarks in the long-run. As outperformance cannot be documented for any of the funds, no decision on the rejection or acceptance of hypotheses *H3a: SRI funds that outperform their SRI benchmarks in the first sub-period will underperform the benchmark in the second sub-period* and *H3b: SRI funds that outperform their conventional benchmarks in the first sub-period will underperform the benchmark in the second sub-periods* can be made.

Table 24: Single-factor analyses for monthly return data in sub-periods

This table shows the regression results for equally weighted portfolios of all SRI funds included in the sample. The results are computed for each category of funds over two sub-periods. Panel A illustrates the regression results for the 1-factor models in the period Jan 2003 to Dec 2007 and Panel B for the period Jan 2008 to Dec 2013. The estimates for alphas (α) are expressed in percentage terms per month. The t-statistics reported in parentheses below the coefficients are calculated using Newey-West (1994) standard errors and lags of order 3 to account for heteroscedasticity and autocorrelation. *** indicates significance at the 1% level.

Panel A: 2003-2007	Conventional indices			SRI indices		
Category	Alpha	Beta	Adj. R^2	Alpha	Beta	Adj. R^2
Equity	-0.206	0.845 ***	0.915	0.005	0.741 ***	0.892
	(-1.55)	(25.49)		(0.04)	(24.60)	
Balanced	-0.296 ***	0.601 ***	0.883	-0.174 ***	0.327 ***	0.830
	(-5.09)	(17.92)		(-2.70)	(16.12)	
Fixed Income	-0.256 ***	0.528 ***	0.740	-0.177 ***	-0.022	0.003
	(-7.83)	(10.22)		(-2.75)	(-1.07)	

Panel B: 2008-2013	Conventional indices			SRI indices		
Category	Alpha	Beta	Adj. R^2	Alpha	Beta	Adj. R^2
Equity	0.061	0.741 ***	0.886	0.043	0.734 ***	0.852
	(0.33)	(15.73)		(0.20)	(13.12)	
Balanced	-0.109	0.504 ***	0.827	-0.054	0.306 ***	0.781
	(-1.14)	(13.42)		(-0.52)	(11.16)	
Fixed Income	-0.246 ***	0.582 ***	0.715	-0.029	0.024	0.026
	(-5.08)	(16.42)		(-0.36)	(1.76)	

Source: Own illustration

As displayed in Table 25, the sub-period analysis for the three-factor regression models shows similar results as the single-factor regression models do: Compared to the one-period analysis, alphas generated by the SRI funds are lower – or more negative – in the first period from 2003 to 2007 and higher – or less negative – in the period 2008 to 2013. For SRI balanced funds, the alpha obtained in the one-period analysis is -0.24% per month, but -0.31% per month in the first and -0.27% per month in the second part of the sub-period analysis. Strikingly, the alpha obtained for SRI equity funds is also significantly negative in the first period. Thus, there is evidence of significant underperformance of SRI equity funds between 2003 and 2007. However, this effect diminishes in the second period of the analysis.

Table 25: Three-factor analyses for monthly return data in sub-periods

This table shows the regression results for equally weighted portfolios of all SRI funds included in the sample. The results are computed for each category of funds over two sub-periods. Panel A illustrates the regression results for the 3-factor models in the period Jan 2003 to Dec 2007 and Panel B for the period Jan 2008 to Dec 2013. The estimates for alphas (α) are expressed in percentage terms per month. The t-statistics reported in parentheses below the coefficients are calculated using Newey-West (1994) standard errors and lags of order 3 to account for heteroscedasticity and autocorrelation.

*, **, *** indicates significance at the 10%, 5%, and 1% level, respectively.

Panel A: Period 2003-2007		Conventional indices			
Category	Alpha	Beta 1	Beta 2	Beta 3	Adj. R^2
Equity	-0.345 ***	0.834 ***	0.221 ***	0.055	0.941
	(-2.81)	(25.99)	(3.99)	(0.99)	
Balanced	-0.309 ***	0.351 ***	-0.019	0.344 ***	0.883
	(-5.43)	(4.89)	(-0.05)	(17.86)	
Fixed Income	-0.250 ***	0.468 **	-0.262	0.037	0.783
	(-7.60)	(2.68)	(-1.15)	(0.21)	

Panel B: Period 2008-2013		Conventional indices			
Category	Alpha	Beta 1	Beta 2	Beta 3	Adj. R^2
Equity	-0.106	0.811 ***	0.202 ***	-0.234 ***	0.926
	(-0.67)	(21.90)	(2.76)	(-4.93)	
Balanced	-0.274 ***	0.607 ***	0.196 ***	0.251 ***	0.884
	(-3.59)	(7.80)	(3.45)	(12.92)	
Fixed Income	-0.226 ***	0.447 ***	0.066 *	0.135 ***	0.735
	(-4.95)	(8.39)	(1.79)	(4.44)	

Source: Own illustration

6.2.6 Interim conclusion

Overall, the alphas generated by the SRI funds are mostly negative, irrespective of the investment period analyzed, the country in which the funds have been established or the category the funds belong to. However, given the results obtained in the empirical analyses conducted so far, no clear indication of significant underperformance of SRI funds compared to their benchmark indices can yet be derived. Although the alphas generated by SRI equity funds are mainly negative, the effect is not significant for funds in this category. Controversially, SRI balanced and fixed income funds significantly underperform their benchmarks in almost all analyses conducted.

Looking at the hypotheses that have been derived to assess SRI fund performance, the following conclusions can be made (see also Figure 26 on page 207): First, hypothesis *H1a: There is a significant difference in the performance of SRI indices compared to conventional benchmark indices* has to be rejected as the SRI benchmark indices generate a lower return than the conventional benchmarks, but the difference is not statistically significant. Second, hypothesis *H1b: There is a significant difference in the performance of SRI funds compared to conventional benchmark indices* can only be accepted for SRI balanced and fixed income funds, but has to be rejected for SRI equity funds.[724] This finding holds true for single- and multi-factor regression models estimated. Although SRI equity funds generate negative alphas, the effect is not significant – neither on the aggregated level when all SRI equity funds are combined into one portfolio, nor on the country-specific level when only SRI equity funds that have been established in one country are combined. Third, and in line with the previous finding, hypothesis *H1c: There is a significant difference in the performance of SRI funds compared to SRI benchmark indices* can only be accepted for SRI balanced and fixed income funds, but has to be rejected for SRI equity funds. Forth, hypothesis *H2a: The performance of SRI equity funds is superior to the performance of SRI funds in other categories* and hypothesis *H2b: SRI fixed income funds underperform other categories of funds* can be accepted as SRI equity funds generate higher alphas than SRI balanced and fixed income funds and SRI fixed income funds provide the lowest alphas, which in most cases even are statistically significant. Fifth, as outperformance of SRI funds against their SRI and conventional benchmarks has not been documented in any analysis, no inference about hypothesis *H3a: SRI funds that outperform their SRI benchmarks in the first sub-period will underperform the benchmarks in the second sub-period* and hypothesis *H3b: SRI funds that outperform their conventional benchmarks in the first sub-period will underperform the benchmarks in the second sub-period* can be made. Finally, hypothesis *H3c: SRI funds that underperform their SRI benchmarks during the entire observation period will also underperform the benchmark in sub-periods* and hypothesis *H3d: SRI funds that underperform their conventional benchmarks during the entire observation period will also underperform in sub-periods* have to be rejected for SRI balanced funds: Although the funds underperform in the short-run, alphas generated by the SRI balanced funds are negative in the long-run as well, but the underperformance effect diminishes.

Economically, the results obtained infer that investors – at least on the European SRI market – on the one hand cannot expect to earn positive excess returns when investing into SRI. But, on the other hand, they also do not have to be afraid of losing significant parts of their money when

---

[724] Exceptions are SRI balanced funds in the UK and the Netherlands for the single-factor models and SRI balanced funds in the UK for multi-factor models. However, the effect for the overall European-based portfolio is significant, which leads to the conclusion that H1b is accepted for balanced funds.

comparing the performance of SRI alternatives to conventional investments: The alphas generated by the SRI funds are negative, but statistically not significant in most cases. Only when investing into SRI fixed income funds, investors should be aware of the potential necessity to bear significantly negative returns.

Group of hypotheses		Description of hypotheses		
The performance of SRI screened relative to socially unscreened investments alternatives	H1a:	There is a significant difference in the performance of SRI *indices* compared to *conventional benchmark indices*.	✗	
	H1b:	There is a significant difference in the performance of SRI *funds* compared to *conventional benchmark indices*.	✗	Equity funds
	H1c:	There is a significant difference in the performance of SRI *funds* compared to *SRI benchmark indices*.	✗	Equity funds
The performance of SRI funds across different categories	H2a:	The *performance of SRI equity funds is superior* to the performance of SRI funds in other categories.	✓	Balanced & fixed income funds
	H2b:	*SRI fixed income funds underperform* other categories of SRI funds.	✓	Balanced & fixed income funds
The performance of SRI funds over time	H3a:	SRI funds that *outperform their SRI benchmarks* in the first sub-period will underperform the benchmarks in the second sub-period.	?	Outperformance not observed for any category of funds
	H3b:	SRI funds that *outperform their conventional benchmarks* in the first sub-period will underperform the benchmarks in the second period.	?	Outperformance not observed for any category of funds
	H3c:	SRI funds that *underperform their SRI benchmarks* during the entire observation period will also underperform the benchmark in sub-periods.	✗	Balanced funds
	H3d:	SRI funds that *underperform their conventional benchmarks* during the entire observation period will also underperform in sub-periods.	✗	Balanced funds

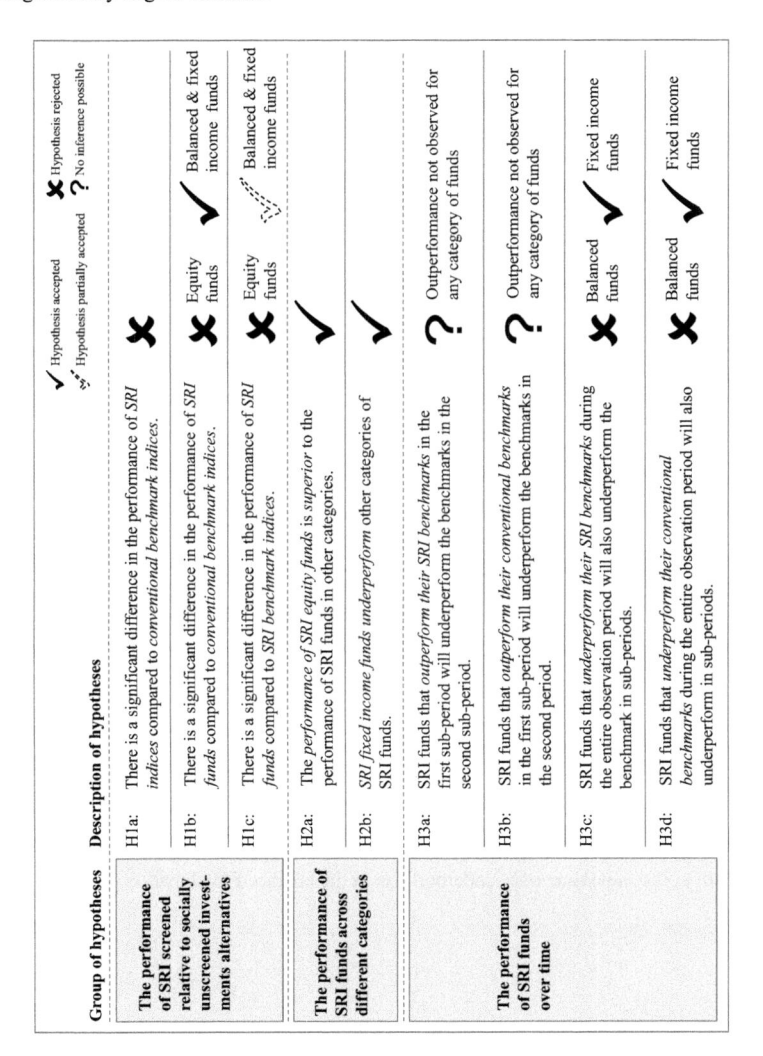

Legend: ✓ Hypothesis accepted; ✓ (partial) Hypothesis partially accepted; ✗ Hypothesis rejected; ? No inference possible

Figure 26: Overview of accepted and rejected hypotheses
Source: Own illustration

In order to further validate the results obtained so far, additional analyses are conducted. These analyses go beyond the ones that are required to merely test the hypotheses developed. Thus, they will provide additional insights on the SRI fund performance and further tests on the robustness on the previous statements on whether to accept or reject a hypothesis. The next section presents the analyses made and the results obtained in these analyses.

6.3 Additional analyses

6.3.1 Index regression

The descriptive statistics for the benchmark indices that are displayed in Table 15 on page 180 indicate that SRI indices tend to perform worse than their conventional counterparts. However, the results presented in Table 16 on page 183 show that the differences in excess returns of the indices are not statistically significant. In order to further validate the finding that SRI indices do not significantly underperform conventional indices, an index regression analysis is conducted. The advantage of the regression analysis is that performance is not only compared on a pure return basis (as it is the case for the results displayed in Table 16), but also on a risk-adjusted basis. Thus, the returns generated by the indices will be compared by also considering the risk that is associated with a certain level of return for each index.

In order to compare risk-adjusted returns for the indices, the returns generated by SRI benchmark indices are regressed against the returns generated by conventional ones. Table 26 shows the results of this regression analysis. The alphas for both, the Euro Stoxx Sustainability Index and the generated SRI index for balanced funds are negative. The alpha for the balanced fund SRI index even is significantly negative (-0.21% per month). These findings support the notion that SRI indices perform worse than the corresponding conventional indices. Conversely, the alpha for the FTSE4Good Index is positive (0.05% per month), but statistically not significant. Thus, SRI indices included in this sample are not able to outperform their conventional counterparts, but at the same time only underperform in the balanced fund market.

Table 26: Index regression

This table shows estimates obtained by regressing SRI indices per category on conventional indices. The estimates for alphas (α) are expressed in percentage terms per month.
*** indicates significance at the 1% level.

Index	Alpha	Beta	Adj. R^2
Euro Stoxx Sust.	-0.058	1.008 ***	0.981
	(-0.89)	(82.59)	
54.4% EuroStoxx Sust.,	-0.210 ***	1.613 ***	0.968
45.6% FTSE4Good	(-2.67)	(62.91)	
FTSE4Good EU	0.052	0.227	-0.006
	(0.12)	(0.50)	

Source: Own illustration

The results obtained in the regression analysis are also of interest for academics, who argue that differences between SRI fund returns and index returns should mainly be attributed to the active management of the funds. Proponents of this argument state that benchmark indices follow passive investment strategies that involve only limited actions for re-balancing the portfolio.[725] SRI funds, however, follow active investment strategies that involve costs such as management fees, load fees or transaction cost.[726] As these costs influence the SRI funds' return, but do not affect the indices' returns, the returns generated by the funds should be lower than the returns generated by the indices.[727]

However, the results displayed in Table 26 indicate that on the equity capital market, the performance of SRI funds and SRI benchmark indices is comparable to the performance of conventional indices, as no significant difference can be observed. On the market for balanced financial securities, significant underperformance not only occurs for SRI funds, but also for SRI indices. Finally, on the fixed income market, SRI funds significantly underperform their benchmarks, but SRI indices perform as good as conventional indices. Overall, the similar results obtained in the regression analyses for SRI funds and SRI indices lead to the conclusion that the fees involved in the active management of the funds do not seem to be the main driver of the underperformance effect observed for SRI balanced and fixed income funds. Moreover, as the performance of SRI indices relative to conventional indices is not significantly negative

---

[725] See Pozen (2002), p. 61.
[726] See Gil-Bazo et al. (2010), p. 245, Malhotra & McLeod (1997), p. 182, Murthi et al. (1997), p. 411.
[727] See Berk & Green (2004), p. 1270, Blanchett (2010), p. 99, Gil-Bazo (2010), p. 251, Sauer (1997), p. 146 and section 5.3.1.

for two of three SRI indices, the index regression analysis provides further evidence that supports the rejection of hypothesis *H1a: There is a significant difference in the performance of SRI indices compared to conventional benchmark indices.*

6.3.2 Gross return analysis

As introduced in section 5.3.1, the excess returns used in the regression analyses are calculated as the difference between the *net* returns of the SRI funds minus the risk-free rate of return. Thus, management fees charged by the SRI funds are deducted from the return prior to calculating the excess returns for each fund portfolio. The exclusion of management fees ensures that the excess returns used for SRI funds are comparable to the excess returns generated by the benchmark indices, which generally do not charge such fees.[728] However, in practice, management fees have to be paid by the investors and thus, influence the investors' perception on the relative performance of such funds against benchmark indices.

In order to test if the regression results change when the management fees that are charged by the funds are not accounted for, the regression analyses are also estimated using gross instead of net returns. Table 27 shows the results obtained in these analyses. Expectedly, the alphas for gross returns are higher than the alphas for net returns for all funds. In the single-factor regression analysis when conventional indices are used as benchmarks, some alphas that have been significantly negative in the initial regression analyses are not significant when gross excess returns are used (e.g. SRI balanced funds on the European level and in France). However, the alphas generated by SRI balanced and fixed income funds mainly remain significantly negative even when gross returns are used in the analysis. Similarly, the alphas obtained for SRI equity funds on the European as well as country-specific level, are not significant. Thus, underperformance only occurs for SRI balanced and fixed income funds and this finding is robust even if management fees are not considered when determining the funds' excess returns.

Table 27: Regression analysis with excess returns net and gross of management fees

This table shows the alpha estimates obtained in single- and multi-factor regression models using conventional and SRI indices as benchmarks. Panel A illustrates the results obtained for each category of funds on a European level, Panel B shows the results per category and country. Alpha net (gross) are estimates calculated using net (gross) excess returns, excluding (including) management fees. The estimates for alpha (α) are displayed in percentage per month for the entire observation period Jan 2003 to Dec 2013. *, **, *** indicates significance at the 10%, 5%, and 1% level, respectively.

---

[728] See section 5.3.1 and Pozen (2002), p. 61.

Panel A: Europe	1-factor conv. indices		1-factor SRI indices		3-factor conv. indices	
Category	Alpha net	Alpha gross	Alpha net	Alpha gross	Alpha net	Alpha gross
Equity	-0.017	0.103	0.028	0.148	-0.151	-0.031
Balanced	-0.170 ***	-0.074	-0.101	-0.004	-0.242 ***	-0.145 **
Fixed Income	-0.249 ***	-0.196 ***	-0.107 *	-0.054	-0.239 ***	-0.186 ***

Panel B: Country split	1-factor conv. indices		1-factor SRI indices		3-factor conv. indices	
Category	Alpha net	Alpha gross	Alpha net	Alpha gross	Alpha net	Alpha gross
Equity						
FR	-0.025	0.104	0.025	0.153	-0.099	0.030
UK	0.063	0.180	0.103	0.220	-0.128	-0.011
NL	-0.056	0.041	-0.013	0.083	-0.250	-0.153
DE	-0.080	0.033	-0.036	0.077	-0.254	-0.141
Balanced						
FR	-0.132 ***	-0.027	-0.056	0.049	-0.171 ***	-0.065 *
UK	-0.038	0.087	0.064	0.189	-0.105	0.020
NL	-0.122	-0.041	-0.057	0.024	-0.228 ***	-0.148 *
DE	-0.262 ***	-0.175 ***	-0.207 ***	-0.121 *	-0.353 ***	-0.267 ***
Fixed Income						
FR	-0.127 ***	-0.080 ***	-0.027	0.020	-0.117 ***	-0.070 ***
UK	-0.654 ***	-0.566 **	-0.299	-0.212	-0.635 ***	-0.548 ***
NL	-0.369 ***	-0.316 ***	-0.202 **	-0.149 *	-0.362 ***	-0.309 ***
DE	-0.414 ***	-0.357 ***	-0.235 ***	-0.179 **	-0.413 ***	-0.356 ***

Source: Own illustration

The similar results obtained in the regression analyses with gross and net returns provide further indication that management fees charged by the funds are not the reason for the (significant) return differences between actively managed SRI balanced and fixed income funds and passively managed indices. Instead, alphas are negative if the performance analyses are done with gross fund returns, net fund returns and even if the performance of SRI indices is regressed against the performance of conventional indices. For SRI equity funds and indices, the results are not significant – neither if gross returns or net returns are used in the regression analysis.

6.3.3 Individual SRI fund performance

The results presented previously have all been calculated on an aggregated level and by running regression models for fund portfolios in each category. For the European panel, excess returns for the funds in a category are calculated as an equally weighted average of the excess returns of all SRI funds in the respective fund category. Accordingly, excess returns for the fund portfolios per category and country have been calculated using a weighted average of the excess returns of the funds in the respective fund category *and* country. Thus, the results obtained in the regression analyses are based on aggregated observations and – strictly speaking – conclusions about the funds' individual performances are only valid on an aggregated level.

Further inferences about individual fund performance cannot be made unless it is assumed that the results for the aggregated level are also valid for the individual fund level. Moreover, as introduced in section 5.2.3.3, the regression analyses are based on the assumption that alphas are constant across the entire sample in each category. This assumption, however, is highly debatable: Although the total sample of SRI funds in a category might generate (significantly) negative alphas, there might also be individual funds that actually generate (significantly) positive alphas. Statman (2000), for example, shows that alphas vary greatly between the individual funds: While the mean alpha for all SRI funds in his sample is statistically insignificant (-2.59% p.a.), there is a broad range of alphas for the individual funds: One SRI fund generates a significantly negative alpha of -12.80% p.a., while another fund generates a significantly positive alpha of +10.14% p.a.[729] Overall, the majority (80.6%) of the individual alphas generated by the funds in his sample is negative, supporting the finding that SRI funds perform worse than conventional funds.

For the SRI funds included in the sample of this thesis, the majority of the funds generates negative alphas as well (see Table 28): When conventional indices are used as benchmarks, 62.3% of the funds (225 in absolute terms) have a negative alpha in the single-factor regression model and 80.9% (292) in the three-factor regression model.[730] Of these, 37.7% and 40.4% are

---

[729] See Statman (2000), p. 35.

[730] Please refer to Appendix IV for a detailed list of the alphas generated by each individual SRI fund.

significantly negative at the 5%-level, respectively. Only in case SRI indices are used as benchmarks, half of the alphas generated by the funds are negative and half positive. Of the negative alphas (180 in absolute terms), only about 23.3% are statistically significant.

In sum, the number of significantly negative alphas on the individual fund level decreases when SRI indices are used as benchmarks instead of conventional ones.[731] This finding is in line with the results obtained in the single-factor regression analyses that show that alphas are slightly higher (less negative) when SRI indices are used as benchmarks (see Table 21 on page 196). At the same time, the number of positive alphas generated by the funds is higher in the models, in which SRI indices are used as benchmarks, but the number of statistically significant positive alphas is lower: While 10 out of the 136 positive alphas generated in the single-factor regression model with conventional indices are statistically significant (about 7.4%), only 9 out of 181 are significant when SRI indices are used as benchmarks (about 5.0%).

Table 28: Individual fund performance for the European fund portfolio

This table shows the number of positive and negative alphas generated in each fund category. The results are calculated for the overall portfolio of SRI funds in each category. The number in brackets refers to the number of funds that are statistically significant at the 5% level.

Category	1-factor conv. indices	1-factor SRI indices	3-factor conv. indices
Equity			
# of alphas ≥0	122 [9]	132 [6]	65 [6]
# of alphas <0	92 [8]	82 [3]	149 [18]
Balanced			
# of alphas ≥0	13 [1]	22 [2]	3 [2]
# of alphas <0	47 [13]	38 [8]	57 [30]
Fixed Income			
# of alphas ≥0	1 [0]	27 [1]	1 [1]
# of alphas <0	86 [64]	60 [31]	86 [70]

Source: Own illustration

---

[731] In the conventional index model, 85 out of 225 SRI funds generate significantly negative alphas; in the SRI index model 42 alphas are significantly negative (out of 180 negative alphas in total).

Table 29: Individual fund performance for country-specific fund portfolios

This table shows the number of positive and negative alphas generated in each category of funds. The results are calculated for the overall portfolio of SRI funds in each category and country. The number in brackets refers to the number of funds that are statistically significant at the 5% level.

Category/Country	1-factor conv. indices	1-factor SRI indices	3-factor conv. indices
Equity			
FR			
# of alphas ≥0	58 [7]	63 [4]	41 [0]
# of alphas <0	45 [8]	40 [3]	62 [15]
UK			
# of alphas ≥0	37 [2]	40 [2]	16 [0]
# of alphas <0	15 [0]	12 [0]	36 [0]
NL			
# of alphas ≥0	12 [0]	14 [0]	4 [0]
# of alphas <0	12 [0]	10 [0]	20 [0]
DE			
# of alphas ≥0	15 [0]	15 [0]	4 [0]
# of alphas <0	20 [0]	20 [0]	31 [3]
Balanced			
FR			
# of alphas ≥0	7 [0]	11 [1]	1 [0]
# of alphas <0	15 [4]	11 [2]	21 [8]
UK			
# of alphas ≥0	4 [1]	5 [1]	1 [0]
# of alphas <0	3 [0]	2 [0]	6 [0]
NL			
# of alphas ≥0	0 [0]	2 [0]	0 [0]
# of alphas <0	8 [0]	6 [0]	8 [6]
DE			
# of alphas ≥0	2 [0]	4 [0]	1 [0]
# of alphas <0	21 [9]	19 [6]	22 [16]
Fixed Income			
FR			
# of alphas ≥0	1 [0]	24 [1]	1 [0]
# of alphas <0	60 [43]	37 [24]	60 [47]
UK			
# of alphas ≥0	0 [0]	0 [0]	0 [0]
# of alphas <0	8 [6]	8 [1]	8 [7]
NL			
# of alphas ≥0	0 [0]	2 [0]	0 [0]
# of alphas <0	6 [4]	4 [2]	6 [5]
DE			
# of alphas ≥0	0 [0]	1 [0]	0 [0]
# of alphas <0	12 [11]	11 [4]	12 [11]

Source: Own illustration

Table 29 provides a more detailed overview of the individual fund performance per category and country. The results displayed lead to similar findings as before: The number of statistically significant alphas (positive and negative) is lower when SRI indices are used as benchmarks instead of conventional ones. SRI fixed income funds have the highest share of significant alphas, e.g. in the three-factor model 70 out of 86 negative alphas are statistically significant.

In France, 65% and 78% of the SRI fixed income funds significantly underperform their benchmark index, depending on the regression model applied. In Germany, the share is even higher: About 90% (11 out of 12 funds) of the SRI fixed income funds generate a significantly negative alpha. Furthermore, only one fund in France generates a positive alpha when conventional indices are used as benchmarks. The alphas obtained for SRI funds in the UK, the Netherlands and Germany are all negative (and most of them statistically significant).

To conclude, the individual fund performance analysis supports the finding that SRI balanced and fixed income funds tend to perform worse than their benchmarks, while SRI equity funds show similar performances as their benchmarks do. Similar to Statman (2000), there are funds that generate positive alphas, but only few of them are significantly positive and thus, able to outperform the market.[732]

6.3.4 Interim conclusion

Additional analyses such as the index regression analyses, gross return analyses and the individual SRI fund performance analyses show similar results as the ones obtained in the single- and multi-factor regression analyses: SRI investment alternatives perform worse than their respective (SRI or conventional) benchmark indices, although the effect is only statistically significant for SRI balanced and fixed income funds.

The index regression analyses show that the negative difference between the returns generated by SRI indices and the returns generated by conventional indices is not significantly different from zero for equity and fixed income SRI funds. Only the SRI benchmark used for balanced funds, which is a composition of the indices used as benchmarks for the equity and fixed income markets, underperforms its conventional counterpart. These findings support the rejection of hypotheses *H1a: There is a significant difference in the performance of SRI indices compared*

---

[732] See Statman (2000), p. 35.

to conventional benchmark indices and undermine the argument that the lower performance of SRI funds compared to benchmark indices is mainly caused by the fees charged by the funds.

The results obtained in the gross return analyses support the argument that fees for active management of the SRI funds do not significantly influence the performance of the funds: Although the alphas obtained are higher (less negative) for the SRI funds, underperformance of balanced and fixed income SRI funds occurs irrespective of the fact if net or gross returns are used in the regression analyses. Thus, the gross return analyses support the acceptance of hypotheses $H1b$: *There is a significant difference in the performance of SRI funds compared to conventional benchmark indices* and $H1c$: *There is a significant difference in the performance of SRI funds compared to SRI benchmark indices* – at least for SRI balanced and fixed income funds.

Finally, the individual SRI fund performance analyses show that, overall, SRI funds seem to perform worse than their benchmark indices. Especially balanced and fixed income funds underperform the market – even on an individual fund performance level. However, there are also SRI funds that have generated significantly positive alphas and thus, outperformed the market during the 10-year observation period. Nonetheless, the majority of the individual alphas obtained are, in fact, negative, indicating underperformance of the SRI (balanced and fixed income) funds against their SRI and conventional benchmark indices.

6.4   Summary of results

The main objective of the empirical part of this thesis has been to assess the performance of socially screened investment alternatives and to test if it is in fact possible for investors to be doing good while doing well when investing in SRI. In order to accompany this objective, three research questions have been defined and answered in the course of the empirical study.

The first research question is how SRI-screened investment alternatives perform relative to the market. In general, SRI-screened investment alternatives such as SRI funds and SRI market indices define non-financial criteria to select the securities that are included in their portfolio. Only those investment securities that meet the criteria defined, e.g. by the funds' managers, can potentially be part of the funds' portfolio. Thus, managers of any SRI-screened investment alternative voluntarily restrict their investment universe by only considering a limited set of securities that meet their investment criteria.

6. Empirical Results

The screening process that is applied by those managers has led to a controversial discussion on potential effects of such constraints on the financial performance of SRI-screened investments.[733] Three possible performance scenarios are discussed: First, proponents of portfolio theory argue that the imposition of additional constraints in the security selection process negatively influences the construction of the efficient portfolio. Consequently, the performance of SRI-screened portfolios should be lower than the performance of SRI-unscreened portfolios that are built based on financial screening criteria. Other researchers, however, argue that – even if the performances of some SRI-screened securities differ from the performances of SRI-unscreened securities – the effects will cancel each other out once the securities are combined into a portfolio. Thus, the second performance scenario states that the screening process will have no effect on the relative performance of SRI-screened investment alternatives and the returns generated by the SRI-screened investments are comparable to the returns generated by SRI-unscreened investments. Finally, advocates of the SRI movement argue that the screening process applied by the managers has a positive effect on the relative performance of SRI-screened investments. The reasoning behind this third performance scenario is that only companies with a high rating on ESG themes can potentially be part of a SRI portfolio. Typically, these companies also exhibit superior long-term performance compared to the market average, which should translate into a higher performance of the SRI-screened relative to the SRI-unscreened investments. As there are existing empirical evidences that support all three theoretically-derived performance scenarios, no inference on the relative performance of SRI-screened investment alternatives can yet be made.

Most of the empirical evidence documented so far is based on the performance of SRI-screened equity investments. SRI-screened equity investments, however, only account for about half of the SRI market in Europe. The data set used in the empirical part of this thesis includes data for SRI equity as well as balanced and fixed income investments and thus, addresses the entire market for SRI. In order to provide an answer to the first research question, the empirical analysis is split into two parts: First, the performances of SRI-screened market indices in each category are assessed relative to the performances of SRI-unscreened or conventional market indices. The SRI-screened and SRI-unscreened indices are used as market proxies in the second part of the analysis, when the performances of SRI-screened (equity, balanced and fixed income) funds are compared to the performances of these benchmark indices.

---

[733] Please refer to sections 4.4 and 5.1.1 for details on the theoretical debate on the performance of SRI-screened relative to SRI-unscreened investments.

The results obtained in the index analyses show that the performance of SRI equity and fixed income indices is comparable to the performance of conventional indices. Only the SRI index used as a proxy for the balanced market underperforms its conventional counterpart. On the SRI fund level, underperformance occurs for SRI balanced and fixed income funds. For equity SRI funds, no significant difference between the returns generated by the funds and the (SRI and conventional) index can be documented. The results are robust even if gross returns are used instead of net returns for the funds.

To conclude, the answer to the first research question depends on the fund category analyzed: On the equity market, no significant difference between SRI-screened and SRI-unscreened investment alternatives can be observed. On the balanced market, the difference between the performances of SRI funds and the SRI index is also not significant. However, SRI balanced funds underperform the conventional index and the SRI index underperforms the SRI-unscreened index. Finally, on the fixed income market, the performance for the SRI index is comparable to the performance of the conventional index, but the SRI funds underperform both indices. Thus, SRI-screened investment alternatives do not generally underperform SRI-unscreened investments, but their performance depends on the category analyzed.

The analyses conducted in order to answer the second research question provide further evidence on the relative performance of SRI-screened funds across the three categories. Specifically, the analyses try to answer the question if there is a difference between the performances of SRI equity, balanced or fixed income funds. Theoretically, one would expect SRI equity funds to perform better, e.g. generate higher returns and have a higher risk, than any other fund category. Conversely, SRI fixed income funds are expected to perform worse, e.g. generate lower returns and have a lower risk, than the other fund categories.[734]

The empirical evidence obtained in the course of the empirical study supports the notion that SRI equity funds on average perform better than SRI fixed income funds: While the average excess return generated by SRI equity funds over the entire observation period is positive, SRI fixed income funds generate a significantly negative return during the same period.[735] Moreover, the alphas generated by the SRI equity funds in all regression models estimated are also higher – but statistically not significant – than the alphas generated by SRI balanced or fixed

---

[734] Please refer to section 5.1.2 for details on the theoretical discussion on the relative performance across different fund categories.

[735] Appendix V shows the return differences as well as t-statistics obtained when comparing average returns of the fund portfolios.

6. Empirical Results

income funds. Thus, the answer to the second research question is: Yes, there is a difference in the performance of SRI equity, balanced and fixed income funds and expectedly SRI equity (fixed income) funds perform better (worse) than funds from the other categories.

Finally, the third research question aims at analyzing if relative SRI fund performance changes over time. Market efficiency hypothesis implies that the price of a security always fully reflects all (financial) information investors or fund managers might need to take the decision on whether or not to invest in a security. Thus, it should not be possible for any individual investors to identify securities that are (temporarily) mispriced and implement trading strategies that exploit the mispricing. Instead, the active management that is needed to regularly re-balance portfolios that are built with the aim to exploit security mispricing involves costs that negatively influence the return generated by such portfolios. Moreover, even if fund managers are able to select securities that outperform passively managed market portfolios in the short-run, the effect should diminish in the long-run.[736]

Given these arguments, two possible scenarios on the relative performance of SRI funds over time can be derived: First, SRI funds should perform worse than their market benchmarks irrespective of the time period analyzed. In other words, SRI funds that underperform their benchmarks over the entire observation period should also underperform in sub-periods; relative performance of SRI funds will not change over time. Second, even if SRI funds perform better than their market benchmarks in the first period, the effect should diminish and result in comparable or slightly lower performance of the SRI funds in the second period.

The results obtained in the empirical study support the first scenario only for SRI fixed income funds: Funds that underperform their benchmarks during the entire period from 2003 to 2013 also underperform in the two sub-periods. Outperformance of SRI funds is not observed, which implies that no inference in the second performance scenario can be drawn. However, the lack of evidence of outperformance supports the efficient market hypothesis: SRI fund managers are not able to identify securities that are (temporarily) undervalued by the market and to use this information to build portfolios that perform better than the market. Investors, in turn, are also not better off when investing into SRI funds as the return generated by the funds are merely comparable to the returns generated by the market indices – if at all. Thus, in order to answer the third research question, the following statements can be made: First, SRI fund performance is stable over time. Second, there is a tendency for SRI fixed income funds to underperform in

---

[736] Please refer to section 5.1.3 for a detailed discussion of market efficiency hypothesis and the theoretical implication on the performance SRI fund portfolios.

the short- and in the long-run. Third, outperformance for the SRI fund portfolios cannot be observed and no inference about the development of outperforming portfolios over time can be made.

The finding obtained in this study reveal several implications that are of interest for investors, fund managers and academic researchers alike. The following section discusses these possible implications. The section thereafter provides ideas how researchers can use the results to further refine their empirical studies and gain additional insights on the relative performance of SRI funds.

6.5 Discussion of results

6.5.1 Implications

6.5.1.1 Investors

The implications that arise from the results obtained in the empirical study can be sorted by the group of stakeholders, which is affected by them: Investors, who consider investing into SRI-screened investments, fund managers, who set up, manage and promote SRI-screened funds and researchers, who aim to get further insights to the relative performance of these investment alternatives.

For investors, the results reveal two major implications. First, irrespective of the category of SRI funds they invest in, it is not possible for them to generate positive abnormal returns – at least for the funds that are included in the sample of this thesis: None of the fund portfolios in the study has outperformed the market portfolio. In best cases and mostly for SRI equity funds, the returns generated by the fund portfolios have not been significantly negative. The results have also shown that there is a difference in the return generated by the fund portfolios of different categories. Thus, the second implication for investors is that they should carefully think about which category of SRI funds they aim to invest in.

Evidence suggests that SRI equity funds perform as good as the market. Except for the alpha generated by SRI equity funds in the multi-factor model for the period 2003 to 2007, none of the alphas is statistically significant. One possible explanation for this finding is that the socially responsible feature does not seem to be priced on equity markets and there is no sacrifice in financial performance when investing into SRI equity funds. Another explanation is that the socially responsible feature of the companies included in these funds represents an investment into the companies' intangible assets, which is immediately incorporated into the price for the fund.[737] Thus, there is no possibility for fund managers to exploit this extra-investment and returns for the funds are not different from the returns generated by the market portfolios. This explanation would also be consistent with the efficient market hypothesis and the notion that all information is fully and immediately incorporated into the price of a security.[738] Both explanations lead to the conclusion that – at least on equity markets – investors can decide to invest in SRI-screened investment securities, which are in line with their personal values and beliefs, and do not have to suffer from inferior financial performance of these securities.[739]

On the balanced and fixed income markets, however, it does not seem to be possible for investors to combine financial and non-financial goals and still earn market returns. As the empirical analysis has shown, SRI balanced and fixed income funds underperform the market benchmarks in almost all settings. This implies that investors have to sacrifice substantial parts of the financial performance of their portfolios, when deciding to invest in SRI balanced and fixed income fund portfolios. Moreover, socially conscious investors face a trade-off between investing according to their personal values and beliefs and generating competitive financial returns with their investments. These findings supports the proponents of portfolio theory, who argue that imposing additional constraints limits the benefits of diversification and ultimately leads to the construction of sub-optimal investment portfolios. Thus, if investors are primarily concerned about the financial performance of their balanced and fixed income portfolio, they are better off with investing into the market portfolio. If investors, however, decide to invest in either SRI balanced or fixed income funds, it should be a conscious decision in which the socially responsible feature of the funds is put ahead of the funds' financial performance.

The finding that the number of SRI balanced and fixed income funds has increased steadily since the mid-1990s[740] indicates that there are investors, who are willing to accept the lower performance of these funds. Alternatively, these investors are not even aware of the fact that SRI balanced and fixed income funds underperform the market, but generally do not care too

---

[737] See Edmans (2011), p. 6, El Ghoul et al. (2011), p. 2389 and Jiao (2010), p. 2549.
[738] See section 5.1.3 as well as Fama (1970), p. 383 and (1991), p. 1575, Jordan (1983), p. 1325 and Malkiel (2003), p. 59.
[739] See also Cortez et al. (2009), p. 584 and Sauer (1997), p. 148.
[740] See Table 12 on page 166.

much about adhering to financial return objectives as long as their non-financial investment objectives are met. Thus, SRI equity funds are presumably attractive investments for investors, who consider both, financial and non-financial objectives in their investment decision process. SRI balanced and fixed income funds, however, are of interest for investors, who assign more weight on non-financial objectives than on financial ones.

6.5.1.2 Fund managers

Fund managers can use the finding that not all investors seem to assign equal weights to financial and non-financial objectives to tailor the marketing strategy when promoting their SRI funds. SRI equity funds, for example, can be promoted as funds that are not only able to generate competitive returns but also address social, ethical and/or environmental problems the society has to cope with. As investors do not have to give up substantial parts of the financial performance, the message of doing well while doing good is well applicable to the performance of SRI equity funds. Thus, fund managers cannot only use this message to attract socially-conscious investors, who are interested in SRI equity funds anyways. They can also use it to develop a new customer base and attract interest of investors, who primarily are interested in generating returns and consider the social aspect of SRI funds as a welcome side-effect.

For SRI balanced and fixed income funds, however, the message needs to be adjusted and focus on the aspect of doing something good while investing. Fund managers could use the socially responsible feature of these SRI funds as a differentiating factor to distinguish the funds from the multitude of other (conventional) funds available. While managers of conventional funds emphasize the historical performance of their funds, SRI fund managers should shift the focus to promoting the social and/or environmental good the companies included in these funds achieve.[741] This will make it easier for investors to identify funds that meet their personal values and beliefs and possibly accept the fact that these funds might generate lower returns than the market does.

The fact that at least parts of the investors are willing to accept lower returns generated by the SRI balanced and fixed funds also has implications on how SRI fund managers can promote the attractiveness of CSR activities to companies. The increasing number of SRI funds in all

---

[741] See Pasewark & Riley (2010), p. 249.

categories in Europe shows that the demand for such funds is growing. Concurrently, the investor base, which is attracted by these funds, is divided into investors that try to combine financial as well as non-financial objectives and investors, which put non-financial objectives ahead of financial ones. Investors, who are "*primarily concerned about social responsibility*"[742] are willing to trade in financial return for achieving social, ethical or environmental good. The return demanded by these investors is lower than the return demanded by investors, who primarily are interested in meeting their financial objectives. Companies, in turn, can benefit from lower return expectations as this can result in a reduction of the companies' cost of capital.[743] Thus, not only fund managers have an incentive to promote their SRI funds to the appropriate investor target group, companies should also be interested in being included in the fund portfolios by implementing and promoting CSR activities and thus, reducing its cost of capital.

Finally, a more advanced step in customizing marketing strategies applied by SRI fund managers would be to promote the funds according to the screens applied when selecting the companies. As the discussion in section 3.2.2 has shown, fund managers apply different types of screens when selecting the companies to invest in. Customized marketing efforts could, for example, promote funds that only invest in companies that are involved in activities targeted towards pollution prevention, recycling and environmental cleanup to investors, who are primarily interested in the environmental impact their investment has. Another example would be to explicitly promote funds that do not invest in companies that are involved in animal testing activities to investors, who are not willing to support such companies. The different funds promoted would attract investors, whose preferences are met with the investment strategy applied by the fund. Contrarily, investors with different preferences would not invest in these funds. Once the funds change their investment strategies, e.g. investing in low pollution companies instead of investing in companies that avoid animal testing, and promote this change accordingly, the types of investors attracted to the funds will change as well. The tendency of a fund or a security to only attract a specific type of investors with similar preferences is also referred to as clientele effect.[744] As the client base might change depending on the investment strategy

---

[742] Nilsson (2009), p. 27.

[743] See Pasewark & Riley (2010), p. 249.

[744] See Besley & Brigham (2014), p. 574 and Brigham & Housten (2015), p. 510. The clientele effect has first been introduced by Miller & Modigliani (1961), p. 411 and 432, who study the effect of varying dividend policies on the current price of a company's shares. Derwall et al. (2011), p. 2146, Muñoz et al. (2014), p. 258 and Renneboog et al. (2011), p. 563 document the presence of the clientele effect in the context of SRI funds and show that investor preferences not only vary across regions but also with regards to the investment objective pursued.

applied by the funds, the marketing strategies to promote the funds to investors need to be set up carefully in order to target the appropriate investor base.

However, the marketing strategies needed to promote these types of funds not only need a careful set up and in-depth knowledge of the investors' preferences. They also require transparency among the funds, which SRI screens the fund managers apply when selecting the companies to invest in. Moreover, companies should report on the CSR activities they have implemented. Today, only a small number of SRI funds provide detailed information on the screens applied and few companies that have implemented CSR activities publicly report them.[745] Once funds and companies with CSR activities are willing to share this information with the public, the promotion of SRI funds according to the screening criteria applied could be an effective marketing tool for fund managers to address the interests of a diverse and broad investor base.[746]

6.5.1.3 Researchers

All implications discussed so far are managerial implications that are of relevance for the stakeholders that are active in the SRI market – either because they want to invest in SRI funds or because they want to promote their SRI funds and attract investors. The results, however, also reveal implications for academia and the researchers, who try to gain further insights into the performance of SRI funds in general.

First, the diverse results obtained for SRI equity funds and balanced and fixed income funds illustrate the necessity to draw separate conclusions for the different fund categories. Previous research has focused on analyzing the performance for SRI equity funds.[747] The findings obtained in these studies are valid only for the equity SRI market; no inference about the balanced or fixed income or entire market for SRI can be made. As there is a difference in the performance of funds from different categories, researchers should refrain from making statements on the entire market – especially if their data set represents only a part of the SRI market.

Second, researchers can use the necessity to distinguish between the fund categories to expand the existing models. The empirical study in this thesis focusses on SRI funds that are established

---

[745] See section 3.1.4 and Table 6.

[746] See Schlegelmilch (1997), p. 52.

[747] See, for example, Bauer et al. (2005), p. 1754 and (2006), p. 36, Humphrey & Lee (2011), p. 526, Kempf & Osthoff (2008), p. 1277 and Renneboog et al. (2011), p. 566 for studies on SRI equity funds. Derwall & Koedijk (2009) examine the performance of SRI balanced and fixed income funds, but exclude SRI equity funds from their analysis.

in Europe. Future research could also include funds from other countries or regions and provide additional evidence on the performance of SRI fund portfolios in other markets. Picking up the idea of customized marketing strategies, researchers could expand their analyses and examine if the application of positive and/or negative screens influences the relative performance of funds in any category. Fund managers could use this information to directly address the "*primarily concerned about profit*" or "*primarily concerned about social responsibility*"[748] investor segment.

Third, the literature review in section 4.5.3 shows that there are already some researchers, who have analyzed the effect of screening intensity on the performance of SRI funds. Although there is evidence in favor of a curvilinear relationship between the screening intensity of a fund and its financial performance, the results have to be interpreted with caution: As the researchers have focused on SRI equity funds, the effect of screening intensity on the performance of SRI balanced and fixed income funds is unclear.[749] Thus, the SRI market again would benefit if researchers expand their existing models and provide further insights for all relevant stakeholder in the market. These are some of the aspects that have not been considered in the empirical study of this thesis, but provide some ideas worth considering in future research. The following sections introduce limitations of this study and provide suggestions on additional areas future research on SRI fund performance could focus on.

6.5.2 Limitations of the empirical study

The empirical study in this thesis has been set up carefully by clearly defining research questions to be answered, deriving hypotheses based on theoretical discussions as well as existing empirical evidences and using regression models that have proven to be successful in assessing SRI fund performance. Nonetheless, there are some limitations readers should have in mind when looking at the results and making inferences about the performance of SRI funds in general. These limitations refer to the data sample used, the fact that the analyses are based on historical performance data and thus, are retrospective, the fact that survivorship bias on the return estimates is neglected and the assumption that alphas and betas of the funds do not change and thus, are constant over time.

---

[748] Nilsson (2009), p. 27.

[749] See, for example, Barnett & Salomon (2006), p. 1117 and Humphrey & Lee (2011), p. 529, who examine the effect of screening intensity on the performance of SRI equity funds.

First, the data set included in the analysis consists of SRI funds established in the four biggest markets for SRI in Europe – the UK, France, the Netherlands and Germany. Together these markets account for about two thirds of the entire European market for SRI. Thus, the data set used is considered to be a representative sample for the total number of SRI funds established in Europe. However, one third of the market is not included in the analysis and no information on the SRI funds established in other European markets such as Belgium, Norway, Denmark or Italy is considered in the empirical study. Therefore, it can only be assumed that SRI funds in the countries that are not included in the analysis exhibit a similar performance pattern as the SRI funds that are part of the data sample do. As a consequence, the results obtained in this study hold true for SRI funds in the four markets that are included in the analysis, but at the same time can only be assumed to also be representative for SRI funds in other European markets. Moreover, conclusions on the performance of SRI funds in the entire European or even global market have to be made with caution and readers should keep in mind that the data set is representative, at least for the European market, but also limited.

Second, the analyses presented in this study are retrospective as they examine SRI fund performance based on historical performance data. Specifically, the analysis provides detailed information on SRI fund performance for fund portfolios across categories, countries and over time. However, performance is assessed in retrospect and thus, results provide insights on the past performance and have to be interpreted with caution.[750] By no means are the results intended to be used as a predictor for the future performance of SRI funds in any category or country. Instead, the results primarily provide an indication about what has happened in the past. Investors should combine this information with their experience on SRI funds in general and make up their own expectation on the future performance of such funds.

Third, the results are calculated for funds that existed in 2013. The price data has been downloaded for the period from January 2003 to December 2013. However, price data has only been obtained for funds that existed over the entire observation period. Funds that ceased to exist between 2003 and 2013 are not included in the sample. As only existing funds are included and dead funds are excluded from the analysis, the data set used could suffer from survivorship

---

[750] See Barnett & Salomon, (2006), p. 1118.

bias.[751] Survivorship bias can lead to an overestimation of average fund returns and thus, influence the inferences made based on the results obtained.[752] In fact, prior research shows that survivorship bias influences fund return estimates by about 0.1% to 0.4% per year.[753] The effect of survivorship bias on the returns of the funds included in this study has not been determined. Moreover, as the data set provided by Morningstar and Vigeo only included funds that existed in 2013, no survivorship-free regression model could have been calculated. Future research could address survivorship bias by setting up a sample that is based on SRI funds that existed at the beginning of the observation period in 2003. In this case, the analysis would still be retrospective, but free of survivorship bias.

A survivorship-free analysis could, for example, examine the performance of the fund sample in accordance with the analysis presented in this study. The knowledge, which funds ceased to exist during the observation period, however, provides possibilities for additional analysis. Separating funds that survived and funds that did not survive until 2013, for example, offers the possibility to also compare the performances of these funds with each other. Thus, future research could provide valuable insights on whether there is a significant difference in the performance between surviving and dead funds and if these differences might be one reason why the funds do not exist anymore.

Finally, the study in this thesis is also based on the assumption that alphas and betas are constant over the sample period. Fund return is assessed for equally weighted fund portfolios in the period from January 2003 to December 2013. Thus, the regression models provide *one* estimation value for the alpha- and beta-factors in each category of funds. Even when fund performance is assessed for the two sub-periods, there is one value for the alpha- and beta-factor in each period. Yearly or monthly alphas are not calculated. Instead, alphas and betas are assumed to remain constant for the funds in one category and over the sample (sub-)periods. Cortez et al. (2009), however, find evidence that alphas and betas for SRI equity funds are time-varying. Studying the performance of 88 SRI funds from seven European countries, the authors show

---

[751] See Elton et al. (1996), p. 1099.

[752] See Brown et al. (1992), p. 572, Chegut et al. (2011), p. 79 and Cogneau et al. (2013), p. 9.

[753] This equals a difference in return of less than 0.05% per month. Thus, the effect on the return estimates obtained for the funds in this study is assumed to be negligible. For details on how to calculate the effect of survivorship bias see Brown & Goetzmann (1995), p. 683, Brown et al. (1992), p. 570, Bu & Lacey (2007), p. 25, Grinblatt & Titman (1989), p. 401, Malkiel (1995), p. 552 and Rohleder et al. (2011), p. 444. For an overview of studies that provide estimates of survivorship bias see Lhabitant (2006), p. 484.

that 45% of the funds have time-varying betas.[754] Nonetheless, the authors also report that the overall result of neutral performance of SRI funds relative to their benchmarks does not change.[755] This finding indicates that the difference in results obtained in models with constant or time-varying betas is limited. Other researchers such as Bauer et al. (2006), Cortez and Nelson (2012) or Renneboog et al. (2008b) find no evidence that the consideration of time-varying betas has a significant effect on the results obtained when analyzing SRI equity fund performance.[756] Thus, although the effect of time-varying alphas and betas is not clearly defined yet, the assumption of constant alphas and betas is a limitation of the empirical study that ought to be considered when looking at the results obtained.

6.5.3 Areas for future research

Addressing the concern of survivorship bias or relaxing the assumption of constant alphas and betas as discussed in the previous section are limitations that can be addressed in future research on SRI fund performance. Other areas further research could focus on are, for example, changing the indices used in the analysis, also including conventional funds or accounting for differences in investment screens applied by the fund managers.

The empirical analysis in this thesis has compared the performance of SRI funds to that of conventional and SRI market indices. The indices chosen as benchmarks are consistent with previous studies that examine SRI fund performance in Europe. For equity funds, for example, the return generated by the Euro Stoxx Index and the Euro Stoxx Sustainability Index are used as proxies for the market return. Other studies that also analyze the performance of SRI funds established in Europe use the MSCI AC Europe Index or the Financial Times World Index as market proxies.[757] Using different market indices as benchmarks in the regression might lead to different results and with this, different inferences about relative SRI fund performance.[758]

---

[754] Cortez et al. (2009) apply conditional models developed by Christopherson et al. (1998) as well as Ferson & Schadt (1996) in order to account for the fact that fund performance can change over time. See Cortez et al. (2009), p. 576 and 579.

[755] See Cortez et al. (2009), p. 584.

[756] See Bauer et al. (2006), p. 42, Cortez et al. (2012), p. 269 and Renneboog et al. (2008b), p. 313.

[757] Cortez et al. (2009), p. 578 analyze the performance of 88 SRI funds from seven European countries and use the MSCI AC Europe as a proxy for SRI equity funds and the MSCI European Capital Markets Index as proxy for SRI balanced funds. Kreander et al. (2005), p. 1475 analyze SRI equity funds from four countries in Europe and use the Financial Times World Index as market proxy.

[758] See Costa & Jakob (2010), p. 100 and (2011), p. 142, Grinblatt & Titman (1993), p. 47, Lehmann & Modest (1987), p. 233, Roll (1978), p. 1056 and Terraza & Razafitombo (2013), p. 37.

6. Empirical Results

In fact, Grinblatt and Titman (1994) show that the benchmarks used have a significant effect on the results obtained for the performance measures.[759] Thus, in order to get more robust results, future research could use another set of market indices and examine if the results are similar to the ones obtained in the empirical part of this thesis.[760]

Researchers interested in gaining future insights on the relative SRI fund performance, could not only change the indices used as benchmarks. They could also expand the data set and, for example, include SRI and conventional funds in the analysis. This approach would not only provide insights on the relative performance of both fund groups relative to the market. It would also offer the possibility to compare the performance of SRI funds to that of conventional funds. The number of conventional funds in each category, however, presumably is larger than the number of SRI funds. Thus, prior to conducting the analysis, an adequate comparison group of conventional funds needs to be defined. In order to find a comparison group, researchers could apply a matched pair analysis like the one applied by Kreander et al. (2005) and compared the performance of SRI funds to a randomly selected sample of conventional funds that are similar in age or asset size.[761]

The advantage of comparing the performance of SRI funds to that of conventional funds would be to get additional insights if the active management of the fund portfolio has an effect on the performance of both fund groups. Researchers could, for example, examine if underperformance of SRI fixed income funds occurs only for SRI funds or if conventional fixed income funds provide similar evidence. The finding that both SRI and conventional fixed income funds underperform against the market index, would provide evidence that the socially responsible feature of the SRI funds is not necessarily the main driver of the lower performance of the funds. Instead, there could be other factors that negatively influence the return of fixed income funds.

In case a comparison between SRI and conventional funds is not possible or desired, researchers could also focus on analyzing if the different screens applied by the SRI funds have an effect on portfolio performance. As no information on the types of screens used by the SRI funds in

---

[759] See Fletcher (1995), p. 136 as well as Grinblatt & Titman (1994), p. 427.

[760] See Lhabitant (2006), p. 509 why the selection of an appropriate performance benchmark is important as well as Bailey (1992), p. 33 for criteria to consider when evaluating and selecting a benchmark.

[761] See Kreander et al. (2005), p. 1470 for a detailed description of the matched pair analysis applied as well as Bauer et al. (2005), p. 1756, Bello (2005), p. 45, Derwall & Koedijk (2009), p. 214, Gregory et al. (1997), p. 705 and Statman (2000), p. 34 for additional studies in which matched pair analyses are applied.

this study is available, no inference about the effect of such screens can be made. Above this, some funds apply more screens than others, which potentially also influences SRI fund return.[762] Previous studies, for example, find evidence that there is a curvilinear relationship between the number of screens applied and the performance of the funds.[763] However, these studies only include SRI equity funds based in the US. Future research could analyze the effect of screening intensity on SRI equity as well as balanced and fixed funds in the US and/or Europe.

Finally, there might be additional factors that have not been accounted for in this study, but potentially also influence fund portfolio performance. Examples used in previous studies on (SRI) equity fund performance are fund age and size, fees charged by the fund and the level of cash inflows to the funds. Grinblatt and Titman (1989), for example, show that smaller fund portfolios (measured by net asset value) perform better than larger fund portfolios. Moreover, the excess returns generated by the smaller fund portfolios are highly significant, indicating that these portfolios outperform the market benchmarks at the 1% significance-level.[764] Controlling for cash inflows, Bu and Lacey (2010) find evidence that smaller funds outperform larger funds and controlling for size, the authors show that funds with higher cash inflows generate higher returns than funds with lower cash inflows do.[765] Conversely, Malhotra and McLeod (1997) conclude that investors should rather invest in older and larger funds than in funds that have been established recently and are smaller in size. Specifically, the authors find evidence that larger and more mature funds on average have lower expense ratios. Funds with lower expense ratios, in turn, generate higher returns.[766]

The list of factors that potentially influence the performance of fund portfolios could be continued further, but would go beyond the scope of this thesis. Especially if the SRI funds included in the sample are extremely heterogeneous, ignoring these factors could lead to incorrect spec-

---

[762] See Barnett & Salomon (2006), p. 1102, Diltz (1995a), p. 64 and (1995b), p. 70 as well as Lee et al. (2010), p. 352.

[763] Barnett & Salomon (2006), p. 1117, Capelle-Blancard & Monjon (2011), p. 26 and Humphrey & Lee (2011), p. 529 show that performance of SRI funds initially decreases with the number of screens applied, but increases again if the number of screens gets large enough.

[764] See Grinblatt & Titman (1989), p. 407. This finding is supported by Chen et al. (2004), p. 1287, who study the relationship between fund size and fund performance. Using a sample of more than 3,000 conventional funds, the authors find a significantly negative relationship between fund size and future fund performance.

[765] See Bu & Lacey (2010), p. 405.

[766] See Malhotra & McLeod (1997), p. 189.

ifications of the regression models applied and thus, result in invalid inferences on the performance of the funds. Few researchers have already addressed some of the factors on SRI equity fund performance.[767] The effect on the performance of SRI balanced and fixed income funds has been neglected so far, but would provide valuable insights on the performance of the entire SRI market. Finally, it should be noted that it would not be possible for researchers to address all of the mentioned factors in one single study. Instead, the list is intended to help them in developing new ideas on how to study SRI fund performance in future analyses.

---

[767] Examples of additional factors examined in studies on SRI equity funds are the investment profile of the SRI funds, the funds' exposure to domestic or international markets, the fact that the funds are retail or wholesale funds, etc. See Humphrey & Lee (2011), p. 520, Jones et al. (2008), p. 190 and Renneboog et al. (2011), p. 587.

7 Conclusion

The main objective of the thesis has been to provide insights on the SRI market on a conceptual and empirical level. On the conceptual level, the thesis aims at providing a comprehensive introduction to the SRI market in general and the various definitions of SRI that can be found in practice and academia. The review of the numerous definitions of SRI available, shows that there is still no clear definition among practitioners and researchers about what SRI is and what it is not. Despite the lack of a common definition of SRI, the market size has increased considerably over the past few years. With increasing market size, the academic interest in this field has emerged as well. The thesis provides an overview of the empirical work on SRI that has been published in recent years: The models used in the existing empirical studies are presented and the results obtained summarized. The literature review is then used as a basis for the derivation of the hypotheses that are to be tested in the empirical part of this thesis.

Thus, the thesis not only addresses socially-conscious investors or readers, who might already have gained experience in SRI and want to get additional insights on the expected financial performance of SRI. It is also of interest for readers with a rather financial background, who might be less experienced with SRI so far. In order to familiarize these readers with the concept of SRI, Chapter 2 provides an in-depth overview of the SRI market, including its historical development and current size, the typical investor base for SRI as well as regulations that are already established to foster the growth of the market. In sum, the European SRI market is the biggest market for SRI globally and has exhibited exceptional growth especially in the past few years. Although a typical SRI investor cannot be defined yet, the investor base for SRI is growing and the concept of SRI is not only interesting for investors, who assign more weights on investing according to their personal values and beliefs than on generating financial returns. Instead, it increasingly attracts the attention from investors, who are concerned about both, achieving a positive impact for society and at the same time generating competitive financial returns with their investments.

Chapter 3 picks up the idea of introducing the concept of SRI to a broad readership and presents the two possibilities how investors can get exposed to SRI. The first possibility is to directly invest in companies that have incorporated CSR activities into their daily business operations. Investors can individually define the SRI criteria that need to be fulfilled and select the companies that meet these criteria. When investing into SRI funds, the indirect investment possibility, the funds' managers are responsible for defining the SRI criteria, selecting the companies that fulfill them and rebalancing the portfolio whenever needed. As SRI funds usually split their investment across a number of companies, investing into one fund already offers investors the possibility of getting exposed to a broad number of companies. Moreover, SRI funds release the individual investor from personally keeping track which companies continuously meet the SRI criteria and which companies might not meet them any longer. Chapter 3 concludes the rather general introduction into the concept of SRI and leads over to the chapters that focus on SRI funds only and present an in-depth literature review as well as the details of the empirical study conducted.

The literature review in Chapter 4 indicates that neither the theoretical debate nor the empirical evidence provides clear or unambiguous evidence on the (expected) performance of SRI funds. From a theoretical perspective, there are arguments in favor of underperformance, outperformance and also similar performance of SRI funds compared to their conventional counterparts or market benchmarks. Empirical studies support this notion. Most of the empirical studies published so far, however, focus on SRI funds established and marketed in the US. Moreover, the data sets used in these studies typically only include SRI equity funds and thus, neglect the presence of SRI balanced and fixed income funds. Consequently, the performance of SRI funds in Europe and across different fund categories is less explored. The empirical study presented in this thesis addresses this research gap by analyzing the performance of SRI equity, balanced and fixed income funds that are established in the four largest European countries for SRI investments – the UK, France, the Netherlands and Germany.

Specifically, the empirical part of the thesis tries to find an answer to the question whether or not it is possible for investors to be doing good while doing well when investing into SRI. In order to answer this question, three research questions are defined and analyzed. The first research question is set up to analyze if there is a difference in the performance of SRI-screened and SRI-unscreened investment alternatives. Therefore, the performance of SRI funds is compared to the performance of SRI and conventional benchmark indices. Moreover, the performance of SRI market indices is assessed relative to that of conventional indices. The second research question tries to provide an answer if there is a difference in the performance of SRI funds from different categories. As the empirical study of this thesis is one of the first to not only examine the performance of SRI equity funds, but also to include SRI balanced and fixed income funds, a performance of the funds can be assessed across the fund categories. Finally, the third research question assesses if there are changes in relative performance of SRI funds over time.

7. Conclusion

In order to assess the performance of the SRI funds – and at the same time provide answers to the research questions defined – the set of hypotheses that is to be tested is derived in Chapter 5. In sum, three sets of hypotheses are defined: The first set contains hypotheses derived in order to analyze the performance of SRI screened relative to socially unscreened investments alternatives. The second set focusses on hypotheses aimed at analyzing the performance of SRI funds across different categories. Finally, the third set contains hypotheses derived in order to assess the performance of SRI funds over time. Chapter 5 also introduces the methodologies applied and the data set used in the analyses.

In Chapter 6, the results obtained in the analysis are presented, implications for various stakeholder groups discussed and limitations as well as ideas for further research introduced. Given the data sample used and the results presented in Chapter 6, the empirical research questions initially defined can be answered as follows: First, there is no significant difference between the performance of SRI and conventional market indices. On the fund portfolio level, SRI equity funds generate similar returns as the SRI and conventional benchmark indices do. Only SRI balanced and fixed income funds significantly underperform their benchmarks. Second, as expected from theory, the performance of SRI equity funds is superior to the performance of SRI balanced and fixed income funds and SRI fixed income funds underperform SRI equity and balanced funds. Third, the performance of SRI funds is stable over time. Funds that underperform the market over the entire observation period also underperform in the two sub-periods; funds that generate similar return levels like the market over the entire period, also show this performance in the sub-periods.

The thesis contributes to existing research on SRI fund performance on a category, geographical and methodological level. On the category level, the empirical study is one of the first to examine the performance of all three fund categories available. While previous studies only address half of the market for SRI funds, the empirical study in this thesis addresses the entire SRI fund market. This approach ensures that the data set is a representative sample for the SRI funds available and that the conclusions made are not subject to the constraint that they are only valid for the equity part of the SRI market. On a geographical level, the study extends existing research as it focusses on European-based SRI funds. Unlike previous studies on SRI fund performance, the data set focusses on funds from four European markets (the UK, France, the Netherlands and Germany), but does not include US-based SRI funds. As these four markets account for about two thirds of the market for SRI in Europe, the data set is considered to be a representative sample for the total number of SRI funds established in Europe.

The models used to assess the performances of the SRI equity funds are models that are already applied excessively in existing studies on SRI fund performance. The models used for SRI balanced and fixed income funds, however, typically are applied to assess the performance of conventional mutual funds only. In the empirical part of this study, these models are applied to the context of SRI. Thus, on a methodological level, the study contributes to previous research by applying existing and broadly applied models in a rather new context of SRI.

The implications that can be drawn from the results obtained in the study are of relevance for investors, fund managers and researchers alike. Investors should be aware of the fact that – at least on the European market and during the sample period from January 2003 to December 2013 – it is not possible for them to generate abnormal returns by investing into SRI funds. The results show that only SRI equity funds perform as good as the market, but there is evidence of significant underperformance of SRI balanced and fixed income funds. None of the SRI fund portfolios, however, outperforms the market. As there are differences in the performance across the SRI fund categories, investors should also carefully think about which market they want to get exposed to and invest accordingly. On the equity markets, investors can expect to earn similar returns when investing into actively managed SRI funds or passively managed SRI market indices. The returns generated by the SRI equity funds are not significantly different from the returns generated by the market indices. Moreover, there is no evidence of underperformance of the SRI market index against the conventional index. SRI balanced and fixed income indices, however, provide evidence in favor of significant underperformance against the market indices. Thus, on the balanced and fixed income markets, investors would be better off investing into the passively managed indices instead of SRI funds. If they decide to invest in SRI balanced and fixed income funds anyways, investors should bear in mind that the returns generated by these funds might be significantly lower than the returns generated by the market indices.

Fund managers, in turn, can use the results obtained in the study to develop tailored marketing strategies that suit different SRI investor target groups. As there is no significant difference in the returns generated by SRI equity funds and the market indices, these funds not only are of interest for socially-conscious investor groups that put SRI objectives ahead of financial ones. Instead, these funds can also be marketed to investor groups that are primarily interested in generating competitive returns and do not require the investments to also have a positive impact for the public, but regard it as a welcome side-effect. When promoting SRI balanced and fixed income funds, fund managers should focus on the aspect of doing something good while investing and use the socially responsible feature of these SRI funds as a differentiating factor to distinguish the funds from the multitude of other (conventional) funds available.

The necessity to differentiate between the different fund categories when promoting SRI funds is also of relevance for researchers interested in gaining additional insights on the performance of these funds. As there are differences in the performances of SRI equity, balanced and fixed income funds, researchers should always consider the category of SRI funds included in the data set when making generalized statements on the performance of these funds. In addition, researchers can use the ideas for future research provided at the end of Chapter 6 to further refine the insights on the performance of SRI funds. Expanding the geographical focus of the data sample, including additional factors such as age and size of the SRI funds or type and number of screens applied by the funds in the security selection process are examples of aspects researchers can consider in future studies.

To conclude, the main objective of this thesis has been to provide an introduction into the market for SRI in general and empirically test whether or not it is possible for investors to be doing good while doing well when investing into SRI. The study conducted shows that the performance of SRI funds is not in principle better or worse than the performance of SRI or conventional market indices. Instead, investors have to consider which kind of fund category they want to invest in and – as with almost every financial investment – have to keep in mind that a potential upside (i.e. doing something good for society) is also related to a potential downside (i.e. earning lower returns than the market). SRI fund categories that perform as good as the market on a portfolio level also include funds that generate significantly positive or negative alphas on the individual fund level. Even if a SRI fund category shows evidence of significant underperformance on a portfolio level, there are individual funds within that category that perform as good as or even better than the market index. Consequently, investors, who invest in individual SRI funds, might still be able to generate above or below market returns, although the fund category in total under- or outperforms against the market. As the evidence provided is retrospective, it is not intended to provide clear predictions on the future performance of individual SRI funds in any category. Instead, investors can use the empirical results obtained in this thesis to make up their own expectations on the future performance of these funds and individually take the decision on whether or not to invest in SRI. The growing market size shows that an increasing number of investors decide to invest in SRI. This, in turn, indicates that SRI already is and most likely will remain an attractive investment opportunity – not only for socially-conscious investors, but also for investors, who are primarily interested in generating financial returns.

Appendices

Appendix I: Total AuM by SRI funds domiciled in Europe
(figures as of June 30 per year)

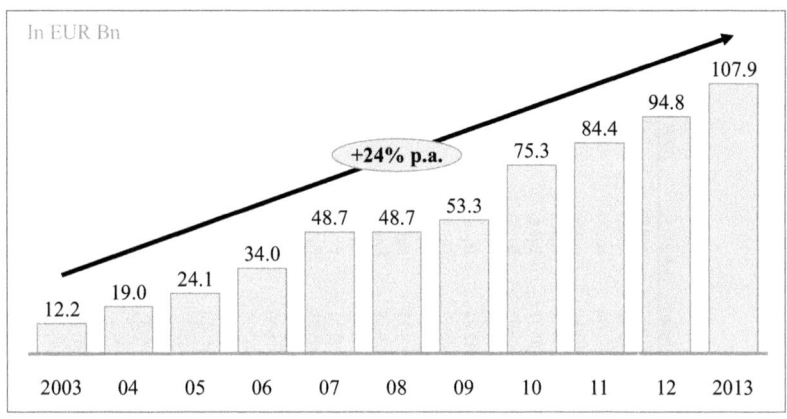

In EUR Bn

Year	2003	04	05	06	07	08	09	10	11	12	2013
	12.2	19.0	24.1	34.0	48.7	48.7	53.3	75.3	84.4	94.8	107.9

+24% p.a.

Source: Own illustration based on Vigeo (2013), p. 8

Appendix II: List of SRI funds included in the empirical analysis

This table shows the number of SRI funds included in the empirical analysis (Panel A: SRI funds in France, Panel B: UK, Panel C: The Netherlands, Panel D: Germany). The values obtained for the total net assets (TNA) of the funds are of mid-2013 and provided by Morningstar and Vigeo.

Panel A: SRI funds in France

ISIN	Fund name	Country	Launch date	Category	TNA 2013 (EUR mln)	Mgmt. Fee (in % p.a.)
FR0010093716	Atout France	FR	1988-01-11	Equity	2,233.4	1.20
FR0010106880	Atout Euroland	FR	1978-10-02	Equity	1,503.6	1.20
FR0010588343	EdR Tricolore Rendement	FR	1998-12-04	Equity	1,481.1	2.00
FR0010321828	Echiquier Major	FR	2005-03-11	Equity	1,070.9	2.39
FR0000018954	LCL Actions Euro	FR	1978-08-11	Equity	713.6	1.50
FR0000018947	LCL Actions France	FR	1965-03-31	Equity	475.0	1.90
FR0010596718	SSgA World SRI Index Equity Fund	FR	2005-03-01	Equity	432.0	0.30
FR0000984346	AG2R Actions ISR Acc	FR	2002-04-26	Equity	415.9	0.50
FR0010668145	BNP Paribas Aqua P	FR	2008-12-03	Equity	373.1	2.00
FR0010028969	BNP Paribas Etheis Inc	FR	2002-05-15	Equity	343.0	1.50
FR0000008963	LBPAM Responsable Actions Euro	FR	2001-11-05	Equity	334.0	1.50
FR0010091116	Ecureuil Bénéfices Responsable Inc	FR	1999-09-21	Equity	326.8	0.80
FR0000017329	Allianz Valeurs Durables R	FR	1991-10-15	Equity	282.4	1.79
FR0007045950	Fédéris ISR Euro C/D	FR	2000-06-16	Equity	267.7	1.00
FR0000970873	Insertion Emplois Dynamique R	FR	1994-05-11	Equity	249.3	1.79
FR0010146530	BNP Paribas Retraite Horizon P 100 Acc	FR	2005-01-21	Equity	240.0	1.20
FR0010153320	Amundi Actions USA ISR P	FR	1993-07-27	Equity	230.9	1.50
FR0010013987	Euro Capital Durable I Acc	FR	2001-11-20	Equity	220.9	1.50
FR0007494703	AG2R La Mondiale Actions Europe ISR	FR	1995-07-07	Equity	214.5	0.50
FR0000982761	AXA Euro Valeurs Responsables Acc	FR	1996-07-25	Equity	211.2	1.50
FR0000970840	Mirova Euro Sustainable Equity	FR	1999-12-20	Equity	206.3	1.75
FR0000437113	HSBC Actions Développement Durable A	FR	1995-12-29	Equity	205.4	1.50
FR0000975880	Allianz Actions Aéquitas A/I	FR	2001-06-29	Equity	201.6	1.79
LU0316218527	AXA WF Framlington Human Capital AC EUR	FR	2007-10-29	Equity	190.6	2.50

Panel A (continued): SRI funds in France

ISIN	Fund name	Country	Launch date	Category	TNA 2013 (EUR mln)	Mgmt. Fee (in % p.a.)
FR0010077412	BNP Paribas Développement Humain	FR	2002-04-11	Equity	174.7	1.50
LU0545089723	AXA WF Framlington Eurozone Ri	FR	2010-11-02	Equity	157.6	1.50
FR0010458760	Amundi Actions Euro ISR I2	FR	1999-05-21	Equity	151.1	0.70
LU0347711466	Parvest Global Environment Classic C Acc	FR	2008-04-09	Equity	149.3	1.75
FR0007083357	Regard Actions Developpement Durable Acc	FR	2003-06-25	Equity	130.5	0.10
FR0010500603	Agipi Monde Durable	FR	2007-09-12	Equity	129.3	2.20
FR0000174526	BNP Paribas Retraite 75 P Inc	FR	1985-12-31	Equity	121.3	1.20
FR0010844365	Amundi Actions France ISR P	FR	2010-01-28	Equity	117.3	1.00
FR0000981441	Ofi Leader ISR	FR	1997-03-14	Equity	116.5	1.30
LU0406802339	Parvest Environmental Opportunities C	FR	2006-05-30	Equity	113.7	2.20
FR0010341800	Palatine Or Bleu A C	FR	2006-07-24	Equity	108.8	1.50
FR0010792465	Label Europe Actions S A/I	FR	2002-07-24	Equity	103.2	1.50
LU0185496469	Ofi Multiselect - Europe SRI A Acc	FR	2006-08-14	Equity	100.4	2.10
FR0000427452	MG Croissance Durable France	FR	1998-08-26	Equity	99.4	1.80
FR0000003998	Objectif Investissement Responsable	FR	2001-06-01	Equity	94.5	1.30
FR0000991432	Amundi Actions Europe ISR P A/I	FR	2003-02-24	Equity	93.4	1.10
FR0000985152	LCL Actions Etats-Unis ISR	FR	1979-12-07	Equity	93.0	0.50
FR0010156216	BNP Paribas Immobilier	FR	2005-01-19	Equity	84.6	1.50
FR0010654830	LFP Actions Euro ISR - Part I	FR	1999-07-01	Equity	72.6	2.25
FR0000991424	Atout Valeurs Durables A/I	FR	2003-02-24	Equity	72.2	1.20
FR0010458539	Mirova Europe Life Quality R(C) EUR	FR	2007-05-29	Equity	71.8	1.50
FR0010822122	Fédéris Sélection ISR Euro A/I	FR	2009-12-16	Equity	64.9	1.00
FR0010237503	Roche-Brune Europe Actions	FR	2003-03-17	Equity	63.0	2.00
FR0010137174	BNP Paribas Euro Valeurs Durables	FR	1998-04-15	Equity	61.1	1.50
FR0000971160	Macif Croissance Durable Euro	FR	2001-01-09	Equity	52.6	1.08
FR0010703355	MAIF Investissement Responsable Europe	FR	2009-01-29	Equity	51.8	1.20
FR0010526079	LFR Euro Développement Durable I	FR	2007-12-10	Equity	47.8	1.60
FR0010689794	Covéa Finance Espace ISR	FR	2008-12-15	Equity	45.7	1.60
FR0000991960	Oddo Génération Europe	FR	1989-12-08	Equity	45.7	1.75
LU0212189012	BNP PARIBAS L2 SUSTAINABLE EQUITY EUROPE	FR	2007-02-06	Equity	44.5	1.50

Panel A (continued): SRI funds in France

ISIN	Fund name	Country	Launch date	Category	TNA 2013 (EUR mln)	Mgmt. Fee (in % p.a.)
FR0000442949	Federal Actions Ethiques A/I	FR	2000-06-30	Equity	44.3	1.50
FR0000444275	SG Actions Europe ISR AC	FR	2000-05-15	Equity	43.7	1.80
FR0000425308	LFP Actions France ISR R	FR	1989-08-29	Equity	43.1	2.00
LU0448199371	Mirova Global Climate Change	FR	2009-10-05	Equity	41.4	1.25
FR0000994816	LCL Actions USA ISR (Euro)	FR	1999-11-26	Equity	32.9	0.50
FR0000989006	LCL Actions Developpement Durable Euro Acc	FR	2002-10-23	Equity	30.8	0.10
LU0245286777	BNP Paribas Islamic Eq Optimiser C	FR	2006-04-05	Equity	29.0	1.50
FR0010091645	MAIF Croissance Durable	FR	2005-08-26	Equity	28.7	0.60
FR0010834457	CPR Progrès Durable Europe P A/I	FR	2009-12-21	Equity	27.1	1.60
FR0007059886	Europe Ethique Expansion Acc	FR	2001-06-29	Equity	22.7	1.39
FR0000448987	MAM Humanis	FR	1998-07-02	Equity	21.4	2.39
FR0010535625	Covéa Finance Actions Solidaires	FR	2007-12-13	Equity	21.4	1.90
FR0010191627	CCR Actions Engagement Durable	FR	2003-07-04	Equity	21.0	1.80
FR0010116137	Allianz Euréco Equity R A/I	FR	2007-07-16	Equity	20.2	1.79
FR0010283838	Roche Brune Zone Euro Actions	FR	2006-03-01	Equity	20.0	2.00
FR0010032169	Fructi Euro ISR (C) EUR	FR	1989-03-13	Equity	19.2	1.50
FR0010622696	LBPAM Responsable Actions Monde A C/D	FR	2008-09-16	Equity	19.0	1.20
FR0010505578	EdR Europe SRI A	FR	1984-07-05	Equity	18.6	2.00
FR0000444366	CM-CIC Actions ISR	FR	2000-06-16	Equity	16.3	2.00
FR0000004970	Epargne Ethique Actions A/I	FR	2000-01-20	Equity	16.0	2.00
FR0010748368	LBPAM Responsable Actions Environnement C	FR	2009-05-11	Equity	16.0	1.80
FR0010632364	Metropole Value SRI	FR	2008-07-09	Equity	15.9	1.80
FR0010521575	Fructi Actions Environnement (C) EUR	FR	2007-11-12	Equity	14.9	0.90
LU0414216498	LFP Trend Opportunities (Part B)	FR	2009-05-12	Equity	14.5	2.00
FR0010716837	Allianz Citizen Care SRI R	FR	2009-03-01	Equity	12.6	1.79
FR0010086520	Performance Environnement A	FR	2004-08-19	Equity	12.3	2.99
FR0010746776	Aviva Valeurs Responsables A	FR	2009-06-03	Equity	11.5	1.25
FR0010700815	Mandarine Engagements R	FR	2009-03-03	Equity	9.6	2.20
FR0000970949	MAM Terra Nova	FR	2000-11-24	Equity	6.5	2.39
FR0010502088	Etoile Environnement Acc	FR	2001-09-18	Equity	6.5	2.00

Panel A (continued): SRI funds in France

ISIN	Fund name	Country	Launch date	Category	TNA 2013 (EUR mln)	Mgmt. Fee (in % p.a.)
FR0010312199	Gérer Multifactoriel France A/I	FR	2001-09-05	Equity	5.8	2.20
FR0010610386	LFR Actions Solidaires I	FR	2008-08-27	Equity	4.7	1.60
FR0007482591	Virtuose Actions France	FR	1993-10-22	Equity	4.4	2.00
FR0010871905	LBPAM Responsable Actions Solidaire	FR	2010-06-21	Equity	4.0	1.80
FR0010502096	Etoile Partenaires Acc	FR	2001-09-05	Equity	4.0	2.00
FR0007023023	Universalis	FR	1998-06-19	Equity	3.7	1.25
FR0000970899	Ethique et Partage - CCFD Inc	FR	2000-12-20	Equity	3.6	2.39
FR0007037130	Euro Active Investors Acc	FR	1999-08-31	Equity	3.4	1.80
FR0010429076	Actions Planète Durable Acc	FR	2007-02-21	Equity	3.3	2.39
FR0007046073	Ethis Vitalité Acc	FR	2000-06-28	Equity	3.1	1.20
FR0010583245	Federal Planète Bleue P	FR	2008-04-15	Equity	2.8	3.00
FR0010609552	Ecureuil Bénéfices Emploi	FR	2008-06-05	Equity	2.3	0.10
FR0010612879	Ecureuil Bénéfice Environnement	FR	2008-06-02	Equity	2.2	0.70
FR0000983819	Macif Croissance Durable&Solidaire Acc	FR	2002-04-26	Equity	2.1	1.08
FR0000990921	Gérer Multifactoriel Euro	FR	1999-02-01	Equity	1.8	2.20
FR0010814400	Avenir Partage ISR A A/I	FR	2009-10-21	Equity	1.2	1.65
FR0010458281	Palatine Actions Défensives Euro A	FR	2007-05-15	Equity	1.2	1.40
FR0010583146	Federal Europe ISR P C/D	FR	2008-02-22	Equity	0.4	3.00
FR0010538033	Proxy Active Investors A	FR	2003-11-01	Equity	0.1	1.44
FR0000174567	BNP Paribas Retraite 5 I Acc	FR	2003-09-19	Balanced	186.6	0.60
LU0087047089	BNP PARIBAS L1 SUSTAINABLE ACTIVE ALLOCATION	FR	1998-06-01	Balanced	109.7	1.50
FR0010821470	ID-Afer	FR	2010-01-12	Balanced	86.7	0.60
FR0010263764	Ethis Valeurs	FR	2000-01-14	Balanced	85.2	1.20
FR0010021576	BNP Paribas Retraite 50 P Inc	FR	1988-01-04	Balanced	79.3	1.20
FR0010698555	Amundi AFD Avenirs Durables P1	FR	2009-03-04	Balanced	69.6	1.50
FR0010303909	Insertion Emplois Equilibre Acc	FR	2006-04-04	Balanced	53.0	0.70
FR0010030049	LBPAM Voie Lactée 2 Acc	FR	2003-11-12	Balanced	29.2	0.55
FR0010177899	Choix Solidaire Acc	FR	2000-03-01	Balanced	25.9	0.90
FR0007447891	Hymnos A/I	FR	1989-05-26	Balanced	24.2	1.20
FR0000004962	Libertés & Solidarité A/I	FR	2001-07-24	Balanced	20.0	1.20

Panel A (continued): SRI funds in France

ISIN	Fund name	Country	Launch date	Category	TNA 2013 (EUR mln)	Mgmt. Fee (in % p.a.)
FR0007048327	Faim et Développement Equilibre Acc	FR	2000-11-02	Balanced	17.7	1.00
FR0010896555	Diamant Bleu Responsable	FR	2010-05-31	Balanced	17.1	0.95
FR0000002164	Covéa Finance Horizon Durable	FR	2001-05-22	Balanced	16.0	2.39
FR0010626184	Agir avec la Fondation Abbé Pierre	FR	2008-07-17	Balanced	15.5	0.10
FR0007014212	LBPAM Voie Lactée 1 Acc	FR	1997-09-10	Balanced	14.2	0.50
FR0000970972	Nouvelle Stratégie 50 Acc	FR	1983-04-22	Balanced	11.9	2.39
FR0010883017	RJ Déploiement Durable	FR	2010-06-09	Balanced	6.4	0.60
FR0007475504	Ecofi Flexible	FR	1993-10-08	Balanced	5.4	1.79
FR0010931576	CPR Reflex Responsable 0-100	FR	2010-09-15	Balanced	2.5	1.80
FR0010400093	Actions Nord Sud Acc	FR	2006-12-27	Balanced	1.6	2.39
FR0010642280	Ecofi Agir Développement Durable	FR	2008-12-18	Balanced	1.0	2.00
FR0007009808	BNP Paribas Mois	FR	1997-04-09	Fixed Income	3,933.3	0.25
FR0007437546	Aviva Monétaire ISR	FR	1991-09-02	Fixed Income	2,395.1	0.40
FR0000009772	Fonsicav	FR	1986-06-19	Fixed Income	926.3	0.40
FR0000008997	Ofi Trésor ISR A/I	FR	1986-08-01	Fixed Income	819.0	0.24
FR0010455683	BNP Paribas Money Prime Euro SRI AC	FR	2007-04-23	Fixed Income	689.5	0.25
FR0010008003	Mirova Sustainable Cash	FR	2003-09-04	Fixed Income	662.6	0.50
FR0000447823	AXA Trésor Court Terme Acc	FR	1995-02-05	Fixed Income	626.9	0.50
FR0010812651	Macif Trésorerie Semestrielle ISR C	FR	2009-11-16	Fixed Income	604.0	0.15
FR0007021324	AG2R La Mondiale Obligations ISR	FR	2000-01-01	Fixed Income	522.6	0.20
FR0010979922	Label Euro Obligations S A/I	FR	2002-07-25	Fixed Income	434.3	1.50
FR0010436980	CPR Monétaire SR A	FR	2007-04-27	Fixed Income	377.8	0.24
FR0010744953	HSBC Monétaire Etat	FR	2009-04-07	Fixed Income	329.0	0.10
LU0265288877	Parvest Euro Corp Bd Sustain Dev Cl Acc	FR	2006-12-19	Fixed Income	299.1	0.75
FR0010702175	Groupama Crédit Euro ISR N C/D	FR	2009-04-14	Fixed Income	213.1	1.20
FR0010035162	Amundi Crédit Euro ISR	FR	2004-01-22	Fixed Income	183.4	0.70
FR0010028985	Fructi ISR Obli Euro R(C) EUR	FR	2003-12-04	Fixed Income	175.3	0.50
FR0010130765	BNP Paribas Obli Etat	FR	2004-12-07	Fixed Income	159.4	0.96
FR0007082458	AG2R La Mondiale Monétaire Euro ISR	FR	2003-04-29	Fixed Income	156.9	0.12
FR0010076943	BNP PARIBAS OBLI ETHEIS	FR	2003-11-24	Fixed Income	113.9	1.08

Appendices   245

Panel A (continued): SRI funds in France

ISIN	Fund name	Country	Launch date	Category	TNA 2013 (EUR mln)	Mgmt. Fee (in % p.a.)
FR0010336560	Allianz Euro Crédit SRI R C/D	FR	2006-06-23	Fixed Income	86.6	0.72
FR0010859785	Federal Taux Variable IR	FR	2010-04-06	Fixed Income	78.2	0.60
FR0010532044	Natixis Impact Nord-Sud Développement	FR	1985-01-03	Fixed Income	75.1	0.80
FR0010061283	HSBC Oblig Développement Durable A	FR	2004-02-13	Fixed Income	72.0	0.80
FR0010291567	CM-CIC Moné ISR	FR	1990-06-07	Fixed Income	71.9	0.70
FR0010915314	LFP Obligations ISR C	FR	2003-05-19	Fixed Income	68.6	1.00
FR0010381681	CPR 1-3 Euro SR P	FR	1987-07-02	Fixed Income	62.7	0.40
FR0010785865	Allianz Sécuricash SRI R	FR	2009-08-27	Fixed Income	61.3	0.60
FR0010376020	CPR 7-10 Euro SR P	FR	1988-12-07	Fixed Income	59.6	0.45
FR0010805788	LBPAM Responsable Tréso E	FR	2009-11-12	Fixed Income	54.9	0.23
FR0010515601	Confiance Solidaire	FR	2007-10-23	Fixed Income	52.2	0.60
FR0010075044	Invest Première	FR	1990-08-03	Fixed Income	51.4	0.41
FR0010018309	LBPAM Responsable Première Long Trm	FR	1997-04-11	Fixed Income	51.3	0.88
FR0010219899	Epargne Ethique Monétaire	FR	1985-07-23	Fixed Income	45.0	0.88
FR0010822130	Regard Obligations Privées ISR	FR	2010-01-07	Fixed Income	44.4	0.10
FR0010941328	CM-CIC Obli ISR	FR	2010-10-01	Fixed Income	35.7	0.70
FR0007479944	CPR 3-5 Euro SR P	FR	1994-04-28	Fixed Income	32.2	0.40
FR0010368159	Palatine Première	FR	1985-12-31	Fixed Income	26.6	1.20
FR0010673491	Insertion Emplois Modéré	FR	2009-01-15	Fixed Income	24.2	0.50
FR0010957860	LBPAM Responsable Obli Crédit E	FR	2010-11-10	Fixed Income	22.9	0.70
FR0010016857	LBPAM Responsable PremièreMoyen Trm	FR	2009-10-05	Fixed Income	20.4	0.50
FR0010721415	CNP Assur-Monet R	FR	2009-02-15	Fixed Income	19.6	0.60
FR0010440156	Danone.Communities Investissement Responsable S3	FR	2007-07-06	Fixed Income	19.2	0.30
FR0007474838	Palatine Trésorerie 1ère	FR	1993-08-02	Fixed Income	18.4	0.50
FR0010439943	Danone.Communities Investissement Responsable S1	FR	2007-06-29	Fixed Income	17.1	0.30
FR0010370528	Uni-MT	FR	2006-09-20	Fixed Income	15.8	1.20
FR0010439935	Danone.Communities D. ISR Prudent	FR	2007-05-04	Fixed Income	15.4	0.30
FR0000934978	Dexia Ethique Gest Oblig Classic C Acc	FR	2000-03-22	Fixed Income	14.3	1.00
FR0010439927	Danone.Communities D. ISR Sérénité	FR	2007-05-04	Fixed Income	11.6	0.30
FR0007413091	Epargne Solidaire	FR	1987-02-06	Fixed Income	11.5	0.00

Panel A (continued): SRI funds in France

ISIN	Fund name	Country	Launch date	Category	TNA 2013 (EUR mln)	Mgmt. Fee (in % p.a.)
FR0007381983	Ecofi Obligations Internationales	FR	1985-11-29	Fixed Income	11.0	0.60
FR0000981425	Ecofi Monédym	FR	1992-10-02	Fixed Income	10.3	0.35
FR0010440164	Danone.Communities Investissement Responsable S2	FR	2007-06-29	Fixed Income	9.8	0.30
FR0010616664	Federal Placement Court Terme IR	FR	2008-06-10	Fixed Income	9.2	0.50
FR0007074844	SG Oblig Corporate ISR	FR	2002-08-23	Fixed Income	8.7	1.20
FR0000971012	MAM Obligations Ethique (C)	FR	1989-07-07	Fixed Income	7.5	1.00
FR0010474577	Gérer Monétaire Trésor	FR	2007-03-23	Fixed Income	6.8	0.18
FR0010766113	Babyfund Taux Fixe 2013 P	FR	2010-01-29	Fixed Income	3.7	1.00
FR0010214650	CMNE Sélections	FR	1996-04-09	Fixed Income	3.4	0.18
FR0010622662	Fédéris Obligations ISR R	FR	2009-05-03	Fixed Income	2.4	0.50
FR0010748848	LFP Trésorerie ISR R	FR	2009-06-22	Fixed Income	1.4	0.25
FR0010433185	Gérer Monétaire Jour	FR	1985-10-21	Fixed Income	1.0	0.60
	Total number of funds in France	186		Sum of TNA	31,781	1.20

Panel B: SRI funds in the UK

ISIN	Fund name	Country	Launch date	Category	TNA 2013 (EUR mln)	Mgmt. Fee (in % p.a.)
GB0001597979	CIS UK Growth Trust Inc	UK	1989-09-25	Equity	1,369.1	1.50
GB0030833981	F&C Stewardship Gr Fd 1 Acc	UK	1984-05-31	Equity	686.8	1.50
GB0005812150	Jupiter Ecology fund Inc	UK	1988-04-01	Equity	468.6	1.50
GB0030833650	F&C Stewardship International 1 Acc	UK	1987-10-13	Equity	450.0	1.50
GB00B1N9DX45	Kames Ethical Equity A Acc	UK	1989-04-17	Equity	410.9	1.25
GB0003506424	AXA Framlington Health Acc	UK	1987-04-03	Equity	390.1	1.50
GB0030835580	F&C Stewardship Income 1 Acc	UK	1987-10-13	Equity	347.1	1.50
GB0005027221	Henderson Glb Care Growth Inc	UK	1991-01-08	Equity	344.3	1.50
GB00B64TS881	First State Global Energ Mkts Sustblty A	UK	2009-04-08	Equity	336.9	1.55
GB00B0TY6S22	First State Asia Pacific Sstnbity A GBP	UK	2005-12-19	Equity	330.0	1.55
GB0008448663	Ecclesiastical Amity International A Inc	UK	1999-09-10	Equity	269.3	1.50

Panel B (continued): SRI funds in the UK

ISIN	Fund name	Country	Launch date	Category	TNA 2013 (EUR mln)	Mgmt. Fee (in % p.a.)
GB0006833718	Aberdeen Ethical World Fd A Acc	UK	1999-05-01	Equity	263.2	1.50
GB0009537407	CIS European Growth Trust Inc	UK	2000-01-31	Equity	258.6	1.38
GB0009243824	L&G Ethical Tr (R) Acc	UK	1999-07-05	Equity	252.4	1.00
GB0031632010	Scottish Widows Environm Investor A Acc	UK	1989-06-29	Equity	216.5	1.50
GB0031811622	Halifax Ethical C Inc	UK	2002-09-16	Equity	213.1	1.50
GB00B3BLRL29	Scottish Widows HIFML Ethical 1	UK	2009-01-19	Equity	213.1	1.50
GB0004331012	Standard Life UK Ethical R Acc	UK	1998-09-21	Equity	199.5	1.50
GB0030028764	Alliance Trust Sustainable Future UK Growth	UK	2001-02-19	Equity	180.3	0.75
GB0030038359	CIS US Growth Trust Inc	UK	2001-02-19	Equity	170.6	1.50
LU0278938138	Aberdeen Glbl Responsible Wld Eq A2	UK	2007-10-17	Equity	140.2	1.50
GB0030029283	Alliance Trust Sustainable Future European Growth	UK	2001-02-19	Equity	135.9	1.50
GB0005297980	AXA Ethical R Acc	UK	1998-05-05	Equity	130.5	1.50
GB0009371310	Ecclesiastical Amity UK A Inc	UK	1988-02-10	Equity	122.8	1.50
IE00B04R3307	Impax Environmental Mkts A GBP Acc	UK	2004-12-09	Equity	121.5	1.00
GB0006685613	Family Charities Ethical Trust Acc	UK	1999-03-31	Equity	115.7	1.50
GB0005027338	Henderson Global Care UK Income Inc	UK	1995-03-07	Equity	108.5	1.50
GB00B05Q3G94	CIS UK FTSE4Good Tracker Tr Acc	UK	2003-09-29	Equity	104.0	1.50
LU0110459103	HSBC Amanah Global Equity Index fund-Inc	UK	2004-01-03	Equity	102.9	0.75
GB00B1ZB0M68	Standard Life Euro Ethical Equity Retail Acc	UK	2007-09-24	Equity	102.2	1.50
GB0032200213	Scottish Widows Ethical Fd A Acc	UK	1987-06-29	Equity	101.8	1.50
GB00B0JZPC21	Old Mutual Ethical Fund A (GBP)	UK	2005-04-08	Equity	91.1	1.25
GB0030029515	Alliance Trust Sustainable Future Absolute Growth	UK	2001-02-19	Equity	85.4	1.50
GB0030029952	Alliance Trust Sustainable Future Global Growth	UK	2000-02-19	Equity	74.1	1.50
GB0004072699	Premier Ethical R Inc	UK	1986-07-28	Equity	71.1	1.50
GB0008337569	Jupiter Responsible Income	UK	1999-11-22	Equity	59.6	1.50
GB0008446626	Ecclesiastical Amity European A Inc	UK	1999-09-10	Equity	58.9	1.50
LU0233833143	SWIP Islamic Global Equity A Acc	UK	2005-11-21	Equity	53.6	0.50
GB00B29KGH36	Virgin Climate Change Acc	UK	2008-01-18	Equity	52.8	1.75
LU0419691059	HSBC Amanah Global Equity A	UK	2009-03-25	Equity	52.0	1.50
LU0318449088	F&C Global Climate Opp A EUR	UK	2008-02-27	Equity	49.9	1.50

Appendices 249

Panel B (continued): SRI funds in the UK

ISIN	Fund name	Country	Launch date	Category	TNA 2013 (EUR mln)	Mgmt. Fee (in % p.a.)
GB0002010634	SLFC Green	UK	1992-06-26	Equity	45.5	1.00
GB0030LNTT93	Aberdeen Multi-Manager Ethical Acc	UK	2002-02-12	Equity	38.1	1.50
GB00B23DJV30	Schroder Global Climate Change Inc	UK	2007-09-28	Equity	32.9	1.50
GB00B131GB92	Aberdeen Responsible UK Equity A Acc	UK	2006-05-09	Equity	30.5	1.50
GB0008317611	Sovereign Ethical Fund Inc	UK	1989-05-23	Equity	28.9	1.50
GB00B4LDCG53	IFDS IM WHEB Sustainability A	UK	2009-05-26	Equity	24.3	1.50
LU0323240290	HSBC GIF Climate Change A Inc	UK	2007-11-09	Equity	19.4	1.50
GB00B1FL7S17	SVM All Europe SRI A Acc	UK	2006-10-31	Equity	15.8	1.50
LU0329070832	Jupiter Global Fund China Sustainable Growth	UK	2009-12-11	Equity	12.1	1.50
LU0231118026	JGF - Jupiter Climate Change Solutions L Acc	UK	2001-08-17	Equity	5.0	1.50
IE00B2PGV129	Guinness Alternative Energy A Inc	UK	2007-12-19	Equity	3.1	1.00
GB00B11TD470	CIS UK Income with Growth Series 3	UK	2006-04-06	Balanced	505.8	1.50
GB0030030281	Alliance Trust Sustainable Future Managed	UK	2001-02-19	Balanced	438.4	1.50
GB00B3PXJV84	CIS Sustainable Diversified Trust	UK	2009-07-24	Balanced	290.8	1.50
GB0031833402	Henderson Glb Care Managed	UK	1998-10-14	Balanced	187.6	1.50
GB00B3PXJX09	CIS Sustainable World Trust	UK	2009-09-21	Balanced	116.3	1.50
GB00B1N9DX45	Kames Ethical Cautious Managed A Acc	UK	2007-03-01	Balanced	99.0	1.25
GB00B1LBFW55	CF 7IM Sustainable Balance A Acc	UK	2007-02-01	Balanced	41.0	1.75
GB0033583427	CIS Corporate Bond Income Trust Inc	UK	2003-09-29	Fixed Income	468.2	1.00
GB0030028988	Alliance Trust Sustainable Future Corporate Bond	UK	2001-02-19	Fixed Income	310.6	1.00
GB0005342646	Kames Ethical Corporate Bond A Acc	UK	2000-04-28	Fixed Income	310.4	1.00
GB00B23YHT07	F&C Ethical Bond 1 Inc	UK	2007-10-01	Fixed Income	227.8	1.00
GB00B4WSJK27	Royal London Ethical Bond A	UK	2007-01-31	Fixed Income	201.5	0.90
GB00B0LNNH51	Standard Life Ethical Corporate Bond Acc	UK	2005-11-02	Fixed Income	187.8	1.00
GB0030957137	Rathbone Ethical Bond Fund Acc	UK	2002-05-07	Fixed Income	140.4	1.25
GB00B2PF8B06	Ecclesiastical Amity Sterling Bond A Inc	UK	2008-04-07	Fixed Income	72.0	1.25
	Total number of funds in the UK	67		Sum of TNA	13,159	1.38

Panel C: SRI funds in the Netherlands

ISIN	Fund name	Country	Launch date	Category	TNA 2013 (EUR mln)	Mgmt. Fee (in % p.a.)
NL0000291086	SNS Euro Aandelenfonds	NL	1997-10-20	Equity	478.7	0.70
LU0187077218	RobecoSAM Sustainable European Equities D EUR	NL	2004-06-07	Equity	448.5	1.25
NL0000441301	ASN Duurzaam Aandelenfonds Inc	NL	1993-04-20	Equity	358.1	1.25
NL0000291037	SNS Nederlands Aandelenfonds Inc	NL	1995-10-30	Equity	322.0	0.70
NL0009347574	Sustainable Europe Index Fund	NL	2010-02-01	Equity	262.9	0.35
LU0278727951	Triodos Sustainable Equity R	NL	2007-06-29	Equity	231.8	1.30
NL0000291144	SNS Wereld Aandelenfonds Inc	NL	1999-11-22	Equity	222.4	1.05
NL0000280501	ASN Milieu & Waterfonds Inc	NL	2001-07-02	Equity	213.4	1.75
LU0119216553	ING (L) Invest Sustainable Gr P Acc	NL	2000-07-10	Equity	177.4	1.50
NL0000113082	Kempen Sense Fund	NL	2002-10-14	Equity	170.6	1.50
NL0009486745	Sustainable North America Index Fund	NL	2010-05-31	Equity	127.7	0.45
NL0006311789	ING Duurzaam Aandelen Fonds Inc	NL	2000-03-03	Equity	113.9	1.40
LU0374106754	RobecoSAM Sustainable Agribusiness Equities D EUR	NL	2008-08-29	Equity	107.9	1.50
LU0264990119	Delta Lloyd L Water & Climate Fund Classe B Acc	NL	2007-11-15	Equity	69.1	1.25
NL0000291136	SNS Amerika Aandelenfonds Inc	NL	1999-11-22	Equity	55.9	0.70
LU0278272843	Triodos Sustainable Pioneer R	NL	2007-03-12	Equity	52.4	1.70
NL0000291151	SNS Euro Vastgoedfonds Inc	NL	2000-07-10	Equity	50.1	0.85
NL0000290518	ASN Duurzaam Small & Midcap Fonds	NL	2006-05-09	Equity	46.0	1.55
NL0000258843	Robeco DuurzaamAandelen Inc	NL	1999-02-09	Equity	45.8	1.20
NL0009347566	Sustainable World Index Fund Inc	NL	2003-05-31	Equity	42.7	0.55
LU0264990036	Delta Lloyd L New Energy Classe B Acc	NL	2007-11-15	Equity	26.6	1.25
NL0000291102	SNS Hoogdividend Aandelenfonds	NL	1997-10-20	Equity	25.7	1.00
NL0000291128	SNS Azië Aandelenfonds	NL	1999-11-11	Equity	22.5	1.00
NL0000293371	SNS Opkomende Landen Aandelenfonds	NL	2007-07-02	Equity	11.6	1.75
NL0000291094	SNS Euro Mixfonds	NL	1997-10-20	Balanced	1,818.4	0.60
NL0000286649	SNS Optimaal Oranje	NL	2002-10-21	Balanced	374.6	1.10
NL0000291193	SNS Optimaal Paars	NL	2005-12-19	Balanced	332.9	1.25
NL0000286656	SNS Optimaal Rood	NL	2002-10-21	Balanced	136.4	1.20
NL0000280089	ASN Duurzaam Mixfonds	NL	1990-10-12	Balanced	129.3	0.70
LU0504302604	Triodos Sustainable Mixed Fund R-dis	NL	2010-06-25	Balanced	94.6	1.05

Panel C (continued): SRI funds in the Netherlands

ISIN	Fund name	Country	Launch date	Category	TNA 2013 (EUR mln)	Mgmt. Fee (in % p.a.)
NL0000286631	SNS Optimaal Geel	NL	2002-10-21	Balanced	84.5	1.00
NL0006056822	SNS Optimaal Blauw	NL	2007-12-03	Balanced	18.0	0.75
NL0000291060	SNS Euro Obligatiefonds	NL	1997-10-20	Fixed Income	888.4	0.50
NL0000440204	Triodos Groenfonds Inc	NL	1998-06-27	Fixed Income	495.0	0.80
LU0278272504	Triodos Sustainable Bond R	NL	2007-07-16	Fixed Income	215.5	1.00
NL0000291011	SNS Euro Liquiditeitenfonds	NL	1995-10-30	Fixed Income	136.4	0.60
NL0000441244	ASN Duurzaam Obligatiefonds	NL	2001-01-15	Fixed Income	115.4	0.55
LU0503372608	Robeco Euro Sustainable Credits D	NL	2010-05-18	Fixed Income	15.3	0.70
	Total number of funds in the Netherlands	38		Sum of TNA	8,538	1.03

Panel D: SRI funds in Germany

ISIN	Fund name	Country	Launch date	Category	TNA 2013 (EUR mln)	Mgmt. Fee (in % p.a.)
LU0273158872	DWS Invest Global Agribusiness LC	DE	2006-11-20	Equity	1,731.6	1.50
LU0061928585	ÖkoWorld ÖkoVision® Classic Acc	DE	1996-05-02	Equity	374.0	1.76
LU0130393993	Postbank Dynamik-Vision Acc	DE	2001-06-16	Equity	155.9	1.30
LU0250028817	Allianz-dit Global EcoTrends A EUR Inc	DE	2006-05-03	Equity	138.9	1.75
DE0009750216	Liga Pax Aktien Union Inc	DE	1997-05-05	Equity	131.0	1.50
DE000A0RHHC8	4Q-Smart Power	DE	2009-12-07	Equity	119.9	1.60
DE000DK0ECS2	Deka-UmweltInvest CF Acc	DE	2006-12-27	Equity	106.1	1.50
DE000DW S0DT1	DWS Klimawandel Inc	DE	2007-02-28	Equity	65.0	1.45
LU0152554803	LIGA-Pax-CattolicoUnion Inc	DE	2002-11-22	Equity	50.0	1.10
DE000A0KEYM4	LBBW Global Warming	DE	2007-01-15	Equity	42.5	1.50
DE0005326532	KCD-Union Nachhaltig Aktien Inc	DE	2001-03-01	Equity	42.0	1.50
DE0001619997	MEAG Nachhaltigkeit A Inc	DE	2003-10-01	Equity	37.2	1.50
IB0005895655	Green Effects NAI-Werte Fonds Acc	DE	2000-10-04	Equity	36.6	0.75
LU0037079380	Öko-Aktienfonds Acc	DE	1999-10-01	Equity	36.5	1.25
LU0315365378	UniSector: Klimawandel	DE	2007-10-01	Equity	29.0	1.55

Panel D (continued): SRI funds in Germany

ISIN	Fund name	Country	Launch date	Category	TNA 2013 (EUR mln)	Mgmt. Fee (in % p.a.)
DE0007560849	Monega FairInvest Aktien Acc	DE	2006-10-19	Equity	26.2	1.00
LU0405846410	LSF Asian Solar & Wind A1	DE	2009-02-02	Equity	25.6	0.90
DE0007045437	WestLB Me Co Fd Pension Dynamic Fonds Acc	DE	2002-08-27	Equity	25.2	1.00
LU0158827195	Allianz RCM Global Sust A EUR Inc	DE	2003-01-02	Equity	24.9	1.50
LU0036592839	SEB ÖkoLux Acc	DE	1992-02-19	Equity	22.7	1.50
DE0009847343	terrAssisi Aktien I AMI Acc	DE	2000-01-21	Equity	20.1	1.35
DE0008470477	INVESCO Umwelt-u.Nachhaltigkeits-Fds Acc	DE	1990-10-18	Equity	19.2	1.50
LU0314225409	DKB Zukunftsfonds Acc	DE	2007-08-20	Equity	13.3	1.40
LU0301152442	Oekoworld ÖkoWorld Klima C Acc	DE	2007-07-31	Equity	12.9	1.76
LU0298649426	DWS Invest Clean Tech LC	DE	2007-05-14	Equity	12.9	1.50
DE000A0NAUP7	LBBW Nachhaltigkeit Aktien R	DE	2006-10-16	Equity	11.2	1.40
LU0332822492	ÖkoWorld Water Life C Acc	DE	2008-01-30	Equity	10.7	1.76
LU0355139220	DKB Ökofonds TNL Acc	DE	2008-04-02	Equity	10.1	1.40
LU0383804431	FG&W Better World	DE	2008-10-20	Equity	9.9	1.30
LU0380798750	ÖkoWorld² Ökotrust C Acc	DE	2008-10-13	Equity	9.8	1.76
DE000A0M8OG4	UniNachhaltig Aktien Global	DE	2009-10-01	Equity	9.0	1.20
LU0309769247	ÖkoWorld Ökovision Europe C Acc	DE	2007-03-25	Equity	6.8	0.20
LU0117185156	Meridio Green Balance Acc	DE	2000-12-04	Equity	6.0	1.20
DE0002605367	ComfortInvest Perspektive	DE	2008-04-15	Equity	4.2	1.00
LU0360172109	Murphy&Spitz-Umweltfonds Deutschland	DE	2008-06-24	Equity	4.1	1.62
DE0005896864	Deka-Stiftungen Balance	DE	2003-04-28	Balanced	1,041.1	1.00
DE000DWS0XF8	WvF Rendite und Nachhaltigkeit	DE	2009-09-03	Balanced	347.0	0.90
DE0005318406	DWS Stiftungsfonds	DE	2002-04-15	Balanced	311.3	1.10
DE0005317127	Sarasin FairInvest Universal Fds Inc	DE	2001-03-30	Balanced	207.9	0.95
DE0009750000	KCD-Union Nachhaltig MIX	DE	1990-12-17	Balanced	192.0	0.70
LU0458538880	FairWorldFonds	DE	2010-03-11	Balanced	143.0	1.14
DE000A0RE972	BERENBERG-1590-Stiftung	DE	2009-05-04	Balanced	74.2	1.28
LU0353730392	Postbank Dynamik Klima Garant Acc	DE	2008-08-07	Balanced	50.8	1.02
DE000A0M80H2	Volksbank Gütersloh Nachhaltigkeitsinvest	DE	2009-12-01	Balanced	39.0	1.00
DE0007045148	WestLB Mellon Werte Fonds Inc	DE	2002-01-31	Balanced	36.7	0.65

Panel D (continued): SRI funds in Germany

ISIN	Fund name	Country	Launch date	Category	TNA 2013 (EUR mln)	Mgmt. Fee (in % p.a.)
DE000A0B7JB7	BfS Nachhaltigkeitsfd Ertrag SEB Inv Inc	DE	2005-09-30	Balanced	33.1	0.90
DE000A0M0317	First Nachhaltig Wachstum PI 4 Acc	DE	2007-10-04	Balanced	31.1	1.20
DE000A0X9SA0	Sparda München nachhaltige Vermögensverwaltung	DE	2009-12-01	Balanced	29.6	1.35
DE000A0LGNP3	NORD/LB AM Global Challenges Index-Fonds	DE	2007-09-03	Balanced	23.9	0.40
DE0008023565	Fonds fur Stiftungen INVESCO Inc	DE	2003-02-17	Balanced	22.7	0.95
DE000A0M03X1	First Nachhaltig Balance PI 4 Acc	DE	2007-10-04	Balanced	22.4	1.20
DE0005314215	LIGA-Pax-Bal-Stiftsfds-Union Inc	DE	2000-05-02	Balanced	21.0	0.95
LU0332822906	ÖkoWorld Garant 20 C Acc	DE	2008-01-30	Balanced	20.6	1.76
LU0206716028	IAM-ProVita World Fund Acc	DE	2005-04-01	Balanced	18.0	1.50
LU0305675109	DJE LUX SICAV - DJE Vermögensmanagement P	DE	2007-07-16	Balanced	12.8	1.60
LU0360706096	BN & P - Good Growth Fonds B Acc	DE	2008-05-14	Balanced	11.7	1.56
DE0007248700	Ampega Responsibility Fonds	DE	2004-12-30	Balanced	9.8	1.75
DE000A0D95R8	FT Navigator Sustainability	DE	2005-12-01	Balanced	6.1	0.75
DE0008491226	LIGA-Pax-RentUnion Inc	DE	1989-12-28	Fixed Income	422.0	0.55
DE0009750141	LIGA-Pax-KUnion Inc	DE	1994-12-01	Fixed Income	306.0	0.50
DE0005326524	KCD-Union Nachhaltig-RENTEN Inc	DE	2001-03-01	Fixed Income	167.0	0.85
LU0199537852	LIGA-Pax-Corporates-Union Inc	DE	2005-01-25	Fixed Income	143.0	0.60
DE000A0M6W36	CSR Bond Plus OP	DE	2008-01-16	Fixed Income	122.8	0.35
LU0182869809	INIK Acc	DE	2003-12-22	Fixed Income	104.5	1.25
DE0008474081	DWS ESG Global-Gov Bonds LC	DE	1972-05-02	Fixed Income	100.4	0.75
DE000A0X97K7	LBBW Nachhaltigkeit Renten	DE	2010-03-01	Fixed Income	20.0	0.75
DE000A0NGJV5	terrAssisi Renten I AMI P(a) Inc	DE	2009-04-22	Fixed Income	18.2	0.46
LU0041441808	SEB Ökorent Inc	DE	1990-11-28	Fixed Income	10.8	0.70
DE0009769844	ACATIS Fair Value Bonds UI A	DE	1997-10-01	Fixed Income	9.5	0.95
LU0183092898	ÖKOTREND Bonds Inc	DE	2004-03-16	Fixed Income	5.4	0.08
	Total number of funds in Germany	70		Sum of TNA	7,516	1.16

Appendix III: Security split of balanced funds

This table shows the security split of the balanced funds included in the sample. The splits are used as weights in order to calculate the benchmark used for SRI balanced funds in the empirical analysis.

ISIN	Fund name	Country	Share of equity securities	Share of fixed income securities
FR0000174567	BNP Paribas Retraite 51 Acc	FR	22.1	77.9
LU0087047089	BNP PARIBAS L1 SUSTAINABLE ACTIVE ALLOCATION	FR	38.9	61.1
FR0010821470	ID-A fer	FR	56.5	43.5
FR0010263764	Ethis Valeurs	FR	74.0	26.0
FR0010021576	BNP Paribas Retraite 50 P Inc	FR	57.3	42.7
FR0010698555	Amundi AFD Avenirs Durables P1	FR	45.2	54.8
FR0010303909	Insertion Emplois Equilibre Acc	FR	53.0	47.0
FR0010030049	LBPAM Voie Lactée 2 Acc	FR	45.1	54.9
FR0010177899	Choix Solidaire Acc	FR	57.1	42.9
FR0007447891	Hymnos A/I	FR	54.0	46.1
FR0000049462	Libertés & Solidarité A/I	FR	24.5	75.6
FR0007048327	Faim et Développement Equilibre Acc	FR	49.0	51.0
FR0010896555	Diamant Bleu Responsable	FR	42.3	57.7
FR0000002164	Covéa Finance Horizon Durable	FR	56.5	43.5
FR0010626184	Agir avec la Fondation Abbé Pierre	FR	42.1	57.9
FR0007014212	LBPAM Voie Lactée 1 Acc	FR	24.1	75.9
FR0000970972	Nouvelle Stratégie 50 Acc	FR	100.0	0.0
FR0010883017	RJ Déploiement Durable	FR	56.5	43.5
FR0007475504	Ecofi Flexible	FR	72.1	27.9
FR0010931576	CPR Reflex Responsable 0-100	FR	98.7	1.3
FR0010400093	Actions Nord Sud Acc	FR	100.0	0.0
FR0010642280	Ecofi Agir Développement Durable	FR	72.8	27.2
GB00B11TD470	CIS UK Income with Growth Series 3	UK	79.4	20.6
GB0030030281	Alliance Trust Sustainable Future Managed	UK	87.1	12.9
GB00B3PXJV84	CIS Sustainable Diversified Trust	UK	51.9	48.1
GB0031833402	Henderson Glb Care Managed	UK	84.7	15.3

ISIN	Fund name	Country	Share of equity securities	Share of fixed income securities
GB00B3PXJX09	CIS Sustainable World Trust	UK	85.6	14.4
GB00B1N9DX45	Kames Ethical Cautious Managed A Acc	UK	62.4	37.6
GB00B1LBFW55	CF 7IM Sustainable Balance A Acc	UK	71.8	28.2
NL0000291094	SNS Euro Mixfonds	NL	53.8	46.2
NL000286649	SNS Optimaal Oranje	NL	48.9	51.1
NL000291193	SNS Optimaal Paars	NL	53.8	46.2
NL000286656	SNS Optimaal Rood	NL	77.1	22.9
NL000280089	ASN Duurzaam Mixfonds	NL	46.6	53.4
LU0504302604	Triodos Sustainable Mixed Fund R-dis	NL	46.8	53.2
NL0000286631	SNS Optimaal Geel	NL	37.1	63.0
NL0006056822	SNS Optimaal Blauw	NL	52.0	48.0
DE0005896864	Deka-Stiftungen Balance	DE	35.4	64.6
DE000DWS0XF8	WvF Rendite und Nachhaltigkeit	DE	38.7	61.3
DE0005318406	DWS Stiftungsfonds	DE	31.7	68.4
DE0005317127	Sarasin FairInvest Universal Fds Inc	DE	35.8	64.2
DE0009750000	KCD-Union Nachhaltig MIX	DE	26.6	73.5
LU0458538880	FairWorldFonds	DE	39.6	60.4
DE000A0RE972	BERENBERG 1590-Stiftung	DE	39.8	60.2
LU0353730392	Postbank Dynamik Klima Garant Acc	DE	50.0	50.0
DE000A0M80H2	Volksbank Gütersloh NachhaltigkeitsInvest	DE	70.3	29.7
DE0007045148	WestLB Mellon Werte Fonds Inc	DE	42.3	57.7
DE000A0B7JB7	BfS Nachhaltigkeitsfd Ertrag SEB Inv Inc	DE	60.4	39.6
DE000A0M0317	First Nachhaltig Wachstum PI 4 Acc	DE	60.7	39.4
DE000A0X9SA0	Sparda München nachhaltige Vermögensverwaltung	DE	73.0	27.0
DE000A0LGNP3	NORD/LB AM Global Challenges Index-Fonds	DE	100.0	0.0
DE0008023565	Fonds fur Stiftungen INVESCO Inc	DE	86.1	13.9
DE000A0M03X1	First Nachhaltig Balance PI 4 Acc	DE	49.8	50.2
DE0005314215	LIGA-Pax-Bal-Stiftsfds-Union Inc	DE	23.8	76.2
LU0332822906	ÖkoWorld Garant 20 C Acc	DE	19.7	80.3
LU0206716028	IAM-ProVita World Fund Acc	DE	76.7	23.3

ISIN	Fund name	Country	Share of equity securities	Share of fixed income securities
LU0305675109	DJE LUX SICAV - DJE Vermögensmanagement P	DE	94.3	5.7
LU0360706096	BN & P - Good Growth Fonds B Acc	DE	76.5	23.5
DE0007248700	Ampega Responsibility Fonds	DE	49.8	50.2
DE000A0D95R8	FT Navigator Sustainability	DE	70.9	29.2
		Average	57.2	42.8

Appendix IV: Individual fund performance

This table shows individual fund performance according to alphas generated in single- and multi-factor regression models. The estimates for alphas (α) are expressed in percentage terms per month. ** Indicates significance at the 5% level.

ISIN	Fund name	Country	1-factor conv. Indices			1-factor SRI indices			3-factor conv. Indices		
			Alpha	t-stat.	Sign.	Alpha	t-stat.	Sign.	Alpha	t-stat.	Sign.
FR0000984346	AG2R Actions ISR Acc	FR	0.162	1.47		0.219	2.04	**	0.153	1.33	
FR0007494703	AG2R La Mondiale Actions Europe ISR	FR	0.070	0.75		0.128	1.42		0.135	1.49	
FR0010429076	Actions Planète Durable Acc	FR	-0.074	-0.38		-0.099	-0.46		-0.146	-0.84	
FR0000975880	Allianz Actions Aéquitas A/I	FR	0.295	1.72		0.344	1.86		0.117	0.74	
FR0010716837	Allianz Citizen Care SRI R	FR	0.551	2.09	**	0.552	1.94		0.141	0.68	
FR0010116137	Allianz Euréco Equity R A/I	FR	-0.193	-0.97		-0.137	-0.60		-0.409	-2.15	**
FR0000017329	Allianz Valeurs Durables R	FR	0.007	0.09		0.063	0.77		-0.007	-0.08	
FR0010458760	Amundi Actions Euro ISR I2	FR	0.122	1.68		0.107	1.17		0.097	1.27	
FR0000991432	Amundi Actions Europe ISR P A/I	FR	-0.085	-0.58		-0.052	-0.32		-0.170	-1.15	
FR0010844365	Amundi Actions France ISR P	FR	0.110	0.53		0.089	0.43		0.043	0.16	
FR0010153320	Amundi Actions USA ISR P	FR	0.116	0.36		0.118	0.37		-0.007	-0.02	
FR0010106880	Atout Euroland	FR	-0.224	-2.63	**	-0.166	-1.65		-0.238	-2.73	**
FR0010093716	Atout France	FR	0.094	0.85		0.110	0.89		0.051	0.44	
FR0000985152	LCL Actions Etats-Unis ISR	FR	0.071	0.27		0.101	0.38		-0.018	-0.07	
FR0000018954	LCL Actions Euro	FR	-0.234	-2.81	**	-0.178	-1.68		-0.261	-2.89	**
FR0000018947	LCL Actions France	FR	-0.242	-1.76		-0.185	-1.19		-0.289	-1.99	**
FR0010994816	LCL Actions USA ISR (Euro)	FR	0.106	0.55		0.150	0.72		0.021	0.11	
FR0010746776	Aviva Valeurs Responsables A	FR	0.214	1.19		0.219	1.43		0.184	0.97	
FR0000982761	AXA Euro Valeurs Responsables Acc	FR	0.059	0.67		0.112	1.07		0.011	0.12	
LU0316218527	AXA WF Framlington Human Capital AC EUR	FR	0.541	2.15	**	0.555	1.95		0.114	0.56	
FR0010792465	Label Europe Actions S A/I	FR	0.339	2.00	**	0.325	1.69		0.035	0.26	
LU0545089723	AXA WF Framlington Eurozone Ri	FR	0.158	0.55		0.113	0.37		-0.004	-0.01	
LU0245286777	BNP Paribas Islamic Eq Optimiser C	FR	0.294	1.11		0.284	1.07		0.168	0.67	
FR0010668145	BNP Paribas Aqua P	FR	0.860	2.42	**	0.870	2.38	**	0.377	1.30	
FR0010077412	BNP Paribas Développement Humain	FR	0.087	0.33		0.095	0.35		-0.013	-0.05	
FR0010028969	BNP Paribas Etheis Inc	FR	-0.093	-1.06		-0.044	-0.43		-0.102	-1.19	
FR0010137174	BNP Paribas Euro Valeurs Durables	FR	-0.035	-0.30		0.001	0.00		-0.076	-0.58	

Appendices

(continued)

ISIN	Fund name	Country	1-factor conv. Indices			1-factor SRI indices			3-factor conv. Indices		
			Alpha	t-stat.	Sign.	Alpha	t-stat.	Sign.	Alpha	t-stat.	Sign.
FR0010156216	BNP Paribas Immobilier	FR	-0.027	-0.07		-0.023	-0.06		-0.163	-0.45	
LU0212189012	BNP PARIBAS L2 SUSTAINABLE EQUITY EUROPE	FR	0.146	1.23		0.112	0.79		0.021	0.17	
FR0000174526	BNP Paribas Retraite 75 P Inc	FR	-0.115	-1.37		-0.080	-0.88		-0.136	-1.68	
FR0010146530	BNP Paribas Retraite Horizon P 100 Acc	FR	-0.004	-0.03		0.009	0.07		-0.048	-0.39	
FR0010703355	MAIF Investissement Responsable Europe	FR	0.399	3.01	**	0.392	2.44	**	0.209	1.51	
LU0347711466	Parvest Global Environment Classic C Acc	FR	0.403	1.23		0.375	1.07		-0.014	-0.05	
FR0010500603	Agipi Monde Durable	FR	-0.291	-0.96		-0.314	-0.96		-0.535	-1.99	**
LU0406802339	Parvest Environmental Opportunities C	FR	0.212	0.60		0.214	0.57		-0.336	-1.09	
FR0010191627	CCR Actions Engagement Durable	FR	-0.294	-1.86		-0.235	-1.22		-0.384	-2.53	**
FR0000444366	CM-CIC Actions ISR	FR	-0.179	-1.85		-0.125	-1.13		-0.184	-1.90	
FR0010535625	Covéa Finance Actions Solidaires	FR	0.204	1.46		0.198	1.26		0.183	1.15	
FR0010689794	Covéa Finance Espace ISR	FR	0.295	1.15		0.303	1.12		0.078	0.29	
FR0010834457	CPR Progrès Durable Europe P A/I	FR	0.193	1.35		0.181	1.08		0.016	0.11	
FR0000991424	Atout Valeurs Durables A/I	FR	-0.061	-0.44		-0.027	-0.18		-0.123	-0.89	
FR0000004970	Epargne Ethique Actions A/I	FR	-0.333	-3.33	**	-0.273	-2.31	**	-0.333	-3.03	**
FR0010609552	Ecureuil Bénéfices Emploi	FR	0.156	1.03		0.107	0.60		0.081	0.47	
FR0010091116	Ecureuil Bénéfices Responsable Inc	FR	-0.166	-1.73		-0.141	-1.21		-0.191	-1.87	
FR0010505578	EdR Europe SRI A	FR	0.091	0.41		0.144	0.60		-0.126	-0.66	
FR0010588343	EdR Tricolore Rendement	FR	0.137	1.03		0.183	1.36		0.113	0.74	
FR0010502088	Etoile Environnement Acc	FR	-0.131	-0.80		-0.080	-0.47		-0.183	-1.01	
FR0010502096	Etoile Partenaires Acc	FR	-0.029	-0.19		0.022	0.15		-0.051	-0.31	
FR0010583146	Federal Europe ISR P C/D	FR	-0.319	-1.99	**	-0.351	-2.06	**	-0.388	-2.17	**
FR0000442949	Federal Actions Ethiques A/I	FR	0.083	0.37		0.137	0.55		-0.185	-1.08	
FR0010583245	Federal Planète Bleue P	FR	-0.564	-1.93		-0.608	-1.87		-0.748	-2.53	**
FR0007045950	Fédéris ISR Euro C/D	FR	0.051	0.64		0.108	1.18		0.052	0.62	
FR0010822122	Fédéris Sélection ISR Euro A/I	FR	0.173	1.39		0.152	1.06		0.053	0.35	
FR0010086520	Performance Environnement A	FR	-0.786	-1.99	**	-0.771	-1.84		-0.945	-2.52	**
FR0010321828	Echiquier Major	FR	0.312	1.44		0.314	1.37		0.144	0.84	
FR0010013987	Euro Capital Durable 1 Acc	FR	0.066	0.77		0.113	1.21		0.040	0.46	
FR0000437113	HSBC Actions Développement Durable A	FR	-0.094	-0.92		-0.037	-0.33		-0.109	-1.00	
FR0007023023	Universalis	FR	0.061	0.41		0.117	0.65		-0.062	-0.48	
FR0007059886	Europe Ethique Expansion Acc	FR	-0.117	-0.93		-0.071	-0.59		-0.138	-0.99	

(continued)

ISIN	Fund name	Country	1-factor conv. Indices			1-factor SRI indices			3-factor conv. Indices		
			Alpha	t-stat.	Sign.	Alpha	t-stat.	Sign.	Alpha	t-stat.	Sign.
FR0010748368	LBPAM Responsable Actions Environnement C	FR	-0.111	-0.43		-0.114	-0.41		-0.409	-1.62	
FR0000008963	LBPAM Responsable Actions Euro	FR	-0.009	-0.10		0.046	0.51		-0.009	-0.10	
FR0010622696	LBPAM Responsable Actions Monde A C/D	FR	0.362	1.53		0.368	1.49		0.104	0.49	
FR0010871905	LBPAM Responsable Actions Solidaire	FR	-0.167	-0.73		-0.183	-0.72		-0.320	-1.18	
FR0010610386	LFR Actions Solidaires I	FR	-0.173	-0.79		-0.182	-0.72		-0.476	-2.13	**
FR0010526079	LFR Euro Développement Durable I	FR	-0.129	-0.70		-0.139	-0.61		-0.338	-1.78	
FR0010654830	LFP Actions Euro ISR - Part I	FR	-0.014	-0.06		0.000	0.00		-0.229	-1.11	
FR0000003998	Objectif Investissement Responsable	FR	0.135	1.25		0.186	1.86		0.144	1.22	
FR0000989006	LCL Actions Developpement Durable Euro Acc	FR	0.074	0.98		0.132	1.48		0.060	0.77	
FR0000971160	Macif Croissance Durable Euro	FR	0.023	0.26		0.077	0.83		0.082	0.99	
FR0000983819	Macif Croissance Durable&Solidaire Acc	FR	0.037	0.35		0.075	0.64		0.086	0.78	
FR0010091645	MAIF Croissance Durable	FR	0.188	1.53		0.200	1.55		0.202	1.50	
FR0000427452	MG Croissance Durable France	FR	-0.072	-0.60		-0.019	-0.14		-0.082	-0.61	
FR0010700815	Mandarine Engagements R	FR	-0.277	-2.19	**	-0.279	-1.83		-0.321	-1.80	
FR0000970899	Ethique et Partage - CCFD Inc	FR	-0.481	-3.22	**	-0.431	-2.78	**	-0.559	-3.60	**
FR0000448987	MAM Humanis	FR	-0.145	-0.88		-0.093	-0.56		-0.252	-1.55	
FR0000970949	MAM Terra Nova	FR	-0.210	-1.00		-0.174	-0.80		-0.369	-2.03	**
FR0010632364	Metropole Value SRI	FR	0.325	1.70		0.281	1.24		0.247	1.22	
FR0010458539	Mirova Europe Life Quality R(C) EUR	FR	0.106	0.53		0.089	0.41		-0.054	-0.31	
FR0010612879	Ecureuil Bénéfice Environnement	FR	0.234	1.11		0.192	0.78		-0.032	-0.20	
FR0010521575	Fructi Actions Environnement (C) EUR	FR	0.206	1.07		0.189	0.86		0.005	0.03	
FR0010032169	Fructi Euro ISR (C) EUR	FR	-0.180	-2.06	**	-0.129	-1.23		-0.185	-2.08	**
LU0448199371	Mirova Global Climate Change	FR	-0.097	-0.29		-0.100	-0.27		-0.534	-2.38	**
FR0000970873	Insertion Emplois Dynamique R	FR	-0.172	-1.70		-0.124	-1.09		-0.213	-1.95	
FR0000970840	Mirova Euro Sustainable Equity	FR	-0.108	-1.20		-0.052	-0.49		-0.148	-1.53	
FR0000991960	Oddo Génération Europe	FR	-0.059	-0.36		-0.003	-0.01		-0.206	-1.47	
FR0010814400	Avenir Partage ISR A A/I	FR	0.071	0.30		0.074	0.28		-0.353	-1.57	
FR0000981441	Ofi Leader ISR	FR	-0.057	-0.55		-0.007	-0.06		-0.087	-0.81	
LU0185496469	Ofi Multiselect - Europe SRI A Acc	FR	0.400	2.02	**	0.413	1.89		0.086	0.52	
FR0000990921	Gérer Multifactoriel Euro	FR	-0.003	-0.03		0.046	0.42		0.006	0.05	
FR0010312199	Gérer Multifactoriel France A/I	FR	0.031	0.26		0.026	0.19		0.004	0.03	
FR0010458281	Palatine Actions Défensives Euro A	FR	-0.054	-0.31		-0.068	-0.38		-0.121	-0.71	

(continued)

ISIN	Fund name	Country	1-factor conv. Indices Alpha	t-stat.	Sign.	1-factor SRI indices Alpha	t-stat.	Sign.	3-factor conv. Indices Alpha	t-stat.	Sign.
FR0010341800	Palatine Or Bleu A C	FR	0.132	1.06		0.120	0.82		0.057	0.49	
FR0007037130	Euro Active Investors Acc	FR	0.079	0.39		0.127	0.57		-0.087	-0.46	
FR0010538033	Proxy Active Investors A	FR	0.140	1.02		0.110	0.76		0.145	0.99	
FR0007046073	Ethis Vitalité Acc	FR	-0.139	-1.15		-0.087	-0.66		-0.180	-1.36	
FR0007083357	Regard Actions Développement Durable Acc	FR	0.227	2.03	**	0.277	2.31	**	0.200	1.70	
FR0010283838	Roche Brune Zone Euro Actions	FR	0.175	0.86		0.165	0.71		0.036	0.25	
FR0011237503	Roche-Brune Europe Actions	FR	0.124	0.79		0.161	0.91		-0.015	-0.11	
FR0000444275	SG Actions Europe ISR AC	FR	-0.065	-0.65		-0.017	-0.15		-0.119	-1.26	
FR0010596718	SSgA World SRI Index Equity Fund	FR	0.543	1.67		0.513	1.51		0.284	1.01	
FR0000425308	LFP Actions France ISR R	FR	0.018	0.13		0.069	0.49		-0.046	-0.33	
LU0414216498	LFP Trend Opportunities (Part B)	FR	0.226	0.60		0.217	0.54		-0.332	-0.96	
FR0007482591	Virtuose Actions France	FR	0.014	0.11		0.066	0.50		-0.018	-0.14	
FR0010400093	Actions Nord Sud Acc	FR	-0.262	-1.95		-0.107	-0.93		-0.166	-1.40	
FR0010698555	Amundi AFD Avenirs Durables P1	FR	-0.055	-0.81		-0.033	-0.44		-0.203	-3.31	**
FR0007447891	Hymnos A/I	FR	-0.056	-0.68		0.027	0.30		-0.137	-1.61	
FR0010821470	ID-Afer	FR	0.235	1.62		0.291	1.66		0.037	0.24	
FR0000174567	BNP Paribas Retraite 5 I Acc	FR	-0.004	-0.10		0.004	0.10		-0.105	-5.99	**
FR0011021576	BNP Paribas Retraite 50 P Inc	FR	-0.249	-3.90	**	-0.156	-2.32	**	-0.298	-4.02	**
LU0087047089	BNP PARIBAS L1 SUSTAINABLE ACTIVE ALLOCATION	FR	-0.076	-1.24		-0.031	-0.46		-0.240	-6.93	**
FR0000002164	Covéa Finance Horizon Durable	FR	-0.108	-1.36		0.019	0.23		-0.091	-1.20	
FR0010931576	CPR Reflex Responsable 0-100	FR	0.084	0.38		0.109	0.51		-0.073	-0.32	
FR0010896555	Diamant Bleu Responsable	FR	-0.128	-0.70		-0.097	-0.48		-0.229	-1.30	
FR0010626184	Agir avec la Fondation Abbé Pierre	FR	0.002	0.04		0.004	0.09		-0.045	-0.85	
FR0010177899	Choix Solidaire Acc	FR	-0.141	-2.30	**	-0.083	-1.25		-0.160	-2.41	**
FR0010642280	Ecofi Agir Développement Durable	FR	-0.294	-1.90		-0.194	-1.20		-0.313	-1.83	
FR0007475504	Ecofi Flexible	FR	-0.284	-3.08	**	-0.179	-1.83		-0.271	-2.89	**
FR0007048327	Faim et Développement Equilibre Acc	FR	-0.214	-4.44	**	-0.161	-3.15	**	-0.200	-3.72	**
FR0007014212	LBPAM Voie Lactée 1 Acc	FR	0.100	1.84		0.125	2.18	**	-0.017	-0.57	
FR0010030049	LBPAM Voie Lactée 2 Acc	FR	0.079	1.43		0.122	1.93		-0.003	-0.06	
FR0000004962	Libertés & Solidarité A/I	FR	-0.042	-0.62		-0.028	-0.40		-0.163	-3.55	**
FR0000970972	Nouvelle Stratégie 50 Acc	FR	-0.347	-1.93		-0.169	-1.02		-0.256	-1.65	
FR0010303909	Insertion Emplois Equilibre Acc	FR	0.029	0.41		0.070	0.85		-0.128	-1.92	

(continued)

ISIN	Fund name	Country	1-factor conv. Indices Alpha	t-stat	Sign.	1-factor SRI indices Alpha	t-stat	Sign.	3-factor conv. Indices Alpha	t-stat	Sign.
FR0010263764	Ethis Valeurs	FR	-0.123	-1.40		0.012	0.13		-0.090	-1.01	
FR0010883017	RJ Déploiement Durable	FR	0.063	0.45		0.079	0.55		-0.043	-0.30	
FR0007021324	AG2R La Mondiale Obligations ISR	FR	0.030	0.23		0.152	1.39		0.057	0.45	
FR0007082458	AG2R La Mondiale Monétaire Euro ISR	FR	-0.011	-1.05		-0.006	-0.74		-0.008	-1.18	
FR0010336560	Allianz Euro Crédit SRI R C/D	FR	-0.168	-2.58	**	0.128	1.14		-0.135	-2.12	**
FR0010785865	Allianz Sécuricash SRI R	FR	-0.079	-15.41	**	-0.080	-16.53	**	-0.079	-15.09	**
FR0010035162	Amundi Crédit Euro ISR	FR	-0.138	-3.00	**	0.060	0.72		-0.097	-3.24	**
FR0010439935	Danone.Communities D. ISR Prudent	FR	-0.111	-3.89	**	-0.033	-1.01		-0.109	-3.58	**
FR0010439927	Danone.Communities D. ISR Sérénité	FR	-0.114	-6.90	**	-0.096	-6.75	**	-0.108	-6.95	**
FR0010439943	Danone.Communities Investissement Responsable S1	FR	-0.105	-7.59	**	-0.089	-7.86	**	-0.100	-7.56	**
FR0010440164	Danone.Communities Investissement Responsable S2	FR	-0.093	-2.14	**	-0.026	-0.48		-0.086	-1.76	
FR0010440156	Danone.Communities Investissement Responsable S3	FR	-0.079	-2.15	**	0.040	0.82		-0.064	-1.79	
FR0007437546	Aviva Monétaire ISR	FR	-0.215	-3.94	**	-0.202	-4.14	**	-0.211	-3.84	**
FR0010979922	Label Euro Obligations S A/I	FR	-0.099	-1.05		0.154	1.04		-0.146	-2.72	**
FR0000447823	AXA Trésor Court Terme Acc	FR	-0.075	-35.60	**	-0.075	-41.02	**	-0.075	-36.59	**
FR0010076943	BNP PARIBAS OBLI ETHEIS	FR	-0.376	-5.87	**	-0.159	-1.43		-0.357	-5.79	**
FR0007009808	BNP Paribas Mois	FR	-0.037	-11.86	**	-0.035	-11.54	**	-0.037	-11.71	**
FR0010455683	BNP Paribas Money Prime Euro SRI AC	FR	-0.042	-11.25	**	-0.038	-9.26	**	-0.041	-11.76	**
FR0010130765	BNP Paribas Obli Etat	FR	-0.174	-2.47	**	0.003	0.03		-0.170	-4.85	**
LU0265288877	Parvest Euro Corp Bd Sustain Dev Cl Acc	FR	-0.235	-1.91		0.174	1.11		-0.105	-1.58	
FR0010291567	CM-CIC Moné ISR	FR	-0.105	-19.88	**	-0.103	18.90	**	-0.106	-20.76	**
FR0010941328	CM-CIC Obli ISR	FR	-0.053	-1.42		0.032	0.52		-0.055	-2.05	**
FR0010381681	CPR 1-3 Euro SR P	FR	-0.017	-0.31		0.044	0.77		-0.040	-1.01	
FR0007479944	CPR 3-5 Euro SR P	FR	-0.084	-1.36		0.084	1.07		-0.091	-2.52	**
FR0010376020	CPR 7-10 Euro SR P	FR	-0.104	-0.84		0.131	0.82		-0.068	-1.33	
FR0010436980	CPR Monétaire SR A	FR	-0.045	-6.11	**	-0.039	-4.80	**	-0.045	-5.83	**
FR0000934978	Dexia Ethique Gest Oblig Classic C Acc	FR	-0.246	-5.40	**	-0.025	-0.31		-0.233	-9.89	**
FR0010766113	Babyfund Taux Fixe 2013 P	FR	-0.126	-3.50	**	-0.041	-0.82		-0.127	-3.35	**
FR0010515601	Confiance Solidaire	FR	-0.074	-2.86	**	-0.032	-1.19		-0.071	-2.87	**
FR0000981425	Ecofi Monédym	FR	-0.056	-3.89	**	-0.054	-4.12	**	-0.053	-3.77	**
FR0007381983	Ecofi Obligations Internationales	FR	-0.095	-2.08	**	0.040	0.66		-0.096	-2.39	**
FR0010219899	Epargne Ethique Monétaire	FR	-0.127	-33.12	**	-0.125	-32.32	**	-0.127	-33.66	**

Appendices 263

(continued)

ISIN	Fund name	Country	1-factor conv. Indices Alpha	t-stat.	Sign.	1-factor SRI indices Alpha	t-stat.	Sign.	3-factor conv. Indices Alpha	t-stat.	Sign.
FR0007413091	Epargne Solidaire	FR	-0.148	-4.64	**	-0.110	-3.54	**	-0.153	-4.55	**
FR0010075044	Invest Première	FR	-0.089	-20.59	**	-0.087	-22.36	**	-0.088	-20.84	**
FR0010616664	Federal Placement Court Terme IR	FR	-0.064	-13.17	**	-0.062	-11.52	**	-0.065	-16.14	**
FR0010859785	Federal Taux Variable IR	FR	-0.037	-0.37		0.019	0.25		-0.027	-0.39	
FR0010622662	Fédéris Obligations ISR R	FR	-0.146	-1.07		0.203	1.37		-0.107	-1.54	
FR0010702175	Groupama Crédit Euro ISR N C/D	FR	-0.283	-1.78		0.081	0.45		-0.312	-2.87	**
FR0010744953	HSBC Monétaire Etat	FR	-0.052	-11.51	**	-0.053	-12.13	**	-0.052	-11.12	**
FR0010061283	HSBC Oblig Développement Durable A	FR	-0.132	-2.47	**	0.102	0.83		-0.082	-1.95	
FR0010018309	LBPAM Responsable Première Long Trm	FR	-0.179	-2.73	**	0.110	0.97		-0.143	-4.89	**
FR0010016857	LBPAM Responsable PremièreMoyen Trm	FR	-0.086	-2.78	**	0.010	0.20		-0.092	-3.82	**
FR0010957860	LBPAM Responsable Obli Crédit E	FR	-0.004	-0.03		0.278	1.71		-0.006	-0.07	
FR0010805788	LBPAM Responsable Tréso E	FR	-0.045	-11.09	**	-0.045	-11.55	**	-0.045	-10.64	**
FR0010214650	CMNE Sélections	FR	-0.048	-2.90	**	-0.042	-3.42	**	-0.041	-4.12	**
FR0010915314	LFP Obligations ISR C	FR	-0.141	-1.66		0.041	0.29		-0.135	-2.28	**
FR0010812651	Macif Trésorerie Semestrielle ISR C	FR	-0.008	-1.28		-0.007	-1.26		-0.007	-1.31	
FR0000971012	MAM Obligations Ethique (C)	FR	-0.142	-4.22	**	-0.037	-0.71		-0.136	-4.45	**
FR0010721415	CNP Assur-Monet R	FR	-0.090	-14.50	**	-0.092	-17.61	**	-0.090	-13.74	**
FR0000099772	Fonsicav	FR	-0.068	-25.85	**	-0.067	-25.42	**	-0.068	-26.26	**
FR0010028985	Fructi ISR Obli Euro R(C) EUR	FR	-0.082	-1.57		0.115	1.20		-0.076	-1.81	
FR0010673491	Insertion Emplois Modéré	FR	-0.081	-1.95		-0.015	-0.26		-0.076	-2.01	**
FR0010008003	Mirova Sustainable Cash	FR	-0.085	-25.53	**	-0.084	-25.34	**	-0.085	-25.45	**
FR0010532044	Natixis Impact Nord-Sud Développement	FR	-0.166	-2.54	**	0.013	0.16		-0.156	-3.02	**
FR0000008997	Ofi Trésor ISR A/I	FR	-0.039	-10.18	**	-0.036	-9.66	**	-0.038	-12.73	**
FR0010433185	Gérer Monétaire Jour	FR	-0.107	-16.00	**	-0.104	-16.89	**	-0.106	-15.60	**
FR0010474577	Gérer Monétaire Trésor	FR	-0.100	-5.18	**	-0.095	-5.40	**	-0.099	-5.18	**
FR0010368159	Palatine Première	FR	-0.199	-2.28	**	0.030	0.31		-0.211	-5.09	**
FR0007474838	Palatine Trésorerie 1ère	FR	-0.095	-21.95	**	-0.094	-22.65	**	-0.095	-21.79	**
FR0010370528	Uni-MT	FR	-0.186	-1.80		-0.022	-0.21		-0.206	-3.30	**
FR0010822130	Regard Obligations Privées ISR	FR	-0.061	-0.45		0.220	1.50		-0.037	-0.50	
FR0007074844	SG Oblig Corporate ISR	FR	-0.329	-3.02	**	-0.085	-0.83		-0.255	-5.57	**
FR0010748848	LFP Trésorerie ISR R	FR	-0.043	-6.76	**	-0.043	-6.39	**	-0.043	-6.59	**
LU0278938138	Aberdeen Glbl Responsible Wld Eq A2	UK	0.269	0.82		0.246	0.73		0.073	0.24	

(continued)

ISIN	Fund name	Country	1-factor conv. Indices			1-factor SRI indices			3-factor conv. Indices		
			Alpha	t-stat.	Sign.	Alpha	t-stat.	Sign.	Alpha	t-stat.	Sign.
GB0006833718	Aberdeen Ethical World Fd A Acc	UK	0.142	0.68		0.182	0.83		0.011	0.05	
GB00B131GB92	Aberdeen Responsible UK Equity A Acc	UK	0.131	0.40		0.118	0.34		-0.026	-0.09	
GB00B0LNTT93	Aberdeen Multi-Manager Ethical Acc	UK	0.046	0.16		0.045	0.14		-0.167	-0.72	
GB0030029515	Alliance Trust Sustainable Future Absolute Growth	UK	0.145	0.61		0.186	0.74		-0.086	-0.46	
GB0030029283	Alliance Trust Sustainable Future European Growth	UK	0.198	1.41		0.240	1.51		0.056	0.44	
GB0030029952	Alliance Trust Sustainable Future Global Growth	UK	-0.049	-0.19		-0.014	-0.05		-0.240	-1.04	
GB0030028764	Alliance Trust Sustainable Future UK Growth	UK	0.265	1.00		0.305	1.09		0.035	0.14	
GB0003506424	AXA Framlington Health Acc	UK	0.277	0.75		0.299	0.82		0.084	0.24	
GB0005297980	AXA Ethical R Acc	UK	-0.113	-0.36		-0.076	-0.24		-0.309	-1.02	
GB0009537407	CIS European Growth Trust Inc	UK	-0.136	-1.09		-0.083	-0.61		-0.188	-1.60	
GB00B05Q3G94	CIS UK FTSE4Good Tracker Tr Acc	UK	-0.039	-0.18		-0.009	-0.04		-0.134	-0.63	
GB0001597979	CIS UK Growth Trust Inc	UK	-0.007	-0.03		0.032	0.14		-0.149	-0.74	
GB0030038359	CIS US Growth Trust Inc	UK	-0.083	-0.28		-0.050	-0.17		-0.237	-0.81	
GB0008446626	Ecclesiastical Amity European A Inc	UK	0.100	0.84		0.145	1.10		0.010	0.08	
GB0008448663	Ecclesiastical Amity International A Inc	UK	0.263	1.34		0.297	1.49		0.120	0.70	
GB0009371310	Ecclesiastical Amity UK A Inc	UK	0.072	0.27		0.109	0.39		-0.124	-0.48	
GB0030833981	F&C Stewardship Gr Fd 1 Acc	UK	0.132	0.47		0.173	0.58		-0.074	-0.29	
GB0030835580	F&C Stewardship Income 1 Acc	UK	0.169	0.57		0.203	0.66		-0.026	-0.09	
GB0030833650	F&C Stewardship International 1 Acc	UK	0.092	0.37		0.127	0.49		-0.111	-0.48	
LU0318449088	F&C Global Climate Opp A EUR	UK	0.143	0.42		0.106	0.28		-0.179	-0.62	
GB0006685613	Family Charities Ethical Trust Acc	UK	-0.095	-0.34		-0.053	-0.18		-0.325	-1.23	
GB00B0TY6S22	First State Asia Pacific Sstnblty A GBP	UK	0.723	2.05	**	0.722	2.01	**	0.496	1.62	
GB00B64TS881	First State Global Emerg Mkts Sustblty A	UK	1.064	2.28	**	1.078	2.27		0.407	1.09	
IE00B2PGVJ29	Guinness Alternative Energy A Inc	UK	-0.929	-1.19		-0.927	-1.18		-1.143	-1.12	
GB0031811622	Halifax Ethical C Inc	UK	0.056	0.24		0.092	0.39		-0.109	-0.52	
GB0005027221	Henderson Glb Care Growth Inc	UK	0.097	0.42		0.134	0.57		-0.099	-0.46	
GB0005027338	Henderson Global Care UK Income Inc	UK	-0.187	-0.72		-0.145	-0.53		-0.341	-1.32	
LU0419691059	HSBC Amanah Global Equity A	UK	0.402	1.07		0.400	1.01		-0.156	-0.63	
LU0110459103	HSBC Amanah Global Equity Index fund-Inc	UK	-0.014	-0.05		0.015	0.06		-0.072	-0.29	
LU0322240290	HSBC GIF Climate Change A Inc	UK	0.105	0.31		0.119	0.34		-0.245	-0.92	
GB00B4LDCG53	IFDS IM WHEB Sustainability A	UK	0.076	0.22		0.086	0.23		-0.413	-1.31	
IE00B04R3307	Impax Environmental Mkts A GBP Acc	UK	0.300	1.02		0.305	0.97		0.056	0.22	

Appendices

(continued)

ISIN	Fund name	Country	1-factor conv. Indices			1-factor SRI indices			3-factor conv. Indices		
			Alpha	t-stat.	Sign.	Alpha	t-stat.	Sign.	Alpha	t-stat.	Sign.
LU0231118026	JGF - Jupiter Climate Change Solutions L Acc	UK	0.139	0.55		0.177	0.67		-0.093	-0.40	
LU0329070832	Jupiter Global Fund China Sustainable Growth	UK	-0.003	0.00		0.002	0.00		-0.966	-1.34	
GB0005812150	Jupiter Ecology fund Inc	UK	0.169	0.64		0.206	0.77		-0.054	-0.22	
GB0008337569	Jupiter Responsible Income	UK	0.217	0.75		0.256	0.86		0.031	0.11	
GB00B1N9DX45	Kames Ethical Equity A Acc	UK	0.091	0.24		0.075	0.19		-0.031	-0.09	
GB0009243824	L&G Ethical Tr (R) Acc	UK	0.159	0.62		0.204	0.75		-0.014	-0.06	
GB00B0JZPC21	Old Mutual Ethical Fund A (GBP)	UK	0.094	0.33		0.091	0.30		-0.118	-0.49	
GB0004072699	Premier Ethical R Inc	UK	0.067	0.32		0.106	0.48		-0.082	-0.39	
GB00B23DJV30	Schroder Global Climate Change Inc	UK	0.288	0.87		0.261	0.73		0.084	0.27	
LU0233833143	SWIP Islamic Global Equity A Acc	UK	0.332	1.06		0.330	1.03		0.135	0.48	
GB00B3BLRL29	Scottish Widows HIFML Ethical 1	UK	0.624	1.80		0.635	1.79		0.232	0.76	
GB0031632010	Scottish Widows Environm Investor A Acc	UK	-0.134	-0.45		-0.095	-0.31		-0.328	-1.15	
GB0032200213	Scottish Widows Ethical Fd A Acc	UK	-0.210	-0.72		-0.171	-0.56		-0.397	-1.37	
GB0008317611	Sovereign Ethical Fund Inc	UK	-0.227	-0.69		-0.184	-0.54		-0.449	-1.44	
GB00B1ZB0M68	Standard Life Euro Ethical Equity Retail Acc	UK	0.094	0.35		0.041	0.13		-0.090	-0.38	
GB0004331012	Standard Life UK Ethical R Acc	UK	0.315	0.97		0.358	1.03		0.005	0.02	
GB0002010634	SLFC Green	UK	0.225	0.89		0.261	1.00		-0.021	-0.09	
GB00B1FL7S17	SVM All Europe SRI A Acc	UK	0.658	1.37		0.644	1.25		0.480	1.21	
GB00B29KGH36	Virgin Climate Change Acc	UK	-0.183	-0.37		-0.215	-0.40		-0.473	-0.99	
GB00B1LBFW55	CF 7IM Sustainable Balance A Acc	UK	-0.271	-0.97		-0.205	-0.76		-0.442	-1.96	
GB0030030281	Alliance Trust Sustainable Future Managed	UK	-0.135	-0.63		-0.027	-0.13		-0.198	-1.00	
GB00B11TD470	CIS UK Income with Growth Series 3	UK	0.032	0.10		0.132	0.42		-0.218	-0.79	
GB00B3PXJV84	CIS Sustainable Diversified Trust	UK	0.323	1.09		0.349	1.15		-0.017	-0.06	
GB00B3PXJX09	CIS Sustainable World Trust	UK	0.693	2.30	**	0.736	2.38	**	0.393	1.23	
GB0031833402	Henderson Glb Care Managed	UK	-0.016	-0.08		0.097	0.51		-0.056	-0.30	
GB00B1N9DX45	Kames Ethical Equity A Acc	UK	0.025	0.07		0.085	0.24		-0.224	-0.78	
GB0030028988	Alliance Trust Sustainable Future Corporate Bond	UK	-0.769	-2.80	**	-0.418	-1.55		-0.725	-3.43	**
GB0033583427	CIS Corporate Bond Income Trust Inc	UK	-0.874	-3.70	**	-0.489	-2.06	**	-0.845	-4.37	**
GB00B2PF8B06	Ecclesiastical Amity Sterling Bond A Inc	UK	-0.931	-2.37	**	-0.173	-0.49		-0.941	-2.74	**
GB00B23YHT07	F&C Ethical Bond 1 Inc	UK	-0.853	-2.54	**	-0.246	-0.67		-0.822	-2.66	**
GB0005342646	Kames Ethical Corporate Bond A Acc	UK	-0.468	-1.79		-0.117	-0.43		-0.427	-1.96	
GB0030957137	Rathbone Ethical Bond Fund Acc	UK	-0.534	-1.92		-0.163	-0.61		-0.485	-2.25	**

(continued)

ISIN	Fund name	Country	1-factor conv. Indices			1-factor SRI indices			3-factor conv. Indices		
			Alpha	t-stat.	Sign.	Alpha	t-stat.	Sign.	Alpha	t-stat.	Sign.
GB00B4WSJK27	Royal London Ethical Bond A	UK	-0.981	-2.51	**	-0.437	-1.10		-0.905	-2.85	**
GB00B0LNNH51	Standard Life Ethical Corporate Bond Acc	UK	-0.535	-2.15	**	-0.147	-0.50		-0.537	-2.31	**
NL0000441301	ASN Duurzaam Aandelenfonds Inc	NL	0.060	0.29		0.090	0.44		-0.084	-0.43	
NL0000290518	ASN Duurzaam Small & Midcap Fonds	NL	0.156	0.42		0.137	0.33		-0.172	-0.72	
NL0000280501	ASN Milieu & Waterfonds Inc	NL	0.253	0.93		0.288	1.04		-0.041	-0.17	
LU0264990036	Delta Lloyd L New Energy Classe B Acc	NL	-0.580	-0.86		-0.610	-0.88		-0.843	-1.12	
LU0264990119	Delta Lloyd L Water & Climate Fund Classe B Acc	NL	-0.209	-0.41		-0.255	-0.47		-0.547	-0.99	
LU0119216553	ING(L) Invest Sustainable Gr P Acc	NL	-0.021	-0.11		0.016	0.08		-0.139	-0.77	
NL0006311789	ING Duurzaam Aandelen Fonds Inc	NL	0.004	0.02		0.042	0.22		-0.091	-0.53	
NL0000113082	Kempen Sense Fund	NL	0.488	1.68		0.540	1.68		0.087	0.44	
NL0000288843	Robeco DuurzaamAandelen Inc	NL	-0.179	-0.88		-0.143	-0.67		-0.320	-1.66	
LU0374106754	RobecoSAM Sustainable Agribusiness Equities D EUR	NL	0.190	0.34		0.159	0.26		-0.253	-0.53	
LU0187077218	RobecoSAM Sustainable European Equities D EUR	NL	-0.045	-0.24		0.001	0.01		-0.211	-1.24	
NL0000291136	SNS Amerika Aandelenfonds Inc	NL	0.013	0.05		0.040	0.15		-0.101	-0.38	
NL0000291128	SNS Azië Aandelenfonds	NL	-0.039	-0.13		-0.009	-0.03		-0.278	-1.02	
NL0000291086	SNS Euro Aandelenfonds	NL	-0.058	-0.40		-0.016	-0.09		-0.189	-1.35	
NL0000291151	SNS Euro Vastgoedfonds Inc	NL	-0.169	-0.43		-0.121	-0.29		-0.423	-1.23	
NL0000291102	SNS Hoogdividend Aandelenfonds	NL	-0.279	-1.54		-0.238	-1.31		-0.327	-1.86	
NL0000291037	SNS Nederlands Aandelenfonds Inc	NL	-0.294	-1.16		-0.242	-0.90		-0.456	-1.64	
NL0000293371	SNS Opkomende Landen Aandelenfonds	NL	-0.019	-0.04		-0.046	-0.09		-0.315	-0.69	
NL0000291144	SNS Wereld Aandelenfonds Inc	NL	-0.035	-0.18		-0.001	0.00		-0.183	-1.04	
NL0009347574	Sustainable Europe Index Fund	NL	0.251	1.74		0.237	1.40		0.083	0.89	
NL0009486745	Sustainable North America Index Fund	NL	0.526	1.26		0.527	1.23		0.188	0.65	
NL0009347566	Sustainable World Index Fund Inc	NL	0.191	0.62		0.186	0.57		-0.070	-0.23	
LU0278271951	Triodos Sustainable Equity R	NL	0.591	1.83		0.562	1.65		0.288	1.10	
LU0278272843	Triodos Sustainable Pioneer R	NL	0.107	0.29		0.086	0.23		-0.062	-0.15	
NL0000280089	ASN Duurzaam Mixfonds	NL	-0.129	-1.15		-0.080	-0.71		-0.254	-2.40	**
NL0000291094	SNS Euro Mixfonds	NL	-0.132	-1.56		-0.052	-0.55		-0.208	-2.68	**
NL0000056822	SNS Optimaal Blauw	NL	-0.066	-0.81		-0.054	-0.63		-0.232	-4.58	**
NL0000286631	SNS Optimaal Geel	NL	-0.148	-1.78		-0.116	-1.30		-0.311	-4.82	**
NL0000286649	SNS Optimaal Oranje	NL	-0.083	-0.96		-0.019	-0.20		-0.214	-2.85	**
NL0000291193	SNS Optimaal Paars	NL	-0.078	-0.41		0.067	0.36		-0.038	-0.21	

Appendices   267

(continued)

ISIN	Fund name	Country	1-factor conv. Indices Alpha	t-stat.	Sign.	1-factor SRI indices Alpha	t-stat.	Sign.	3-factor conv. Indices Alpha	t-stat.	Sign.
NL000286656	SNS Optimaal Rood	NL	-0.087	-0.70		0.018	0.14		-0.156	-1.35	
LU0504302604	Triodos Sustainable Mixed Fund R-dis	NL	-0.245	-1.94		-0.232	-1.77		-0.494	-4.06	**
NL000441244	ASN Duurzaam Obligatiefonds	NL	-0.450	-4.39	**	-0.221	-1.76		-0.439	-5.97	**
LU0503372608	Robeco Euro Sustainable Credits D	NL	-0.018	-0.13		0.273	1.65		-0.017	-0.23	
NL000291011	SNS Euro Liquiditeitenfonds	NL	-0.289	-5.09	**	-0.276	-4.73	**	-0.289	-4.98	**
NL000291060	SNS Euro Obligatiefonds	NL	-0.423	-4.73	**	-0.183	-1.51		-0.404	-4.97	**
NL000440204	Triodos Groenfonds Inc	NL	-0.378	-5.18	**	-0.254	-3.17	**	-0.383	-6.49	**
LU0278272504	Triodos Sustainable Bond R	NL	-0.156	-1.47		0.168	1.04		-0.171	-3.23	**
LU0158827195	Allianz RCM Global Sust A EUR Inc	DE	0.069	0.35		0.097	0.46		-0.074	-0.40	
LU250028817	Allianz-dit Global EcoTrends A EUR Inc	DE	-0.060	-0.13		-0.075	-0.16		-0.343	-0.73	
DE0009847343	terrAssisi Aktien I AMI Acc	DE	0.033	0.17		0.072	0.34		-0.138	-0.75	
LU0117185156	Meridio Green Balance Acc	DE	-0.118	-0.41		-0.081	-0.28		-0.322	-1.22	
DE000A0KEYM4	LBBW Global Warming	DE	0.321	1.03		0.291	0.83		0.095	0.31	
DE000A0NAUP7	LBBW Nachhaltigkeit Aktien R	DE	0.133	0.59		0.140	0.60		-0.097	-0.41	
LU0355139220	DKB Ökofonds TNL Acc	DE	-0.563	-1.27		-0.593	-1.25		-0.815	-1.88	
LU0314225409	DKB Zukunftsfonds Acc	DE	0.069	0.26		0.040	0.15		-0.045	-0.17	
DE000DK0ECS2	Deka-UmweltInvest CF Acc	DE	-0.099	-0.24		-0.126	-0.29		-0.332	-0.82	
LU0130393993	Postbank Dynamik-Vision Acc	DE	-0.123	-0.89		-0.075	-0.50		-0.165	-1.16	
DE000DWS0DT1	DWS Klimawandel Inc	DE	-0.518	-1.53		-0.547	-1.51		-0.719	-2.18	**
DE0298649426	DWS Invest Clean Tech LC	DE	-0.575	-1.75		-0.602	-1.71		-0.785	-2.45	**
LU0273158872	DWS Invest Global Agribusiness LC	DE	0.261	0.51		0.235	0.43		0.010	0.02	
LU0405846410	LSF Asian Solar & Wind A1	DE	-0.846	-0.50		-0.868	-0.50		-0.981	-0.47	
IE0005895655	Green Effects NAI-Werte Fonds Acc	DE	0.214	0.85		0.251	0.95		-0.031	-0.14	
DE000A0RHHC8	4Q-Smart Power	DE	0.308	0.67		0.301	0.59		-0.296	-0.85	
DE0008470477	INVESCO Umwelt-u.Nachhaltigkeits-Fds Acc	DE	0.018	0.10		0.055	0.29		-0.097	-0.54	
DE0037079380	Öko-Aktienfonds Acc	DE	0.150	0.52		0.190	0.64		-0.062	-0.21	
LU0383804431	FG&W Better World	DE	-0.292	-0.62		-0.295	-0.60		-0.553	-1.22	
DE0002605367	ComfortInvest Perspektive	DE	0.057	0.15		0.023	0.06		-0.283	-0.89	
DE0001619997	MEAG Nachhaltigkeit A Inc	DE	-0.114	-0.60		-0.077	-0.38		-0.227	-1.27	
DE0007560849	Monega FairInvest Aktien Acc	DE	-0.059	-0.28		-0.066	-0.27		-0.250	-1.26	
DE3600172109	Murphy&Spitz-Umweltfonds Deutschland	DE	-0.373	-0.86		-0.405	-0.89		-0.525	-1.13	
LU0309769247	ÖkoWorld Ökovision Europe C Acc	DE	-0.161	-0.56		-0.190	-0.61		-0.390	-1.38	

(continued)

ISIN	Fund name	Country	1-factor conv. Indices Alpha	t-stat.	Sign.	1-factor SRI indices Alpha	t-stat.	Sign.	3-factor conv. Indices Alpha	t-stat.	Sign.
LU0332822492	ÖkoWorld Water Life C Acc	DE	0.237	0.72		0.222	0.65		-0.093	-0.33	
LU0380798750	ÖkoWorld² Ökotrust C Acc	DE	-0.148	-0.65		-0.142	-0.60		-0.473	-2.41	**
LU0301152442	Oekoworld ÖkoWorld Klima C Acc	DE	-0.099	-0.28		-0.130	-0.34		-0.375	-1.04	
LU0061928585	ÖkoWorld ÖkoVision® Classic Acc	DE	0.073	0.30		0.115	0.45		-0.153	-0.68	
LU0036592839	SEB ÖkoLux Acc	DE	-0.066	-0.24		-0.025	-0.08		-0.299	-1.09	
LU0152254803	LIGA-Pax-Cattolico Union Inc	DE	-0.044	-0.42		-0.006	-0.05		-0.084	-0.87	
LU0315365378	UniSector: Klimawandel	DE	-0.432	-1.02		-0.463	-1.05		-0.687	-1.49	
DE0005326532	KCD-Union Nachhaltig Aktien Inc	DE	-0.119	-0.68		-0.078	-0.44		-0.162	-0.94	
DE0009750216	Liga Pax Aktien Union Inc	DE	-0.106	-1.10		-0.059	-0.55		-0.155	-1.77	
DE000A0M80G4	UniNachhaltig Aktien Global	DE	0.577	1.77		0.578	1.68		0.257	1.00	
DE0007045437	WestLB Me Co Fd Pension Dynamic Fonds Acc	DE	0.133	0.86		0.174	1.14		0.077	0.51	
DE0007248700	Ampega Responsibility Fonds	DE	-0.455	-2.80	**	-0.417	-2.57	**	-0.512	-3.35	**
DE0005896864	Deka-Stiftungen Balance	DE	-0.206	-2.08	**	-0.189	-1.91		-0.342	-5.13	**
LU0353730392	Postbank Dynamik Klima Garant Acc	DE	0.098	0.79		0.100	0.84		-0.021	-0.23	
LU0305675109	DJE LUX SICAV - DJE Vermögensmanagement P	DE	-0.164	-0.49		-0.095	-0.27		-0.562	-1.51	
DE000DW S0XF8	WvF Rendite und Nachhaltigkeit	DE	-0.033	-0.30		-0.010	-0.08		-0.273	-3.83	**
DE0005318406	DWS Stiftungsfonds	DE	-0.376	-3.36	**	-0.346	-3.03	**	-0.480	-4.44	**
DE000A0D95R8	FT Navigator Sustainability	DE	-0.114	-0.76		-0.061	-0.39		-0.200	-1.41	
LU0360706096	BN & P - Good Growth Fonds B Acc	DE	-0.271	-1.93		-0.259	-1.81		-0.363	-2.30	**
DE0008023565	Fonds fur Stiftungen INVESCO Inc	DE	-0.105	-0.98		-0.075	-0.71		-0.157	-1.47	
LU0206716028	IAM-Pro Vita World Fund Acc	DE	-0.499	-2.62	**	-0.444	-2.27	**	-0.502	-2.77	**
DE000A0X9SA0	Sparda München nachhaltige Vermögensverwaltung	DE	-0.165	-1.98		-0.153	-1.75		-0.257	-2.97	**
DE000A0LGNP3	NORD/LB AM Global Challenges Index-Fonds	DE	0.179	0.49		0.304	0.85		0.068	0.21	
LU0332822906	ÖkoWorld Garant 20 C Acc	DE	-0.139	-0.85		-0.118	-0.73		-0.465	-3.06	**
DE000A0M03X1	First Nachhaltig Balance PI 4 Acc	DE	-0.029	-0.28		0.016	0.14		-0.233	-2.73	**
DE000A0M0317	First Nachhaltig Wachstum PI 4 Acc	DE	-0.061	-0.48		0.005	0.04		-0.233	-1.98	
DE000A0B7JB7	BfS Nachhaltigkeits fd Ertrag SEB Inv Inc	DE	-0.293	-2.61	**	-0.256	-2.29	**	-0.361	-2.93	**
LU0458538880	FairWorldFonds	DE	-0.064	-0.62		-0.048	-0.47		-0.232	-3.52	**
DE0009750000	KCD-Union Nachhaltig MIX	DE	-0.174	-1.70		-0.132	-1.25		-0.340	-5.27	**
DE0005314215	LIGA-Pax-Bal-Stifts fds-Union Inc	DE	-0.288	-2.59	**	-0.255	-2.31	**	-0.399	-3.68	**
DE000A0M80H2	Volksbank Gütersloh Nachhaltigkeits Invest	DE	-0.109	-0.77		-0.064	-0.46		-0.046	-0.30	
DE000A0RE972	BERENBERG-1590-Stiftung	DE	-0.443	-2.51	**	-0.409	-2.20	**	-0.551	-3.81	**

Appendices

(continued)

ISIN	Fund name	Country	1-factor conv. Indices			1-factor SRI indices			3-factor conv. Indices		
			Alpha	t-stat.	Sign.	Alpha	t-stat.	Sign.	Alpha	t-stat.	Sign.
DE0005317127	Sarasin FairInvest Universal Fds Inc	DE	-0.183	-2.12	**	-0.136	-1.58		-0.306	-4.05	**
DE0007045148	WestLB Mellon Werte Fonds Inc	DE	-0.202	-2.15	**	-0.154	-1.63		-0.334	-3.95	**
DE000A0NGJV5	terrAssisi Renten I AMI P(a) Inc	DE	-0.175	-2.15	**	-0.101	-1.37		-0.169	-2.17	**
DE000A0X97K7	LBBW Nachhaltigkeit Renten	DE	-0.272	-2.44	**	-0.052	-0.37		-0.270	-2.59	**
DE0008474081	DWS ESG Global-Gov Bonds LC	DE	-0.405	-3.40	**	-0.160	-1.19		-0.434	-3.87	**
LU0182869809	INIK Acc	DE	-0.265	-3.11	**	-0.138	-1.95		-0.220	-3.43	**
LU0183092898	ÖKOTREND Bonds Inc	DE	-0.237	-2.15	**	-0.205	-2.04	**	-0.253	-2.38	**
DE000A0M6W36	CSR Bond Plus OP	DE	-0.067	-0.53		0.094	0.85		-0.092	-0.95	
LU0041441808	SEB Ökorent Inc	DE	-0.593	-3.26	**	-0.326	-1.75		-0.662	-4.56	**
LU0199537852	LIGA-Pax-Corporates-Union Inc	DE	-0.525	-3.26	**	-0.271	-1.81		-0.429	-4.01	**
DE0005326524	KCD-Union Nachhaltig-RENTEN Inc	DE	-0.438	-5.19	**	-0.193	-1.73		-0.407	-5.27	**
DE0009750141	LIGA-Pax-KUnion Inc	DE	-0.361	-4.45	**	-0.270	-3.20	**	-0.361	-4.46	**
DE0008491226	LIGA-Pax-RentUnion Inc	DE	-0.470	-4.37	**	-0.270	-2.27	**	-0.468	-4.66	**
DE0009769844	ACATIS Fair Value Bonds UI A	DE	-0.545	-3.40	**	-0.345	-2.31	**	-0.571	-4.32	**
	Average alpha		-0.045			0.012			-0.165		
	Min alpha		-0.981			-0.927			-1.143		
	Max alpha		1.064			1.078			0.496		

Appendix V: SRI fund difference portfolios

This table shows the differences in monthly excess returns between the fund portfolios for the entire observation period from January 2003 - December 2013. Monthly returns are continuously compounded returns and reported in percentage terms.

Difference portfolio	Difference in excess returns (%)	t-stat.
Equity minus balanaced SRI funds	0.20	0.703
Equity minus fixed income SRI funds	0.16	0.528
Balanced minus fixed income SRI funds	0.03	0.236

References

Acock, Alan C. (2008). *A gentle introduction to Stata.* College Station: Stata Press.

Affleck-Graves, John/McDonald, Bill. (1989). Nonnormalities and tests of asset pricing theories. *The Journal of Finance, 44*(4), 889–908.

Aguilera, Ruth V./Rupp, Deborah E./Williams, Cynthia A./Ganapathi, Jyoti. (2007). Putting the S back in corporate social responsibility: A multilevel theory of social change in organizations. *Academy of Management Review, 32*(3), 836–863.

Amenc, Noel/Goltz, Felix/Lioui, Abraham. (2011). Practitioner portfolio construction and performance measurement: Evidence from Europe. *Financial Analysts Journal, 67*(3), 39–50.

Anderson, Jerry W. Jr. (1986). Social responsibility and the corporation. *Business Horizons, 29*(4), 22–27.

Anson, Mark J. P. (2008). *Handbook of alternative assets* (2nd ed.). Hoboken: John Wiley & Sons, Inc.

Antunovich, Peter/Laster, David S. (1998). Do investors mistake a good company for a good investment? *FRB of New York Staff Report No. 60.*

Areal, Nelson/Cortez, Maria C./Silva, Florinda. (2015). The conditional performance of US mutual funds over different market regimes: Do different types of ethical screens matter? *Financial Markets and Portfolio Management, 27*(4), 397–429.

Auer, Benjamin R./Schuhmacher, Frank. (2016). Do socially (ir)responsible investments pay? New evidence from international ESG data. *The Quarterly Review of Economics and Finance, 59(2016)*, 51-62.

Ayadi, Mohamed A./Kryzanowski, Lawrence. (2011). Fixed-income fund performance: Role of luck and ability in tail membership. *Journal of Empirical Finance, 18*(3), 379–392.

Bailey, Jeffery V. (1992). Evaluating Benchmark Quality. *Financial Analysts Journal, 48*(3), 33–39.

Baker, H. Kent. (2009). Dividends and dividend policy: An overview. In H. Kent Baker (Ed.), *Dividends and Dividend Policy* (1st ed., pp. 1–20). Hoboken: John Wiley & Sons, Inc.

Baltagi, Badi H. (2002). *Econometrics* (3rd ed.). Berlin: Springer Science & Business Media B.V.

Banegas, Ayelen/Gillen, Ben/Timmermann, Allan/Wermers, Russ. (2013). The cross section of conditional mutual fund performance in European stock markets. *Journal of Financial Economics, 108*(3), 699–726.

Barnett, Michael L./Salomon, Robert M. (2006). Beyond dichotomy: The curvilinear relationship between social responsibility and financial performance. *Strategic Management Journal*, *27*(11), 1101–1122.

Barreda-Tarrazona, Iván/Matallín-Sáez, Juan C./Balaguer-Franch, Maria R. (2011). Measuring investors' socially responsible preferences in mutual funds. *Journal of Business Ethics*, *103*(2007), 305–330.

Bassen, Alexander/Meyer, Katrin/Schlange, Joachim. (2006). The influence of corporate social responsibility on the cost of capital. *Working Paper*, University of Hamburg. Retrieved from http://ssrn.com/abstract=984406.

Bauer, Rob/Derwall, Jeroen/Otten, Roger. (2007). The ethical mutual fund performance debate: New evidence from Canada. *Journal of Business Ethics*, *70*(2), 111–124.

Bauer, Rob/Günster, Nadja/Otten, Roger. (2004). Empirical evidence on corporate governance in Europe: The effect on stock returns, firm value and performance. *Journal of Asset Management*, *5*(2), 91–104.

Bauer, Rob/Koedijk, Kees/Otten, Roger. (2005). International evidence on ethical mutual fund performance and investment style. *Journal of Banking & Finance*, *29*(7), 1751–1767.

Bauer, Rob/Otten, Roger/Rad, Alireza T. (2006). Ethical investing in Australia: Is there a financial penalty? *Pacific-Basin Finance Journal*, *14*(1), 33–48.

Beal, Diana J./Goyen, Michelle. (1998). Putting your money where your mouth is: A profile of ethical investors. *Financial Services Review*, *7*(2), 129–143.

Beal, Diana J./Goyen, Michelle/Philips, Peter. (2005). Why do we invest ethically? *The Journal of Investing*, *14*(3), 66–78.

Becchetti, Leonardo/Ciciretti, Rocco/Dalò, Ambrogio/Herzel, Stefano. (2015). Socially responsible and conventional investment funds: Performance comparison and the global financial crisis. *Applied Economics*, *47*(25), 2541–2562.

Bello, Zakri Y. (2005). Socially responsible investing and portfolio diversification. *Journal of Financial Research*, *28*(1), 41–57.

Benartzi, Shlomo/Thaler, Richard H. (2001). Naive diversification strategies in defined contribution saving plans. *American Economic Review*, *91*(1), 79–98.

Benson, Karen L./Brailsford, Timothy J./Humphrey, Jacquelyn E. (2006). Do socially responsible fund managers really invest differently? *Journal of Business Ethics*, *65*(4), 337–357.

Berk, Jonathan B./DeMarzo, Peter. (2014). *Corporate finance* (3rd ed.). Essex: Pearson Education Limited.

Berk, Jonathan B./Green, Richard C. (2004). Mutual fund flows and performance in rational markets. *Journal of Political Economy, 112*(6), 1269–1295.

Berry, Thomas C./Junkus, Joan C. (2012). Socially responsible investing: An investor perspective. *Journal of Business Ethics, 112*(4), 707–720.

Besley, Scott/Brigham, Eugene F. (2014). *Principles of finance* (6th ed.). Mason: Cengage Learning.

Betker, Brian/Sheehan, Joseph. (2013). A comparison of single factor and multiple factor alphas used in measuring mutual fund performance. *Financial Services Review, 22*(4), 349–365.

Blake, Christopher R./Elton, Edwin J./Gruber, Martin J. (1993). The performance of bond mutual funds. *Journal of Business, 66*(3), 371–403.

Blanchett, David M. (2010). Exploring the cost of investing in socially responsible mutual funds: An empirical study. *The Journal of Investing, 19*(3), 93–103.

Bodie, Zvi/Kane, Alex/Marcus, Alan J. (2007). *Essentials of investments* (6th ed.). New York: McGraw-Hill/Irwin.

Bodie, Zvi/Kane, Alex/Marcus, Alan J. (2011). *Investments* (9th ed.). New York: McGraw-Hill/Irwin.

Bogle, John C. (2015). *Bogle on mutual funds: New perspectives for the intelligent investor.* Hoboken: John Wiley & Sons, Inc.

Bollen, Nicolas P. B. (2007). Mutual fund attributes and investor behavior. *Journal of Financial and Quantitative Analysis, 42*(3), 683–708.

Bradfield, James. (2007). *Introduction to the economics of financial markets.* New York: Oxford University Press.

Brammer, Stephen/Brooks, Chris/Pavelin, Stephen. (2006). Corporate social performance and stock returns: UK evidence from disaggregate measures. *Financial Management, 35*(3), 97–116.

Brealey, Richard A./Myers, Stewart C./Allen, Franklin. (2014). *Principles of corporate finance* (11th ed.). New York: McGraw-Hill Education.

Brekke, Kjell A./Nyborg, Karine. (2004). Moral hazard and moral motivation: Corporate social responsibility as labor market screening. *Working Paper No. 25*, University of Oslo Economics. Retrieved from http://ssrn.com/abstract=645741.

Breusch, Trevor S./Pagan, Adrian R. (1979). A simple test for heteroscedasticity and random coefficient variation. *Econometrica: Journal of the Econometric Society, 47*(5), 1287–1294.

Brigham, Eugene/Housten, Joel. (2015). *Fundamentals of financial management* (14th ed.). Boston: Cengage Learning.

Brooks, Chris. (2008). *Introductory econometrics for finance* (2nd ed.). New York: Cambridge University Press.

Brooks, Lee J. (1989). Corporate ethical performance: Trends, forecasts and outlooks. *Journal of Business Ethics, 8*(1), 31–38.

Brown, Stephen J./Goetzmann, William N. (1995). Performance persistence. *The Journal of Finance, 50*(2), 679–698.

Brown, Stephen J./Goetzmann, William N./Ibbotson, Roger G./Ross, Stephen A. (1992). Survivorship bias in performance studies. *The Review of Financial Studies, 5*(4), 553–580.

Bu, Qiang/Lacey, Nelson. (2007). Exposing survivorship bias in mutual fund data. *Journal of Business & Economic Studies, 13*(1), 22–37.

Bu, Qiang/Lacey, Nelson. (2010). Smart money meets smart size. *Journal of Asset Management, 10*(6), 392–405.

Bugg-Levine, Antony/Emerson, Jed. (2011). *Impact investing: Transforming how we make money while making a difference*. San Francisco: John Wiley & Sons, Inc.

Capelle-Blancard, Gunther/Monjon, Stéphanie. (2011). The performance of socially responsible funds: Does the screening process matter? *Working Paper No. 2011-12*, Finance and Corporate Governance Conference. Retrieved from http://ssrn.com/abstract=1734764.

Capelle-Blancard, Gunther/Monjon, Stéphanie. (2012). Trends in the literature on socially responsible investment: Looking for the keys under the lamppost. *Business Ethics: A European Review, 21*(3), 239–250.

Carhart, Mark M. (1997). On persistence in mutual fund performance. *The Journal of Finance, 52*(1), 57–82.

Carroll, Archie B. (1999). Corporate social responsibility: Evolution of a definitional construct. *Business & Society, 38*(3), 268–295.

Carroll, Archie B./Shabana, Kareem M. (2010). The business case for corporate social responsibility: A review of concepts, research and practice. *International Journal of Management Reviews, 12*(1), 85–105.

Cazden, Elizabeth. (2013). Quakers, slavery, anti-slavery, and race. In Stephen W. Angell & Pink Dandelion (Eds.), *The Oxford Handbook of Quaker Studies* (pp. 347–362). Oxford University Press.

Chatfield, Chris. (2013). *The analysis of time series: An introduction* (6th ed.). Boca Raton: CRC Press LLC.

Chegut, Andrea/Schenk, Hans/Scholtens, Bert. (2011). Assessing SRI fund performance research: Best practices in empirical analysis. *Sustainable Development, 19*(2), 77–94.

Chen, Joseph/Hong, Harrison/Huang, Ming/Kubik, Jeffrey D. (2004). Does fund size erode mutual fund performance? The role of liquidity and organization. *American Economic Review, 94*(5), 1276–1303.

Christopherson, Jon A./Ferson, Wayne W./Glassman, Debora A. (1998). Conditioning manager alphas on economic information: Another look at the persistence of performance. *Review of Financial Studies, 11*(1), 111–142.

Climent, Francisco/Soriano, Pilar. (2011). Green and good? The investment performance of US environmental mutual funds. *Journal of Business Ethics, 103*(2), 275–287.

Cogneau, Philippe/Bodson, Laurent/Hübner, Georges. (2013). Is there a link between past performance and fund failure. In Virginie Terraza & Hery Razafitombo (Eds.), *Understanding investment funds: Insights from performance and risk analysis* (pp. 9–36). Hampshire: Palgrave Macmillan.

Cohen, Mark A./Fenn, Scott A./Konar, Shameek. (1997). Environmental and financial performance: Are they related? *Investor Responsibility Research Center, Environmental Information Service*.

Comer, George/Larrymore, Norris/Rodriguez, Javier. (2009). Controlling for fixed-income exposure in portfolio evaluation: Evidence from hybrid mutual funds. *Review of Financial Studies, 22*(2), 481–507.

Cooper, Ian. (1996). Arithmetic versus geometric mean estimators: Setting discount rates for capital budgeting. *European Financial Management, 2*(2), 157–167.

Cortez, Maria C./Silva, Florinda/Areal, Nelson. (2012). Socially responsible investing in the global market: The performance of US and European funds. *International Journal of Finance & Economics, 17*(3), 254–271.

Cortez, Maria C./Silva, Florinda/Areal, Nelson. (2009). The performance of European socially responsible funds. *Journal of Business Ethics, 87*(4), 573–588.

Costa, Bruce A./Jakob, Keith. (2010). Enhanced performance measurement of mutual funds: Running the benchmark index through the hurdles. *Journal of Applied Finance, 20*(1), 95–102.

Costa, Bruce A./Jakob, Keith. (2011). Are mutual fund managers selecting the right benchmark index? *Financial Services Review, 20*(2), 129–143.

Cowton, Christopher J. (1999). Playing by the rules: Ethical criteria at an ethical investment fund. *Business Ethics: A European Review, 8*(1), 60–69.

Crown, William H. (1998). *Statistical models for the social and behavioral sciences: Multiple regression and limited-dependent variable models*. Westport: Greenwood Publishing

Group, Inc.

Cullis, John G./Lewis, Alan/Winnett, Adrian. (1992). Paying To Be Good? U.K. Ethical Investments. *Kyklos, 45*(1), 3–24.

Cumby, Robert E./Glen, Jack D. (1990). Evaluating the Performance of International Mutual Funds. *The Journal of Finance, 45*(2), 497–521.

Cummings, Lorne S. (2000). The financial performance of ethical investment trusts: An Australian perspective. *Journal of Business Ethics, 25*(1), 79–92.

Curcio, Richard J./Kyaw, Nyonyo A./Thornton, John H. (2003). Do size, book-to-market, and beta factors explain mutual fund returns? *The Journal of Investing, 12*(2), 80–86.

Cuthbertson, Keith/Nitzsche, Dirk. (2013). Performance, stock selection and market timing of the German equity mutual fund industry. *Journal of Empirical Finance, 21*(1), 86–101.

D'Agostino, Ralph B./Belanger, Albert/D'Agostino, Ralph B. Jr. (1990). A suggestion for using powerful and informative tests of normality. *The American Statistician, 44*(4), 316–321.

D'Antonio, Louis/Johnsen, Tommi/Hutton, R. Bruce. (2000). Socially responsible investing and asset allocation. *The Journal of Investing, 9*(3), 65–72.

Datamonitor. (2011). Best practice in corporate social responsibility. Retrieved October 2, 2014, from http://www.datamonitor.com/store/Product/best_practice_in_corporate_social_responsibility?productid=CM00047-004.

Davis, Keith. (1973). The case for and against business assumption of social responsibilities. *Academy of Management Journal, 16*(2), 312–322.

de Colle, Simone/York, Jeffrey G. (2009). Why wine is not glue? The unresolved problem of negative screening in socially responsible investing. *Journal of Business Ethics, 85*(1), 83–95.

DeBondt, Werner F. M./Thaler, Richard H. (1985). Does the stock market overreact? *The Journal of Finance, 40*(3), 793–805.

DeCarlo, Lawrence T. (1997). On the meaning and use of kurtosis. *Psychological Methods, 2*(3), 292–307.

DeFusco, Richard A./McLeavey, Dennis W./Pinto, Jerald E./Runkle, David E. (2011). *Quantitative investment analysis* (2nd ed.). Hoboken: Wiley & Sons, Inc.

den Hond, Frank/de Bakker, Frank G. A. (2007). Ideologically motivated activism: How activist groups influence corporate social change activities. *Academy of Management Review, 32*(3), 901–924.

den Hond, Frank/de Bakker, Frank G. A./Neergaard, Peter. (2007). *Managing corporate so-*

cial responsibility in action: Talking, doing and measuring. Burlington: Ashgate Publishing Company.

Derwall, Jeroen/Guenster, Nadja/Bauer, Rob/Koedijk, Kees. (2005). The eco-efficiency premium puzzle. *Financial Analysts Journal, 61*(2), 51–63.

Derwall, Jeroen/Koedijk, Kees. (2009). Socially responsible fixed-income funds. *Journal of Business Finance & Accounting, 36*(1-2), 210–229.

Derwall, Jeroen/Koedijk, Kees/Ter Horst, Jenke. (2011). A tale of values-driven and profit-seeking social investors. *Journal of Banking & Finance, 35*(8), 2137–2147.

Dialynas, Chris P./Ritchie, John C. (2005). Convertible securities and their investment characteristics. In Frank J. Fabozzi (Ed.), *The handbook of fixed income securities* (7th ed., pp. 1371–1396). Boston: McGraw-Hill, Inc.

Diderich, Claude. (2009). *Positive alpha generation: Designing sound investment processes*. West Sussex: John Wiley & Sons Ltd.

Dietze, Leif H./Entrop, Oliver/Wilkens, Marco. (2009). The performance of investment grade corporate bond funds: Evidence from the European market. *The European Journal of Finance, 15*(2), 191–209.

Diltz, J. David. (1995a). Does social screening affect portfolio performance? *The Journal of Investing, 4*(1), 64–69.

Diltz, J. David. (1995b). The private cost of socially responsible investing. *Applied Financial Economics, 5*(2), 69–77.

Drobetz, Wolfgang. (2001). How to avoid the pitfalls in portfolio optimization? Putting the Black-Litterman approach at work. *Financial Markets and Portfolio Management, 15*(1), 59–75.

Dumas, Christel/Michotte, Emmanuelle. (2014). Where do-gooders meet bottom-liners: Disputes and resolutions surrounding socially responsible investment. In Céline Louche & Tessa Hebb (Eds.), *Socially responsible investment in the 21st century: Does it make a difference for society* (pp. 119–148). Bingley: Emerald Group Publishing Limited.

Durbin, James/Watson, Geoffrey S. (1950). Testing for serial correlation in least squares regression: I. *Biometrika, 37*(3), 409–428.

Durbin, James/Watson, Geoffrey S. (1951a). Corrections to Part I: Testing for Serial Correlation in Least Squares Regression: I. *Biometrika, 38*(1), 177–178.

Durbin, James/Watson, Geoffrey S. (1951b). Testing for serial correlation in least squares regression: II. *Biometrika, 38*(1), 159–177.

Edmans, Alex. (2011). Does the stock market fully value intangibles? Employee satisfaction and equity prices. *Journal of Financial Economics, 101*(3), 621–640.

Eisenhardt, Kathleen M. (1989). Agency theory: An assessment and review. *The Academy of Management Review*, *14*(1), 57–74.

Eisenhofer, Jay W./Barry, Michael J. (2005). *Shareholder activism handbook*. Aspen Publishers.

El Ghoul, Sadok/Guedhami, Omrane/Kwok, Chuck C. Y./Mishra, Dev R. (2011). Does corporate social responsibility affect the cost of capital? *Journal of Banking & Finance*, *35*(9), 2388–2406.

Elton, Edwin J./Gruber, Martin J./Agrawal, Deepak/Mann, Christopher. (2001). Explaining the rate spread on corporate bonds. *The Journal of Finance*, *56*(1), 247–277.

Elton, Edwin J./Gruber, Martin J./Blake, Christopher R. (1995). Fundamental economic variables, expected returns, and bond fund performance. *The Journal of Finance*, *50*(4), 1229–1256.

Elton, Edwin J./Gruber, Martin J./Blake, Christopher R. (1996). Survivorship bias and mutual fund performance. *The Review of Financial Studies*, *9*(4), 1097–1120.

Elton, Edwin J./Gruber, Martin J./Brown, Stephen J./Goetzmann, William N. (2009). *Modern portfolio theory and investment analysis* (8th ed.). Hoboken: John Wiley & Sons, Inc.

Equator Principles Association. (2013). The equator principles. Retrieved October 2, 2014, from http://www.equator-principles.com/resources/equator_principles_iii.pdf.

Erhardt, Michael/Brigham, Eugene. (2008). *Corporate finance: A focused approach* (3rd ed.). Mason: Cengage Learning.

European Commission. (2013). Corporate social responsibility (CSR). Retrieved July 11, 2013, from http://ec.europa.eu/growth/industry/corporate-social-responsibility/.

EUROSIF. (2003). European SRI study 2003. Retrieved July 12, 2014, from http://www.eurosif.org/research/eurosif-sri-study/2003.

EUROSIF. (2006). European SRI study 2006. Retrieved July 12, 2014, from http://www.eurosif.org/research/eurosif-sri-study/2006.

EUROSIF. (2010). European SRI study 2010. Retrieved July 12, 2014, from https://www.eurosif.org/publication/view/european-sri-study-2010/.

EUROSIF. (2012). European SRI study 2012. Retrieved July 12, 2014, from http://www.eurosif.org/research/eurosif-sri-study/sri-study-2012.

EUROSIF. (2014). European SRI Study 2014. Retrieved October 14, 2015, from http://www.eurosif.org/wp-content/uploads/2014/09/Eurosif-SRI-Study-2014.pdf.

Fabozzi, Frank J./Gupta, Francis/Markowitz, Harry M. (2002). The legacy of modern portfolio theory. *The Journal of Investing*, *11*(3), 7–22.

Fabozzi, Frank J./Ma, K. C./Oliphant, Becky J. (2008). Sin stock returns. *The Journal of Portfolio Management*, *35*(1), 82–94.

Fama, Eugene F. (1970). Efficient capital markets: A review of theory and empirical work. *The Journal of Finance*, *25*(2), 383–417.

Fama, Eugene F. (1991). Efficient capital markets: II. *The Journal of Finance*, *46*(5), 1575–1617.

Fama, Eugene F./French, Kenneth R. (1989). Business conditions and expected returns on stocks and bonds. *Journal of Financial Economics*, *25*(1), 23–49.

Fama, Eugene F./French, Kenneth R. (1992). The cross-section of expected stock returns. *The Journal of Finance*, *47*(2), 427–465.

Fama, Eugene F./French, Kenneth R. (1993). Common risk factors in the returns on stocks and bonds. *Journal of Financial Economics*, *33*(1), 3–56.

Fama, Eugene F./French, Kenneth R. (1995). Size and book-to-market factors in earnings and returns. *The Journal of Finance*, *50*(1), 131.

Fama, Eugene F./French, Kenneth R. (1996). Multifactor explanations of asset pricing anomalies. *The Journal of Finance*, *51*(1), 55–84.

Fama, Eugene F./French, Kenneth R. (2010). Luck versus skill in the cross section of mutual fund returns. *The Journal of Finance*, *65*(5), 1915–1947.

Fama, Eugene F./Jensen, Michael C. (1983). Separation of ownership and control. *Journal of Law and Economics*, *26*(2), 301–325.

Feibel, Bruce J. (2003). *Investment performance measurement*. Hoboken: John Wiley & Sons, Inc.

Ferson, Wayne W./Schadt, Rudi W. (1996). Measuring fund strategy and performance in changing economic conditions. *The Journal of Finance*, *51*(2), 425–461.

Fisher, Lawrence. (1975). Using modern portfolio theory to maintain an efficiently diversified portfolio. *Financial Analysts Journal*, *31*(3), 73–85.

Fisman, Ray/Heal, Geoffrey/Nair, Vinay B. (2008). A model of corporate philanthropy. *Unpublished Manuscript*. Retrieved from http://d1c25a6gwz7q5e.cloudfront.net/papers/1331.pdf.

Fletcher, Jonathan. (1995). The evaluation of managed fund performance. *The British Accounting Review*, *27*(2), 127–138.

Fombrun, Charles/Shanley, Mark. (1990). What's in a name? Reputation building and corporate strategy. *Academy of Management Journal*, *33*(2), 233–258.

Foo, Jennifer/Witkowska, Dorota. (2015). Mutual funds efficiency comparison between U.S.

and Europe. *International Journal of Business, Accounting, & Finance, 9*(1), 1–12.

Fowler, Stephen J./Hope, C. (2007). A critical review of sustainable business indices and their impact. *Journal of Business Ethics, 76*(3), 243–252.

Francis, Jack C. (1993). *Management of investments* (3rd ed.). New York: McGraw-Hill, Inc.

Francis, Jack C./Kim, Dongcheol. (2013). *Modern portfolio theory: Foundations, analysis, and new developments.* Hoboken: John Wiley & Sons, Inc.

Franke, Jürgen/Härdle, Wolfgang K./Hafner, Christian M. (2011). *Statistics of financial markets.* Berlin: Springer Verlag.

Freireich, Jessica/Fulton, Katherine. (2009). Investing for social & environmental impact. Retrieved July 9, 2013, from http://monitorinstitute.com/downloads/what-we-think/impact-investing/Impact_Investing.pdf.

French, Craig W. (2002). Jack Treynor's "Toward a theory of market value of risky assets." *Working Paper.* Retrieved from http://ssrn.com/abstract=628187.

Freund, Rudolf J./Wilson, William J./Sa, Ping. (2006). *Regression analysis.* San Diego: Academic Press.

Friedman, Milton. (1970). The social responsibility of business is to increase its profits. Retrieved September 2, 2012, from http://query.nytimes.com/gst/abstract.html?res=9E05E0DA153CE531A15750C1A96F9C946190D6CF&legacy=true#.

Galema, Rients/Plantinga, Auke/Scholtens, Bert. (2008). The stocks at stake: Return and risk in socially responsible investment. *Journal of Banking & Finance, 32*(12), 2646–2654.

Geczy, Christopher C./Stambaugh, Robert F./Levin, David. (2005). Investing in socially responsible mutual funds. *Working Paper*, Wharton School, University of Pennsylvania. Retrieved from http://ssrn.com/abstract=416380.

Gevlin, Kathy. (2007). The coming of age of socially responsible investing. *Financial Planning, 37*(8), 56a–56b.

Gil-Bazo, Javier/Ruiz-Verdú, Pablo/Santos, André A. P. (2010). The performance of socially responsible mutual funds: The role of fees and management companies. *Journal of Business Ethics, 94*(2), 243–263.

Gitman, Lawrence/Joehnk, Michael/Billingsley, Randy. (2010). *Financial planning* (12th ed.). Mason: Cengage Learning.

Glac, Katherina. (2009). Understanding socially responsible investing: The effect of decision frames and trade-off options. *Journal of Business Ethics, 87*(1), 41–55.

Goldberg, Jennifer/Goldberg, Stephen R./Ratliff-Miller, Paulette. (2008). Investing in socially responsible companies. *Journal of Corporate Accounting & Finance, 20*(1), 53–59.

References

Goldreyer, Elizabeth F./Diltz, J. David. (1999). The performance of socially responsible mutual funds: Incorporating sociopolitical information in portfolio selection. *Managerial Finance*, 25(1), 23–36.

Gompers, Paul A./Ishii, Joy/Metrick, Andrew. (2003). Corporate governance and equity prices. *The Quarterly Journal of Economics*, 118(1), 107–155.

Gonzalez-Perez, Alejandra M. (2013). *Corporate Social Responsibility and International Business: A Conceptual Overview. Advances in Sustainability and Environmental Justice* (Vol. 11). Emerald Group Publishing Limited.

Graham, John/Smart, Scott/Megginson, William. (2009). *Corporate finance: Linking theory to what companies do* (3rd ed.). Mason: Cengage Learning.

Greer, Robert J. (1997). What is an asset class, anyway? *The Journal of Portfolio Management*, 23(2), 86–91.

Gregory, Alan/Matatko, John/Luther, Robert G. (1997). Ethical unit trust financial performance: Small company effects and fund size effects. *Journal of Business Finance & Accounting*, 24(5), 705–725.

GRI. (2013). GRI sustainability reporting guidelines. Retrieved July 12, 2013, from https://www.globalreporting.org/resourcelibrary/GRIG4-Part1-Reporting-Principles-and-Standard-Disclosures.pdf.

Grinblatt, Mark/Titman, Sheridan. (1989). Mutual fund performance: An analysis of quarterly portfolio holdings. *Journal of Business*, 62(3), 393–416.

Grinblatt, Mark/Titman, Sheridan. (1992). The persistence of mutual fund performance. *The Journal of Finance*, 47(5), 1977–1984.

Grinblatt, Mark/Titman, Sheridan. (1993). Performance measurement without benchmarks: An examination of mutual fund returns. *The Journal of Business*, 66(1), 47–68.

Grinblatt, Mark/Titman, Sheridan. (1994). A study of monthly mutual fund returns and performance evaluation techniques. *The Journal of Financial and Quantitative Analysis*, 29(3), 419–444.

Grossman, Blake R./Sharpe, William F. (1986). Financial implications of South African divestment. *Financial Analysts Journal*, 42(4), 15–29.

Guerard, John B. (1997). Is there a cost to being socially responsible in investing? *The Journal of Investing*, 6(2), 11–18.

Haigh, Matthew/Hazelton, James. (2004). Financial markets: A tool for social responsibility? *Journal of Business Ethics*, 52(1), 59–71.

Hall, Alvin D. (2010). *Getting started in mutual funds* (2nd ed.). Hoboken: John Wiley & Sons.

Hamilton, Sally/Jo, Hoje/Statman, Meir. (1993). Doing well while doing good? The investment performance of socially responsible mutual funds. *Financial Analysts Journal*, *49*(6), 62–66.

Haslem, John. (2009). *Mutual funds: Risk and performance analysis for decision making*. Hoboken: John Wiley & Sons, Inc.

Heal, Geoffrey. (2005). Corporate social responsibility: An economic and financial framework. *The Geneva Papers on Risk and Insurance Issues and Practice*, *30*(3), 387–409.

Hearth, Douglas/Zaima, Janis K. (1998). *Contemporary investments: Security and portfolio analysis* (2nd ed.). Orlando: Harcourt Brace & Company.

Heinkel, Robert/Kraus, Alan/Zechner, Josef. (2001). The effect of green investment on corporate behavior. *Journal of Financial and Quantitative Analysis*, *36*(4), 431–449.

Henriksson, Roy D. (1984). Market timing and mutual fund performance: An empirical investigation. *Journal of Business*, *57*(1), 73–96.

Heywood, John. (1546). *A dialogue conteinyng the nomber in effect of all the prouerbes in the englishe tongue: Compacte in a matter concernyng two maner of mariages*. T. Berthelet.

Hirt, Geoffrey A./Block, Stanley B. (2012). *Fundamentals of investment management* (10th ed.). New York: McGraw-Hill/Irwin.

Hong, Harrison/Kacperczyk, Marcin. (2009). The price of sin: The effects of social norms on markets. *Journal of Financial Economics*, *93*(1), 15–36.

Horowitz, Ira. (1966). The "reward-to-variability" ratio and mutual fund performance. *Journal of Business*, *39*(4), 485–488.

Huberman, Gur/Jiang, Wei. (2006). Offering versus choice in 401(k) plans: Equity exposure and number of funds. *The Journal of Finance*, *61*(2), 763–801.

Hummels, Harry/Timmer, Diederik. (2004). Investors in need of social, ethical, and environmental information. *Journal of Business Ethics*, *52*(1), 73–84.

Humphrey, Jacquelyn E./Lee, Darren D. (2011). Australian socially responsible funds: Performance, risk and screening intensity. *Journal of Business Ethics*, *102*(4), 519–535.

Humphrey, Jacquelyn E./Lee, Darren D./Shen, Yaokan. (2012). Does it cost to be sustainable? *Journal of Corporate Finance*, *18*(3), 626–639.

Hutton, R. Bruce/D'Antonio, Louis/Johnsen, Tommi. (1998). Socially responsible investing: Growing issues and new opportunities. *Business & Society*, *37*(3), 281–305.

ICI. (2007a). A guide to mutual funds. Retrieved August 2, 2015, from https://www.ici.org/pdf/bro_g2mfs_p.pdf.

ICI. (2007b). A guide to understanding mutual funds. Retrieved August 2, 2015, from https://www.ici.org/pdf/bro_understanding_mfs_p.pdf.

Ilmanen, Antti. (1995). Time varying expected returns in international bond markets. *The Journal of Finance, 50*(2), 481–506.

Ippolito, Richard A. (1989). Efficiency with costly information: A study of mutual fund performance, 1965-1984. *The Quarterly Journal of Economics, 104*(1), 1–23.

IRIS. (2014). IRIS & GIIRS. Retrieved October 2, 2014, from http://giirs.org/about-giirs/how-giirs-works/163.

J.P. Morgan. (2014). Knocking on the door – Shareholder activism in Europe: Five things you need to know. Retrieved December 4, 2013, from https://www.jpmorgan.com/cm/Blob-Server/mabriefing_activism_july2014.pdf?blobkey=id&blob-where=1320656894344&blobheader=application/pdf&blobheadername1=Cache-Control&blobheadervalue1=private&blobcol=urldata&blobtable=MungoBlobs.

Jacquier, Eric/Kane, Alex/Marcus, Alan J. (2003). Geometric or arithmetic mean: A reconsideration. *Financial Analysts Journal, 59*(6), 46–53.

Jansson, Magnus/Biel, Anders. (2011). Motives to engage in sustainable investment: A comparison between institutional and private investors. *Sustainable Development, 19*(2), 135–142.

Jegadeesh, Narasimhan/Titman, Sheridan. (1993). Returns to buying winners and selling losers: Implications for stock market efficiency. *The Journal of Finance, 48*(1), 65–91.

Jensen, Michael C. (1968). The performance of mutual funds in the period 1945-1964. *The Journal of Finance, 23*(2), 389–416.

Jensen, Michael C. (1969). Risk, the pricing of capital assets, and the evaluation of investment portfolios. *The Journal of Business, 42*(2), 167–247.

Jensen, Michael C. (1972). Capital markets: Theory and evidence. *The Bell Journal of Economics and Management, 3*(2), 357–398.

Jensen, Michael C./Meckling, William H. (1976). Theory of the firm: Managerial behavior, agency costs and ownership structure. *Journal of Financial Economics, 3*(4), 305–360.

Jiao, Yawen. (2010). Stakeholder welfare and firm value. *Journal of Banking & Finance, 34*(10), 2549–2561.

Jobson, John D./Korkie, Bob M. (1980). Estimation for Markowitz efficient portfolios. *Journal of the American Statistical Association, 75*(371), 544–554.

Jones, Charles P. (2009). *Investments: Analysis and management* (11th ed.). Hoboken: John Wiley & Sons, Inc.

Jones, Stewart/van der Laan, Sandra/Frost, Geoff/Loftus, Janice. (2008). The investment performance of socially responsible investment funds in Australia. *Journal of Business Ethics*, *80*(2), 181–203.

Jordan, J. S. (1983). On the efficient markets hypothesis. *Econometrica: Journal of the Econometric Society*, *51*(5), 1325–1343.

Juravle, Carmen/Lewis, Alan. (2008). Identifying impediments to SRI in Europe: a review of the practitioner and academic literature. *Business Ethics: A European Review*, *17*(3), 285–310.

Kempf, Alexander/Osthoff, Peer. (2007). The effect of socially responsible investing on portfolio performance. *European Financial Management*, *13*(5), 908–922.

Kempf, Alexander/Osthoff, Peer. (2008). SRI funds: Nomen est omen. *Journal of Business Finance & Accounting*, *35*(9/10), 1276–1294.

Kennedy, Peter. (2003). *A guide to econometrics*. Malden: Blackwell Publishing Ltd/Inc.

Kleinbaum, David/Kupper, Lawrence/Nizam, Azhar/Rosenberg, Eli. (2013). *Applied regression analysis and other multivariable methods* (5th ed.). Boston: Cengage Learning.

Knoll, Michael S. (2002). Ethical screening in modern financial markets: The conflicting claims underlying socially responsible investment. *The Business Lawyer*, *57*(2), 681–726.

Konno, Hiroshi/Kobayashi, Katsunari. (1997). An integrated stock-bond portfolio optimization model. *Journal of Economic Dynamics and Control*, *21*(8-9), 1427–1444.

KPMG. (2013). The KPMG survey of corporate responsibility reporting 2013. Retrieved September 21, 2015, from https://assets.kpmg.com/content/dam/kpmg/pdf/2015/08/kpmg-survey-of-corporate-responsibility-reporting-2013.pdf.

Kreander, Niklas/Gray, Robert H./Power, David M./Sinclair, Christopher D. (2005). Evaluating the performance of ethical and non-ethical funds: A matched pair analysis. *Journal of Business Finance & Accounting*, *32*(7-8), 1465–1493.

Kritzman, Mark. (1999). Toward defining an asset class. *The Journal of Alternative Investments*, *2*(1), 79–82.

Kurtz, Lloyd. (1997). No effect, or no net effect? Studies on socially responsible investing. *The Journal of Investing*, *6*(4), 37–49.

Langbein, John H./Posner, Richard A. (1980). Social investing and the law of trusts. *Michigan Law Review*, 72–112.

Lavine, Alan. (1994). *Getting started in mutual funds*. New York: John Wiley & Sons, Inc.

Le Sourd, Véronique. (2010). The performance of socially responsible investment: A study of the French market. *Bankers, Markets & Investors*, *3*(106), 15–40.

Lean, Hooi H./Ang, Wei R./Smyth, Russell. (2015). Performance and performance persistence of socially responsible investment funds in Europe and North America. *The North American Journal of Economics and Finance, 34,* 254–266.

Lee, Cheng F./Lee, John C./Lee, Alice C. (2000). *Statistics for business and financial economics, volume 1* (2nd ed.). Singapore: World Scientific Publishing Co. Pte. Ltd.

Lee, Darren D./Humphrey, Jacquelyn E./Benson, Karen L./Ahn, Jason Y. K. (2010). Socially responsible investment fund performance: The impact of screening intensity. *Accounting & Finance, 50*(2), 351–370.

Lehmann, Bruce N./Modest, David M. (1987). Mutual fund performance evaluation: A comparison of benchmarks and benchmark comparisons. *The Journal of Finance, 42*(2), 233–265.

Leite, Paulo/Cortez, Maria C. (2014). Style and performance of international socially responsible funds in Europe. *Research in International Business and Finance, 30,* 248–267.

Leite, Paulo/Cortez, Maria C. (2015). Performance of European socially responsible funds during market crises: Evidence from France. *International Review of Financial Analysis, 40,* 132–141.

Levy, Haim/Sarnat, Marshall. (1995). *Capital investment and financial decisions* (5th ed.). Hertfordshire: Prentice Hall International.

Lewis, Alan/Mackenzie, Craig. (2000). Support for investor activism among UK ethical investors. *Journal of Business Ethics, 24*(1993), 215–222.

Lewis, Alan/Webley, Paul. (2002). Social and ethical investing: Beliefs, preferences and the willingness to sacrifice financial return. In Alan Lewis & Karl-Erik Wärneryd (Eds.), *Ethics and Economic Affairs* (pp. 171–182). London: Routledge.

Lhabitant, Françoise-Serge. (2006). *Handbook of hedge funds.* West Sussex: John Wiley & Sons Ltd.

Lindström, Erik/Madsen, Henrik/Nielsen, Jan N. (2015). *Statistics for finance.* Boca Raton: Taylor & Francis.

Lintner, John. (1965a). Security prices, risk, and maximal gains from diversification. *The Journal of Finance, 20*(4), 587–615.

Lintner, John. (1965b). The valuation of risk assets and the selection of risky investments in stock portfolios and capital budgets. *Review of Economics and Statistics, 47*(1), 13–38.

Lo, Andrew W. (2010). *Hedge funds - An analytic perspective.* Princeton: Princeton University Press.

Lowry, Ritchie P. (1993). *Good money: A guide to profitable social investing in the '90s.* London: W. W. Norton & Company.

Luther, Robert G./Matatko, John/Corner, Desmond C. (1992). The investment performance of UK "ethical" unit trusts. *Accounting, Auditing & Accountability Journal, 5*(4), 57–70.

Lydenberg, Steve/Graham, Sinclair. (2009). Mainstream or daydream? The future for responsible investing. *Journal of Corporate Citizenship, 2009*(33), 47–68.

Mackenzie, Craig/Lewis, Alan. (1999). Morals and markets: The case of ethical investing. *Business Ethics Quarterly, 9*(3), 439–452.

Madura, Jeff. (2014). *Financial markets and institutions* (11th ed.). Mason: Cengage Learning.

Maindonald, John/Braun, W. John. (2010). *Data analysis and graphics using R: An example-based approach* (3rd ed.). New York: Cambridge University Press.

Malhotra, Deepak K./McLeod, Robert W. (1997). An empirical analysis of mutual fund expenses. *Journal of Financial Research, 20*(2), 175–190.

Malkiel, Burton G. (1995). Returns from investing in equity mutual funds 1971 to 1991. *The Journal of Finance, 50*(2), 549–572.

Malkiel, Burton G. (2003). The efficient market hypothesis and its critics. *Journal of Economic Perspectives, 17*(1), 59–82.

Mallin, Chris A./Saadouni, Brahim/Briston, Richard J. (1995). The financial performance of ethical investment funds. *Journal of Business Finance & Accounting, 22*(4), 483–496.

Margolis, Joshua D./Elfenbein, Hillary A./Walsh, James P. (2009). Does it pay to be good... and does it matter? A meta-analysis of the relationship between corporate social and financial performance. In *MIT Sloan Management Review* (Vol. 50, pp. 61–68).

Margolis, Joshua D./Walsh, James P. (2003). Misery loves companies: Rethinking social initiatives by business. *Administrative Science Quarterly, 48*(2), 268–305.

Markit. (2014). Markit iBoxx Indices. Retrieved November 27, 2015, from https://www.markit.com/Product/File?CMSID=915f800efc0643f3bbf8c064c9715c2e.

Markowitz, Harry M. (1952). Portfolio selection. *The Journal of Finance, 7*(1), 77–91.

Markowitz, Harry M. (1959). *Portfolio selection: Efficient diversification of investments*. London: John Wiley & Sons, Inc.

Markowitz, Harry M. (1976). Markowitz revisited. *Financial Analysts Journal, 32*(5), 47–52.

Markowitz, Harry M. (1991). Foundations of portfolio theory. *The Journal of Finance, 46*(2), 469–477.

Markowitz, Harry M. (1999). The early history of portfolio theory: 1600-1960. *Financial Analysts Journal, 55*(4), 5–16.

Matten, Dirk/Moon, Jeremy. (2008). "Implicit" and "Explicit" CSR: A conceptual framework for a comparative understanding of corporate social responsibility. *The Academy of Management Review, 33*(2), 404–424.

Mayo, Herbert B. (2013). *Investments: An introduction* (11th ed.). Mason: Cengage Learning.

McDonald, John G. (1974). Objectives and performance of mutual funds, 1960-1969. *Journal of Financial & Quantitative Analysis, 9*(3), 311–333.

McWilliams, Abagail/Siegel, Donald. (2000). Corporate social responsibility and financial performance: Correlation or misspecification? *Strategic Management Journal, 21*(5), 603–609.

McWilliams, Abagail/Siegel, Donald. (2001). Corporate social responsibility: A theory of the firm perspective. *Academy of Management Review, 26*(1), 117–127.

Menz, Klaus-Michael. (2010). Corporate social responsibility: Is it rewarded by the corporate bond market? A critical note. *Journal of Business Ethics, 96*(1), 117–134.

Michelson, Grant/Wailes, Nick/Van Der Laan, Sandra/Frost, Geoff. (2004). Ethical investment processes and outcomes. *Journal of Business Ethics, 52*(1), 1–10.

Miller, Merton H./Modigliani, Franco. (1961). Dividend policy, growth, and the valuation of shares. *The Journal of Business, 34*(4), 411–433.

Mobius, Mark. (2007). *Mutual funds: An introduction to the core concepts*. Singapore: John Wiley & Sons Ltd.

Montgomery, Douglas C./Peck, Elizabeth A./Vining, G. Geoffrey. (2015). *Introduction to linear regression analysis* (5th ed.). Hoboken: John Wiley & Sons, Inc.

Morningstar. (2004). Fact sheet: The Morningstar equity style box. Retrieved October 13, 2015, from http://corporate.morningstar.com/US/documents/MethodologyDocuments/FactSheets/MorningstarStyleBox_FactSheet_.pdf.

Mossin, Jan. (1966). Equilibrium in a capital asset market. *Econometrica: Journal of the Econometric Society, 34*(4), 768–783.

Muñoz, Fernando/Vargas, María/Vicente, Ruth. (2014). Fund flow bias in market timing skill. Evidence of the clientele effect. *International Review of Economics and Finance, 33*, 257–269.

Murthi, B. P. S./Choi, Yoon K./Desai, Preyas. (1997). Efficiency of mutual funds and portfolio performance measurement: A non-parametric approach. *European Journal of Operational Research, 98*(2), 408–418.

Neter, John/Wasserman, William/Whitmore, G. A. (1993). *Applied statistics* (4th ed.). Needham Heights: Simon & Schuster, Inc.

Newey, Whitney K./West, Kenneth D. (1994). Automatic lag selection in covariance matrix estimation. *The Review of Economic Studies, 61*(4), 631–653.

Nilsson, Jonas. (2008). Investment with a conscience: Examining the impact of pro-social attitudes and perceived financial performance on socially responsible investment behavior. *Journal of Business Ethics*, *83*(2), 307–325.

Nilsson, Jonas. (2009). Segmenting socially responsible mutual fund investors: The influence of financial return and social responsibility. *International Journal of Bank Marketing*, *27*(1), 5–31.

Nofsinger, John/Varma, Abhishek. (2014). Socially responsible funds and market crises. *Journal of Banking & Finance*, *48*, 180–193.

Obama, Barack. (2009). Executive Order 13514. Retrieved February 13, 2014, from http://www.whitehouse.gov/assets/documents/2009fedleader_eo_rel.pdf\nhttp://www.whitehouse.gov/administration/eop/ceq/sustainability.

OECD. (1976). OECD guidelines for multinational enterprises. Retrieved October 2, 2014, from http://www.oecd.org/daf/inv/mne/50024800.pdf.

OECD. (2007). Recent trends and regulatory implications in socially responsible investment for pension funds. Retrieved August 3, 2014, from http://www.oecd.org/investment/mne/38550550.pdf.

OECD Watch. (2013). Calling for corporate accountability: A guide to the 2011 OECD guidelines for multinational enterprises. Retrieved August 3, 2013, from http://oecdwatch.org/publications-en/Publication_3962/at_download/fullfile.

Orlitzky, Marc. (2015). The politics of corporate social responsibility or: why Milton Friedman has been right all along. *Annals in Social Responsibility*, *1*(1), 5–29.

Orlitzky, Marc/Benjamin, John D. (2001). Corporate social performance and firm risk: A meta-analytic review. *Business & Society*, *40*(4), 369–396.

Orlitzky, Marc/Schmidt, Frank L./Rynes, Sara L. (2003). Corporate social and financial performance: A meta-analysis. *Organization Studies*, *24*(3), 403–441.

Otten, Roger/Bams, Dennis. (2004). How to measure mutual fund performance: Economic versus statistical relevance. *Accounting and Finance*, *44*(2), 203–222.

Pasewark, William/Riley, Mark. (2010). It's a matter of principle: The role of personal values in investment decisions. *Journal of Business Ethics*, *93*(2), 237–253.

Pension Federation. (2007). Weighing up social interests and transparency in the investment process. Retrieved September 2, 2013, from http://www.pensioenfederatie.nl/Document/Publicaties/English publications/Weighing up social interests and transparency in the investment process.pdf.

Perold, André F. (2004). The capital asset pricing model. *Journal of Economic Perspectives*, *18*(3), 3–24.

Pivato, Sergio/Misani, Nicola. (2008). The impact of corporate social responsibility on consumer trust: The case of organic food. *Business Ethics: A European Review, 17*(1), 3–12.

Porter, Michael E./van der Linde, Claas. (1995). Green and competitive: Ending the stalemate. *Harvard Business Review*, 120–134.

Pozen, Robert C. (2002). *The mutual fund business* (2nd ed.). Boston: Houghton Mifflin Company.

Preu, Friederike J./Richardson, Benjamin. (2011). German socially responsible investment: Barriers and opportunities. *German Law Journal, 12*(3), 865–900.

PRI Initiative. (2012). Annual report 2012. Retrieved February 3, 2014, from http://www.unpri.org/wp-content/uploads/Annualreport20121.pdf.

PRI Initiative. (2013). Annual report 2013. Retrieved February 2, 2014, from http://d2m27378y09r06.cloudfront.net/viewer/?file=wp-content/uploads/AnnualReport20131.pdf.

PwC. (2010). CSR trends 2010. Retrieved August 3, 2014, from www.pwc.com/ca/en/sustainability/publications/csr-trends-2010-09.pdf.

Razali, Nornadiah M./Wah, Yap B. (2011). Power comparisons of Shapiro-Wilk, Kolmogorov-Smirnov, Lilliefors and Anderson-Darling tests. *Journal of Statistical Modeling and Analytics, 2*(1), 21–33.

Reilly, Frank K./Akthar, Rashid A. (1995). The benchmark error problem with global capital markets. *The Journal of Portfolio Management, 22*(1), 33–52.

Reilly, Frank K./Brown, Keith C. (2011). *Investment analysis and portfolio management* (10th ed.). Mason: Cengage Learning.

Renneboog, Luc/Ter Horst, Jenke/Zhang, Chendi. (2008a). Socially responsible investments: Institutional aspects, performance, and investor behavior. *Journal of Banking & Finance, 32*(9), 1723–1742.

Renneboog, Luc/Ter Horst, Jenke/Zhang, Chendi. (2008b). The price of ethics and stakeholder governance: The performance of socially responsible mutual funds. *Journal of Corporate Finance, 14*(3), 302–322.

Renneboog, Luc/Ter Horst, Jenke/Zhang, Chendi. (2011). Is ethical money financially smart? Nonfinancial attributes and money flows of socially responsible investment funds. *Journal of Financial Intermediation, 20*(4), 562–588.

Research, National Bureau of Economic. (n.d.). Determination of the December 2007 peak in economic activity. Retrieved December 1, 2015, from http://www.nber.org/cycles/dec2008.pdf.

Revelli, Christophe/Viviani, Jean-Laurent. (2015). Financial performance of socially responsible investing (SRI): What have we learned? A meta-analysis. *Business Ethics: A European Review*, *24*(2), 158–185.

Reyes, Mario G./Grieb, Terrance. (1998). The external performance of socially-responsible mutual funds. *American Business Review*, *16*(1), 1–7.

RIA. (2013). Canadian SRI review 2012. Retrieved August 13, 2013, from https://riacanada.ca/wp-content/uploads/CSRIR-2012-English.pdf.

RIAA. (2013). The 2013 responsible investment benchmark report. Retrieved January 13, 2014, from http://www.responsibleinvestment.org/wp-content/uploads/2013/07/2013-Benchmark-Report.pdf.

Richardson, Benjamin. (2008). *Socially responsible investment law: Regulating the unseen polluters*. New York: Oxford University Press.

Richardson, Benjamin/Cragg, Wes. (2010). Being virtuous and prosperous: SRI's conflicting goals. *Journal of Business Ethics*, *92*(1), 21–39.

Rivoli, Pietra. (2003). Making a difference or making a statement? Finance research and socially responsible investment. *Business Ethics Quarterly*, *13*(3), 271–287.

Rockefeller Foundation. (2010). Impact investments: An emerging asset class. Retrieved August 13, 2013, from http://www.rockefellerfoundation.org/uploads/files/2b053b2b-8feb-46ea-adbd-f89068d59785-impact.pdf.

Rockefeller Foundation. (2012). Accelerating Impact: Achievements, challenges and what's next in building the impact investing industry. Retrieved August 13, 2013, from https://www.rockefellerfoundation.org/app/uploads/Accelerating-Impact-Full-Summary.pdf.

Rohleder, Martin/Scholz, Hendrik/Wilkens, Marco. (2011). Survivorship bias and mutual fund performance: Relevance, significance, and methodical differences. *Review of Finance*, *15*(2), 441–474.

Roll, Richard. (1978). Ambiguity when performance is measured by the securities market line. *The Journal of Finance*, *33*(4), 1051–1069.

Roll, Richard. (1980). Performance evaluation and benchmark errors (I). *The Journal of Portfolio Management*, *6*(4), 5–12.

Roll, Richard. (1981). Performance evaluation and benchmark errors (II). *The Journal of Portfolio Management*, *7*(2), 17–22.

Rosen, Barry N./Sandler, Dennis M./Shani, David. (1991). Social issues and socially responsible investment behavior: A preliminary empirical investigation. *Journal of Consumer Affairs*, *25*(2), 221–234.

Ross, Stephen A. (1973). The economic theory of agency: The principal's problem. *American Economic Review*, *63*(2), 134–139.

Ross, Stephen A. (1976). The arbitrage theory of capital asset pricing. *Journal of Economic Theory*, *13*(3), 341–360.

Ross, Stephen A./Westerfield, Randolph/Jaffe, Jeffrey F. (2010). *Corporate finance* (9th ed.). New York: McGraw-Hill, Inc.

Rowland, Mary. (1996). *A commonsense guide to mutual funds*. Princeton: Bloomberg Press.

Rubinstein, Mark. (2002). Markowitz's "Portfolio Selection": A fifty-year retrospective. *The Journal of Finance*, *57*(3), 1041–1045.

Rudd, Andrew. (1981). Social responsibility and portfolio performance. *California Management Review*, *23*(4), 55–61.

Ruppert, David. (2004). *Statistics and finance: An introduction*. New York: Springer Science & Business Media B.V.

Ruppert, David. (2010). *Statistics and data analysis for financial engineering*. New York: Springer Science & Business Media B.V.

Ruppert, David/Matteson, David. (2015). *Statistics and data analysis for financial engineering: with R examples* (2nd ed.). New York: Springer Science & Business Media B.V.

Russo, Michael. (2010). *Companies on a mission: Entrepreneurial strategies for growing sustainably, responsibly, and profitably*. Stanford: Stanford University Press.

Sampford, Charles/Ransome, Bill. (2013). *Ethics and socially responsible investment: A philosophical approach*. Surrey: Ashgate Publishing, Ltd.

Sandberg, Joakim/Juravle, Carmen/Hedesström, Ted Martin/Hamilton, Ian. (2008). The heterogeneity of socially responsible investment. *Journal of Business Ethics*, *87*(4), 519–533.

Sauer, David A. (1997). The impact of social-responsibility screens on investment performance: Evidence from the Domini 400 Social Index and Domini Equity Mutual Fund. *Review of Financial Economics*, *6*(2), 137–149.

Scalet, Steven/Kelly, Thomas. (2010). CSR rating agencies: What is their global impact? *Journal of Business Ethics*, *94*(1), 69–88.

Schlegelmilch, Bodo B. (1997). The relative importance of ethical and environmental screening: Implications for the marketing of ethical investment funds. *International Journal of Bank Marketing*, *15*(2), 48–53.

Scholtens, Bert/Zhou, Yangqin. (2008). Stakeholder relations and financial performance. *Sustainable Development*, *16*(3), 213–232.

Schroder, Michael. (2003). Socially responsible investments in Germany, Switzerland and the

United States. *ZEW Discussion Paper No. 03-10*. Retrieved from http://ssrn.com/abstract=421462.

Schueth, Steve. (2003). Socially responsible investing in the United States. *Journal of Business Ethics, 43*(3), 189–194.

Schwartz, Mark S. (2003). The "ethics" of ethical Investing. *Journal of Business Ethics, 43*(3), 195–213.

Sclove, Stanley L. (2012). *A course on statistics for finance*. Boca Raton: Taylor & Francis.

Shapiro, Samuel S./Wilk, Martin B. (1965). An analysis of variance test for normality (complete samples). *Biometrika, 52*(3), 591–611.

Sharfman, Mark P./Fernando, Chitru S. (2008). Environmental risk management and the cost of capital. *Strategic Management Journal, 29*(6), 569–592.

Sharpe, Norean R./De Veaux, Richard D./Vellemann, Paul F. (2015). *Business statistics* (3rd ed.). Essex: Pearson Education Limited.

Sharpe, William F. (1964). Capital asset prices: A theory of market equilibrium under conditions of risk. *The Journal of Finance, 19*(3), 425–442.

Sharpe, William F. (1966). Mutual fund performance. *The Journal of Business*, 119–138.

Sharpe, William F. (1987). Integrated asset allocation. *Financial Analysts Journal, 43*(5), 25–32.

Sharpe, William F. (1992). Asset allocation. *The Journal of Portfolio Management, 18*(2), 7–19.

Sharpe, William F./Alexander, Gordon J./Bailey, Jeffery V. (1995). *Investments* (6th ed.). Englewood Cliffs: Prentice Hall International.

Sheskin, David J. (2003). *Handbook of parametric and nonparametric statistical procedures* (3rd ed.). Boca Raton: CRC Press LLC.

Shleifer, Andrei/Vishny, Robert W. (1997). A survey of corporate governance. *The Journal of Finance, 52*(2), 737–783.

SIF Japan. (2011). 2011 review of socially responsible investment in Japan. Retrieved July 15, 2013, from http://www.sifjapan.org/document/en2011.pdf.

Silva, Florinda/Cortez, Maria C./Armada, Manuel R. (2003). Conditioning information and European bond fund performance. *European Financial Management, 9*(2), 201–230.

Smith, Craig N. (2003). Corporate social responsibility: whether or how? *California Management Review, 45*(4), 52–77.

Smith, Keith V./Smith, Jane A. (2005). *Strategies in personal finance: Basic investment principles for today and tomorrow*. West Lafayette: Purdue University Press.

Spanos, Aris. (1999). *Probability theory and statistical inference: Econometric modeling with observational data.* Cambridge: Cambridge University Press.

Sparkes, Russell. (1998). Through a glass darkly: Some thoughts on the ethics of investment. *Epworth Review, 25*(3), 13–27.

Sparkes, Russell. (2001). Ethical investment: Whose ethics, which investment? *Business Ethics: A European Review, 10*(3), 194–205.

Statman, Meir. (1987). How many stocks make a diversified portfolio? *The Journal of Financial and Quantitative Analysis, 22*(3), 353–363.

Statman, Meir. (2000). Socially responsible mutual funds. *Financial Analysts Journal, 56*(3), 30–39.

Statman, Meir/Glushkov, Denys. (2009). The wages of social responsibility. *Financial Analysts Journal, 65*(4), 33–46.

Stock, James H./Watson, Mark W. (2007). *Introduction to econometrics* (2nd ed.). Boston: Pearson Education, Inc.

Studenmund, A. H. (2011). *Using econometrics: A practical guide* (4th ed.). Boston: Pearson Education, Inc.

Taylor, Robert. (2000). How new is socially responsible investment? *Business Ethics: A European Review, 9*(3), 174–179.

Terrazza, Virginie/Razafitombo, Hery. (2013). The fund synthetic index: An alternative benchmark for mutual funds. In Virginie Terrazza & Hery Razafitombo (Eds.), *Understanding investment funds: Insights from performance and risk analysis* (pp. 37–56). London: Palgrave Macmillan.

The Corporate Register. (2008). The corporate climate communications report 2007: A study of climate change disclosures by the Global FT500. Retrieved September 2, 2013, from www.corporateregister.com/pdf/CCCReport_07.pdf.

Thomson Reuters Lipper. (2012). Holdings-based fund classification methodology. Retrieved January 14, 2014, from http://www.lipperweb.com/docs/Research/Methodology/Lipper_HBC_Classification_Methodology_v2_2.pdf.

Thomson Reuters Lipper. (2013). European fund market review: 2013 edition. Retrieved January 14, 2014, from http://share.thomsonreuters.com/PR/Lipper/European_Fund_Market_Review_2013.pdf.

Tobin, James. (1958). Liquidity preference as behavior towards risk. *The Review of Economic Studies, 25*(2), 65–86.

Tobin, James/Brainard, William C. (1977). Asset markets and the cost of capital. *Cowles*

Foundation Discussion Papers No. 427. Retrieved from http://econpapers.repec.org/RePEc:cwl:cwldpp:427.

Treynor, Jack L. (1961). Toward a theory of market value of risky assets. *Unpublished Manuscript*. Retrieved from http://www.empirical.net/wp-content/uploads/2014/12/Treynor-Toward-a-Theory-of-Market-Value-of-Risky-Assets.pdf.

Treynor, Jack L. (1964). How to rate management of investment funds. *Harvard Business Review*, *43*(1), 63–75.

Tsay, Ruey S. (2005). *Analysis of financial time series* (2nd ed.). Hoboken: John Wiley & Sons, Inc.

Tschopp, Daniel. (2005). Corporate social responsibility: A comparison between the United States and the European Union. *Corporate Social Responsibility and Environmental Management*, *12*(1), 55–59.

Tschopp, Daniel/Huefner, Ronald J. (2015). Comparing the evolution of CSR reporting to that of financial reporting. *Journal of Business Ethics*, *127*(3), 565–577.

Tversky, Amos/Kahneman, Daniel. (1981). The framing of decisions and the psychology of choice. *Science*, *211*(4481), 453–458.

Ullmann, Arieh A. (1985). Data in search of a theory: A critical examination of the relationships among social performance, social disclosure, and economic performance of US firms. *Academy of Management Review*, *10*(3), 540–557.

United Nations. (2013). What is CSR? Retrieved July 11, 2013, from http://www.unido.org/what-we-do/trade/csr/what-is-csr.html.

USSIF. (2006). 2005 report on socially responsible investing trends in the United States. Retrieved July 12, 2013, from www.ussif.org/files/Publications/05_Trends_Report.pdf.

USSIF. (2010). Report on socially responsible investing trends in the United States.

USSIF. (2012). Report on sustainable and responsible investing trends in the United States 2012. Retrieved October 2, 2014, from http://www.ussif.org/files/publications/12_trends_exec_summary.pdf.

USSIF. (2013). SRI basics: What is sustainable and responsible investing? Retrieved July 10, 2013, from http://www.ussif.org/sribasics.

van de Velde, Eveline/Vermeir, Wim/Corten, Filip. (2005). Corporate social responsibility and financial performance. *Corporate Governance*, *5*(3), 129–138.

Vandekerckhove, Wim/Leys, Jos/Van Braeckel, Dirk. (2007). That's not what happened and it's not my fault anyway! An exploration of management attitudes towards SRI-shareholder engagement. *Business Ethics: A European Review*, *16*(4), 403–418.

VBDO. (2012). Benchmark responsible investment by insurance companies in the Netherlands 2012. Retrieved August 2, 2013, from www.vbdo.nl/files/download/1106/VBDO_BM_pensioenen_LR1.pdf.

Verbeek, Marno. (2012). *A guide to modern econometrics* (4th ed.). Chichester: John Wiley & Sons Ltd.

Vigeo. (2013a). Green, social and ethical funds in Europe: The retail market. Retrieved June 11, 2014, from http://www.vigeo.com/csr-rating-agency/en/etude-fds-verts-112013.

Vigeo. (2013b). What is CSR? Retrieved June 11, 2014, from http://www.vigeo.com/csr-rating-agency/en/rse-la-rse/blog.

Villasenor Alva, José A./Estrada, Elizabeth G. (2009). A generalization of Shapiro-Wilk's test for multivariate normality. *Communications in Statistics: Theory & Methods, 38*(11), 1870–1883.

Vogel, David. (2006). *The Market for virtue: The potential and limits of corporate social responsibility*. Washington, D.C.: Brookings Institution Press.

Vose, David. (2008). *Risk analysis: A quantitative guide* (3rd ed.). Hoboken: John Wiley & Sons, Inc.

Vyvyan, Victoria/Ng, Chew/Brimble, Mark. (2007). Socially responsible investing: The green attitudes and grey choices of Australian investors. *Corporate Governance: An International Review, 15*(2), 370–381.

Waddock, Sandra A./Graves, Samuel B. (1997). The corporate social performance-financial performance link. *Strategic Management Journal, 18*(4), 303–319.

Wan-Ni, Lai. (2012). Faith matters? A closer look at the performance of belief-based equity investments. *Journal of Asset Management, 13*(6), 421–436.

White, Halbert. (1980). A heteroskedasticity-consistent covariance matrix estimator and a direct test for heteroskedasticity. *Econometrica: Journal of the Econometric Society, 48*(4), 817–838.

Wood, Donna J. (1991). Corporate social performance revisited. *Academy of Management Review, 16*(4), 691–718.

Wooldridge, Jeffrey. (2013). *Introductory econometrics: A modern approach* (5th ed.). Mason: Cengage Learning.

Yamashita, Miwaka/Sen, Swapan/Roberts, Mark C. (1999). The rewards for environmental conscientiousness in the US capital markets. *Journal of Financial and Strategic Decision, 12*(1), 73–82.

Zimmer, Ben. (2011). "Have Your Cake and Eat It Too." Retrieved October 12, 2012, from http://www.nytimes.com/2011/02/20/magazine/20FOB-onlanguage-t.html?_r=0.